TRADITION & CHANGE IN ETHIOPIA

Social and Cultural Life as Reflected in Amharic Fictional Literature (1930-1974)

REIDULF KNUT MOLVÆR

Tradition & Change in Ethiopia: Social and Cultural Life as Reflected in Amharic Fictional Literature (1930-1974)
Copyright © 2008 by Reidulf Knut Molvær. All rights reserved.

Apart from any fair dealing for the purpose of private study, research, criticism or review, as permitted under the Copyright Act, no part of this publication may be reproduced in any form, stored in a retrieval system or transmitted in any form by any means—electronic, mechanical, photocopy, recording or otherwise—without the prior permission of the publisher. Enquiries should be sent to the undermentioned address.

Tsehai books may be purchased for educational, business, or sales promotional use. For more information, please contact our special sales department.

Tsehai Publishers and Distributors
P. O. Box: 1881, Hollywood, CA 90078

www.tsehaipublishers.com
info@tsehaipublishers.com

ISBN 10: 1-59907-037-5 | ISBN 13: 978-1-59907-037-7

Second Print 2008 | First Published in 1980 by E. J. Brill, Leiden, The Netherlands

Publisher: Elias Wondimu | Marketing and Sales Director: Sara Gezahegne
Cover Designer: Samuel Taye and Lisa Fang
Cover Photography: Adam Overton (www.adamoverton.com)

Library of Congress Catalog Card Number
A catalog record for this book is available from the Library of Congress.

British Library Cataloguing in Publication Data.
A catalogue record for this book is available from the British Library.

2 1 10 9 8 7 6 5 4 3

Printed in the United States of America.

Printed on acid-free, recycled paper

TRADITION & CHANGE
IN ETHIOPIA

TSEHAI
Publishers & Distributors

To Gebre Yohannes

TABLE OF CONTENTS

Preface. IX

Introduction 1
  Aims and methods 1
  Some general remarks on Amharic literature, with notes on the authors studied in this book 8
  Works selected as primary sources for this study 11

Abbreviations 19
Mode of transcription 19

PART ONE
TRADITIONAL ASPECTS OF MODERN ETHIOPIA

  I. The class structure of the society. 23
    1. The classes in traditional society 23
    2. Social interrelationships 28
      a) The Emperor and the people 28
      b) Landlords and tenants 33
      c) Status symbols 40
      d) Politeness 45
      e) Litigation 51

  II. Beliefs and ethics. 58
    1. Christianity. 58
      a) Popular Christian beliefs. 58
      b) Christian life and worship 72
    2. Pagan practices 101
    3. Syncretism in Christianity and paganism 113
    4. Ethics 121
    5. Some traditional beliefs, ideals, and customs . . . 127
    6. Views on sickness and health 130

  III. Private relationships and individual life. 133
    1. Forms of social intercourse in the local community 133
    2. Family life 135
    3. Food and drink 138
    4. Sex and marriage 143
    5. The position of women 154

IV. National characteristics: how Ethiopians see themselves. 159

PART TWO
CHANGING ETHIOPIA

V. Influences for change 165
   1. Indigenous influences. 165
   2. Foreign influences 168

VI. Attitudes to change. 172
   1. Conservatives 172
   2. Radicals 180
   3. Escapists 190

VII. Main areas of change 201
   1. Progress 201
      a) Education 201
      b) Urbanization 206
      c) Economic development 211
   2. Decay 217
      a) Relaxation of traditional ties and mores 217
      b) Moral decay 222
      c) Increase of crime and deceit 225

VIII. Building a new society: visions of change. 231
   1. New aspirations 231
   2. A changed society envisaged 235
      a) Education 235
      b) Patriotism 237
      c) Moral values 238
      d) Prosperity 240

Conclusions 243

Alphabetical list of the primary sources for this study . . . 246
Bibliography 248

Index of Amharic terms 254
Index of translated passages 261
General index 262

PREFACE

Fictional literature can be read for its style or story, to learn about the author or the society in and by which it is created. I have found the last approach particularly rewarding and instructive in the case of Amharic literature. In the West, such an approach could easily lead astray, as we have perhaps got used to writing about the special, the unusual, the extraordinary. Ethiopian authors, on the other hand, seem to prefer to describe the general, the typical, people and experiences readers can identify with. J. Jahn's words about African literature I think apply, on the whole, also in the case of Amharic fiction: "No figure is portrayed for the sake of his experiences or his interesting situation, but for the sake of the instruction which the author hopes to achieve through his story."*

I have sometimes supplemented fictional descriptions with information from other sources. In such cases I have tried to rely on Ethiopian material so as to let Ethiopians speak for themselves. I have, however, not wanted to make a study of fictional works a pretext for talking about things that are extraneous to this literature, so I have kept additional explanations to a minimum. I have thus, for example, made no attempt to reduce the prevailing confusion concerning the divisions within the Ethiopian Orthodox Church. Neither have I referred to studies on the Stephanites, which concentrate on the first couple of centuries of their existence or the development of the sect at Gunda Gunde but have not tried to find out how centuries of isolation have influenced the pockets that survive in Lake Tana. Here, as elsewhere in this book, I have paid most attention to views held by the common people.

I have not mentioned the role of censorship nor speculated about what might have been different without it. Official policy may account for the almost total neglect of Islamic culture in Amharic literature. Otherwise, I have come to admire the dexterity Ethiopian authors have displayed in order to circumvent the obstacles set by this institution, and many years as an editor in Addis Ababa made me well acquainted with its workings. Amharic is eminently suited to express more than one meaning in the same word or

---

*) J. Jahn. *Muntu*, Düsseldorf, 1958 (English translation, *Muntu*, London, 1961), chapter 5, v.

phrase, and this characteristic of the language must for centuries have been used for fun to create puns and riddles, but also poetry, and, like most poetic devices, it was probably intended to clarify and open the mind and vision rather than to obscure the sense. Minstrels and scholars have, however, used it to express delicate views at royal and noble courts. During the Italian occupation of Ethiopia, journalists used it to pass messages to the people under the very noses of the censors. Later, political awakening and a new social consciousness made authors seek ways of expressing protest and dissent and still getting their books printed, especially from the 1950's onwards. The same old technique of *double entendre* served their purpose well. The political and social situation rather than an archetypal Ethiopian mentality may explain the complicated literary style of the last few decades. By contrast, the earliest writers I have discussed are outstandingly clear, simple and straightforward.

The time I have covered is chosen because the first book I consider suitable for inclusion in this type of study was published in 1930, and in 1974 I started research at the University of London. The fact that Haile Sellassie's reign as emperor coincides with this period may add to the semblance of cohesion during these years. As 1974 also marks the end of one era in Ethiopian history and the beginning of a new, the preceding years may be of special interest and can possibly explain subsequent events.

The Introduction deals exclusively with the Ethiopian literary scene. The rest of the book gives a survey of the social and cultural life in the country.

This book was originally written as a Ph. D. thesis, with which the staff at the School of Oriental and African Studies gave me most valuable assistance. Professor E. Ullendorff, my supervisor, helped to give form and shape to my material and kept a close eye on my renderings of the Amharic originals. Ato Girma Sellassie Asfaw's willing cooperation over the more complicated literary passages proved invaluable. Dr. D. Appleyard suggested a great number of improvements and corrections in the language. Dr. A. Irvine contributed to both form and content, and his tutoring in Geez during three years was useful also for an understanding of Amharic literature. Dr. R. Pankhurst made available some reference material I would otherwise have had difficulties in obtaining.

The greatest debt I owe of course to the authors whose works I have studied in this book. Many other Ethiopians have stimulated my mind and given me valuable insights and information, both while the research lasted and during ten years in Ethiopia. I also want to mention Mr. M. Lundgren, who has taken a personal interest in my studies and obtained a grant for me from the Church of Sweden Mission. The printing has been subsidised by the Norwegian Research Council for Science and the Humanities.

It is a pleasure to thank all those who have given me help and encouragement during the work with this book.

R. K. Molvaer

January 1979

INTRODUCTION

Aims and Methods

Ethiopian authors of fiction are strongly concerned with the social and cultural life of their time, and it would not do Amharic literature full justice to evaluate it only on aesthetic grounds. This literature is not purely art for art's sake, or for entertainment; proper appreciation of the modern Ethiopian literary scene can be gained if one relates fictional writing to society.

It is the aim of this book to study the society modern authors live in and describe in their fictional work, paying equal attention to how traditional culture survives today and how customs and ways of thinking have changed during the last few decades, and how writers of works of fiction want to influence and guide the future development of Ethiopia.

The first author whose work is central to the theme of this study is Blattengeta Hǝruy Wäldä Sǝllase, and the period surveyed here starts with the publication of his novel *Yäləbb hassab* in 1923 E.C., i.e. A.D. 1930-31. The work of a dozen authors has been studied, ending with Bä'alu Gǝrma's *Yähǝllina däwäl*, which was published in 1974, the year research for this book started.

When studying society on the basis of fictional literature, one does not always get an objective picture of social conditions. Authors have at all times acted as a kind of "conscience" of society, and in their writings they include their own evaluation of social institutions and customs in the country. We may therefore find they emphasize abuses and glorify their ideals, and the resulting picture may be somewhat distorted if it is evaluated against objective reality. But their intellectual discussion of values is part of the modern Ethiopian social and cultural scene, and from the point of view of this study such personal value judgments that perhaps give a slightly exaggerated picture of a situation, add to the value of the literature. Both facts and viewpoints are discussed here. Amharic literature is very much part of the cultural life of modern Ethiopia. Fictional literature is thus studied for its own sake, and it is set against the social background, so that literary and social considerations go hand in hand.

The fictional work of twelve authors has been selected as a basis for this study. The twelve writers are (in order of the date of the first publication included in this study):

1. Həruy Wäldä Səllase [1]
2. Käbbädä Mika'el
3. Gərmaččäw Täklä Hawaryat
4. Mäkonnən Əndalkaččäw
5. Haddis Alämayyähu
6. Taddäsä Libän
7. Daňňaččäw Wärku
8. Ṣäggaye Gäbrä Mädhən
9. Abbe Gubäňňa
10. Bərhanu Zärihun (also Zäryəhun)
11. Mängəstu Lämma
12. Bä'alu Gərma.

All these authors are well known and widely read in Ethiopia and can be considered representative of the best in Ethiopian literary tradition. Others could naturally be included; but some prominent ones deal with questions not immediately relevant to this study, and others (e.g. Mängəstu Gädamu and Pawlos Ňoňňo) write about contemporary social questions in rather allegorical form which may be interpreted in different ways. I have not included these categories of writers among my primary sources. I have also excluded a fine poet like Gərma Taddäsä, because his poems are often "thoughts" and do not deal concretely with social issues in a descriptive manner, although many of his observations could very well be relevant to themes treated here.

Among the authors studied, only Həruy Wäldä Səllase wrote before the Italian occupation of Ethiopia, but much of *Araya* by Gərmaččäw Täklä Hawaryat and probably all of *Fəkr əskä mäkabər* by Haddis Alämayyähu are set in the pre-war period (although the latter is rather vague about the time during which the story takes place). Mäkonnən Əndalkaččäw has written about the war (e.g. *Almotkum bəyye alwaṣəm*), but most of his books, and those of the other authors studied here, deal with the post-war era. Some, though, are not specific about the time setting, even when they

---

[1] The authors in this book are referred to by their full names, or occasionally by their first names only; but Həruy Wäldä Səllase is here normally called Blattengeta Həruy, as he is commonly known in Ethiopia.

clearly deal with contemporary issues. Several authors have written works of historical fiction, particularly about the Emperor Tewodros II, which are considered here for the light they throw on modern authors' views of Ethiopia's past, and for the use they make of history to exercise social criticism of the society they live in.

A perusal of Amharic literature written between A.D. 1930 and A.D. 1974 reveals a society that strongly holds on to traditions and values inherited from previous centuries.[2] The first part of this thesis surveys the institutions, relationships, beliefs and attitudes that bear the stamp of long tradition. The material shows a heavy leaning towards religion and the supernatural, and one could well look at Ethiopian society and culture starting as it were from the "otherworldly" and working one's way down to more individual relationships and to "things", such as food.[3] I have, however, chosen to arrange the material in relation to institutions, starting with the state and matters that relate to all or most of the country, passing on to large organizations and commonly held views (dealing here also with religion and ethical values), and then taking up relationships that affect or concern people in more individual ways. This part concludes with a short chapter where I make an attempt to give a general picture of the character of the Ethiopian people as the authors of fiction see it.

Part Two of the book deals with changes that have taken place in Ethiopia during the period 1930-1974, and with the Ethiopian authors' views of these changes and of how they want their country to develop in future.

Ethiopian authors are strongly concerned with questions related to the future of their country, and a preoccupation with the moral issues involved in social and cultural change is prominent in much of Amharic literature, much more than, for example, a discussion of economic growth. Traditional viewpoints are strongly felt in this discussion, and concrete proposals are few, and usually tentative. Some authors conceal their social criticism and views on development under the form of historical novels or plays. The works of historical fiction are therefore considered in Part Two of this book.

---

[2] For comparison, see, for example, J. Doresse, *La vie quotidienne des Éthiopiens chrétiens (aux XVIIe et XVIIIe siècles)*, Paris, 1972.

[3] Cf. I. M. Lewis, *Social Anthropology in Perspective*, (Penguin) 1976, p. 10: "My preference, which will not commend itself to everyone, is to start with religion, so in effect beginning at the top and working down."

Some reservations must be made when Amharic literature is used as a source for an examination of Ethiopian society and culture.

Amharic is only one of many languages spoken in the country, and, although it is the official national language, it is not known by large sections of the population. Naturally, Amharic literature deals mostly, but not exclusively, with areas and cultures where this language is widely understood and written by authors who are familiar with Amharic and live in a social setting penetrated by what has been called Amhara civilization. Although not all of these authors are ethnic Amharas, their writing reflects primarily this "Amhara" society and culture.

The "Amhara" cultural area is limited to the central highlands, where the inhabitants are predominantly Christian. There is little mention of Islam or Muslims in Amharic literature, and this lack is reflected in this book. Several traces of paganism are noted, but these refer mostly to pagan practices kept alive by Christians or at least in Christian surroundings.

The locale can be even more closely defined than the central highlands. Except for the literature on Tewodros, Gondar and its surrounding areas are rarely the setting for works of fiction in Amharic (although for example Bərhanu Zärihun comes from Gondar). About half the works studied for this book are set in Addis Ababa, or, in a few cases, some other town. When the action of other works takes place in the countryside, the main character is frequently from the capital, and has come temporarily to live in a village. In such works, the contrast, and frequently conflict, between urban and rural customs and viewpoints are set out. (In other works, Ethiopian and European customs are contrasted, by having the main character return to a traditional society from studies abroad.) The rural areas used as settings in Amharic literature are primarily northern Shoa, Gojjam, and Hararge; one novel is set in Illubabor.

Ethnic differences are noticed here and there in Ethiopian literature, but they are rarely accentuated. (The literature uses the term Galla rather than Oromo; I have followed the use of the literature in this book.)

Only a small percentage of Ethiopia's population is literate, and the authors therefore write with a comparatively small potential readership in mind, students or others with some degree of education. This is a group of frequently privileged members of an intelligentsia (to whom they belong) that may have come from a poor background but can expect to be influential in shaping the country's future. The anticipated readership gives form to a writer's style and presentation to a large extent, so we may expect a certain repetition of favourite themes. This is particularly noticeable in books about life in Addis Ababa. We do not find, on the other hand, the conscious presentation of the country with a foreign audience in mind which mars much African literature written in European languages. The picture we get of Ethiopia is one reflecting the daily experiences of inhabitants of the country, seen and interpreted by Ethiopians for Ethiopians. In some places it has therefore been necessary to supplement the narrative with additional information from non-fictional sources to make the text comprehensible to non-Ethiopian readers. But whenever this occurs in this book, passages or concepts in fictional literature have given rise to the thought or the exposition; and such cases do not occupy much space in this study.

The emphasis in the book is on the life of the common people. Fiction does not go into details about legislation relating to land ownership, or philosophical expositions of the finer points of theology in the Ethiopian Orthodox Church (mostly referred to as "the Church" in this book); but it goes to great lengths in describing how people experience—or suffer under—the system of tenancy and arbitrary rule by landlords, and we often see how people react on the basis of a faith that may be simpler than or departs from what is sanctioned by the hierarchy in the Church. The daily life of ordinary citizens is what emerges most clearly from such an examination as the one undertaken here. In some cases it has been found most suitable to give a rather "systematic" (rather than chronological) presentation of the material, for example in the chapters on religion. The situation in which a reference to God or some other supernatural being occurs is not always significant, and it is sufficient on such occasions to treat religious concepts separate from the particular setting in each case. When the circumstances are essential or important, they are of course mentioned. In other cases a knowledge of the situation in which a remark is made, etc., is necessary for a proper understanding of what is implied. In some such cases a statement may be made on the basis of a work examined without specific mention of the work in the text. A look at the footnotes will tell what specific passage a certain observation is founded on. This is done to save space when it is felt that little or nothing is gained by very frequent mention of a work in the main body of the book. Some books are referred to more often than others. This can have several causes. The big books contain, of course, more detail than the smaller ones—which form the bulk of Amharic literature. There are also books that deal specifically with the themes of various chapters in this study, and these will be quoted more frequently than other works. Thus, both *Fəkr əskä mäkabər* and *Adäfrəs* are large in volume and deal in great detail with many religious questions and with the relationship between landlord and tenant, and the life of the aristocracy. Even where there is a preponderance of references to or quotations from certain works, it should be kept in mind that all works selected for this study have been consulted for each chapter. Sometimes a brief quotation or a reference to a few lines is given to support an argument in the body of this work, but it should also be borne in mind here that such quotes are representative of the whole works that have been studied and should not be read in isolation. A few passages may succinctly give expression to a thought, but they are of course no substitute for the works themselves.

In Part Two of the book, the thoughts and arguments of the authors are followed more closely than in Part One, where the "background" or situation is given prominence. In the second part there are, therefore, also several references to the works as a whole, and the story of an entire book may underpin the argument in a certain context. Otherwise, no general surveys or summaries of the works under discussion will be found here, nor will there be much biographical detail about the authors, as these tasks have been performed by others.

Among Ethiopians, few have written extensively about modern Amharic literature. Both Mängəstu Lämma and Solomon Deressa have produced articles about recent fictional works in their country, the former about the literature of quality,[4] the latter about the more ephemeral books that are published.[5]

---

[4] Mängəstu Lämma, "From Traditional to Modern Literature in Ethiopia", in *Zeitschrift für Kulturaustausch*, Sonderausgabe, 1973, pp. 81-83.
[5] Solomon Deressa, "The Amharic Dime-Novel", in *Addis Reporter*, Vol. I, No. 1, (January 3, 1969), pp. 17-22.

Italian scholars (e.g. E. Cerulli and M. M. Moreno) have written about Amharic literature prior to 1935, and some have also made contributions in more recent years (especially L. Ricci). In France, in particular P. Comba has penned several articles on publications in Amharic.

Stephen Wright wrote a general survey of Amharic literature in 1963.[6] But the fullest accounts of Amharic literature have been given by A. Gérard and T. L. Kane. In 1968, Gérard published an article on early Amharic literature,[7] and this was expanded and brought up to date in a book published three years later.[8] The author has done an admirable job in collecting biographical data and background material, and he shows a clear understanding of the general trends of modern Amharic writing. He gives a summary of much of the literature written in Ethiopia in this century, although there are some rather serious mistakes, which is not surprising, as the author does not read Amharic.[9]

T. L. Kane's book on Amharic literature was published in 1975.[10] He gives a summary of a great many works, thematically arranged. A useful survey of what has been written in Amharic is found here, and the book serves rather well as a reference work of the Ethiopian literary scene. I feel, though, that it is difficult to accept many of his generalizations. Both he and Gérard have several lacunae in their Amharic bibliographies. It would enhance the value of both these works if some criteria for sifting the obvious trash from works of greater literary merit had been applied.

As very many topics have been discussed in this book, the general bibliography has had to be selective rather than compre-

---

[6] S. Wright, "Amharic Literature", in *Something*, Vol. I, No. 1, (1963), pp. 11-23.

[7] A. Gérard, "Amharic creative literature: the early phase", in JES, Vol. VI, No. 2 (July 1968), pp. 39-55.

[8] A. Gérard, *Four African Literatures*, Berkeley, 1971.

[9] Some of these mistakes are questions of emphasis, and sometimes a book is summed up so as slightly to distort the story. Some value judgments may be hasty. More serious errors are: (a) Wäldä Giyorgis Wäldä Yohannəs the author (an employee in the Ministry of Information) is confused with the eponymous Minister of the Pen (pp. 313ff.); (b) Bərhanu Zärihun, one of Ethiopia's finest stylists and an influential writer, is very briefly treated, and of his seven books (all published before Gérard wrote his book) only the first is briefly mentioned, and almost all that is said about this book is wrong. His other works are dismissed with the phrase that "there is too little information on them for a discussion here" (p. 359f.).

[10] T. L. Kane, *Ethiopian literature in Amharic*, Wiesbaden, 1975.

hensive. Fairly full lists of Amharic literature can be found in the works of Gérard and Kane referred to above.

SOME GENERAL REMARKS ON AMHARIC LITERATURE, WITH NOTES ON THE AUTHORS STUDIED IN THIS BOOK

Although Amharic may have existed as a spoken language for about a thousand years, written literature in the language was rather scanty before the present century. Songs in praise of ruling monarchs go back to the fourteenth century, and in the sixteenth and seventeenth centuries some didactic and polemical religious writings were produced as a result of the presence of Portuguese missionaries in the country. Tewodros II in the nineteenth century supported the use of Amharic in written literature, and the chronicles of his reign are in Amharic. Some original works and some translations appear later in the century, mostly of a religious and historical nature.

This century has seen a great increase in the production of books in Amharic, and the first printed fictional work proper appeared in 1908, when Afäwärḳ Gäbrä Iyäsus published his novel *Ləbb wälläd tarik*, later also named *Ṭobbiya*. It is set in the remote past, and can hardly be called a realistic work. The book is valued for its style, and the author may have written it as a purely artistic exercise; it is "art for art's sake". It is not relevant to this study, as it does not deal with the social or cultural scene of modern Ethiopia. The first author of fiction to deal directly with social issues is Blattengeta Həruy Wäldä Səllase, and of his works (many of which were factual or, as e.g. *Wädaje ləbbe*, purely religious) two are highly relevant to the theme of this study. He wanted to be understood by as many as possible, and he uses a simple style that appeals to the heart as well as the head, and his art is rather "art for man's sake", eager as he is to improve the human condition.

After the Italian occupation, the reformist ideas of Həruy were continued by Käbbädä Mika'el (whose style seems also strongly influenced by Həruy) and Gərmaččäw Täklä Hawaryat whose style seems to combine both Afäwärḳ's and Həruy's: it is simple, but it probably appeals to the intellect rather than the emotions. Mäkonnən Əndalkaččäw, who writes in an emotive style rather reminiscent of Həruy, represents a reaction against the zeal for innovation found in most previous authors. He stresses the ethical values of the Church and the benefits of a social system dominated by a benevolent aristocracy.

Attitudes to social change become more differentiated and complex with the next generation of writers. Haddis Alämayyähu can be nostalgic about traditional Ethiopia, but he clearly sees that the culture of the past is waning, destroyed first of all as the result of abuses by conservative traditionalists. His language and style are perhaps unsurpassed in Amharic literature. Taddäsä Libän writes well-told short stories from Addis Ababa and he describes life there, full of deceit and sorrows, with great compassion. Daňňaččäw Wärḵu's most valuable contribution to Amharic literature is a novel giving a panoramic view of the social situation and the intellectual climate in Ethiopia in the 1960's. Ṣäggaye Gäbrä Mädhən writes mostly plays and poems about the confusion of modern urban life and the conflicts encountered by people (particularly young people) in contemporary society.

Abbe Gubäňňa is a prolific writer, and not only of fiction. He writes stories which, by their simplistic presentation and relentless pursuit of single themes, can make a great emotional impact on the reader. He vigorously defends the idea of Ethiopia's speedy conversion into an industrial democracy, much like the more advanced western countries. Mängəstu Lämma is at the same time progressive and nostalgic about the past, and his writing may reflect his views of 1952, "that Ethiopian culture must be and remain till the end nationalist in form and progressive in content".[11] Bərhanu Zärihun is a fine stylist who, as editor of the newspaper *Addis Zämän*, changed journalistic style from the obtuse longwindedness that had been the fashion previously to an easy presentation in clear and concise sentences.[12] His best novels are among the finest writings in Amharic. He wants to see his country develop spiritually as well as materially and observes with regret that the morals of the younger generation are deteriorating; but he also attacks abuses of the traditional society. Bä'alu Gərma, also at one time editor of *Addis Zämän*, has published two well-written novels, one about the confused generation of young Ethio-

---

[11] Mängəstu Lämma, "Muggət", in *New Times and Ethiopia News*, 9 February 1952.
[12] Pawlos Ñoňňo has also strongly influenced Ethiopian journalism in the same direction.

pians in Addis Ababa, the second about building a new Ethiopia through communal, cooperative efforts.

The style of Amharic employed in modern fiction has developed along the patterns set by the earliest writers. Afäwärḳ has perhaps his most direct successors in this respect in Daňňaččäw Wärḳu and Ṣäggaye Gäbrä Mädhən who are both fond of innovations in language and style and have used words which were probably not current in the literary language before. This had also been the case with Afäwärḳ.

With regard to style, Həruy was followed by Käbbädä Mika'el, Mäkonnən Ǝndalkaččäw and Haddis Alämayyähu. Simplicity and at the same time precision characterize these authors, and many readers are greatly attracted by their way of writing. It is likely that their background in church schools explains the style they have developed; but other authors who employ more "artistic" language have also had church education and often create new words from Ge'ez roots.

The "third" style in Amharic fiction that goes back to Gərmaččäw, combining the intellectual challenge of Afäwärḳ's language with the simplicity and emotional appeal of Həruy's writing, seems to have become predominant in most recent Amharic literature. Abbe Gubäňňa, Bərhanu Zärihun, Mängəstu Lämma, and Bä'alu Gərma can be said to continue this tradition, and some have developed and refined it as well as created their own individual styles.

There seems to have been an increase in the use of *double entendre* in the last couple of decades. At the same time, an increasing number of colloquialisms and foreign borrowings enrich the literary language during this period.

In terms of form, it seems that Ethiopian authors have found Western models suitable for presenting what they want to convey. This is most noticeable in their writing of novels and plays. Poetry bears many marks of the traditional *ḳəne* poetry taught in church schools for the creation of hymns. The religious climate in Ethiopia may also account for the overriding moral concern that can be discerned in all Amharic writing. Many authors have attended church schools, and much of Amharic literature has benefited from this influence.

All authors discussed here have been (or are) in government employ, some in high positions. This may, to some extent, account for the preoccupation with matters of national concern, so salient a feature in almost all Amharic literature.

WORKS SELECTED AS PRIMARY SOURCES FOR THIS STUDY

Authors have been listed chronologically in order of publication of their first work included in this study. The short characterization given of each work is meant to show how it relates to this study. All books in the following list are published in Addis Ababa, with the exception of *Araya* by Gərmaččäw Täklä Hawaryat, which was first published in Asmara (but later editions appeared in Addis Ababa). (Some reprints of Amharic works seem to have retained earlier dates of publication.)

1. Həruy Wäldä Səllase wrote more non-fiction than fiction; among his fictional work two novels are of particular interest for this study:
Yäləbb hassab (sub-titled *Yäbərhanenna yäṣəyon mogäsa gabəčča*), published 1923 E.C. (A.D. 1930-31).[13] It deals with education, especially of women, the age of marriage, and the upbringing and care of children, with emphasis on the need for modern medical knowledge. (52 pp.)
Addis aläm (sub-titled *Yäkənočənna yädägg adragiwoč mänorya*), 1925 E.C. (1932-33).[14] Awwäḳä, a young man educated in France, wants to bring about many reforms in his community and in the Church. He succeeds after much opposition. (63 pp.)

2. Käbbädä Mika'el has a rich production of factual and fictional works to his credit. Relevant for this study are:
Tarikənna məssale, Book III, 1934 E.C. (1941-42). This is a textbook for elementary school children, and consists of short stories and poems, only some of which were composed by this author. (The 1961 E.C. edition is used here. 71 pp.)
Yäḳəne azmära, 1956 E.C. (1963-64). This is a collection of the best of his poetry (much of which had been published previously in various places). Many poems deal with morality and Ethiopian ideals. (158 pp.)
Kaleb, 1958 E.C. (1965-66). This is a play about the sixth century

---

[13] The 1963 E.C. edition, in a collection called *Dərsätoč*, pp. 129-180, is used here.
[14] The 1948 E.C. edition by Zämänfäs Ḳəddus Abrəha is used here.

Ethiopian emperor's defeat of Dhu Nuwas at Najran (in 525). It sets out Ethiopia's greatness based on Christian ideals. (70 pp.)

Yätənbit ḵäṭäro, 1959 E.C. (1966-67). In this play, a soothsayer predicts the fall of a pagan king and the establishment of a Christian kingdom. It emphasizes the value of Ethiopia's Christian heritage. (1964 E.C. edition used. 105 pp.)

3. Gərmaččäw Täklä Hawaryat has written two books, both of importance for this study:

Araya, 1941 E.C. (1948-49), a novel. Araya goes to France for education and wants to institute wide-ranging social reforms on his return to Ethiopia. He is frustrated both by the envy of his colleagues and later by the Italian invasion and occupation of Ethiopia. (1960 E.C. edition used. 350 pp.)

Tewodros, 1950 E.C. (1957-58), a play about Tewodros II and his nationalistic struggles and aspirations, and the forces of opposition he had to contend with from nobles, clergy, and the common people. (1960 edition used. 109 pp.)

4. Mäkonnən Əndalkaččäw was a prolific writer. Of interest here are:

Arrəmuññ, 1947 E.C. (1954-55). This is a collection of several works, some of which, according to the author's preface, had been written many years prior to their publication. (1960 E.C. edition used. 360 pp.) It contains:

Yäḵayäl dəngay, a playlet purporting to show that evil is both the cause and result of inventions and material progress (pp. 29-42);

Aläm wärätäñña, a play (or largely dramatized narrative—as is the case with many of this author's works) about a girl's escape from the hardships of this world to the peace of a convent and finally paradise (pp. 43-77);

Yädäm dəmṣ, a play about Abunä Peṭros and his refusal to collaborate with the Italian occupiers; he is killed and becomes a great inspiration for the patriotic struggle (pp. 79-104);

Yädəhoč kätäma, a novel about a man's moral and mental degeneration and death owing to his greed and pursuit of money all over the world; appended is a series of maxims (pp. 105-192);

Salsawi Dawit, a "novel" (with large parts written as a play) containing mostly discourses between King David III's son Ya'ḳob and a noble youth, Ləjj Mäsfən, about kingship and leadership, leading to Prince Ya'ḳob's renunciation of the world (pp. 193-245);

Assabənna säw is a novel about the biblical king David, attempting to show how man is driven by his passions (pp. 247-272);

Almotkum bəyye alwašəm is a novel telling the story of a man who went to Hararge in 1935 to fight the Italians; on his return home, several months later, he finds his wife is living with an Italian officer. He commits suicide, and his wife, when she recognizes him, kills her lover and incites Ethiopians to resist the invaders (pp. 273-338);

Yä-May Čäw ṭorənnätənna baččəru yä'aläm polätika, an essay relating one of Ethiopia's last major battles with the Italians in 1936 to world events (pp. 339-360).

Yäfəḳər čora, 1949 E.C. (1956-57) is a novel telling the story of the illicit love and adulterous relationship between a man and a woman who are separately married and go to Europe to be together for some time. The book ends with a series of religious and philosophical thoughts. (197 pp.)

Ṣähay Mäsfən, 1949 E.C. (1956-57), a novel about an impoverished young woman of noble family who has lost her parents, is widowed early and left with three children. Ləjj Alämu is a parvenu who wants to marry her, but on one occasion is ashamed of her traditional dress and causes her to run out into the rain; she contracts pneumonia and dies. As an act of repentance, he gives all his wealth to her children who go abroad for education. Back in Ethiopia, they build a rest-home for old people; Ləjj Alämu comes there to die. (1960 E.C. edition used. 102 pp.)

Ṭaytu Bəṭul, 1950 E.C. (1957-58), an historical novel about Ṭaytu Bəṭul's virtuous resistance to Emperor Tewodros's amorous advances; she is rewarded with marriage to Menelik II. (79 pp.)

Joro ṭäbi, 1951 E.C. (1958-9). In this novel, a man contrives the death of a rich couple and is able to get hold of their property in the name of his own child; but finally he comes to a bad end at the hand of his own son who does not believe he is his father. (180 pp.)

5. Haddis Alämayyähu is a master at telling a good story in very beautiful Amharic.

Tärät tärät yämäsärät, 1948 E.C. (1955-56), is a collection of stories or fables written in the style of traditional folk-tales. Most of them point a moral, often about the use or abuse of power. (1962 E.C. edition used. 112 pp.)

Fəkr əskä mäḳabər, 1958 E.C. (1965-66), is one of Ethiopia's largest fictional works.[15] It is built round the life story of Bäzzabbəh, a man of humble origins who is educated and makes his career in the Church; he is involved with Fitawrari Mäšäša's household and falls in love with his daughter Säblä Wängel. With the help of Guddu Kasa, they are able to elope and marry a short time before Bäzzabbəh dies. The novel is rich in material about the Church and situations showing how the nobility live and exercise their power. (1962 E.C. edition used. 555 pp.)

6. Taddäsä Libän has published two well-written collections of short stories:

Mäskäräm, 1949 E.C. (1956-57) (118 pp.), and

Lelaw mängäd, 1952 E.C. (1959-60) (115 pp.), both describe life in Addis Ababa, especially among the slightly educated and slightly liberated youth. He writes with much understanding and sympathy about people whose experiences often lead to suffering for the participants.

7. Daňňaččäw Wärku has published two works in Amharic:

Säw allä bəyye, 1950 E.C. (1957-58), is a verse drama about a boy who tries to fool and then to kill a boy who has left home rather than abandon his friend to his fate. No one can be trusted, is the point made in the play. (135 pp.)

Adäfrəs, 1962 E.C. (1969-70), is a novel that has much to say about religion, and the aristocracy and their way of life. Adäfrəs, a student, and others from Addis Ababa stay with a landlady in the country for some time, and rural and urban views and customs are contrasted. A great number of topics are discussed in this book. (330 pp.)

---

[15] If the non-fictional parts of *And lännatu* by Abbe Gubäňňa are excluded, *Fəkr əskä mäḳabər* is probably the longest work of fiction in the Amharic language.

8. Ṣäggaye Gäbrä Mädhən is a playwright and poet. Of his works in Amharic, the following have been published:

Yäšoh aklil, 1952 E.C. (1959-60), a play showing the difficulties in accepting a man for what he is, regardless of his family background. The occasion is that a boy who has been adopted by a nobleman wants to marry a nobleman's daughter and is then found wanting. (105 pp.)

Bälg, 1958 E.C. (1965-66), a play about people who learn to love and accept each other after all their romantic illusions about love have been shattered. (140 pp.)

Yäkärmo säw, 1958 E.C. (1965-66), a play showing the problems of two young people who have left the countryside for the easy life of the town, and the dilemmas they encounter when they have given up their inheritance. In town they lose their sense of purpose. (85 pp.)

Эsat wäy abäba, 1966 E.C. (1973-4), is a collection of poems written over a period of many years and covering a wide range of subjects. (208 pp.)

9. Abbe Gubäñña has written a great number of books, not all fictional. Of importance for this study are:

Yä'amäṣ nuzaze, 1955 E.C. (1962-63), a novel containing the story of a man who has lived in drunkenness and adultery, as told by himself. (1962 E.C. edition used. 85 pp.)

Aləwwällädəm, 1955 E.C. (1962-63), is a novel where the main character begins to tell his own story in his mother's womb and goes on telling it after he is dead. He achieves great things for his country, but is hampered at each step by envious people. (1966 E.C. edition used. 236 pp.)

Məlkam säyfä näbälbal, 1956 E.C. (1963-64), tells the story of a prime minister who achieves tremendous progress for his country in a short time. The book gives a brief sketch of his life, and contains a series of speeches he gave on different occasions. (4th edition, 1957 E.C. used. 171 pp.)

Kältammawa əhəte, 1957 E.C. (1964-65), is a novel about a girl who runs away from home to escape the harsh treatment of a stepmother and, after living with a few lovers, ends up as a low-class prostitute until her brother finds her. (1962 E.C. edition used. 52 pp.)

Yähamet susäññoč[16] contains essays and poems on a favourite theme of the author: people's envy and propensity for calumny. (70 pp.)

And lännatu, 1961 E.C. (1968-69), is a large historical novel covering the life of Tewodros II, giving an idealized picture of this monarch, with much attention paid to his family background in an attempt to prove his royal descent. (602 pp.)

Әddəl näw? bädäl?, 1962 E.C. (1969-70), is a novel about a peasant who is impoverished because of demands made by the Church when his wife dies; he is driven to desperation when he cannot win compensation in a lawsuit over a stolen ox. (139 pp.)

Mäskot, A.D. 1971,[17] is a collection of poems, mostly of a moralistic nature. The author tries, in introductions to each section, to show that traditional Ethiopian forms of poetry are adequate for any need of modern poetic expression. (192 pp.)

Gobland ačbärbariw țoța, A.D. 1971,[18] a brief novel about an ape who talks and behaves like a human, but because it is cunning and lacks a conscience becomes utterly destructive. Appended (pp. 87-121) is a section on modern literary forms. (121 pp.)

Yäräggäfu abäboč, 1964 E.C. (1971-72), is a novel about a group of young people who wantonly spend their time mostly in different bars in Addis Ababa, seeking pleasure and discussing all kinds of topics, including some of great social importance. (270 pp.)

Әretənna mar, 1965 E.C. (1972-73), is a collection of poems, mostly of a nationalistic and moralistic nature. The author writes largely within the traditional rules of versification. (64 pp.)

Yäddäkamoč wäțmäd, 1965 E.C. (1972-73), a play set in the Era of the Judges (or Princes), strikes a nationalistic note, pointing to the harm done to the country by corrupt and selfish leaders in that period. (144 pp.)

10. Bərhanu Zärihun (or Zäryəhun in later works) wrote six novels and a collection of short stories between 1952 and 1960 E.C.; since he was ousted from his job as editor of *Addis Zämän*, after a controversy about Tewodros, no more works from his pen have been published.

---

[16] My copy, the only I have been able to consult, lacks the page with the date of publication.
[17] The only date given is the 41st year of Emperor Haile Sellassie's reign.
[18] The only date given is the 41st year of Emperor Haile Sellassie's reign.

Yä'ənba däbdabbewoč,[19] 1952 E.C. (1959-60), tells of a woman who is lured away from her husband and child to become the mistress of a well-to-do young man from Addis Ababa. Because of her country manners, he soon gets tired of her, and she becomes a prostitute and dies of sickness and deprivation. (1961 E.C. edition used. 136 pp.)

Dəll kämot bähwala 1955, E.C. (1962-63), tells about the struggle against oppression of and injustice against the black people of South Africa. (211 pp.)

Amanu'el därso mäls, 1956 E.C. (1963-64), tells the story of a man who suddenly comes into money which he spends on prostitutes and alcohol for his own destruction. His abandoned wife rescues him after he has spent some time in Amanu'el Hospital, i.e. the Addis Ababa lunatic asylum. (91 pp.)

Yäbädäl fəṣṣame, 1956 E.C. (1963-64), perhaps Ethiopia's first detective story, tells of embezzlement and the difficulties of bringing powerful people to justice. (157 pp.)

Čäräka sətwäṭa (no date) tells of a man's love for, and trust in, a girl who does not seem as promiscuous as most girls in Addis Ababa; but when he learns that she has had a sexual relationship with, and is going to marry, one of his friends, he comforts himself with a prostitute. (93 pp.)

Yätewodros ənba, 1958 E.C. (1965-66), is an historical novel about Tewodros and particularly the attempts to undermine his power and estrange his closest friends and helpers. (140 pp.)

Bərr ambar säbbärälləwo, 1960 E.C. (1967-68), is a collection of four stories describing marriage customs in different parts of Ethiopia. (108 pp.)

11. Mängəstu Lämma has written a collection of poetry and two comedies that are included in this study:

Yägəṭəm guba'e, 1955 E.C. (1962-63), contains poems based on his experiences abroad, especially in England and India, as well as others where he expresses more philosophical ideas, stressing traditional Ethiopian values. (69 pp.)

Yalačča gabəčča, 1957 E.C. (1964-65), is a play about a teacher of good family and with high education who settles down to teach

---

[19] On an inside page, the alternative title *Hulätt yä'ənba däbdabbewoč* is also given.

in a small village, marries his maid, and prefers this life to the grander plans of his rich aunt. (166 pp.)

Ṭälfo bäkise, 1961 E.C. (1968-69), a play about a group of young men from Addis Ababa who abduct a girl whom they plan to marry to one of them, in imitation of the customs of their fathers. (71 pp.)

12. Bä'alu Gərma has published two novels:

Kä'admas bašagär, 1962 E.C. (1969-70), tells about the aimless life of restless young intellectuals in Addis Ababa, and how, finally, love seems to give meaning to two people when they have been brought to an almost hopeless situation. (186 pp.)

Yähəllina däwäl, 1966 E.C. (A.D. 1974), describes how a student succeeds in uniting the people of a small town in a communal effort to build their own school when government support is not forthcoming. He has to contend with opposition from local authorities, but this is overcome, and the school is built and is seen as a symbol of a brighter future for Ethiopia. (248 pp.)

ABBREVIATIONS

DTW   Dästa Täklä Wäld, *Addis yamarəñña mäzgäbä ḵalat*, Addis Ababa, 1962 E.C. (A.D. 1970).
E.C.   Ethiopian Calendar.
JES   *Journal of Ethiopian Studies*.
KBT   Täsämma Habtä Mika'el, *Käsatä bərhan täsämma. Yä'amarəñña mäzgäbä ḵalat*, Addis Ababa, 1951 E.C. (1958-59).
KWK   Kidanä Wäld Kəfle, *Mäṣhafä säwasəw wägəss wämäzgäbä ḵalat haddis*, Addis Ababa, 1948 E.C. (1955-56).

MODE OF TRANSCRIPTION

The Amharic syllabary is transcribed as follows:

a) "alphabetical" order:
    h, l, m, r, s, š, ḵ, b, t, č, n, ñ, a, k, w, z, ž, y, d, j, g, ṭ, č̣, p, ṣ, f, p̣.

b) vowel orders:
    ä, u, i, a, e, ə, o.

PART ONE

TRADITIONAL ASPECTS OF MODERN ETHIOPIA

CHAPTER ONE

THE CLASS STRUCTURE OF THE SOCIETY

1. *The classes in traditional society*

Ethiopians are very class conscious, and everyone has his clearly defined place in the social structure and will generally behave and function in accordance with the role assigned to him. "Class" is called *akəm*, "strength; status", *bota*, "place", or *wäsän*, "limit", and the words *zär*, "family", *däm*, "blood", or *aṭənt*, "bones" may convey the same idea, as status or class is normally, but not exclusively, tied to one's family background.[1]

Ato Ṭəso, a rather conservative judge who is also acquainted with modern ideas (in *Adäfrəs*) explains his view of the Ethiopians' attitude to class:

> "We have this tradition of authority and superiority that causes respect to be paid to us and that protects our right.—What does it mean, then, to say we have the tradition of honouring authority and obeying superiors? It means, for example, that unity in the family remains strong by the father's authority and superiority. It means that if the father's authority is destroyed, if the father's superiority meets with a competitor or rival, the house that was united will scatter in all directions - -. Furthermore, the clergy has spiritual authority, and the state has governmental authority and superiority which serve to guarantee a peaceful life." [2]

Those who have done well and are comfortable in this system are inclined to defend it as the best way to organize society, and many regard it as the expression of God's will supported by reason.[3] One rich landowning lady says that appointment to high office or position is given to the best of men, as the best wood is chosen for the altar in a church. "Now, for example—my servants, even if I say they are created in the likeness of God, should I say they are equal to me? No my child," she tells Adäfrəs, a university student, and she advises him to take the realities of the situation into

---

[1] *Fəkr əskä mäḳabər*, 126:22-25, 335:11.20; 84:3.11, 86:29, 221:18, 334:7.
[2] *Adäfrəs*, 72ult.-73:9.
[3] *Ib.*, 8:25-31, 157:1-14.

consideration, instead of putting forward only theoretical arguments.[4]

The ranks of the nobility were not closed, and many could advance from simple status into a higher class, but the old noble families tended to guard their privileges jealously and look down upon those who had a short noble lineage, particularly if the title was thought to have been obtained through payments which they regarded as bribes.[5] Guddu Kasa, the wise "fool" who is also a nobleman in *Fəkr əskä mäkabər*, explains how the nobles have become prisoners of a system where they enjoy so many privileges, and because of their intransigent defence of their position they will eventually be driven into confrontations in which they will inevitably lose. He mentions as an example how he could freely use his maid for sexual pleasures, but as soon as he married her, he became an outcast from his own class and family, and his children were not accepted by his relatives.[6] Women who have married above their class or status may continually be reminded of their lower origins and have to defend themselves through arguments other than class. Defiantly they may counter, "Who am I inferior to?"[7] The proud attitude of such a woman may elicit admiration and acceptance from some, as Bälläṭäč in *Yalačča gabəčča* gains the approval of the conservative and authoritarian landowner Wzo Alganäš after her nephew Bahru had married Bälläṭäč although she had been his maid.[8] Wzo Asäggaš in *Adäfrəs* admonishes one of her tenants who has revealed some ambition and a tendency towards self-assertion but holds out the hope that he might advance to a higher status one day.[9] A proverb says that to do well in life, one should either be born well or stick close to someone of good family.[10]

Noble status is strongly coveted, and special pride is taken in a long line of noble forefathers and in having oneself obtained nobility through bravery. One's forefathers are often referred to as "grandfather, great-grandfather", but many more generations are usually

---

[4] *Adäfrəs*, 101:3-8.
[5] *Fəkr əskä mäkabər*, 86:4-13.
[6] *Fəkr əskä mäkabər*, 334:2-335:16.
[7] *Kä'admas bašagär*, 141:11-20, *Yähəllina däwäl*, 68:19.22.
[8] *Yalačča gabəčča*, 161:1-6.
[9] *Adäfrəs*, 12:13-19.
[10] *Ib.*, 66:25f., 133:17.

implied by this phrase.[11] One who has a long noble pedigree, a "heavy, noble parentage that cannot be lifted with two hands", considers himself better than one who has only recently acquired a title.[12] The landed gentry felt strongly attached to the land, and built their power on the accumulation of land and entrenched themselves in the local community through always adding to their prerogatives.[13] The government would often reward faithful servants through grants of land, or rights to the tax or tribute, in part or in full, from government land, rights that could expire after a specified number of years, or on a person's death, or could be inherited by his family. Such grants could be given on condition that the recipient would raise soldiers or provide for troops during military campaigns, and he would be expected to be an *akəñ*, i.e. one who protects the government's interests and is a civilizing influence in the area.[14]

As high position and wealth were frequently regarded as gifts from God and the king, it is natural that many nobles would be strong supporters of the Church and the Emperor.[15]

The presence of the clergy is strongly felt at all levels of society. Apart from performing ritual functions connected with the Church, they act as advisers to their parishioners. In Amharic literature, they are often depicted as conservative supporters of the nobility and the powerful who would like to see things remain as they are, without much change. The Church often demands heavy sacrifices that can further impoverish poor farmers.[16]

Ordinary peasants are often described as an oppressed class, and we meet them mostly in situations of confrontation with landlords or other people who exploit them in their humble and defenceless position. This is the situation in *Fəkr əskä mäkabər*, where the

---

[11] *Fəkr əskä mäkabər*, 84:2-7. 11f., 221:9-17, *Adäfrəs*, 12:17, 43:12, 82:29, *Şähay Mäsfən*, 5:10-14, 16:15-17. An Ethiopian is likely to know at least seven generations of his forefathers. These are designated, beginning with the father, grandfather, etc.: *abbat, ayat, kədmayat (əmmita,* "great-grandmother"), *kəmat* or *kəmayat, šämmat, məzlat,* and *əndəlat.* CF. DTW, p. 507, on *zär kotäva.*

[12] *Fəkr əskä mäkabər*, 83:21f., 88:12, 89:14, 108:4f., 121:3f., 412:9.

[13] *Ib.*, 209ult.-210:27, *Adäfrəs*, 12:16-19.

[14] *Adäfrəs*, 29:1, 66:21.24f., 93:3-6, 134:6f., (cf. DTW on *gəndä bäl*), *Fəkr əskä mäkabər*, 211:22-212:1, 213:17-19, 452:26f.

[15] *Adäfrəs*, 8:3f. 25-31, 172:12-24.

[16] *Adäfrəs*, 101:9-11, *Fəkr əskä mäkabər*, 215;10-12, 220:20-25 *Yalačča gabəčča*, 72:20ff., *Əddəl näw? bädäl?*, 11:1-17:10, 18:15-22:4 (esp. 20:11-17, 21:3f., 21:24-22:4), 30:1-33:20.

peasants appear to protest when the burden of taxes and tributes becomes intolerable;[17] and in *Adäfrəs* tenants and smallholders are equally shown as humiliated and exploited by their masters, because they have no one else to turn to in times of trouble.[18] *Əddəl näw? bädäl?* is a novel totally dedicated to this theme: a peasant is driven to desperation because of difficulties and demands made by priests and bureaucrats. The farmer who had a small piece of land and was a tax-payer, the *gäbbar*, could be entangled in debts and difficulties that made his situation sometimes worse than that of the tenant, *čəsäñña*, who paid rent and tribute to the landlord but was otherwise free to leave the land if his lot became intolerable. The *gäbbar*, by trying to hold on to his land, could enter into a relationship little better than slavery to one who had *gult*-rights (i.e. rights to claim tribute) on his land.[19] Strict measures could be taken by landlords against peasants who did not meet their obligations. Ato Mäšäša in *Fəkr əskä mäkabər* makes an armed attack on them;[20] another landlord is said to have taken a tenant's pretty wife as a mistress when her husband could not pay his debts.[21] In other cases, wives might be sent to grind grain at the mill, weed and harvest, or to spin, and a tenant's children be used as shepherds, or incorporated in the landlord's retinue.[22] Peasants had many obligations and had to give many gifts to their lords, and tenants could easily be evicted.[23]

Shepherds may not be regarded as a separate class, but they have developed a direct, earthy, frequently vulgar directness in behaviour and speech, and their poetry is celebrated for its down-to-earth rudeness.[24]

Servants, male and female, are present in almost all households, performing a variety of jobs. Some servants can be treated almost as members of the family,[25] whereas others are treated practically

---

[17] *Fəkr əskä mäkabər*, chapters 18 and 20, esp., pp. 209-36, 251-75.
[18] *Adäfrəs*, 6:30-12:28.
[19] *Adäfrəs*, 93:1-94:10.
[20] *Fəkr əskä mäkabər*, chapter 21, pp. 276ff.
[21] *Yäšoh aklil*, 17:24-30, cf. 58:26-34.
[22] *Adäfrəs*, 13:29, 17:26, 157:4-6.
[23] *Fəkr əskä mäkabər*, 137:24-27, 176:10ff., 180:3, 209:10. 210:15.17, 212:12, 219:29-31, 253ult., *Yähəllina däwäl* 62:6-17.
[24] *Əddəl näw? bädäl?* 100:9-101:16, cf. DTW on *ənka səlantiyyah*, p. 942, *Bälg*, 74:6. (*And lännatu*, 327:1-11.)
[25] *Adäfrəs*, chapter 10, pp. 70f., *Araya*, 183:2.

as slaves.²⁶ A servant in Fitawrari Mäšäša's house (in *Fəkr əskä mäkabər*) describes her own sad situation:

"The happiness of a slave mother and father is only the love they make sleeping together before bearing a child! It (i.e. the happiness) is not in thinking that the child I bore will help me when I am tired, nurse me when I am sick, look after me when I am old! A slave's motherly relationship to her child lasts only while she is pregnant and has labour pains until she gives birth, and while she suckles him, until he begins to eat *ənjära*-bread. After that she counts for nothing. After that, both the child and the mother are equally the master's property." ²⁷

There are other references to slave status, too, in Amharic literature, although this can be indirect, as when it is related that a servant is given his "freedom",²⁸ or others are given names only applied to slaves, e.g. *Sättäñ*, "He (God) gave me (this slave)", *Aräru*, a male slave's name, according to DTW, who also gives the translation "black donkey" for this word; ²⁹ or a "name-phrase", so that he is called by the first part of the phrase, and has to respond by the second half of the phrase to complete the meaning of the name, e.g. a girl is called *ləkura bähullu*, "I have reason to be proud towards everyone", and she has to respond by the words *əmmete sallu!* "as long as my mistress is there, or because of my mistress!" ³⁰

When a female slave bears a child by her master, it is called *yäbet wəld*, "born in the house", or *dikala*, "bastard", and has rights of inheritance.³¹

Worst off socially are the artisans or craftsmen (and minstrels) of all kinds who are often looked down upon and treated as outcasts by other classes of people. "The cast or group of manual workers" is despised, and called by derogatory names, especially *țäyyəb*, a

---

[26] *Arrəmuññ*, pp. 49ff. Cf. *Yähəllina däwäl*, 237:15-238:7.
[27] *Fəkr əskä mäkabər*, 311:2-10.
[28] *Araya*, 206:11f.
[29] DTW, p. 960.
[30] *Fəkr əskä mäkabər*, 86:15, 280:23, 281:8ff. 17-22.Cf. Säyfu Mättafäriya Frew, "*Yäbariya səm bä'amaraw bahəl*", in JES, Vol. X, No. 2 (July 1972), pp. 127-200.
[31] *Yäšoh aklil*, 70:32, *Yähəllina däwäl*, 70:6-8, *Joro țäbi*, 30:13-31:1, 6oult., 100:13-101:1, 103:3-9. Also slaves have their "genealogies" according to the number of generations they have been serving the same household; starting with the last generation of slaves born of a slave or slaves in the household, they are: *wəlaj, fənaj, kənaj, asäläț, amäläț, man bete, däräba bete, dur bete*; cf. DTW on *bariya*.

word that also associates them with the possession of "the evil eye" and the ability to cause harm to others by magical means.[32]

The attitude to manual workers is set out by a student in *Yähəllina däwäl*:

> "In our land, beginning from of old, those who have tasted academic learning do not like to work with their hands. This did not begin with us. They used to insult and humiliate those who work with their hands, calling them hammerers (i.e. blacksmiths), masters of the hand (i.e. manual workers), *ṭäyyəb* (a word associating artisans with "the evil eye"), scrapers (i.e. tanners). Those who work with their hands have not become priests or *däbtära* (cantors or scholars), officials or soldiers. The merchant is called "one who bites the strap used to tie the load on the donkey", the farmer, "one who pushes soil"."[33]

Merchants are treated kindly in some cases. Ato Wäldu, an important character in *Adäfrəs*, is well born and rather well educated, but has given up a government job and his right to his father's land in order to become a merchant in Däbrä Sina. He is portrayed with sympathy; and he is a tolerant and gentle, though also a somewhat weak character.[34] In *Fəḵr əskä mäḵabər*, merchants from Gojjam help Bäzzabbəh to reach Addis Ababa when he flees from the wrath of Fitawrari Mäšäša, and in the capital one of them helps him to pay the fee required to get a particular teaching job in the Church.[35] Other merchants are shown as grasping people who do not shy away from using doubtful or dishonest means of acquiring wealth.[36]

Although oppression and misuse of power are frequently pointed out in Amharic literature, Ethiopian authors seem on the whole to accept the class structure of their society.

2. *Social interrelationships*

a) *The Emperor and the people*

It is common in Amharic books printed during the period 1930-74 to meet a picture of the Emperor at the front, and the year of

---

[32] *Fəḵr əskä mäḵabər*, 334:7, *Yäšoh aklil*, 31:33f. Cf. DTW on *ṭäyyəb* for different insulting terms applied to smiths, potters, weavers (always men), tanners and carpenters or masons.
[33] *Yähəllina däwäl*, 179:1-6; cf. *Yäḵəne azmära*, 49:6-14.
[34] *Adäfrəs*, 27:29f., 34:8ff., 151:1ff., 317:1ff.
[35] *Fəḵr əskä mäḵabər*, 433:5ff., 455:15-456:2.
[36] *Ṣähay Mäsfən*, 18:8ff., 36:12-38:16, *Yäḵəne azmära*, 100:5-101:13.

publication is often accompanied by the year of the Emperor's reign in which the book was published. A few have laudatory words addressed to the Emperor, and, in rare cases, an author may preface a "letter" to him at the beginning of the book. This may be done in admiration of the Emperor or to show one is a loyal subject, or to be noticed and possibly rewarded, or maybe also in the hope of making one's views known to him and thus becoming a kind of unofficial guide or adviser to the Emperor.

In the body of the fictional works themselves, the Emperor is quite frequently referred to, but there are few descriptions of actual meetings with him.

Generally, great loyalty to the Emperor is demonstrated by the characters in Amharic literature. Even when changes in the land are sought, the imperial power should not be affected, as one *aläḵa* says:

> "Today, both the times and the knowledge of man have changed, and it is better to function in accordance with the times. Only matters relating to faith time does not change, but there is no problem if matters relating to custom change after their usefulness has been evaluated, unless this harms the king, the government or the people." [37]

The Emperor is referred to as *nəgus*, "king", *nəgusä nägäst*, "king of kings, emperor", *gərmawi*, "Majesty", *janhoy*, approximately "Your/His Majesty", and *aṣe*, approximately "Emperor".[38] Ethiopian emperors are also known by a "horse name", or *nom-de-guerre*; Haile Sellassie's was *ṭäḵəl(l)*, "encompass, unify, wrap up!" [39] It is common practice to swear by the name of a ruling monarch, e.g. *haylä səllase yəmut*, "May Haile Sellassie die (if I tell a lie)".[40]

Gərmaččäw Täklä Hawaryat writes in *Araya* for his own part, it seems, that the Ethiopians have always been obedient to their emperor and have great faith in and love for him, more than other

---

[37] *Addis aläm*, 50:25-30.
[38] *Araya*, 7:1-3, 163:16, 166:5.10.22.25, 210:10, 242:9, 255:15, 319:17f. (cf. 168:23), 338:1.5.8, *Säw allä bəyye*, p. 1, 124:3 (cf. *Kaleb*, 65:14); see KWK on *ḥäde* and *ḥädege*, p. 457, and DTW on *jan hoy*, p. 399.
[39] *Yäḵəne azmära*, 46:9, 47:7. Cf. *če bäläw (yäfäräs səm)*, by Blattengeta Mahtämä Səllase Wäldä Mäsḵäl, Addis Ababa, 1961 E.C.; also in JES, Vol. VII, No. 2 (July 1969), pp. 195-303. Haile Sellassie is known as *abba ṭäḵəl*, "father of *Ṭäḵəl*"; cf. DTW on *ṭäḵəl*.
[40] *Adäfrəs*, 257:21 (cf. *Araya*, 338:1f).

peoples have for their leaders. In Ethiopia, the king is regarded as anointed by God and created to lead the people. He is both judge and head, and at the same time he is considered the *pater familias* who is ever kind and helpful to small and big alike. He is not remote from the people but can be approached and appealed to by any ordinary man.[41] To swear "in the name of Haile Sellassie" vouches for the truth of a statement.[42] The Emperor is looked upon as shepherd of his people, a just judge, guardian of the faith, and a national leader who has been anointed by God to his high position.[43]

Some see Haile Sellassie as the one chosen to bring civilization and a better life to the Ethiopian people and to lead Ethiopia into modern times; and to complete the work begun by Menelik.[44] As supreme judge, the Emperor has his own court, *čəlot*.[45] He is an inspiration to soldiers who, it is said, do not fight well unless they see the king,[46] and the people are ready to die for the honour of their Emperor.[47] Käbbädä Mika'el writes that Haile Sellassie has caused work to be honoured, and laziness or idleness to be "demoted".[48] The Emperor grants titles and appoints high officials, such as governors and political leaders;[49] he made the Ethiopian Church independent of Egypt, united Church and state, and placed the Church under the power of the state; he is himself head of both and is seen as the one who lends splendour to both.[50] In the administration of the country, he tried to break the power of the old noble families by appointing to high office what aristocrats used to call "the children of any poor man", people who owed allegiance only to him; all his troubles, the old ruling class maintained, came from this policy.[51]

After the Italian occupation of Ethiopia, the Emperor wanted to put emphasis on what he called "the new civilization", i.e. education, hard work, unity, cooperation, love, equality before

---

[41] *Araya*, 168:1f.10-21.
[42] *Adäfrəs*, 278:18.
[43] *Tarikənna məssale*, 2nd page after list of contents, ll. 13-20.
[44] *Araya*, 143:8-10, 168:29-169:3, 170:1-5 (cf. 44:20-24).
[45] *Ib.*, 166:14.
[46] *Ib.*, 242:8-10, 243:13.
[47] *Yähəllina däwäl*, 177:26.
[48] *Yäkəne azmära*, 48:6f., 49:4f., 50:3f., 51:20f., 52:15f.
[49] *Adäfrəs*, 8:2-4.27f., 77:8, 172:19-22.
[50] *Ib.*, 73:15-74:3, 90:23f.
[51] *Ib.*, 172:19-22.

the law, and freedom; he would improve agriculture, promote trade, and encourage art and science.[52] Araya considers Haile Sellassie as equal to and even surpassing the great emperors of Ethiopia's past.[53]

Scenes where the Emperor appears are rare in Amharic literature, and most of them occur in *Araya*. In *Fəkr əskä mäḵabər* there is a vague royal presence at a royal banquet, but no clear image emerges; we are only told that the feast is resplendent, and that the food is plentiful.[54] The most detailed and colourful description of the royal entourage is given in *Araya*. The Emperor with retinue passes through the palace grounds, the *gəbbi*, where a large crowd is gathered. The Emperor greets the people, "How did you spend the night?" and a chamberlain repeats his words in a loud voice, and the people throw themselves to the ground. Araya finds the Emperor has refined traits and a fair complexion; his great natural majesty is not diminished by his short stature, and it is rather increased by his silk-like beard. Araya is clearly impressed and is filled with longing, love, joy and pride when he sees the Emperor for the first time.[55]

Araya's own interview with the Emperor is rather tersely described:

> "His Majesty was leaning over a big desk and was looking at and turning over papers heaped in front of him. As Araya arrived in front of him, he greeted him in a proper way. After His Majesty had asked him, with a smile that revealed kindness, about his health, about his family, and about his studies, he asked him in what way he meant to serve the country. And although Araya had made a special study of agriculture, he explained to him that he was prepared to perform any work His Majesty commanded him.
> And His Majesty, realizing this young man's sincerity and willingness to work, and wanting to put him in a position where he was urgently needed and where he could benefit (from working), told him to go and serve in the ministry of....., and ordered him to go to the minister and ask him (about it)."[56]

Both Gərmaččäw Täklä Hawaryat and Mäkkonən Əndalkaččäw have written about the battle of Mayčäw and the Emperor's participation in it;[57] the former has also described his return after

---

[52] *Araya*, 346:15-26.
[53] *Ib.*, 170:16-23; cf. *Adäfrəs*, 90:13-91:12.
[54] *Fəkr əskä mäḵabər*, 448:1-20 (cf. 447:18).
[55] *Araya*, 166:21-167ult. See also 168:1-170:23.
[56] *Araya*, 176:12-28.
[57] *Ib.*, chapter 17; *Arrəmuññ*, 341-360.

his exile in 1941 and reports a speech where the Emperor outlines some of his programme for the future.[58]

When the Emperor travelled about in the country, the local population had a duty to provide him with food and drink, referred to as *mäṭən*,[59] strictly speaking ten *ənjära*-bread, one jar of beer, and a pot of stew, according to DTW. The Emperor could normally be approached only by permission of "the one who gives access", the *ligaba*, a functionary who also reads royal proclamations to the people, such as the proclamation of the general mobilization in 1935, and who also has some legal duties.[60]

There are a few expressions of criticism of, or disagreement with, the Emperor in Amharic literature. Araya says: "I consider the battle of May Çäw a great error",[61] and he thinks the Emperor should not have gone into exile, but stayed in Ethiopia as leader of the freedom fighters, the *arbäññoč*.[62] One gets also the feeling that Araya is disappointed with the way power has been centralized and the inefficient way the bureaucracy is run,[63] and he rejects the view of the Ethiopian consul in Djibouti that development and change in Ethiopia should be slow and gradual.[64] In both cases, it is likely Araya opposes policies originating from the Emperor. Particularly the latter point, that the country should be modernized slowly, might have been indirectly criticized by authors like Abbe Gubäñña, whose heroes in *Məlkam säyfä näbälbal* and *Aləwwällädəm* advocate and practise rapid change as national leaders. The voluminous fictional literature about Tewodros, who was impatient and wanted to change Ethiopia fast, may also be an expression of the view that Ethiopia was developing too slowly.

In more recent times, opposition could become more radical, so that university students are reported to have refused to obey the Emperor.[65] He could be blamed for the backwardness of the country and for the oppression in the Church.[66]

Ato Wäldu, a merchant who has been to France for education,

---

[58] *Araya*, chapter 30.
[59] *Ib.*, 255:16.
[60] *Araya*, 233:25, 234:2, *Fəkr əskä mäḳabər*, 392:25f. Cf. DTW on *ligaba*, p. 216.
[61] *Araya*, 284:27f.
[62] *Ib.*, 285:12-21.
[63] *Ib.*, chapter 11.
[64] *Ib.*, 115:7-23.
[65] *Adäfrəs*, 172:12-24.
[66] *Ib.*, 73:18-74:3, 87:12-88:6.

believes people have an unrealistic view of the Emperor, and would therefore blame him for hunger, thirst, that they cannot cope (with life), for troubles from the heat of the sun, tiredness or drought. He is asked to do what even God refuses to do for man, he says.[67] Adäfrəs thinks people do not appreciate the good the Emperor has done because it was granted to them without a struggle, as was the case with the granting of a constitution and the right to vote for members to a parliament.[68]

Although justice was not always found in "the king's court",[69] a simple man like Gärrämäw in *Əddəl näw? bädäl?* who only meets frustration in his vain search for justice, could still express his love for the country and the Emperor.[70]

b) *Landlords and tenants*

The relationship between tenants (*čəsänña*) and tax or tribute paying farmers (*gäbbar*), on the one hand, and landlords who receive the tribute in kind or money, on the other, is especially important in *Fəkr əskä mäkabər* and *Adäfrəs*. Wzo Alganäš in *Yalačča gabəčča* is a landowning lady and is portrayed as a rather pompous but also kindly woman. She is used to ordering people about, including her own family, and to being obeyed,[71] and she tells a boy to greet people on her behalf while she reads the Psalter [72] in an even more detached way than the Emperor, whose own greeting is repeated in a louder voice by a chamberlain.[73] She is a capable woman who can look after her affairs and hold on to her land; [74] but she can also see reason and be kind and forgiving.[75]

In *Araya*, also, we meet a landlord who is depicted with sympathy, and whereas Araya criticizes to his face the system he represents,[76] he defends it by saying landlord and tenants are like one big family who look after each other's needs, and he says they share what they have; and the system has divine sanction and gives

---

[67] *Adäfrəs*, 155:11-28.
[68] *Ib.*, 155:1-8.
[69] *Fəkr əskä mäkabər*, 462:23ff.
[70] *Əddəl näw? bädäl?* 93:13.
[71] *Yalačča gabəčča*, 69:15-18, 82:13-19, 89:1ff., 93:17-94:5, 95:9-12, 111ult.-112:2.
[72] *Ib.*, 27:10-16.
[73] *Araya*, 166:21-167:2.
[74] *Yalačča gabəčča*, 55:7f., 144:3-6, 165:3ff.
[75] *Ib.*, 161:1-162:2.
[76] *Araya*, 159:1-4, 159:16-160:6, 160:19-26, 160:30-161:7, 161:12-21.

happiness to everyone, in his opinion.[77] But his sumptuous life style is in sharp contrast to that of the common people Araya sees.[78] The argument is here a general one, and any attack on the landlords is made without acrimony, and without representing them as evil, corrupt people.

Later literature is more outspoken in attacking the way land was acquired and tribute exacted from the peasantry, and authors become more vociferous in defending the rights of the tenants, or farmers in general. This is probably caused by the deterioration in the relationship between the two groups, as a result of increased demands on the farmers. The new, additional taxes and gifts they had to pay are a main grievance of the peasants who ask Fitawrari Mäsäša in *Fəkr əskä mäkabər* to alleviate their lot after a series of natural disasters. They do not complain of taxes that have a long tradition, but recent additions are too heavy for them.[79] Fitawrari Mäsäša's view is that "if the peasant is sated, he does not know his limit", i.e. he becomes arrogant, insubordinate and aggressive.[80]

A tenant in *Adäfrəs* also complains to his mistress, Wzo Asäggaš, that their lot is getting worse. "The old days were better", he says, "not like today, when the landlord and the farmer have to account to each other (for everything)".[81]

Fitawrari Täkka in *Yähəllina däwäl* is kind and helpful to the local peasantry, but when it comes to eviction of tenants, there is nothing he can do to help them. "It is a problem brought by the times", he tells them, and adds that "time will heal it".[82] The landowner or the master with rights to taxes and tributes on the land had great powers in regulating the size of these fees (the legal maximum was 75 % of the harvest).[83] The situation for the peasants deteriorated so badly that one of the most insistent of demands for change in the country centred on a cry for land reform: "land to the tiller".[84]

In a confrontation between peasants and their master, Fitawrari

---

[77] *Araya*, 158:10-13, 159:5-15, 160:7-18. 27-29, 161:22-163:9.
[78] *Ib.*, 156:3-158:2, 162:10-14; cf. 129:6-27, 151:15-152:16.
[79] *Fəkr əskä mäkabər*, 212:16ff., 213:15-23, 213:31ff., 215:2ff.
[80] *Ib.*, 211:13f.
[81] *Adäfrəs*, 9:1f.
[82] *Yähəllina däwäl*, 62:6-17. Cf. S. Pausewang, "Die Landreform in Äthiopien" (in *Afrika Spectrum*, No. 1, 1977, pp. 17-36), pp. 21-24.
[83] *Adäfrəs*, 93:4-7; cf. S. Pausewang, *op. cit.*, p. 24.
[84] *Yähəllina däwäl*, 176:18, 177:8.

Mäšäša, in *Fəkr əskä mäkabər*, an elder who speaks for the peasants tells Fitawrari that "we cannot live without you, and you also cannot live without us", and he advises him to come to a reasonable settlement with the peasants.[85] Then he states their problem:

> "After New Year, we poor ones who live on your three *gult* lands (i.e. who pay tribute to you) have sold our cattle and paid three bullocks for (the celebration of) the Feast of the Cross (*mäskäl*), and three for Christmas. And this in addition to the quarter of the harvest (*ərbo*) (paid by) those who till your hereditary land (*rəst*) and the stipulated tribute (*gämäta*) (paid by) those who live on and till your *gult* land. In addition, there are obligations to pay money to and to work for the district (*wäräda*), for the governor (*məsläne*), the local headman (*čəka šum*): all this is beyond our capacity." [86]

The tribute called *ərbo* in this passage is one of the major forms of rent paid by tenants. Another is known as *siso*, literally "one third".[87] The tenants first pay one tenth (*asrat*) of the harvest to the landowner, and the *siso araš* pays one third, the *ərbo araš* one fourth of the remainder.[88]

In the further argument with Fitawrari Mäšäša, he is reminded that his three *gult*-holdings are *näṭala gultoč*, not *rəstägult*, i.e. they are given to him to last only during his lifetime and are not hereditary in his family. This involves a difference in the tribute: to a holder of *näṭala gult* only *gämäta*, i.e. a stipulated, or estimated and agreed fee, should be paid, in money or in kind.[89] Gifts on holidays used to be voluntary gifts and no obligation. Only recently have landlords tried to demand as a duty what started as an expression of friendship and good will, and this has led to heavy burdens on the peasants.[90]

---

[85] *Fəkr əskä mäkabər*, 212:3ff.

[86] *Ib.*, 212:16-22. The country is divided into provinces (*ṭäklay gəzat*), sub-provinces (*awrajja*), districts (*wäräda*) and sub-districts (*məkəttəl wäräda*); *məsläne* can be used both of the governor of a province and of one of his deputies or an administrator under him; the *čəka šum* is a minor official who deals with the peasants on behalf of the *gult*-holder.

[87] *Yähəllina däwäl*, 86:7, *Əddəl näw? bädäl?* 27:18-20.

[88] Cf. J. M. Cohen and D. Weintraub, *Land and peasants in Imperial Ethiopia*, Assen, 1975, p. 53. The authors write that the practice of *ərbo* steadily decreased and the practice of *siso* increased. Many even required 50%, after the 10% (*əkkul araš*).

[89] *Fəkr əskä mäkabər*, 213ult.-214:9.

[90] *Ib.*, 214:9-29; cf. 219:29-31.

Wzo Asäggaš in *Adäfrəs* had inherited land from her deceased husband, an officer, and her father, the head of a main church. The husband had left her at least ten *gašša* [91] that had originally been given to his father for the upkeep of himself and his troops (*yämadäriya märet*), and although such government land (*yämängəst hudad*) usually reverted to the state at a person's death, the *gult* rights over this land had been made hereditary (*rəstä gult*). Most valuable was the right to decide the size of the tribute (*gəbər*) the peasants (*gäbbar*) should pay; and his demands were severe: for each *gašša* he requested payment of one hornful (*gundo*) of honey, one third of the harvest (*siso*) (after one tenth had been paid, as noted above), three sacks (*dawəlla*, ca. 100 kg. each) of grain, that five *ḵunna* (ca. 5 litres each) of grain be ground at the mill, that his silos be guarded and that firewood be brought to him.[92] From her father Wzo Asäggaš had inherited land, including the right of tribute on church land pertaining to his position as *aläḵa*, head of a main church. Her husband was harsh in exercising the right of tribute on this land, too. He asked for honey and chickens, and that the peasants weeded and ploughed his land, and threshed his grain, and even fetched water, gathered wood and reared his cattle. These peasants, who owned their own small pieces of land, had to give tribute and, together with their whole families, work for the *aläḵa*, or a local military officer, or the *mälkäñña*, representing the governor or a rich landowner and often a landowner himself, or all of them, especially during planting and harvesting times; and no one dared to disobey their masters. If a peasant or his family were lazy in performing what was required of them, they would suffer hunger and have to leave their house and land; the children would then become shepherds, the women would grind at the mill or sew, and the farmers themselves would become farmhands, retainers, part of the landlord's retinue. In the end they would be totally demoralized, give up their land and the family would be scattered, or become servants of the local officer, the *aläḵa*, or the *mälkäñña*.[93] Wzo Asäggaš herself had given most of the supervision of her land to a "helper" after her husband's death, and, as a result, most of the obligations of the farmers had been relaxed. She had a couple of shepherd-boys who worked for her in lieu of

---

[91] One *gašša* is ca. 40 hectares.
[92] *Adäfrəs*, 93:1-13.
[93] *Adäfrəs*, 93:14-28.

tribute, until their fathers would be able to pay their debts; but even this arrangement was done on the suggestion of the fathers of the boys.[94] Still she is capable of looking after her land and her interests. As she is thus presented as a tough, though not overly severe master, it is of interest to quote at some length a conversation she has with one of her tenants. It shows her understanding of the position, privileges and obligations of both of them, and the basic views underlying the arguments she uses to drive her points home. She talks in detail about God's interest in the matter, and of man's duty to God, and of God's ability to punish people for pride and dereliction of duty through sending locusts, sorrow and plague, with resulting famine.[95] Then she goes on:

"To fear God is the first wisdom.—Next is to honour your superiors—the nobility, the landlords, those who were not cut off from the generosity of their king, from the goodness of God - - - - Yes, "If flies gather (their efforts), they cannot undo threads twisted together" - -.''

"I know, Madam!"

"Maybe you know it, but if you consider a bit, you can understand it was not put into practice. Now, for example, you have come to borrow some millet (mašəlla). True enough, it does not apply to your behaviour today, you have honoured me and been a nice man. But last year, if you remember,—you remember, I am sure—, when I asked you to help me with the mowing and the threshing, what was it you answered me? Didn't you say (like the proverb), " "Goodbye, sack; I have put the fruit inside"—I haven't even mown my own—I haven't even threshed my own; I even need someone to help me!"? Didn't you even say, "I pay tax to the government, you see; I have no obligation (to help you)"? You had become arrogant towards us, you see—you had become conceited ("inflated") against us! "When there is no rain, everywhere can be a house (or home); when no guest comes, everyone can do the work of a woman!" (i.e. do not under-estimate me because I am a woman). Yes, you are right, you have no obligation—but look here ... look here ... when the times are against you, you wag your tail like a whelp, timidly like this—! "If one cannot find people one likes, one will sponge on people one hates!" You were giving yourself airs against me, me - - -.''

"Doesn't one say, "If one tells him (i.e. a beggar) that there is a shaggy dog, he will die of hunger (fearing to go there to beg)'' - - ?''

"You are very vain; that is why you are crushed by all these troubles - - -.'' [96]

---

[94] *Adäfrəs*, 94:1-10.
[95] *Ib.*, 6:30-8:1.
[96] *Ib.*, 8:2-23.

She says that both God and the Emperor have honoured her and elevated her to high position because of her humility, and returns to the matter at hand:

> "Well now then, you said you came to borrow some sorghum (zängadda) - -?"
> "Yes, I did, Madam, if I am not causing too much trouble - - -."
> "Do you want to buy it, then - -?"
> "Where, Madam, where is the money to be found? No, it is to be paid in the same way, in kind, in December - -." [97]

When she again rebukes him for past arrogance, he says he has nowhere else to go. She is pleased with his humiliation and promises to help him, although not gladly, and in spite of the fact that the price of sorghum has become "fire", i.e. very expensive. Then she goes on:

> "What happiness ("world") is there like helping each other? Helping each other is not bad - - If I lend you today, then tomorrow maybe I shall come to you and ask you to lend to me - - -."
> "Maybe, maybe, Madam - - However - - -."
> "Oh no; I did not mean maybe - - - It is like saying what there is no doubt about - - And now then, what you want is fifteen ḳunna (ca. 5 litres each) - -?"
> "Yes, Madam, if you please - - -."
> "Very well - - fifteen ḳunna - - - That means I give you nine ḳunna; in December you will return fifteen - -."
> "Oh no, what I, however - - -."
> "As you see, I do not want any interest; it is the same, kind for kind, from what you will gather in of your rich harvest. Yes, it is not much. And it will also be measured up to you to overflowing. "A bone swallowed with pleasure tastes better than (soft) meat from the breast"."
> "Isn't it a bit much, Madam - -?"
> "Is it too much? Well then, if it is too much, it is better you ask someone else.—I am not so very enthusiastic about the whole business; I lend you because I feel sorry for you—It was you who came to me; I didn't come to you - - -."
> "Well, yes, Madam, I was just thinking you felt sorry for me - - -."
> "I never stopped feeling sorry for you - - - And furthermore, if our talk leads to bickering, what is the point -."
> "That's right; only, I reply that I think it is a bit too much - -."
> "Well, well, well; but don't pierce me with talk. Are you making me a usurer who takes more from you than the government has permitted me? Your talk is misguided (or subversive)...." [98]

---

[97] *Adäfrəs*, 9:9-14.
[98] *Adäfrəs*, 10:22-11:16.

THE CLASS STRUCTURE OF THE SOCIETY

She complains of all her expenses: tax to the government, food (dərgo) to every monk who comes, a wedding to arrange. After some bickering, the tenant asks:

"Let that be, and now then, well, what do I do - - -?"
"Yes, that is better - - this year is not last year. There is nothing for you to do - - - By the way, when I do something for you, you should probably also do something for me - - that is the sign of Christians - - -."
"I don't mind if there is something I can do - - -."
"The sign of Christians is to do as one is done by; a great lesson; and, well then, if you help me to cut the grass that is adjacent to you (your land) - - - I mean, it is like a favour! So that my favour will not weigh heavily upon you - - - If we help each other, God helps us; it makes Him happy, when He looks down upon us - - - And also, it does not do you any harm to cut that grass; as for me, I shall not forget this favour of yours in future - - As you know, I am a gentle person - - - Now then, as I mentioned to you earlier, your speed has become too fast (i.e. you want to move up in society too quickly); "What (i.e. clothes) one ties on while running, fall off while one is running" - - restrain it a bit - - Yes, you will be able once to hold your head high ("to hold your nose horizontally"). Even as for me, don't think I could have reached this level at once by myself; it is because my forefathers left behind rich land ("that makes it possible to drink mead"), because they did not only urinate on it and pass on (i.e. they settled). Yes, "a man lives (or has to live) by the standard of his own family, not by that of his neighbour". - - Now then, after you have cut the grass - - it may be about eighty loads - - don't forget to bring it and heap it in front of my door - - The way is a bit far for you - - therefore I don't ask you to hurry - In a fortnight or maybe a month you'll be able to finish it - -." [99]

As mentioned, Wzo Asäggaš is not presented as a particularly harsh master: her husband's exploitation had driven peasants from their land so that he could acquire it, and the peasants became his tenants or servants. Fitawrari Mäšäša in *Fəkr əskä mäkabər* is also unbending in his demands to the peasants who owe him tribute, and when they are unable to pay up, he tries to subjugate them by going on an armed campaign against them.[100]

Many landowners are shown in a fairly good light and not as harsh exploiters. This is the case with Ṣähay Mäsfən's father as well as earlier generations of her family.[101] Fitawrari Täkka in

---
[99] *Adäfrəs*, 12:1-23.
[100] *Fəkr əskä mäkabər*, chapter 21, pp. 276-303.
[101] *Ṣähay Mäsfən*, 16:18-17:5.

Yähəllina däwäl is progressive and tries to help the local peasants.[102] Even Fitawrari Mäšaša's relatives try to restrain him and are clearly of more moderate views and more liberal in the exercise of their rights and privileges than he is, although they fear that leniency and compromise with the peasants may reduce their power and therefore advise against it.[103] But the landowning nobility is judged as a group from the excesses of the most exploitative of their number.[104] Guddu Kasa says this will lead to their eventual downfall.[105] The situation for poor farmers became so difficult that many were forced to be quite outspoken in their complaints. Even where we have a kind landowner, as in *Yähəllina däwäl*, a farmer laments that troubles only come to the poor, not to the rich. The poor hunger and thirst, and also God is partial, because He says that more shall be added to the one who has. The poor who do not succeed on earth do not even enter heaven.[106] Many demanded a change in the system.[107]

c) *Status symbols*

The way used to show one's status and if possible to give an exaggerated impression of it is mostly to display wealth or signs of wealth. But if one can obtain titles, this too is a matter of importance for the bearers and is greatly coveted.[108] Some Ethiopian authors had high noble titles. Mäkonnən Əndalkaččäw was *ras bitwäddäd*, "beloved *ras*" (and *ras*, "head", was, as most noble titles, originally a military title, signifying "head or commander of the army"); and Gərmaččäw Täklä Hawaryat was *däjjazmač*, "commander of the (ruler's) gate". After the Emperor or king (both titles signifying Haile Sellassie I during most of the period this book deals with, since Haile Sellassie did not appoint regional kings as had been the practice previously) came the *ras*, then the *däjjazmač*, or *däjjač* for short; then the *fitawrari*, "commander of the vanguard"; the *ķäññazmač*, "commander of the right wing of the army"; the *grazmač*, "commander of the left wing of the army"; the *balambaras*, "commander of a fortress". Most titles occur

---

[102] *Yähəllina däwäl*, 36:15-26, 57:11-20, 61:6-17, 62:19.
[103] *Fəķr əskä mäķabər*, 217:2-220:2.
[104] *Ib.*, 462:23-463:16.
[105] *Ib.*, 221:6-31.
[106] *Yähəllina däwäl*, 86:1-4.
[107] *Ib.*, 176:18, 177:8.
[108] *Yalačča gabačča*, 42:6ff.

frequently in Amharic literature, and the authors seem to have a slight preference for the *fitawrari* and the *käññazmač* among the nobility.[109] Less important were the *nägadras*, "head of the merchants", the *baldäras*, "keeper of the (king's) horses", and the *čəka šum*, an appointed village elder or headman.[110] Həruy Wäldä Səllase was given the courtly title *blattengeta* as a tribute to his scholarly work, a title conferred by the Emperor; this title could also signify a "steward in charge of the ruler's estates of gwilt land".[111] The less important title *blatta* was also given for scholarly distinction.[112] Of other courtly titles, we encounter the *aggafari*, a supervisor of the servants in the royal household, or majordomo or chamberlain. But the title can be used of a head servant in any nobleman's household.[113] The titles of the clergy also denote one's place in the ecclesiastical hierarchy. (See chapter II, 1b.)

A warrior who had taken part in battles and killed an enemy, and particularly the *arbäñña*, the patriot or freedom fighter during the Italian occupation of Ethiopia (1935-41), would grow long hair and shape it like a mane, a *gofäre*. Often he would appear with his weapons at banquets or in audiences with the Emperor, although the practice was dying out.[114]

Titles are not hereditary, but sons of nobles are very often ennobled themselves.[115] Some took an inordinate pride in their long line of noble forefathers. Fitawrari Mäšäša in *Fəkr əskä mäkabər* had great difficulties in finding a worthy husband for his daughter Säblä Wängel, because he always found something lacking in the family tree of the suitors. A *käññazmač* was found insolent because he wanted her for his son; a *grazmač* was rejected because "his father is not a man, he is a peasant"; a *fitawrari* fares no better, because "his father was a biter of the leather strap used to tie donkey loads, a merchant"; a *balambaras* because "his father was a vulgar countryman who had many cows". All had bought their titles for money and therefore did not deserve them, nor his daugh-

---

[109] *Fəkr əskä mäkabər*, 8oult., 81:2, 85:4.13.17.25, 86; 11f., 135:18, 217:3, 220:2, *Ṭälfo bäkise*, 50:1f., *Yähəllina däwäl*, 26:1, *Adäfrəs*, 168:12, *Araya*, 254:26f.
[110] *Adäfrəs*, 213:26.32, *Fəkr əskä mäkabər*, 136:13.
[111] Cf. A. Hoben, *Land tenure among the Amhara of Ethiopia*, Chicago and London, 1973, p. 250.
[112] *Fəkr əskä mäkabər*, 16:25.
[113] *Ib.*, 444:18.21, *Araya*, 166:23.30f.; 155:20.
[114] *Əddəl näw? bädäl?*, 39:15.23, *Araya*, 155:10f.29, 165:12-16.
[115] *Əddəl näw? bädäl?*, 96:7-9.

ter, in Fitawrari Mäšäša's view.[116] A long line of noble forefathers was thus a source of great pride.[117]

Other signs of status the rich or mighty are glad to display are a great number of cattle, and many tenants on one's land, or many peasants from whom one has the right to claim tribute or tax.[118] Rich feasts with plenty to eat and drink add to the honour of the hosts.[119] Even external signs of affluence like a big paunch, and a rolling gait due to obesity, or smooth hands could be valued as signs of class and wealth.[120] The great lord or lady would ride with a retinue, frequently armed, when moving away from home, and importance was attached to the horse and the saddle.[121] To have a number of mistresses or concubines was also a sign of an important man.[122] People have to be addressed with respect, and one must take care to use titles properly; if the title is right, the name is not necessary. So one can ask, "How is your father, the *käññazmač*?" without mentioning his name; important men can be addressed as *getoč*, literally "lords", the plural signifying a person of great wealth and authority; and ladies as *əmmete*, "my lady", etc.[123] A sign of good upbringing for a noble youth was that he had acquired skills in daring, martial arts and games, such as horse-riding, *gugs* (a kind of polo), shooting, etc.[124]

Wealth is a principal sign of high status, and poverty is felt to be shameful. One man is insulted by being called "a child of ten poor (forefathers)", and a girl talks of her misery by saying she is "the daughter of a seller of *ənjära* (Ethiopian bread), poor of seven houses (i.e. generations)", where the numbers are only used to signify great poverty.[125] An impoverished nobleman is deeply

---

[116] *Fəkr əskä mäkabər*, 85:4-86:27.
[117] *Ib.*, 221:6-31, *Ṣähay Mäsfən*, 5:10ff., 16:15ff.
[118] *Adäfrəs*, 30:18-20.
[119] *Yä'ənba däbdabbewoč*, 12:11-25, *Bərr ambar säbbärälləwo*, 25:2ff., *Araya*, 159:1ff., 189:4-11.
[120] *Fəkr əskä mäkabər*, 85:29-31, *Yalačča gabəčča*, 114:8-10, *Yähəllina däwäl*, 181:18-22 (cf. 195:17).
[121] *Yähəllina däwäl*, 152:1-3.22, 153:1-6, *Fəkr əskä mäkabər*, 149:22ff., 154:19ff., 162:30ff., 460:26ff.
[122] *Fəkr əskä mäkabər*, 113:5-29.
[123] *Ib.*, 87:16, 90:1, *Adäfrəs*, 168:12, *Yalačča gabəčča*, 37:1.
[124] *Fəkr əskä mäkabər*, 266:11ff. Cf. Blattengeta Mahtämä Səllase Wäldä Mäskäl, "Portrait retrospectif d'un gentilhomme éthiopien", in *Proceedings of the Third International Conference of Ethiopian Studies*, Addis Ababa, 1970, Vol. III, pp. 60-68.
[125] *Adäfrəs*, 70:20, *Bälg*, 75:12.

humiliated when it is revealed that his own wife and daughter fetch water from the river because he cannot afford servants.[126]

In everyday life, the situation of one's house and homestead is the main manifestation of a person's status.

Most people live in a simple house (*bet*) or hut (*gojjo*), which may be rectangular or circular. A poor hut or shanty (*däsasa gojjo*) is built of wattle and daub, the texture of the mud being strengthened by straw; a better kind of hut is built of white stone and black mud. The roof is normally grass or straw, supported by bamboo sticks, and the house is called a "grass house"; but corrugated iron roofs are becoming common on square houses.[127] The windows are small holes, *fuka*, to let the smoke escape; window panes are not common. The house may be divided into sections by partitions, which can be a curtain; there is a larder, where only women should enter; common furniture is wickerwork chairs, tripod stools made from one piece of wood (*barčumma/bərčumma*), and hides or skins, mostly of sheep and oxen, are spread over earthen benches (*mädäb*), and used as bedspreads. In the centre of the hut is a pole (*məsäso*) to support the roof; bigger huts may have several poles.[128]

The description of the more imposing houses of the nobility is given in great detail, particularly the houses of Fitawrari Mäšäša in *Fəkr əskä mäkabər* and of Wzo Asäggaš in *Adäfrəs*. A stately, well-equipped, "warm" house is called a *betä nəgus*, literally "royal house", and used of a large circular house, mansion, manor; or an *əlfəñ*, "main house", a word used also of a hall, a reception room, a bedroom, or any room in a large house; or a *sägännät*, literally "balcony".[129] A noble's house is usually built on an elevated place in the landscape, his compound fenced in, mostly by a fence of branches. Such a compound may house a great many members of the family, with their dependants and servants, and the homestead is referred to as a village or hamlet, *mändär*. Thus is, for example, "Ato Gälagəle's hamlet" (a passing reference in *Bərr ambar säbbärälləwo*)[130] named after the head of the family living there. In

---

[126] *Bərr ambar säbbärälləwo*, 5:14-19, 8:4-11.

[127] *Fəkr əskä mäkabər*, 62:25, 285:12f., *Yähəllina däwäl*, 195:5.9, *Adäfrəs*, 31:5-10, 32:1.23-25, *Yalačča gabačča*, 19:5f., 20:10, 37:2. (The word *tukul*, often used to designate an Ethiopian hut, is unknown in Ethiopia.)

[128] *Yalačča gabačča*, 19:8-17, 20:9, *Fəkr əskä mäkabər*, 27:20, 28:1, 56:6f., 91:4, *Adäfrəs*, 18ult., 31:10f.16, *Mäškäräm*, 13:7-18.

[129] *Fəkr əskä mäkabər*, 91:2-4, 255:8, 259:30f., 285:12f., *Adäfrəs*, 29:14, 70:18, *Säw allä bəyye*, 125:11.

[130] *Adäfrəs*, 29:4-10, 32:31, *Bərr ambar säbbärälləwo*, 3:20f.

the compound of a man of importance, there can be a great number of buildings, in addition to the dwellings of the members of the family. There are living quarters for the servants, and cattle-sheds; there are houses where the food and drink are prepared, and several storage bins or silos for the grain. The crops are protected from predators by boys keeping watch from an elevated platform (*mamma*) erected in a cultivated field.[131]

The main house is built with special care. Choice wood is used in the structure. On top of the roof is placed an inverted pot, *gullǝlat*, that can be made of clay or metal, sometimes even silver. This addition to the house symbolizes the wealth and high status of the occupant.[132] Such a stately house would contain several rooms properly partitioned off by walls; there would be men's quarters and women's quarters, a storage room or vestry, a sewing-room, and a room where the food is kept after it has been brought in from the outside kitchen and before it is served.[133] A rich man's house has fine carpets and silk-covered cushions, and curtains that are used for temporary partitions or to screen off parts of the room, or to cover doors (rather than windows, which are frequently paneless and covered by shutters). The furniture is also good, such as the armchair cut out of a single piece of wood, the *gǝrǝmbud*, and the wooden pillow, the *bǝrkumma*. Weapons, well-bound prayer-books and different utensils may decorate the walls. The master of the house will take great pride in displaying his outfit from military campaigns. A well-equipped house can boast a great number and variety of tools and pots, baskets and tables, fine, coloured basket-tables (*mäsobä wärḵ*) and aquamanile and wash-bowl, etc.[134]

It was part of a young lady's education to be able to handle awl and straw (*akrǝma*, or *alala* if coloured) to weave baskets (as well as to make food).[135]

Agriculture and animal husbandry are, as Araya says, the basis

---

[131] *Fǝḵr ǝskä mäḵabǝr*, 26:28, 277:24-27, *Arrǝmuññ*, 279:8f., *Adäfrǝs*, 31:4, 32:1-6.23.31f., 61:25, *Araya*, 204:31f., 205:5, 325:1-3.

[132] *Adäfrǝs*, 29:16-26.

[133] *Ib.*, 29:14, 30:13, 143:12, *Fǝḵr ǝskä mäḵabǝr*, 91:2-4, 259:3f.

[134] *Yalaččä gabǝččä*, 37:1-15, *Kä'admas bašagär*, 17:21, *Adäfrǝs*, 30:5-7.13f., 30:26-31:3, 94:29, *Fǝḵr ǝskä mäḵabǝr*, 21:25, 22:18f., 234:32, 255:29, 280:23f., 293:19, *Lelaw mängäd*, 36:22, *Yalaččä gabǝččä*, 115:3f., *Araya*, 157:11.

[135] *Fǝḵr ǝska mäḵabǝr*, 306ult.-307:3.

and mainstay of Ethiopia's wealth and development,[136] and a prosperous landlord will have a great number and assortment of farm animals and plants. Plenty of cows is a symbol of prosperity and power; the animal is used almost as a currency. Bullocks and oxen, sheep and goats, mules and donkeys and chickens are common, and many keep bees to get honey for the mead.[137] Cereals, vegetables, spices and fruits are grown in great variety, and a rich man will want to be self-sufficient in supplying all his needs.[138]

A wealthy landowner is turned to in times of need, and as he has more than he needs, he can lend to the poorer farmers or to his tenants, usually asking much more in return than what he lends; but this is not always so.[139]

A landlord's status is shown by the number of peasants who pay rent, tribute or tax to him, by the size of his land and by the number of cattle he has. Cattle are well looked after as they represent an important part of the wealth of the owner.[140] To keep up one's standards, hard work on the land is required, "to run (up and down) the lowlands and the highlands", as Wzo Asäggaš in *Adäfrəs* expresses it.[141] The children of rich landowners may not be permitted to do the work of the children of ordinary peasants, such as taking part in the work on the farm, however much they would like to.[142]

d) *Politeness*

In addition to showing respect and friendliness, polite behaviour, whether in words or deed, also gives expression to social relationships based on relative position and authority.

Great importance is attached to the right forms of address. The use of polite pronouns and verb endings is called "to say *antu*", although *ərswo/əsswo*, "you (polite form)", is in fact used.[143] Säblä Wängel, of noble birth, has been addressed by Bäzzabbəh, her

---

[136] *Araya*, 221:24-28.
[137] *Ib.*, 204:22, *Adäfrəs*, 12:30-13:4, 15:20, 31:27f. 30-32, 32:15.
[138] *Araya*, 202:8-10, 204:25f., 205:6, 218:20f., *Adäfrəs*, 6:15-17, 7:30f., 8:9, 9:5f., 13:14-22, 33:1f., 85:4, 95:11, 124:8, 133:7, 161:9, 235:14, 261:8, 292:3f.
[139] *Adäfrəs*, 9:9ff., *Yähəllina däwäl*, 56:1-63:9.
[140] *Adäfrəs*, 30:7-9.18-20.
[141] *Ib.*, 42:5f.
[142] *Ib.*, 188:1-4.
[143] *Kä'admas bašagär*, 75:8, *Adäfrəs*, 123ult.-124:2, *Yalačča gabəčča*, 117:5-7.

teacher but social inferior, in the familiar form, on her instigation, until her father rebukes him for doing so. When he thereafter uses the polite form to her, she thanks him, a bit discomfited, for "the (use of the form) əsswo".[144] Her father had in fact asked him in the presence of his relatives about the progress of her studies. Bäzzabbəh praises her ability and is bewildered when he is abruptly asked to leave the room. Fitawrari Mäšäša then explains his anger to the others by saying Bäzzabbəh had taken an inadmissible liberty in talking of his daughter in the familiar form. Not even his wife's explanation that Bäzzabbəh had been enjoined by her and their daughter to do so placates him entirely.[145]

There are fine nuances in the use of the polite and the familiar forms. A wife can use the familiar forms to her husband but still address him by means of his title, without the name, whereas the husband may use an endearing short form of her name when talking to her.[146] Both wife and daughter use the polite forms when addressing Fitawrari Mäšäša, while he uses the familiar form, not only to them, but to social equals who are somewhat younger than him, as well. Säblä Wängel uses the familiar form to her mother, however.[147] Adäfrəs and Ṣiwäne, young people close both in age and in social standing, talk to each other in the familiar form, but he uses the familiar form to Roman, who is nearly the same age as Ṣiwäne but socially inferior, whereas she uses the polite form to him.[148]

Advanced age is usually reason enough for addressing someone in polite verbal forms. An unidentified speaker in a discussion in *Adäfrəs* is referred to in the familiar form; but others are written of in the polite forms only because they are said to be "an elder of advanced age" or "an elderly woman".[149] This may also apply when an old tenant is referred to by his master, as it occurs in *Adäfrəs* which is set in northern Shoa,[150] but in *Fəkr əskä mäkabər*, which is set in Gojjam, the point is stressed strongly that any noble can address an old man of poor family in familiar forms.[151] It is

---

[144] *Fəkr əskä mäkabər*, 239:5-9.
[145] *Ib.*, 192:15ff., 193:9-14.19-22.31ff.
[146] *Bərr ambar säbbärälläwo*, 9:1, 18:17.
[147] *Fəkr əskä mäkabər*, letters pp. 140-42, 144f.; 408:31ff., 480:1ff.
[148] *Adäfrəs*, 144:17.19, 185:8.11.
[149] *Ib.*, 41:1.3, 42:26, 43:3f.
[150] *Ib.*, 68:15f.
[151] *Fəkr əskä mäkabər*, 334:14-16; cf. *Yähəllina däwäl*, 57:14ff.20f., 58:21-25.

THE CLASS STRUCTURE OF THE SOCIETY 47

difficult to say whether this regional difference is of importance.[152]

God, the Virgin Mary, or a *tabot* ("church") can be talked of in the familiar form, but saints in the polite form, although this latter usage may not be universal.[153]

Young people, particularly in towns, have more and more come to use familiar forms in addressing their parents and older relatives.[154]

An oral petition to a king may start with the word *abetu*, approximately "please", the same word that is used when pleading to God in prayer.[155] A man of very high social status may be addressed as *getoč*, literally "lords, sirs" (but used as a singular); *getaye*, "my lord or master", is used approximately like "sir"; *əmmät/əmmete/əmmäbet/əmmäbete/əmmäyte*, "Madam, my lady", and *wäyzäro*, "Lady, Madam, Mrs." (which can be used as an honorific mode of address to both married and unmarried women) are used to ladies of standing, the former often being used alone, the latter with the person's name added.[156] *Gašše* and *abəyye* should, according to DTW, properly be used of and to the eldest and the second brothers respectively, but in actual usage *gašše* is a mode of address implying both respect and familiarity, often used when addressing a middle-aged person; *abəyye* is commonly used of and to an uncle. In one case a girl refers to her own father as *gašše*, but that is probably because everyone else talks of him by that appellation.[157] *Wändəmme*, "my brother", can be both friendly and respectful. It is used, for example, by an old nobleman to Araya, and later he calls him "my child"; Araya calls the noble deferentially "my father".[158] *Aya*, "Mr." is less formal and shows a higher degree of familiarity than *ato*, "Mr.", and can even be used by a wife when addressing her husband.[159] "My father" is also used as a term of affection by a wife to her husband (almost as endearing an expres-

---

[152] Cf. S. J. Hoben, "The Meaning of the Second-person Pronouns in Amharic", in M. L. Bender, J. D. Bowen, R. L. Cooper, C. A. Ferguson, (eds.), *Language in Ethiopia*, London, 1976, pp. 281-88.
[153] *Fəkr əskä mäkabər*, 195:15-18, *Adäfrəs*, 220:17-19, etc. (cf. 170:2-4).
[154] *Yalačča gabəčča*, 17:8-14.
[155] *Tarikənna məssale*, Book III, 1:5, 48:23.
[156] *Fəkr əskä mäkabər*, 20:10, 37:1, 59:16.21, 60:3f., 62:10, 90:1, 184:18f., *Yäləbb hassab*, 152:4-6.
[157] *Adäfrəs*, 120:14.16.21; 25:1, *Yalačča gabəčča*, 138:8, *Yäkärmo säw*, 10:6.13.
[158] *Araya*, 171:11.23, 173:23, cf. *Adäfrəs*, 6:30f.
[159] *Fəkr əskä mäkabər*, 15:19, 29:26.

sion as "my intestines", i.e. my heart), and he calls her "my beloved, my dear one".[160] "My mother" (ənnate) is also a friendly and respectful expression, but is often used without much meaning, except perhaps ironically, as when a great lady calls a maid ənnate.[161] "My sister" is also frequently used, especially by women, without its literal meaning; it expresses mostly surprise, and a mother can say "my sister" in this way to her own daughter; or it can be a friendly and polite way of addressing a young woman.[162] ət abäba, literally "sister flower", is used of and to an elder sister or female relative.[163]

Nobody wants to be yäwaza säw, "someone taken or treated lightly".[164] There is an elaborate etiquette regulating courteous, urbane or affable demeanour. In the countryside, people who meet greet each other, even if they are strangers. When Bäzzabbəh does the same in Addis Ababa, his motives are questioned: no honest person is expected to behave like that.[165] When a superior approaches, one will rise up, step aside, and drape the shawl (šämma) in a respectful manner. A tenant may greet the landlord by bowing low, to the level of the knee, or "cause the forehead to be hit", i.e. to let it touch the ground; if riding, he will dismount, maybe kiss the landlord's feet or the ground, and "tremble", i.e. show a humble, submissive attitude, and leave the road to let the master pass. It is a sign of utter humility, often as a sign that one has a request, or asks forgiveness, if a person carries a stone on his head, at the same time draping the šämma in a deferential way. To "fall" on someone's foot to kiss it designates both respect and a certain degree of familiarity and frequently gratitude.[166] The one who is thus greeted can graciously catch the other person's chin and lift him up and kiss his cheeks, before he gets a chance to stoop very low. But delicate expressions of feeling can be communicated by the way this is done. On one occasion, Wzo Asäggaš in *Adäfrəs* lets Gorfu (a young man she suspects of having behaved

---

[160] *Fəkr əskä mäḳabər*, 52:21, 54:3f.; cf. *Adäfrəs*, 81:10.
[161] *Yalačča gabəčča*, 69:2.
[162] *Fəkr əskä mäḳabər*, 305:14-16, *Araya*, 280:5.
[163] *Kältammawa əhəte*, 12:7.
[164] *Fəkr əskä mäḳabər*, 15:31.
[165] *Fəkr əskä mäḳabər*, 436:18ff.
[166] *Ib.*, 94:14-16, 211:5-7, 292:31f. (cf. 293:10f.), *Yalačča gabəčča*, 47:10, *Adäfrəs*, 10:9f., 37:2-4, 208:3-5, *Yähəllina däwäl*, 57:20f. (cf. 62:1-21), 148ult., 222:19-23.

THE CLASS STRUCTURE OF THE SOCIETY 49

with some levity towards one of the girls in her house) stoop a bit deeper than usual, and she holds him in that position long enough to confuse him and instil in him the proper attitude of awe and humility, in preparation for the ensuing discussion about his behaviour:

> "While she is saying, "How are you, my friend - - how are you - - how are you - - how are you!" she stretches her hand down and keeps him low for a long time in such a way as to confuse him, instead of catching his chin and kissing him at once. "How are you then!" she still continues; and after having raised him up and kissed him, she says, "And how is your father, the käññaz-mač - - - ?" "[167]

People do not only kiss hands, feet, cheeks, or the ground, but out of reverence they kiss crosses and, as Adäfrəs puts it, "stone", i.e. the steps and porch of churches, and "paper", i.e. the Bible and other sacred books. Wzo Asäggaš maintains the custom persists because people cherish it, and it would fall into disuse as soon as it had exhausted its social usefulness.[168]

Prior to entering the house of a person of high status, a visitor may arrange the šämma in a way that shows proper respect. He may only throw a flap or corner of the šämma over the left shoulder (women throw it over the right shoulder), but it will show greater respect if he also lowers the šämma and ties it round the waist, "under the chest", and keeps it "folded under the arm" (the right arm for men, the left for women). When approaching a man of importance, one will also bow low.[169]

When someone enters a room, those of inferior status or younger in years rise up (these always stand up when someone more senior is on his feet), and the host will greet the newcomer in words like, "I am glad you arrived well"; the new arrival asks those in the house to sit down with the words, "By (or in the name of) God, sit down, by the fathers, by the saints—it is not proper (that you should stand up)!", or some such phrase.[170] After kisses have been exchanged in the proper way, on feet, knee, hand or cheek, as the

---

[167] *Adäfrəs*, 168:8-12.
[168] *Ib.*, 207:4-8 (cf. 206:11-13.19f.25), 208:7-14 (cf. 37:4-7).
[169] *Araya*, 155:12-14, 165:8f. (cf. 165:21f., *Kaleb*, 67:3f.), *Yalačča gabəčča*, 165:13, *Kä'admas bašagär*, 94:14-16, *Adäfrəs*, 74:26f., 168:4 (cf. 170:14-16), *Əddəl näw? bädäl?* 60:13, 68:15-17.
[170] *Yalačča gabəčča*, 53:2f., 138:17f., *Bälg*, 125:2f., 128:8, *Țälfo bäkise*, 50:31f.

case may be, the older person will normally ask about the health and situation of the younger, and of his parents and other relations. Questions may relate to the cattle, crops, the house, etc., and are frequently repeated. The younger person will only respond, without asking similar questions of the older one, at least not immediately; and his replies are generally to the effect that all is well, whether this is true or not, and he uses phrases such as, "I am well, praise be to the good God", "let the Creator be honoured and praised", "let His honour increase" (because all is well). Only later is more exact and truthful information exchanged. If there is a particular message that will please the person it is brought to, it is introduced by the word "Congratulations! (or Good news!)", to which the other person, for unknown reasons, retorts, "Eat lentils!". Then follows the happy message itself. Messages of grief, such as the news of someone's death, are brought very gradually.[171]

Hospitality is important, also to strangers, "God's poor", "God's guests", because this is considered to be of value to the host's soul. The guest may not be able to pay for such hospitality, but a blessing on those who have received him, such as, "May the Mother of God give you rest of soul", is regarded as a sufficient recompense.[172]

When a guest leaves, it is polite, and expected, that the host sees him off by accompanying him part of the way, at least to the gate of the compound.[173] On parting, one expresses the wish to meet again by the phrase, "May He make us come together in peace". Greetings are sent to relatives in words like, "Kiss her shoe for me", if the relationship is a close one, or less cordial if the situation demands it. Relatives and friends are expected to, and usually do, visit each other frequently. One can say as a pretext for a visit that "I have come for God's greeting", i.e. to greet you in God's name; but it can be expected that the real motive for a visit is more serious.[174]

---

[171] *Yalačča gabačča*, 121:2.7.9f., *Adäfrəs*, 168:8-20, *Fəḳr əskä mäḳabər*, 416:28, 417:2; 62:13-63:22.

[172] *Tarikənna məssale*, Book III, 61:20f., *Fəḳr əskä mäḳabər*, 60:3f., 501:12, 509:7. Blessings should only be given by an older to a younger person (except by clergymen); otherwise it can be a veiled insult, unless said jokingly to a friend (but one can say, "May He forgive you" to one who sneezes); *Ṭälfo bäkise*, 18:14 (cf. 22:2f), 28:14f.

[173] *Yähəllina däwäl*, 234:7, cf. *Yalačča gabačča*, 144:2, 166:3f.

[174] *Yalačča gabačča*, 130:9, 138:18, 152:10f., *Säw allä bəyye*, 76:7f., 126:2, 127:24f., *Tarikənna məssale*, 19:25-30, *Fəḳr əskä mäḳabər*, 67:24-26, *Adäfrəs*, 169:1-16, 178:12-14.

A common phrase meaning "to greet" is *əjj nässa*. Greetings may be accompanied by gifts, particularly when greeting important people; *əjj mänša*, signifying such a gift, is in our days seen as a form of bribery.[175]

There are many taboos in polite social intercourse. Thus it is *näwr*, "rude, vulgar, not proper, bad form", persistently to refuse food when it is offered to a guest, or not to accept hospitality; it is *näwr* to cause someone to feel ashamed or slighted in front of others, especially when older people are affected. One should avoid all insolent or impudent words or deeds.[176] It is expected of young people, especially girls, to show a kind of timidity or pretend to be bashful. Only close friends can speak and behave freely, "without pretending". One does not stare people in the eyes except as a gesture of defiance or arrogance, or to make a point of showing one is an equal of the other person.[177]

A servant may pretend to sneeze if his master sneezes, to preclude any feeling of embarrassment on his behalf.[178] But subordinates may not always be so considerate or subservient, so a man in authority may keep a whip as a sign of his position, and occasionally use it to enforce obedience or submission.[179]

These patterns of polite behaviour are closely related to Ethiopian concepts of status and class.

e) *Litigation*

Court cases occupy a large amount of time for many Ethiopians. A man can be taken to court for petty crimes such as "going too far with one's mouth", i.e. expressing criticism of, or insulting another person,[180] as well as more serious offences. The most common cases brought to court appear to be disputes about land-ownership and concerning marital problems, with demands of divorce settlements. Such lawsuits can be time-consuming, and drag on for years, "like (i.e. with the speed of) a snail", as Wzo

---

[175] *Araya*, 166:28, *Adäfrəs*, 169:16, *Fəkr əskä mäkabər*, 253ult., *Yätewodros ənba*, 47:20, 51:10f.
[176] *Adäfrəs*, 273:22-274:16, 280:15-21, *Araya*, 206:11-24, 281:26, *Yalačča gabəčča*, 40:3.
[177] *Araya*, 239:15, 278ult.-279:4, *Adäfrəs*, 70:19f.
[178] *Tälfo bäkise*, 47:4f.
[179] *Adäfrəs*, 7:17, 148:24, 149:14.
[180] *Tälfo bäkise*, 53:9.

Alganäš, a landowning lady in *Yalačča gabəčča* complains.[181] One of her disputes about a piece of land has lasted twelve years, and another even longer, since her nephew Bahru, who is now teaching after having completed his university education, was "a fruit", i.e. a small child.[182] Marital problems could also go from one court to another and take many years before a final settlement is reached.[183]

There are several kinds of courts and judges. The "family judge" seeks to arbitrate between the contesting parties in order to help them reach an agreement, and the council of elders, the *šängo*, is also primarily established to bring about reconciliation.[184] A traditional court (*yäləmad čəlot*) conducts its cases in accordance with customary law.[185] Simple cases can be settled by a "neighbourhood judge" (/*yä/aṭbiya dañña*) who may be a member of the local landed gentry and have authority in his village only.[186] More serious charges were referred to a higher judge.[187] When litigants appeal their cases to higher courts, they may have to go to Addis Ababa.[188] But to facilitate the conducting of some proceedings, high court judges are sent to provincial towns to settle cases that are beyond the jurisdiction of local judges, and that have lasted for a long time, often several years. Normally they will be sent there during the long rainy season, when the peasants are not busy on their land. Such judges are mentioned to have come yearly to Illubabor; and Ato Ṭəso in *Adäfrəs* is sent on such a mission to Däbra Sina in northern Shoa.[189] Judges are usually called *dañña* or *färaj*, or sometimes *wänbär*, "chair", after the seat of authority they occupy.[190] Normally only a king is referred to as

---

[181] *Yalačča gabəčča*, 57:11-13.
[182] *Ib.*, 55:7f., 144:3-6; cf. *Joro ṭäbi*, 103:10-104:3, 175:12ff.
[183] *Adäfrəs*, 34:3-6, 39:15-17.
[184] *Fəkr əskä mäḳabər*, 393:25, *Yäkärmo säw*, 69:11.
[185] *Fəkr əskä mäḳabər*, 394:10.
[186] *Əddəl näw? bädäl?* 39:11.17f.20, 41:19f., *Yähəllina däwäl*, 69:10-14. Officially, the neighbourhood judge could hear civil disputes for claims of up to E$25, and criminal disputes for damages up to E$15, and conduct cases at any time or place, in or out of doors. He must be assisted by two elders who advise him. He receives small fixed fees. See A. Hoben, *Land Tenure among the Amhara of Ethiopia*, p. 79.
[187] *Əddel näw? bädäl?* 43:1-10, 45:10-13.
[188] *Yalačča gabəčča*, 144:1-5.
[189] *Yähəllina däwäl*, 202:2-5, *Adäfrəs*, 34:1-6.
[190] *Yäšoh aklil*, 26:11f., *Fəkr əskä mäḳabər*, 393:1, *Adäfrəs*, 108:32. According to *Area Handbook for Ethiopia*, 2nd ed., Washington, 1971, by I. Kaplan *et al.*, p. 110, *wänbär* is used in Shoa, *liḳ* ("scholar") in Gondar, for the more general term *azzaž* ("commander") to designate a royal judge.

THE CLASS STRUCTURE OF THE SOCIETY 53

fälaṭ ḳoraṭ, i.e. one who decides absolutely, a final judge whose judgment cannot be questioned.[191] Criminal proceedings are conducted by "the middle judge", but at each lawsuit three judges must be present.[192] There was a time when justice rested with men of authority, and the change from personally administered justice dispensed according to the pleasure of the judge to more formal proceedings conducted according to statutory law is confusing to the older generation who do not understand this kind of litigation. This is the case with Fitawrari Mäšäša in *Fəkr əskä mäkabər* who loses in his dispute with the peasants on his land.[193] Others have become specialists in procedure and the finer points of law so they can twist its provisions to suit their interests; they are called "legal, or law-abiding criminals".[194] So both previous and present ways of conducting legal hearings could turn out as the judges wanted, and it is a general complaint that magistrates and lawyers are influenced by bribes.[195] Still, the common plea to a judge is, "May God show you (i.e. the truth)",[196] and people have a strong love of justice and might pursue it till death, trusting they will find it finally, and not holding life worth living without justice.[197]

Corrupt judges are so common that the "bidding" to win over the judges starts ahead of the time a case is presented at court.[198] The fee for a judge can be call a *wərərrəd*, which also means a bet, a wager.[199] Gifts "by which one may be seen, noticed, received" are sent to a judge and frequently also to members of his family that may be mediators and influence his decision.[200] It is commonly believed that to win a case in court one must start early to try to attract the attention of the judge, to bribe and flatter him, and also be helped by some good fortune.[201] When a judge is won over to one party and has made up his mind, he will demand

---

[191] *Yätənbit ḳäṭäro*, 53:1f.; cf. *Aləwwällädəm*, 154:25f.
[192] *Yähəllina däwäl*, 217:11, *Kä'admas bašagär*, 162ult.-163:1.4f., *Yäbädäl fəṣṣame*, 149:11.
[193] *Fəkr əskä mäkabər*, 392:1-400:16.
[194] *Ǝddəl näw? bädäl?* 61:5.
[195] *Ib.*, 50:8-15, 52:5-16, 53:3-8, 76:21f., 89:14.
[196] *Ib.*, 122:4.
[197] *Ib.*, 79:25f., 81:1 (and the whole of this book), *Adäfrəs*, 251:8-17.
[198] *Fəkr əskä mäkabər*, 393:1-7, 394:19-395:11.
[199] *Fəkr əskä mäkabər*, 254:6, 263:19.
[200] *Adäfrəs*, 35:15-28, 36:32-37:13, 39:3f., 43:28-31.
[201] *Ib.*, 44:22-25, 45:1-3.

bribes the other party cannot pay, "the hump of a chicken", as a proverb says.[202] In *Yäfəkər ṭora* it is told about people who come to church and throw themselves down on the ground of the compound, and on the road, pleading for justice,

> "because, having been robbed of justice, they did not have the key, money, to open and enter the iron door of justice".[203]

One way of depriving people of justice is to delay passing judgment for so long that one party cannot afford to go on with the case, or just to let it continue indefinitely.[204]

Sentence can in some cases be comparatively mild, and in other cases rather severe. When Fitawrari Mäšaša has been very harsh in his treatment of recalcitrant peasants, he is let off with a fine, and it is enough for him to present a guarantor to avoid being sent to prison. In case the fine is not paid, the guarantor's cattle may be impounded.[205] Compensation may also be paid for having killed "a soul",[206] but the more usual penalty for murder is death, often by hanging.[207]

Legal procedures in court have been changing during this century. The traditional ways are, however, still practised and are mentioned briefly in Amharic literature.

Ato Ṭəso is a judge in *Adäfrəs*, and on one occasion he tells of what he calls "the previous *täṭäyyäḵ ləṭäyyəḵəh* (i.e. approximately: defend yourself, I accuse you)", which is the name given to this kind of litigation. When he refers to it as an earlier practice, he probably means that it is not common in towns and places influenced by legal customs there, since he mentions to Adäfrəs, who is young and has lived all his life in the capital, that he will not have witnessed this kind of presenting one's grievances before a judge. He uses the term *täṭäyyäḵ ləṭäyyəḵəh* also about judicial practices of today, but says they take a different form (i.e. cross-examination by trained lawyers).[208] He recalls two cases of this

---
[202] *Adäfrəs*, 91:8.
[203] *Yäfəkər ṭora*, 172:14-173:1.
[204] *Əddəl näw? bädäl?*, 98:11-20.
[205] *Fəḵr əshä mäḵabər*, 396:3-397:8; cf. 382:18, *taggätä käbt*, "confiscated cattle of a guarantor".
[206] *Ib.*, 393:14.38, *Araya*, 214:16-30.
[207] *Yähəllina däwäl*, 190:6-194:22, *Adäfrəs*, 257:1-4 (cf. 261:25-262:9. 19-25, 263:25-264:6.11-15.
[208] *Adäfrəs*, 250:1-4. 8-12, 255:16-21; cf. *Kä'admas bašagär*, 165:17. See also D. Levine, *Wax and Gold*, Chicago, 1965, p. 231 for a more recent experience of this kind of court hearing.

former procedure. The plaintiff and the defendant conduct their own cases, and accusation and defence are put into verse. An accuser says:

> "I the slave
> have arrived
> flowing like (i.e. as fast as) water (or a river)
> blowing like grass (i.e. coming with the speed of the wind);
> my wife is a *gäbbar* (i.e. she pays her tax),
> my mule is a trotter (i.e. fast) - - -".

The defendant, a man of authority, gives a conciliatory reply:

> "You the slave,
> if you arrived
> flowing like water
> I shall have you dig ditches;
> if you blew like grass
> I shall have you cut grass for the horse;
> if your wife pays tribute
> she will have her house to dwell in,
> if your mule trots
> you will (be able to) spend the night wherever evening (or night) overtakes you (i.e. you will be made welcome anywhere)."[209]

This illustrates the unequal case between a master and a slave. The other case Ato Ṭəso recollects shows the attempt of two litigants to outsmart each other with arguments:

> "The plaintiff brings his case saying,
> "As my heifer vanished from the highlands,
> I came searching for her;
> in front of your door I found a chunk of meat,
> which makes you liable to compensation ("a debtor")".
> The defendant answers him saying,
> "If a heifer vanishes from the highlands
> and if you come searching for her,
> and if you find a chunk of meat at my door
> there is a big (main) road below my house
> which is used by soldiers (or many people) by day and wild animals at night;
> above my house there is a big sycamore
> where birds of prey and beasts scream -
> if a bird of prey and a wild animal, when they grab (or fight about) and then drop ("spit out") a chunk of meat,
> and if a chunk of meat is found in front of my door,
> this does not make me your debtor"." [210]

---
[209] *Adäfrəs*, 255:22-256:8.
[210] *Adäfrəs*, 250:13-251:4.

Ato Ṭəso says that although this way of conducting lawsuits may sound amusing today, "it worked for its time", and even Adäfrəs finds it "marvellous" and very pleasing.[211]

Another traditional form of criminal investigation is the *afärsata*, which consists of calling all the people together and administering an oath to all that they will tell the judges if they know who has committed the crime being heard, or where he is hiding. In Amharic literature there is not much direct description of the *afärsata*.[212] In *Ǝddəl näw? bädäl?* a plaintiff who has lost his ox is made aware of the possibility of holding an *afärsata* hearing if he wants it.[213] When a goat disappears, the village people are similarly called to be present at an *afärsata* in *Yalačča gabəčča*.[214] A more serious case is presented in *Yähəllina däwäl*. A man has been murdered for having raped a farmer's daughter, and the local population is ordered "to sit" for an *afärsata* and reveal the culprit, and the questioning of each individual often makes such a sitting of long duration, maybe a week or two. As nobody is permitted to leave or be absent, trade and farming stop.[215] Haddis, the teacher from Addis Ababa, comments on the practice to a local policeman:

> "I realize the benefit of the *afärsata* for earlier times. But I don't see its use for the present time. It makes people idle. It stops work on the land, profits, education, health-tax, development contributions! Isn't the investigation of you policemen preferable in order to find the criminal quickly? You who say you don't overlook the scratch of a hen......"[216]

The policeman replies that it is not only a thing of the past but is still practised and is based on the principle of collective responsibility, as a few policemen cannot alone prevent all crimes.[217] Many days later the *afärsata* is over, without having led to the apprehension of the criminal, not even to a slight clue being found. "Nowadays not even someone who tells a rumour can be found." Both the previous year and the year before that equally fruitless gatherings had been held.[218] It is thus not presented as a worthwhile process, and it is seen to be unsuitable for our times.

---

[211] *Adäfrəs*, 250:5f., 255:18.
[212] Cf. *The Afersata*, by Sahle Sellassie, London, 1968.
[213] *Ǝddəl näw? bädäl?* 130:12-14.
[214] *Yalačča gabəčča*, 97:13-21.
[215] *Yähəllina däwäl*, 90:14-24.
[216] *Ib.*, 91:1-6.
[217] *Ib.*, 91:7-9.
[218] *Ib.*, 98:11-21.

THE CLASS STRUCTURE OF THE SOCIETY 57

The court cases that are described most fully in Amharic literature are much more like European court practice than the cases referred to above. Bä'alu Gərma's two novels, *Kä'admas bašagär* and *Yähəllina däwäl*, have long sections about the main characters' appearances before a court and time in prison. Legal procedures and discussions also take some considerable space in Bərhanu Zärihun's *Yäbädäl fəṣṣame*. The vocabulary used as well as the proceedings clearly betray Western influences in modern law practice.[219]

Accused and arrested people are detained in a "house of appointment" where they wait for their cases to come up before a judge,[220] and although a policeman in *Joro ṭäbi* threatens to whip a witness unless he tells him what he wants to know,[221] brutality against, or torture of witnesses or prisoners is not a theme Ethiopian authors write about.

---

[219] See e.g. *Kä'admas bašagär*, 162:14, 163:10f.16, 165:17. 170:23, 175:22, 180:5, *Yähəllina däwäl*, 210:4.20, 217:18-22, 218:24, 219:4, *Yäbädäl fəṣṣame*, 144:14-18, 145:13, 147:13f., 149:4ff., etc.
[220] *Kä'admas bašagär*, 181:1-6.
[221] *Joro ṭäbi*, 63:2-10, 69:4-10.

CHAPTER TWO

BELIEFS AND ETHICS

1. *Christianity*

a) *Popular Christian beliefs*

In everyday life Ethiopians frequently mention religious concepts. It would be difficult to converse normally and politely without referring explicitly or implicitly to God, the saints, or the Church, although this may be as much a cultural as a religious manifestation.

Wzo Asäggaš, a landowner, greets Gorfu, son of a neighbouring nobleman, in a typical manner, asking about his health and then about his father's:

" "He is well! He is well!" says Gorfu while greeting her.
"And your mother - - -?"
"God be praised, she is well - -."
"And the children - - and the cattle - -."
"The Creator be honoured and praised - -."
"And you, how has He done by you - -?"
"May His honour increase, may His honour increase! He has certainly kept me well until now - -."
"The harvest, the weeding, the rains - - -."
"We get along all right - - everything considered - - -."
"Now we do not even meet at church - - -."
"One could say our work does not let us free - - -."
"Even so! Even so! While our cattle graze in the same field - - you maybe (are too busy), but your cattle (we should have seen) ---."
"As for that, it was not convenient for them, the cattle (to graze where your cattle graze) - - -."
"Last Micha'el's day (i.e. the 12th) of Säne, it was three months since I saw either you or your father - -"." [1]

God, əgzi'abəher or əgzer, literally "Lord of the land", or amlak, is fäṭari, "Creator", and "the one and only God", (andəyye).[2] God is frequently called "the Trinity" (səllase) and it is common to use the trinitarian concept. People are "created in the image of the Trinity"; oaths are taken "by, or in the name of, the three

---

[1] *Adäfrəs*, 168:13-169:5.
[2] *Ib.*, 5:23.28, 40:19, 109:4, 213:21, 274:14f., *Fəkr əskä mäḳabər*, 233:13, 524:13, *Araya*, 237:8, 262:8, *Ṭälfo bäkise*, 55:19, 56:20.

persons of the Trinity!"³ When the persons of the Trinity are mentioned individually, it is often in the trinitarian formula: "In the name of the Father and the Son and the Holy Spirit, one God, Amen" is used at the beginning of a prayer; "Go out, evil spirit, in the name of the Father, the Son, and the Holy Spirit" is a formula of exorcizing an evil spirit.⁴

Indirect references to God are numerous: "What if He cuts me down; or, Let Him cut me down (if I tell a lie)"; "May His honour increase"; "May He get honour and praise"; "May His honour increase; may He be praised"; "I am glad He released the bridle, or constraint, of fasting for you" (said at the end of a fasting season).⁵

Explicit references to God are of course also frequent: "May God bring you home well"; "May God make us meet in peace, or: Goodbye"; "May God give, or help, you" (which may imply a refusal to give anything to a beggar); "May God give you success, or: Good luck".⁶

The belief in God's interference with, or control of, man's life is expressed indirectly in the above quotations, but this view can also be stated directly:

> "As for me, I plan to return soon, if God makes this possible! Who except He knows what will happen between today and the day I say I plan to return?"⁷

The same view is expressed in *Araya*:

> "- - - there is no one except God who knows which works or deeds are ordained in a man's life, what he shall accomplish".⁸

God is "God the disposer", or "the God who makes things happen".⁹

God is man's "helper"; ¹⁰ but He can also be thought of as severe;

---

³ *Adäfräs*, 5:22, 263:18, *Bärr ambar säbbäralläwo*, 13:23, *Kä'admas bašagär*, 97:7, *Yalačča gabačča*, 56:1.
⁴ *Arrämuñň*, 90:17f., *Fäḳr äskä mäḳabär*, 140:20f., *Adäfräs*, 205:15.
⁵ *Adäfräs*, 70:6, *Bärr ambar säbbäralläwo*, 23:16, 45:17, *Araya*, 185:5, *Kä'admas bašagär*, 68:1.
⁶ *Arrämuñň*, 320:9f., 125:23f., *Kä'admas bašagär*, 100:11-13, *Ṭälfo bäkise*, 8:17, *Adäfräs*, 168:15.17, *Araya*, 237:8f., 262:8.
⁷ *Fäḳr äskä mäḳabär*, 377:25-28.
⁸ *Araya*, 169:12f.
⁹ *Ib.*, 169:18f.
¹⁰ *Yä'änba däbdabbewoč*, 118:17.

cf. the pleading of the wounded on a battlefield: "For the sake of the Bäläs,[11] give me water! For the sake of the God of the brave, finish me off, or kill me!" [12]

References to Christ are often connected with external symbols associated with him, especially the cross; e.g. "(The Feast of) the Cross", i.e. the feast on 17 Mäskäräm, celebrating the finding of the cross.[13] Christ is "the Saviour of the world", *mädhane aläm*, a title frequently used to signify a church.[14] An oath can be taken "in the name of the crucified!" [15] Käbbädä Mika'el in his play *Yätənbit ḳäṭäro* refers to Christ as a saviour and a teacher (Christ is speaking):

"After I have spilt my blood as a compensation for your sins, I shall make you enter paradise." [16]
"He (Christ) preached the Gospel, having renewed the Torah." [17]

Divisions and schisms in the Church are occasionally mentioned, but mostly indirectly.[18] Wzo Asäggaš in *Adäfrəs* belongs to "the family, or group of Grace (*ṣägga*)".[19]

The story in *Fəḵr əskä mäḵabər* about the Abba who says he has a cross that came down to him from heaven [20] indicates that he is an adherent of the sect of Karra.[21] It is said of Bäzzabbəh that he went to Däbrä Wärḵ to study exegesis of the books of the Church.[22]

---

[11] Bäläs is the only river and source of water in a desolate area near Gondar and Lake Tana. People in desperate need plead for help with the words, "Give me water, for the sake of the Bäläs" (see KBT sub *bäläs* /4/).
[12] *Araya*, 256:15f., (cf. line 23).
[13] *Adäfrəs*, 5:28 (cf. lines 21-23).
[14] Ib., 5:27, *Yäkärmo säw*, 23:3, *Fəḵr əskä mäḵabər*, 161:10f.
[15] *Bərr ambar säbbärälləwo*, 6:14f.
[16] *Yätənbit ḳäṭäro*, 104:10f.
[17] Ib., 104:22 (cf. 105:13f.).
[18] The term *täwahdo* ("monophysite") (cf. *Bərr ambar säbbärälləwo*, 80:13.17) is claimed by all the sects into which the Church has split (and there is no pure *täwahdo* church separate from these sects). The main groups are the Ṣägga (or House of Täklä Haymanot, or the believers in the Three Births), and Ḳəbat (or House of Ewosṭatewos, or the believers in the Two Births). Karra, "The Knife" is a sect that is closely related to the Ḳəbat group. All maintain that they have preserved the pure, original *täwahdo* doctrine of Christ. Cf. Ayala Takla-Haymanot, *La Chiesa etiopica e la sua dottrina cristologica*, Rome, 2nd ed., 1974, p. 194; see KWK on *täwahdo*, and *ṣägga* (2), DTW on *ṣägga* (2) and *ṣäggoč*.
[19] *Adäfrəs*, 29:3.
[20] *Fəḵr əskä mäḵabər*, 420:14-30.
[21] See KWK, p. 492, 1st col., ll.1-3. (He writes about *karra* under its Geez name *mäṭbaḥtawi*.)
[22] *Fəḵr əskä mäḵabər*, 59:6-8.

Däbrä Wärk, in Gojjam, is, according to DTW, a parish adhering to the doctrines of the Kəbat sect.

The "mediator, intercessor, go-between" (ammalaj), is primarily Christ, but the term can be used of "Jesus Christ.... Mary, the prophets, the apostles, the saints, the martyrs, the angels".[23]

Mary is the "mother of God" (əmmä amlak or wäladitä amlak), or "the mother of light". Oaths are taken in her name: "by, for the sake of, in the name of the mother of God", and beggars appeal for alms for her sake. She is "the compassionate one", and thanks are given her for her help: "Thank you, my mother, the merciful or compassionate one". She is also called "the redemptrix of the world" (bezawitä aläm).[24] Many days in the church calendar are celebrated in her memory: her birth, her entry into the temple, her conception, and her death.[25] Many churches are dedicated to her; she is often depicted in religious paintings, and then mostly referred to as "our Lady" (əmmäbetaččən) or "covenant of mercy" (kidanä məhrät).[26]

Vows are made to Mary, and if she helps, the believer has to fulfil promises given, such as Bäzzabbəh's mother's vow when her child was ill: "he will serve you by studiously saying your hourly prayers in your church".[27] She makes similar vows for the health of her child to the Virgin Mary, to St. George and St. John, to Michael and Gabriel, the archangels, and, it is said:

> "be it by the protection of the saints or by strength of faith: he conquered death and succeeded to grow up".[28]

---

[23] *Adäfrəs*, 208:2, *Kaleb*, 51:7-9, 80:18f., *Fəkr əskä mäkabər*, 172:24f., *Yähəllina däwäl*, 114:4, 119:10, DTW p. 775. (Cf. Ayala Takla-Haymanot, *op. cit.*, pp. 205ff., on the position of Mary in the Ethiopian Church.)

[24] *Yäšoh aklil*, 61:20, *Fəkr əskä mäkabər*, 12:28, 32:8, 60:3, 112:13, *Yäkärmo säw*, 67:21, 78:18, *Yalačča gabačča*, 104:18, *Arrəmuńń*, 322:2.11-13, *Bərr ambar säbbärälləwo*, 4:19.

[25] *Adäfrəs*, 5:20f.26, 177:27, *Yä'ənba däbdabbewoč*, 12:11f., *Fəkr əskä mäkabər*, 59:9.

[26] *Adäfrəs*, 5:25, 70:19, 77:16. A "covenant", *kidan*, "besteht aus der Zusage Christi, nicht nur dem Heiligen selbst grosse Gnaden und die ewige Seligkeit zu verleihen, sondern auch all denen, die ihn anrufen, die sein Leben niederschreiben etc., bestimmte geistliche und leibliche Segnungen diesseits und besondere Gnaden im Jenseits zu verleihen." (R. Kriss and H. Kriss-Heinrich, *Volkskundliche Anteile in Kult und Legende äthiopischer Heiliger*, Wiesbaden, 1975, p. 3.)

[27] *Fəkr əskä mäkabər*, 30:25-31:1.

[28] *Ib.*, 32:12-18.

Mary is a special helper for women giving birth: "you, shepherdess of those who give birth", one woman cries to St. Mary when she is in distress.[29]

Ethiopian "saints, holy ones" (*kəddusan*), include the angels. Prayers are directed to them, and they are thanked for help given.[30]

Some areas have developed a strong attachment to a particular saint. St. Michael is said to be particularly favoured in Yəfat in northern Shoa, with many churches dedicated to him:

> " "The-e-ere!" She points far away, "what do they call that church, do you think - - -!?"
> "Which?"
> "There! There! The one which is to our left - - -?"
> "Well, it must be St. Michael's church, don't you think! What else can it be? It is he who covers the whole countryside, isn't it - - -?" "[31]
>
> "On every hilltop - Gəft Michael, Gurj Michael, Ramse Michael, Maniyamba Michael, Yälətoki Michael, Waylo Michael - - - if one is on top of Ṭarmabärr mountain and looks at the districts of Yəfat and Ṭəmuga, it seems as if God, when he had finished creating the world, put the leftover junk into this storehouse." [32]

Michael comes easily to mind in this area when people make vows, or need a heavenly witness: "Michael is my witness".[33]

Saints are admired for their holiness and their ability to work miracles. Adäfrəs once discusses the matter with Abba Yohannəs:

> " "And what has he (i.e. Täklä Haymanot) done to be called holy - - - to have a sanctuary (*tabot*) built for him - - -?"
> "What do you imply - do you maybe doubt his holiness - - -?"
> "Yes, I doubt it - - -"
> "To hear the Devil speaking - -! It is the Devil who gives you such doubts, my friend! Täklä Haymanot is the holiest of men. - But surely! you should not have any doubts. He who changed someone like Mätolomi,[34] the pagan Wollamo king, into doing good, taught him, baptized and converted him - - he who stood seven full years on one leg, praying for the country, for the people, until the leg

---

[29] *Bälg*, 72:10.
[30] *Fəkr əskä mäḳabər*, 31ult., *Ṭälfo bäkise*, 58:23, 63:2.
[31] *Adäfrəs*, 188:25-189:2.
[32] *Ib.*, 5:9-16.
[33] *Ib.*, 171:2f., 242:7f.
[34] DTW calls him *Motälämi*; Taddesse Tamrat, *Church and State...*, pp. 121f., says "Motälamī" was "a legendary monarch of Damot" who was said to have "invaded the Shäwan region as far north as the Jäma river, and almost completely annihilated the small Christian communities in the area."

BELIEFS AND ETHICS 63

he stood on fell off - - he who was given such honour that six wings were made to grow out - - - but he is holy, my child! Where can one find a holier man than he - - -?" [35]

Later, Ato Ṭəso, the judge, joins in the conversation:

" "Previously we started talking about Abunä Gäbrä Mänfäs Ḳəddus," [36] comments Ato Ṭəso calmly; "he was Egyptian, we said. - He is a known saint in Ethiopia, we said. - As his *gädl* (i.e. story of a saint) details it, it is said he did not taste his mother's breast from the moment he was born. - He was holy even in his being born: it is said he was conceived because, after his father's sperm had flowed on the papyrus, his mother absorbed it while cutting the papyrus absent-mindedly." " [37]

" "- - And to get for himself Satan's place in Zəḳwala, he prayed for a long time, kneeling, with his head to the ground. - Because of the abundance of his compassion, he gave his eye to a thirsty bird that came. - But the witness of a fly, namely that he had killed her with the fly-whisk he held in his hand, caused his death. - He was able to command lions, leopards, lightning - - -." " [38]

Ato Ṭəso, who is not likely to believe in the "historicity" of the legendary aspects of stories about saints, gives an interpretation of the stories and their value that is more enlightened than is usual in his society, when he explains to Adäfrəs that they represent spiritual truths and ethical values:

"The saints are our symbols of a just life: of truthfulness, of compassion, of spiritual strength, of the greatness of man - - of the multiplicity of our humanity - - -." [39]

Abba Yoḥannəs then tells a story of a compassionate female saint, Krəstos Sämra, that illustrates Ato Ṭəso's point:

"- - - Now Krəstos Sämra's greatest desire was to save all men, after having first caused Satan, who misleads men, to be forgiven. - And God, well - - He said, "The devil won't agree to it, but if he does, why should I mind", and made an agreement with her. She went to the edge of Sheol and called him, saying, "Dear Devil, Dear Devil", to allure him. - And he, hearing her unusual loving call, straightened up to see with his own eyes, revealing his evil nature by the way his body was shaped, and he pulled her by the

---

[35] *Adäfrəs*, 217:21-218:3.
[36] This saint is also known as Abbo, Abunä Gäbrä Həywät, Abuyä Ṣadəḳu (*Adäfrəs*, 219:1-3).
[37] *Adäfrəs*, 220:17-23.
[38] *Ib.*, 221:7-12.
[39] *Ib.*, 222:17-19.

eyelashes into Sheol. - But the merciful God saw all this and commanded Michael to help her, saying, "That meek woman has entered Sheol, and please go and get her out", and immediately she got out. - And many souls came out, following her, and were saved."[40]

In Ethiopia, great numbers of saints are remembered, both imported and indigenous ones.[41] Among the most popular, in addition to those mentioned above, are the Nine Saints (*täs'atu ḳəddusan*), from Syria according to tradition.[42] Best known among them are probably Abunä Arägawi, who is said to have founded the monastery of Däbrä Damo, and Abba Gärima, so called because, "having planted at dawn, he harvested at dusk, and because even the trees obeyed when they heard his words".[43]

A special place is given to St. George, who is also called "the head, or first of the martyrs",[44] and is probably meant by "the quick to help".[45] It might be that the popularity of St. George is due to the appeal of the warrior motif in Ethiopian tradition and to the similarity between his story and the much older stories of the hero who killed the serpent Arwe and was elevated to kingship;[46] so St. George, the dragon-killer, became the head of the martyrs. The stories of St. George who killed the dragon or serpent and rescued the maiden Brutawit or Birutayət are well known.[47]

The importance of saints in the daily lives of the people is possibly best illustrated by the fact that saints' days are more commonly used in the countryside for dating than actual dates of the calendar month. The main saints do not only have a yearly festival, with *nəgs*, "coronation", in their honour but are remembered monthly, and sometimes on several days each month under different designations. Thus, the Virgin Mary has a day, the 16th, each month, and a particular yearly feast on Yäkkatit 16, under the name *kidanä məhrät*. The 21st of each month is also Mary's day, but then called Mary (Maryam) or Zion. The 19th is Gabriel's

---

[40] *Adäfrəs*, 222:20-31.
[41] *Ib.*, chapter 35.
[42] Cf. E. Ullendorff, *Ethiopia and the Bible*, London, 1968, pp. 52f., and Sergew Hable Sellassie, *Ancient and Medieval Ethiopian History to 1270*, Addis Ababa, 1972, pp. 115-121.
[43] Cf. DTW on *Gärima*; *Adäfrəs*, 220:10f.
[44] *Adäfrəs*, 220:11, Fəkr əskä mäḳabər, 169:13; cf. DTW on *liḳä säma'ətat*.
[45] Bərr ambar säbbäralləwo, 3:10; cf. DTW on *fäṭṭəno däraš*.
[46] Cf. DTW on *Gäbgäbo*; Sergew Hable Sellassie, *op. cit.*, p. 95, J. Doresse, *Ethiopia*, p. 15.
[47] *Adäfrəs*, 42:29, 297:16-24; cf. DTW on *Giyorgis*.

day, the 23rd is for St. George, the 24th for Täklä Haymanot, etc.[48] So appointments can be made for, e.g. *Hədar Giyorgis*, "the 23rd of Hədar"; "what about Abbo's day, i.e. the 5th, of the month after next then?" To make doubly sure, one can use both secular and ecclesiastical dating: "the 12th of Yäkkatit, St. Michael's day".[49] "The feast of God" or "the feast of the Son" probably refers to the monthly day celebrating the Nativity, the 29th, which is also called *Iyäsus*, "Jesus"; and the yearly feast of the Nativity, i.e. Christmas, is celebrated on Tahsas 29th, i.e. January 7th.[50]

Spirits can be good or evil but are mostly seen as evil. Good spirits are thought of as angels or as the Holy Spirit. Neutral in a sense is the term *wəkabi*, which DTW defines as "guardian angel"; "good, or benevolent spirit"; "evil spirit, *zar*,[51] *ḳolle*,[51] demonic companion".[52] But in common parlance the word *wəkabi* is associated with evil spirits, although in some expressions it signifies "helper, guardian angel". "The spirit has left them" is used in *Adäfrəs* of small landowners who are severely exploited by *gult*-right holders, and the expression means "they were demoralized, lost courage, gave up hope", so that they sold their property and entered the service of one of their masters.[53]

Man is seen as being manipulated by spirits, and often he submits to their evil influences. If a man harbours doubts about any of the doctrines of the Church, it is because he is dominated by satanic influences.[54] Ṣiwäne, the landowner's daughter in *Adäfrəs*, loves *zäfän*, "secular song and music", and to play the *krar*, "a six-stringed lyre". When her mother's father-confessor finds out, he realizes she is under the influence of an evil spirit that must be driven out:

> "As one day by chance Abba Addise, her mother's father-confessor, spent the night in her uncle's house and heard her playing one night, the matter took on a different interpretation altogether. In the morning, when he heard it was she who had been playing, he

---

[48] *Yäləbb hassab*, 150:17, *Fəkr əskä mäḳabər*, 33:3-6.
[49] *Fəkr əskä mäḳabər*, 147:1, *Bərr ambar säbbärälləwo*, 7:22, *Araya*, 306:1f., 274ult., 315:15f., *Yalačča gabəčča*, 17:3.6.
[50] *Fəkr əskä mäḳabər*, 34:17, DTW on *baläwäld*. One of the controversies in the Church has been concerning the date of Christmas: the *Karra* sect says it is the 28th. (KWK, p. 492, 1st col., ll.4-12.)
[51] Kinds of evil spirits.
[52] The demon called *fəlsäṭa* records a person's sins.
[53] *Adäfrəs*, 93:26.
[54] *Adäfrəs*, 217:22-26.

became very sad and confused, and he called her baptismal name and repeated it several times; then he said, "Come out, evil spirit! Come out, evil spirit!" and sprinkled her with water, so much so that he almost immersed her. Then, after he had understood she would not stop playing the *krar*, he talked to her mother, saying she was possessed by a demon of levity called Legewon. Therefore she was made to discontinue her education in a government school and return to Armaniya, the village of her birth." [55]

When the same priest hears about a moral lapse on the part of Adäfrəs, he comes again with water and exorcises the evil spirit, probably the same spirit referred to in a previous discussion among them, when it is called "the demon of fornication", with the name Legewon.[56]

Although the spirits are invisible, they are believed to appear at times in human form.[57] Aya Ləzzəbu, in *Yalačča gabəčča*, when he realizes his magic has not been effective, looks in his surprise like "a demon who has dropped his wand of invisibility".[58] This refers to a stick or wand, usually called *əṭä mäsäwwər*, "wand of invisibility" which unites the magician with a demon and makes him invisible.[59] When a demon possesses a man and through him appears in human form, he is called *ləbusä səga*, "(a demon) who has put on human form".[60]

Both Christians and pagans believe in spirits. The difference is seen primarily in attitudes to spirits and in the ways and means of dealing with them. Christians seek to avoid evil spirits and to fight them, as Abba Addise in the passage quoted above. Pagans seek rather to placate evil spirits and use means of manipulating them that are not accepted by the Church, such as becoming mediums of spirits or making them serve their own ends. Cf. chapter II, 2, on pagan practices.

The view of man tends to be pessimistic.[61] "There is no beast worse than man", says a priest, Abba Yohannəs in *Adäfrəs*, and he adds that efforts should be made to subdue one's evil instincts: "How can this bestiality in man be overcome?" It is possible

---

[55] *Adäfrəs*, 28:1-11.
[56] *Ib.*, 165:14-17; 117:28f.
[57] *Ib.*, 297:22f.; cf. DTW on *yäzar wälaj*, p. 437.
[58] *Yalačča gabəčča*, 161:7.
[59] DTW on *əṭä mäsäwwər*, p. 917.
[60] Cf. *Adäfrəs*, 158:6.
[61] *Yä'ənba däbdabbewoč*, 23:1, *Yäräggäfu abäboč*, 174:1ff., 192:18.

through unity and strength.[62] But usually more drastic means are called for, especially fasting; and if fasting does not help, God steps in to chastise man through natural disasters, etc.

Fitawrari Mäšäša, a rich landowner, says that "when the peasant has enough to eat, he does not know his limit", i.e., he becomes arrogant and unruly.[63] The concept of satiety as a source of insubordination seems to be very firmly held. Humility and knowing one's place are much praised virtues, and pride and arrogance great moral failings. One who has become puffed up and quarrelsome through much food must be humbled.[64] DTW translates *ṭäggäbä* not only as "to be sated", etc., but also as "to be puffed up, to be well-fed/fat; hence, to look down upon or despise people; to be haughty, to be arrogant or proud"; and he calls a *ṭəgabäňňa* not only "one who is sated", but also an "oppressor of the poor".

If the arrogant spirit cannot be subdued through voluntary weakening of the body through fasting, God takes a hand in the matter; and His methods include humbling man through destroying his harvest, as Wzo Asäggaš explains her views to one of her tenants:

> "God is here, there, everywhere - now He is with us when we talk together - He hears everything - He sees everything - He knows everything. True, he chooses sometimes to appear as if He does not see, hear, or know. Kneeling, He washes the feet of the people who have wronged Him; in his wisdom (or cunning), He seems to say: live as you like - as you are used to - as you desire. One day, when we are not mindful of His greatness, His infiniteness, His inscrutability, He will destroy us. He will bring catastrophe." [65]

The punishment is severe:

> "Locusts, snow and plague devastate what you should eat, so that they spread famine among you - until the proud youth, the inflated, quarrelsome person, the one who relies on his strength, the farmer who is disobedient to the landowner, to his master, bend their necks and pull the tail between their legs like dogs. - He will tell (i.e. show) us! He will bring His crushing whip - -", says Wzo Asäggaš to one of her tenants.
> "Well, I see, now I understand", the tenant answers.
> "Yes, there you see, now you understand - - Do you know why you understand - -?" Wzo Asäggaš continues, "because God has

---

[62] *Adäfrəs*, 84:6.14-18.
[63] *Fəḳr əskä mäḳabər*, 411:13f.
[64] *Ib.*, 126:22-25, *Adäfrəs*, 7:13-17.
[65] *Adäfrəs*, 6:31-7:6.

allied Himself with your mistress against you, stripped your (vain) glory from your shoulders and reduced your wealth. If your fields were weighed down (with plenty) and you had harvested much, you would have been inflated with pride - -." [66]

Conversely, God rewards the humble with wealth and high position, in Wzo Asäggaš's view:

"Look at me, for example - Yes, God did not take dignity, and my emperor did not take honour away from me. Still, I have not become proud; how can I be proud? For what am I? I am but a worm! A small creature - insignificant! But as you see, by putting myself very low, God and my king have placed me very high in front of them - - -." [67]

God is seen as interfering in human affairs very directly, and a bad harvest comes because God is angry, as the farmers on Fitawrari Mäšäša's land explain their situation:

"And particularly this year, God is angry with us; and if we sowed grain, worms would eat the shoots, and what was left after that, hail would descend upon at the time it was to be gathered, and so we went home, each to his home, wringing our hands. If God had only had mercy with us and stopped at this, we would not have become bitter. But now, cattle disease has entered our land, and as each day one or two heads of cattle die on each of us, we stand there weeping, while looking at it".[68]

God is regarded as the ultimate source of justice. When Wzo Wəddənäš, Bäzzabbəh's mother, hears that people may be spreading unfavourable rumours about her, she appeals to God for justice: "May God see to it (i.e., that justice is done)!" God is seen as the cause of success, and He has decided the span of human life, says Wzo Wəddənäš's father-confessor.[69]

There seems to be a belief that one's life is, in the main, decided at one's baptism. When things go against one's wishes or expectations, there is a tendency to blame "his luck of forty days", which seems to refer to the fate that is decided for a man at the time of his baptism, which occurs on the 40th day for boys. As the expression has become an idiom, it can equally be used by or about women, who are baptized on the 80th day. One woman says:

---

[66] *Adäfrəs*, 7:12-24.
[67] *Ib.*, 8:25-29.
[68] *Fəkr əskä mäkabər*, 212:22-29.
[69] *Fəkr əskä mäkabər*, 12:2-7, 16:8, 13:10-13.

"I don't blame men; it is my fate that was decided at my baptism". "The lot of one's forty days" cannot be changed.[70]

Araya's mother believes that God looks after man's health and well-being:

> "But it is God who looks after man; when can a doctor give him health! To be healed from evil, it is enough to believe in the Creator alone." [71]

Man can improve or aggravate his lot by his attitude to God, as an old man tells Araya:

> "It was not by Western knowledge that we got victory at Adwa and seized Harärge: it was by our faith. But today you have ceased respecting religion and you say that fasting is a private matter; you have started smoking tobacco and eating pork; but when His wrath comes, it will even reach us." [72]

When disaster comes, the cause is seen as lack of religion, as one *däbtära* says after Addis Ababa was bombed:

> "Sin has become over-abundant! Fasting has been neglected, religion is forgotten. It is love of money and pleasure that has brought this disaster upon us!" [73]

In times of disaster and grief, the question of guilt and punishment from God often arises:

> "How did I offend God? What did I do so that He brought His wrath upon me?" [74]

Especially when the cause of a misfortune is unknown, such questions are asked. "I do not know how I sinned against my Creator", says a man who has not been able to get children, in spite of the fact that he has observed the rules of his religion and implored God about this matter morning and evening.[75] Childlessness is commonly seen as punishment for sins. "It is because of the multitude of my sins that He did not give me a child: I have sinned against my Creator"; and a woman weeps when she does not get grandchildren: "How did I sin against God since He put me into this trouble?" Other misfortunes, such as ill health, can

---

[70] *Bərr ambar säbbärälləwo*, 3:9, *Kä'admas bašagär*, 61:2f., *Bälg*, 68:9.
[71] *Araya*, 185:30-32.
[72] *Araya*, 174:14-18.
[73] *Ib.*, 306:6-8; cf. *Yähəllina däwäl*, 85:7.
[74] *Yäšoh aklil*, 92:4f.
[75] *Kä'admas bašagär*, 22:22-24.

also be ascribed to the neglect of some religious duty, although it may not be known to the person what this sin consists of.[76]

To make life especially troublesome and full of danger for man, the Devil pesters and tempts him away from God:

> "But the Devil was the head of the angels - -!" begins Abba Addise, speaking like a man who has become a bit annoyed; "and even today, what is impossible for him - ? If he wants, he can shine like an angel of light - so that he can even manage to lead astray those who have renounced the world to become honoured and holy. He strives to be like the Creator to man by showing him endless worldly opportunities and hope - - by saying that "all this is mine, and if you are with me, it will be yours, too" - -; he appears in dreams, in visions - - he appears in human form - - -." [77]

As the world is considered evil, the best way to achieve holiness is to renounce the world and live removed from the affairs and temptations of human society. Holy men are *yäbäkkut*, "those who have had enough (of the world), or renounced (the world, and especially sexual relationships)"; *bəkat*, "satiety (with the world)" means also "holiness".[78]

The social order is regarded as created by God; it is, therefore, the evil in rebellious human nature that wants to introduce changes in society. When new and strange things happen, it is a sign that the end of the world has come near. The last age of this world is known as "the eighth millennium", *səmməntäññaw ši(h)*, and to express one's surprise at the mores of the times, one refers to this concept: "Oh, eighth millennium! The end of the world has truly come near". People living in those times will be a weak, spineless generation.[79]

Modern times are full of the signs of the coming doom:

> "The *Mämre* answered him saying, "There is no end to the strange things happening to fulfil the prophecies of *Fəkkare Iyäsus*.[80] It is a sign that the end of the world is near." [81]

---

[76] *Tarikənna məssale*, Book III, 1:10f., *Käʾadmas bašagär*, 60:19f., *Adäfrəs*, 170:7ff.

[77] *Adäfrəs*, 157:31-158:6.

[78] *Ib.*, 220:21, 221:25.

[79] *Ṭälfo bäkise*, 53:22, *Adäfrəs*, 40:17.

[80] The prophecies concerning the signs expected to precede the end of the world or take place in the eighth millennium, are contained in *Fəkkare Iyäsus*, "The Explanation of Jesus". Cf. Zämänfäs Ḳəddus Abrəha, *Hatäta mänafəst wäʾawdä nägäst*, pp. 285-294. DTW calls the eighth millennium "the name of an epoch; a time when flattery, subterfuge, treachery, wickedness and deviousness abound" (p. 1186).

[81] *Bərr ambar säbbärälləwo*, 23:8f.

There is a strong expectation of the (second) coming of Christ (*məṣat*).[82] This day, because of man's wickedness, will be a day of wrath and disaster, Doomsday, the Day of Wrath or Judgment (*yämä'at ḳän*).[83] The reward the pious can expect is graded according to the amount of righteousness (*ṣədḳ*) they have accumulated. When a certain woman, for money, agrees to look after an unknown traveller who has been attacked by robbers, she does it "thinking it would serve both for righteousness and for profit". Some merchants gave her ten dollars so that she would look after him, because "it will be for the good of both our and your soul".[84] People go to church "in the pursuit of righteousness".[85] The word "righteousness" implies also "completeness", or being a full, genuine human being; thus it occurs in contexts that are not directly religious; e.g., marriage will, for a girl, "make her righteous", and Gorfu, a nobleman's son, quotes the saying, "a coward is not made righteous".[86] These "secular" uses of the concept of righteousness have religious overtones: it is part of a full, godly life both to marry and to be fearless and brave in danger (trusting God). The last example shows clearly this religious implication: cowardice leads to disaster, because God does not help the coward. To overcome tribulations also brings righteousness.[87]

God's final reward is received in heaven (*sämay*, or *mängəstä sämayat*), which is graded, the seventh or highest section being *ṣərha aryam*.[88] At the death of the righteous, it is God who "takes" or "calls" the soul to heaven, by sending his "angel of death" (*ṭarä mot*), a term associating death with agony, and thus more commonly used of the death of sinners (*haṭ'an*).[89]

There seems to be a belief that punishments are accorded to people commensurate with the evil they have perpetrated, so that there are degrees of suffering in "hell" (*gähannäm*; *gähannämä*

---

[82] *Ib.*, 92:8, *Kaleb*, 54:18, *Addis aläm*, 61:13, *Fəḳr əskä mäḳabər*, 170:1.
[83] *Yäḳəne azmära*, 20:8.
[84] *Fəḳr əskä mäḳabər*, 536:4-14.
[85] *Ib.*, 42:5ff.
[86] *Yalačča gabəčča*, 133:7f, *Adäfrəs*, 198:19 (cf. *Revelation*, 21:8).
[87] *Araya*, 334:1f.
[88] *Adäfrəs*, 156:12, *Ṭälfo bäkise*, 19:23, 42:12, *Yäbädäl fəṣṣame*, 146:5, *Yähəllina däwäl*, 148:16. KWK, sub *sämay*, lists the seven parts of heaven as: *Erär, Rama, Iyor, Iyärusalem sämayawit, Sämay wədud, Mänbärä mängəst*, and *Ṣərha aryam*.
[89] *Araya*, 185:4.8, *Yäḳəne azmära*, 13ult., 103:2, *Fəḳr əskä mäḳabər*, 170:2, *Adäfrəs*, 143:7; 33:13.

ǝsat, "hell-fire", si'ol "Sheol", associated with darkness).[90] The word mäk̬ is used approximately like "pit, depth", and mäk̬amäk̬ is approximately "the deep pit", an intensified form of the former.[91] Maybe even deeper is anṭorätos/anṭorṭos, approximately "the deepest pit".[92] One particularly evil person told of in Adäfrǝs is said not to have been received in hell right away, but his body was thrown out of the ground because the ground rejected it till it was commanded to rest in the name of a saint, and only then his body descended into hell with a loud cry, the descent taking several years till the bottom was reached.[93]

Traditionalists have a strong feeling that the end of the world is imminent and that we live in the eighth millennium, because of all the changes that have taken place recently.[94]

b) *Christian life and worship*

The religious life of the Ethiopian Christian centres upon the church, where the faith of the community is celebrated under the leadership of the clergy. The religious feasts and fasts promulgated by the Church are the principal occasions for expressions of the faith. Private expressions of the faith are manifested for example through prayer and at moments of grief.

The church is the centre of the village, and it can be built on a hilltop with the rest of the village spread round it, as Bäzzabbǝh saw Dima when he travelled towards the place:

> "- - - on the flat field he saw a village. With the church in the middle and the houses of the village crowded around it, it resembled a hen that gathers her chickens around her." [95]

The church, which is "the house of Christians", *betä krǝstiyan* or "the house of God", *betä ǝgzi'abǝher*, is elevated above all other houses in the village, as a sign of respect,[96] and Wzo Asäggaš, the most important person in her village, is well aware of this:

---

[90] *Fǝk̬r ǝskä mäk̬abǝr*, 93:20.28f., 392:3, *Ǝsat wäy abäba*, 184:2, 185:6, *Tärät tärät yämäsärät*, 83:26, *Adäfrǝs*, 222:20-31, 251:11.
[91] *Adäfrǝs*, 64:29, 65:9.
[92] *Ib.*, 64:8; cf. DTW, who defines the word as "the deepest deep, the ultimate depth; Sheol, Gehenna" (p. 121).
[93] *Adäfrǝs*, 64:26-65:8.
[94] *Bälg*, 120:5-7.
[95] *Fǝk̬r ǝskä mäk̬abǝr*, 71:8-11.
[96] *Ib.*, 71:9, 428:13, *Adäfrǝs*, 143:2, 188:26, *Yalačča gabǝčča*, 25:21, *Yäk̬ǝne azmära*, 54:14, *Tarikǝnna mǝssale*, Book III, 1:3; *Adäfrǝs*, 5:9f.

"As was customary in the countryside, and as she was of noble birth, she had built her compound on the hilltop just below where Michael's church in Doḳaḳit was established; "Well, it is like this because it shall not appear as if I make myself equal to the Archangel", she says sometimes when she talks and the topic touches upon the matter." [97]

A main church is called *däbər*, a word that also means hill or elevated place; and *adbar* is used for a (usually pagan) place of worship, on an elevated place, and it can be a heap of stones or a tall tree.[98]

The most important part of a church is the box with the tablets made in imitation of the Tablets of the Law and dedicated to a saint, and both the tablets and the church are called *tabot*, although the word strictly speaking refers to "the Tablets of the Law" and to

"a Christian tablet, one cubit and a span by one cubit wide and three inches thick, called a *tabot* and put inside a box. On top of it are written the name of God, Alpha and Omega; and the words, *Tabot* of So-and-so, with the name of an angel, a prophet, St. Mary, an apostle, a saint, or a martyr; on top of the corners are engraved (or drawn) the images of the four animals (or creatures). The first *tabots* that were in Axum, having come from Egypt, are the *Tabot* of Mary and the *Tabot* of Michael." [99]

A church is always dedicated to a saint or holy being, *ḳəddus*, and some saints are more popular than others for such purposes, e.g. Michael.[100] The expression "the forty four *tabots*" [101] refers to the totality of saints that churches are dedicated to, and the expression thus means "all the churches of Ethiopia" or "one of each church dedicated to any saint a church can be dedicated to in Ethiopia".[102] To visit one Michael's church was equal to visiting them all, since homage was paid to Michael himself, who is one and

---

[97] *Adäfrəs*, 29:4-8.
[98] *Ib.*, 77:24f.; 77:15-18.
[99] DTW sub *tabot* (2). The four animals or creatures, *arba'tu ənsəsa*, called Cherubs, *kirub*, are the carriers of the throne of God; in conformity with the faces with which they are pictured they are called "lion face", "cow face", "eagle face" and "human face". (Cf. Ezekiel, Ch. 1, Revelation, 4:6-8, DTW sub *gäṣṣ*.)
[100] *Fəḳr əskä mäḳabər*, 33:26-28, *Adäfrəs*, 5:9ff.
[101] *Yalačča gabəčča*, 26:6f.
[102] The expression used to be applied to the churches of Gondar (J. Doresse, *Ethiopia*, London, 1959, p. 198), but is now used of all churches in Ethiopia.

not divided among all his churches. The holiness of the *tabot* is seen in the case of Fitawrari Mäšäša: when all other means of persuasion have failed, he finally gives in when the *tabots* from two churches are taken out and carried in procession, and he is beseeched in the names of the saints to desist from his foolhardy challenge to fight with his much younger and stronger opponent.[103] The strongest expression of recalcitrance is to refuse "even if one begs him and at the same time takes out the *tabot*".[104]

The *tabot* is also the place in the church where the elements of the Eucharist, "His flesh and blood", *səga wädämu*, are deposited, and the *tabot* serves as an altar.[105] It is in the central part of circular churches, or in the "holy of holies", *mäkdäs*, of any church. All churches are divided into the *mäkdäs*, "the holy of holies", the inner sanctum accessible only to senior priests and the king; the middle part, the *kəddəst*, "the holy", which is used by priests and communicant laymen and where couples are wed; and the outer part of the church, the *kəne mahlet*, where the congregation assembles, where the service is listened to, prayers offered, and where the church music and dances are performed by the *däbtära*, the "cantors".[106]

The proper way of showing reverence to a holy place or object, such as churches and crosses, is to greet it by bowing three times from a distance, or, if approachable, to kiss it; this is expressed by the verb *täsalläma*, approximately "kiss, greet or visit a holy place or object"; a church can also be called *mässallämiya*, approximately "place of obeisance or worship".[107]

Not much attention is paid in Amharic literature to religious paintings, that are part and parcel of all Ethiopian churches. There are occasional references to such paintings, but they are mostly by the way, such as the observation that a group of people met for consultation in a "prayer room" that is also called "the room of paintings", and it seems to be part of a private house, not a church.[108] This neglect in the literature may be due to lack

---

[103] *Fəkr əskä mäkabər*, chapter 14.
[104] *Ib.*, 229:6f.
[105] *Addis aläm*, 25:11f.
[106] *Bərr ambar säbbärälləwo*, 78:16-22, *Fəkr əskä mäkabər*, 72:10f., 156:21ff. Cf. E. Ullendorff, *Ethiopia and the Bible*, p. 88.
[107] *Fəkr əskä mäkabər*, 72:10, *Adäfrəs*, 155:39f., 205:24f.; 177:2.
[108] *Fəkr əskä mäkabər*, 419:3-7.

of appreciation of the art form among young intellectuals. Traditionally, it is a highly developed and respected art, and a religious professional painter in the church is given the honourable title *aläka*, here approximately, "master, maestro, expert".[109]

In *Adäfrəs* a maid explains how Kəbrät, a painter, had behaved when he showed someone a painting he had made; she says: "Even when he showed her the painting, he did it while turning his face aside".[110] Turning aside in front of a picture is a gesture of respect usually reserved for a saint, as it would be an expression of arrogance to stare him in the face. In this case, the painting is of a girl, and the maid finds this gesture is evidence enough that the painter is in love with her.

The same painter had made a painting of St. Michael and presented it to Wzo Asäggaš, his host and a very religious woman. After the picture had been scrutinized, she talks to Gorfu, a rather conservative youth about it:

> "One hears strange things, doesn't one? He said to me, I tell you,[111] "I have made a picture of Michael", and he gave it me - - -! The sword that he had pulled out with his right hand flashed. - In

[109] Cf. Habtä Maryam Wärkənäh, *Təntawi....*, p. 273. He mentions (*ibid.*) the following points regarding the execution of religious paintings: a) evil people are looking aside so that only one eye is seen; good people are painted frontally, with both eyes seen; b) on the cross, Christ always leans his head to the right; c) in pictures of Madonna with child, *məslä fəkur wälda*, our Lord is (held leaning) from left to right, our Lady leans her head to the left; d) in church, paintings are always done on the four walls of the *mäkdäs* as follows: 1. *on the east wall*: the miracles and stories of Christ, the work and struggle of the apostles, and of our Lady of St. Ephraim the Syrian, *yä'efrem əmmäbet* (after the reputed author of *Wəddase Maryam*, and illustrating the text of this book); 2. *the west wall*: Christ's baptism, crucifixion, resurrection, Madonna and child, and St. George; 3. *the north wall*: the stories of the martyrs, and of our Lady suffering with the martyrs: 4. *the south wall*: stories of Mary from birth to resurrection, and of Christ's second coming (Doomsday); 5. (the panels) *close to the floor* (*məhwar*): the resurrection to the east, the Trinity to the west, Mount Tabor (the Transfiguration) to the north, scenes of His (Christ's) baptism to the south, 6. *on the doors of the mäkdäs*: on the doors which are on the west, scenes showing St. Michael drowning Pharaoh and his soldiers, and St. Rufael piercing the sea monster; 7. *on all four sides also*: scenes showing holy deeds of the angels. The author says (p. 272) that the aim of Ethiopian painting is to tell a story and to teach a lesson, and that painters therefore do not pay attention to perspectives and proportions.

[110] *Adäfrəs*, 70:19f.

[111] *Alälləh* could grammatically mean "he said to you, or on your behalf", but the context shows he makes use of a rather unusual construction, meaning approximately "he said, i.e. to me—I now tell you for your benefit".

his left hand, he held the scales high, showing the Creator's justice in a proper way. - His wings covered with gold are a fearful sight - - anyhow, the flashing of his brightness is incredible - - because he was standing on the Devil's belly, his, the Devil's, tongue was stretching out - - the way he twisted his tail - - he was between life and death - - anyway, I was pleased when he brought it to me - - - Immediately I sent someone to Däbrä Sina to buy white silk, and I covered it up, and when the priest came, well, I brought it to him - - - "Well done, my child! Well done, my child! That's fine! That's fine! May he, Michael, shade you and protect you from your left and from your right - - - and may also the hand that painted it be blessed" - While saying this he turned the painting to the right and to the left, looking at it for a long time, from a distance and from close by, and then suddenly his face frowned and he looked at me - - - "What is it, what happened to you?" I asked him then - - - "What fault have you found with it?" - - - "He has painted the Archangel's face dark and the Devil's face light - - O! O! all this work for nothing", he said, and he was annoyed. - - Well, I had also seen it (the painting) - - now then, I thought the Devil's face was a suffering face, but the light colour I had not noticed at the time - - - "Unless you have this changed I will not take it with me", the priest said, will you believe it - -!"

"As for him, he is too particular about everything - - -."

"As he had told me to, I called the painter and asked him to make the Archangel's face light, the Devil's dark - - - and doesn't he answer, "I'd rather die!""

"What? Did he refuse to change it?"

"Exactly!"

"Did he say why?"

"May shame be left behind, like a tail! - Didn't he say to me that "the face of the old man is dark"? "Which old man?" I didn't say anything except, "Which old man?" - - - "Your tenant - - the one living on (or near) the ridge of hills" - - -"

"God of Wrath!"

"May God preserve you from His wrath, my brother - -! Then I looked carefully at it - - the portrait he had made - - it was exactly Aya Ajjəbe's likeness - - and the souls in the balance, they had faces exactly like those of Roman and Ṣiwäne - - - if it was my eyes that tricked me I don't know, but then the Devil's face looked to me like my own face - - - if he had told me it was my own face - - - if he had told me it was my portrait that he had used as a model it could not have been worse - - -."

"What a terrible thing to have happened!"

"Well, I tell you I chased him out of my room, saying, "Here, take it where you want, I don't want to set eyes on it again" - - - I tell you the truth, it was that day I should have chased him with his friend (i.e. Adäfrəs) from my house - - -."

"And what did the priest say - - ? when you told him he (the painter) refused (to change the painting) - - - ?"

"He said, "Never mind, let him return it (the painting, to us) - we will have the faces changed by a local painter." - - But I was shattered - - To have paid homage to the face of Aya Ajjəbe! - - - I did not tell him (the priest) - - if I tell him, just because he has touched it with his hands, only God knows how many days he will spend in prayerful seclusion to seek cleansing - - -."

"By the way, what did he do with the painting - - - ?"

"They told me he gave it to a church of St. Michael's that is built down there towards Adal - -." " [112]

Both the strict adherence to the rules and the way a picture is treated with the same reverence as the object of the painting are illustrated in this passage. The fact that Wzo Asäggaš had not paid attention to the likenesses in the picture points to the fact that this is not an important aspect of traditional Ethiopian art.[113] In this case, the painting was made by a painter who had received a modern European artistic education.

Churches are surrounded by a copse, with trees such as *ṭəd*, "juniperus procera", or African cedar; *wäyra*, "olea chrysophyla", or olive tree; *gamme*, "ehretia cymosa", a highland tree characterized by curved or bent branches and stem; or *bəsanna*, "croton macrostachys", a tree that grows mostly in the *wäynadäga* zone (ca. 5,000-7,000 feet); et al. Believers often stand under a tree to pray.[114] In the church compound, which is often fenced in, there is a house where the elements of the Eucharist are prepared; it is called "the house of secrets or mysteries", or "the house of bread".[115] The most common church bell, *däwäl* or *märäwa*, or *kaçəl* if small, is made of a flat stone, a lithophone, suspended from a tree.[116]

Of the clergy, *betä kəhənät*, we mostly encounter the ordinary

---

[112] *Adäfrəs*, 173:26-175:16.
[113] Cf. Habtä Maryam Wärkənäh, *Təntawi* ..., p. 272; he writes: "Intending to make the lesson and message complete, the painter is not limited to painting alone, but adds a (written) explanation. And to make the paintings explicit (literally to magnify the paintings), all details are also drawn in black and heavy colours." Much Amharic fiction is illustrated, and the influence from traditional Ethiopian religious painting is visible, not least in the treatment of perspective and proportions, and the rejection of lifelike representation as a desirable achievement or aim. On Ethiopian traditional painting, see J. Leroy, *Ethiopian Painting*, London, 1967.
[114] *Adäfrəs*, 77:25f., *Yäləbb hassab*, 159:18f.
[115] *Adäfrəs*, 84:26, DTW sub *betä ləhem*.
[116] *Adäfrəs*, 77:27-78:1, 143:2, 146:7.

priest, especially in his function as adviser and father confessor. There are, in Amharic literature, sometimes references to the higher clergy. The *əčäge* is mentioned in *Addis aläm*, a novel written before the war, when the *əčäge* and the Patriarch had the highest offices in the Church (now both titles are held by the Patriarch). The Patriarch, who is also called "the Bishop", is referred to as "our father", and as a bishop he confers ecclesiastical ranks.[117] The highest officials in the Church are always referred to with respect. In one case, a bishop has become a national hero for his resistance against the Italians during their occupation of the country, namely Abunä Peṭros, about whom Mäkonnən Əndalkaččäw wrote a play, *Yädäm dəmṣ*.[118]

A few of the higher titles of the clergy that occur in Amharic literature are, e.g. *gra geta*, "master of the left", as opposed to the "master of the right", *käňň geta*, who have their position to the left and to the right of the *aläka* (and these positions can only be held in a *däbər*, a main church), and they are in charge of supervising the church chant and dancing from the left and the right sides. The *rə'sä däbər*, literally "head of the main church" is in charge of the chant and dance on a slightly higher level, and above him is the *liḵa ṭäbäbt*, "master of the arts", and above him again, the *märi geta*, "leading, or head master". All these are responsible for the church rituals, primarily the chanting and dancing, and they are thus heads of the *däbtäras*, and below the *aläka*, the administrator and head of the *däbər*.[119]

On the lower levels of the hierarchy, deacons are mentioned a few times; they belong to the clergy, partake in the celebration of Mass, and perform duties connected with burials, saying prayers for the dead, etc.[120]

The priests, both the *aläka* and the ordinary priest, *kes*, are mentioned often by Ethiopian authors. It might be preferable to treat them together, as the term *aläka*, besides being a genuine title, is also used of and to an ordinary priest; the title *mämhər/*

---

[117] *Addis aläm*, 18:10, 60:8f.; 52:20; *Fəḵr əskä mäḵabər*, 527:4.9; 509:32-510:1.
[118] *Arrəmuňň*, pp. 79-104.
[119] *Fəḵr əskä mäḵabər*, 202:13; 312:8.15; 121:17-19; 349:13, 241:19-25, *Yähəllina däwäl*, 172:12f. On titles in the Church, cf. Habtä Maryam Wärḵənäh, *Təntawi...*, pp. 300-303; see also DTW under the respective titles.
[120] *Fəḵr əskä mäḵabər*, 39:2-7, 41ult.-42:4, *Bərr ambar säbbärälləwo*, 79:24.

mämər or *mämre*, which should properly be used of the head or administrator of a monastery, is also used of and to a priest. *Abba*, "father", or *abbate*, "my father", which should be used of or to a monk, is also used of and to a priest.[121]

A priest is required to marry one wife at a *täklil* wedding in church, with Communion, whereby he is forbidden divorce or remarriage; he is then referred to as "a priest married according to the law".[122]

Priests in their function of "father confessors" (literally "father of the soul", *yänäfs abbat*, or "father of repentance", *yänəssəha abbat*) are called on for help in marital conflicts, and they are used as middlemen to arrange marriages, or they are consulted on any important question, especially by members of the nobility, whom they sometimes visit daily, as for example *Ḳes* or *Abba* Mogäse in *Fəḳr əskä mäḳabər*, or *Abba* Addise in *Adäfrəs*.[123] When a priest wants to stress a point with all his authority, he threatens those who disobey him with excommunication. When Bäzzabbəh's mother is hesitant about marrying again after she has survived many husbands, her father confessor tells her:

> "Well, then, I shall excommunicate you, by the compassionate (Virgin Mary)! God does not like such things." [124]

They confirm oaths by similarly threatening with excommunication, or banning from the Church, or excluding a person from the grace of God:

> "Everyone swore while slapping the Book, and finally the priest rose up and said, "If you break the oath you have made here, then be banned from the Merciful One", thus threatening them with excommunication." [125]

One hesitant father who is asked to give his daughter in marriage requires an oath that the other party will not break the engage-

---

[121] *Bərr ambar säbbärällawo*, 4:6, 20:3.22f., *Fəḳr əskä mäḳabər*, 167:13f., *Yäləbb hassab*, 134:16.22, 139:7f., *Araya*, 325:18.22, 326:1; *Fəḳr əskä mäḳabər*, 11:23, 12:25, 13:1f., 59:9.11-13, 510:1-7.

[122] *Fəḳr əskä mäḳabər*, 36:25; cf. DTW sub *balähəgg*, p. 175.

[123] *Yäləbb hassab*, 134:15ff., *Fəḳr əskä mäḳabər*, 11:22ff.; 99:3, 215:13. The institution of the father confessor goes back to the time of Zär'a Ya'ḳob (1434-68). There was, and is, "close personal and economic relationship between the Father Confessor and the individual family." (T. Tamrat, *op. cit.*, p. 244.)

[124] *Fəḳr əskä mäḳabər*, 13:26f.

[125] *Ib.*, 263:31-33.

ment;[126] the priest who is used as mediator immediately administers an oath:

> "And thereupon he prayed the Paternoster and In the Peace of Gabriel,[127] and he offered a final prayer saying, "May He fulfil for us what we planned, may He bless for us what we sowed, may He make plentiful for us what we reap; if you give your consent to us (our proposal), may the One God consent to grant you what you want", and everyone said "Amen!" and accepted the agreement."[128]

The priest is recognized by his turban, his cross held in a piece of cloth, his cloak, and the seemingly inevitable fly-whisk.[129] He is usually described as conservative, opposed to social change; Abba Addise in *Adäfrəs* gives his views to Adäfrəs, particularly opposing the curtailing of any of the rights and privileges of the nobility:

> "Listen to me, "It is not good to take the children's bread and give it to the dogs" - - - and what benefits has Ethiopia got (i.e. from the changes that already have taken place)? - - and isn't it because our king has gathered about him people who are not sons of known people (i.e. of noble birth) that he sees all his troubles - - - ?"[130]

Priests are often ridiculed for their ignorance. Sometimes it is done good-naturedly, as when a priest advises Bäzzabbəh's mother, Əmmät Wəddənäš, on how many times a woman can marry if her husbands all die:

> " "How many times does the Book permit a woman whose husband has died to marry?" Because Abba Taməru this time got a question he had never heard, his forehead began to perspire slightly as if his thoughts were troubled; he soon tilted his fly-whisk and supported his chin on the horny handle, and fixed his eyes on the ceiling, just as if the answers were written on the ceiling. After he had been thus looking upwards for some time, he slowly released the handle of the fly-whisk from under his chin and returned his gaze to Əmmät Wəddənäš.
> "The Book .... sets no limit; as it thus does not set any limit, it means she can marry even beyond the fourth, even the tenth", Abba Taməru said hesitatingly.

---

[126] *Bərr ambar säbbärälləwo*, 21:21-22:8.
[127] *Sälamä gäbrʾel* is "a blessing or praise St. Gabriel said to Our Lady, and it is prayed together with Our Lord's prayer". (DTW)
[128] *Bərr ambar säbbärälləwo*, 22:10-15.
[129] *Ib.*, 22:9f., *Adäfrəs*, 123:23-27, *Yähəllina däwäl*, 114:5f., 246:23f., *Əddəl näw? bädäl?*, 11:2-7.
[130] *Adäfrəs*, 100:19-23.

"The tenth?" said Əmmät Wəddənäš, opening her eyes widely.
"Well, when I say ten, it is just a manner of speech to explain what I said, that no limit is set; it does not mean there ever was a woman who lost nine husbands by death and married a tenth, whether at the time of the Book or later; it is well known that even in future such a thing will not happen. But it means that if such a thing happens, the Book does not forbid it. I ask you to note that this is not a thing to be repeated to others, it remains (should remain) between you and me", said Abba Taməru, putting on a stern face, worrying because he was not sure himself if what he had told Wzo Wəddənäš was true.

"What is it, Father, has all that is said between you and me ever stopped being as secret as the Eucharist?"

"Well, I only thought it is not bad to be careful (or to take precautions)." " [131]

At other times, priests are shown as weaklings who only try to curry favour with people, without any moral guidance to give. Once some starving peasants ask to be released from duties to pay part of the tribute due to their landlord, and the words become harsh from the representative of the peasants. Abba Mogäse, Fitawrari Mäšäša's father confessor (in *Fəkr əskä mäḵabər*), tries to rebuke the spokesman of the peasants:

" "Keep silent, you! What kind of person is this, lacking completely the character of an elder? Did you come here in order to stir up a quarrel, being the messenger of Satan (or a demonic messenger)?" said Abba Mogäse because he saw that the Fitawrari became very angry.

"What is it, Father, did I tell any lies?" the elder said.

"Even if you do not tell any lies, your insolence and your speech is not the speech of an elder!"

"So! (What do you mean:) "If he does not tell a lie!" What is true in what he said?" said Fitawrari, looking at his father confessor in anger.

"As for what he said, what truth is there in it? I only mean that of all of it, his insolence is worst!" " [132]

Later, Guddu Kasa characterizes the priest in no uncertain words, and in his presence:

"Abba Mogäse, as you know him, is a person who has no thought of his own, but who only has the gift of interpreting other people's thoughts from watching their eyes and foreheads; the one who

---

[131] *Fəkr əskä mäḵabər*, 14:13-15:11.
[132] *Fəkr əskä mäḵabər*, 215:10-21.

fills his belly can lead him along the road he desires; he has sold and exchanged his obligations for, or to, his belly." [133]

How the same priest is completely servile to the noble who supports him is seen in his total defence of the unreasonable claims of the landlord against poor peasants in times of hardship, supplying theological arguments in the dispute:

> "It is not true what you say, that to bring gifts to be noticed by and gifts to celebrate the holiday is not an old custom. When the Book says, "Do not stand naked before the Messiah of God", it means, "Do not come empty-handed into the presence of the one whom God has anointed". And it means that when an ordinary man with no title comes before a noble lord to say "Happy festival" on a holiday, or when he comes to him to draw his attention to troubles he has met, he comes with a gift to be noticed by, a gift of greeting, an offering, a gift to celebrate the holiday, but he does not come empty-handed. Therefore, it is a well-known fact that the Book prescribes the giving of gifts for celebration and the paying of homage on holidays." [134]

Abba Mogäse has his parallel in Abba Addise, the father confessor of Wzo Asäggaš, the landowner in *Adäfrəs*. Although the latter priest displays more authoritative behaviour and pronouncements, both have much the same frame of mind. When Ato Wäldu, a Western educated merchant, says to him, "The Ethiopian people - - what they believe in is miracles rather than the intellect", Abba Addise replies:

> "Of course! What doubt can there be about it? It was the work of the intellect that drove Adam and Eve out of Paradise (literally, "the kingdom of the heavens"). - - The Lord said, "Believe me with all your heart, with all your soul"; He did not say, "Investigate me", when He gave us the Law. As the Ethiopian people know that justice is not obtained through investigation, they believe in miracles - -." [135]

The clergy are in a sense servants of the state as well as of the Church, particularly as the close link with the Patriarchate in Egypt was severed with the appointment of an Ethiopian Patriarch. Ato Țəso, the judge, explains the implications of this change to an autocephalous church:

---

[133] *Fəkr əskä mäkabər*, 220:20-25.
[134] *Fəkr əskä mäkabər*, 273ult.-274:10.
[135] *Adäfrəs*, 156:10-17.

BELIEFS AND ETHICS

> "- - until recently, because our ecclesiastical jurisdiction was in the hands of the Egyptians, it certainly appeared as if the governmental and ecclesiastical jurisdictions were divided. But today, the two jurisdictions have become one. The Ethiopian leader has for the first time redeemed the clergy from being under foreign jurisdiction and has made the church to be under her own jurisdiction. - It means, then, that an Ethiopian authority leads her." [136]

And he adds a bit later:

> "And also, on this basis, because the indigenous ecclesiastical jurisdiction is manifested in the king, it means that it has coalesced and become one with the secular jurisdiction." [137]

To come to terms with his attachment both to the state and to his Church, Abba Addise experiences difficulties. Ethiopia and the king become bearers of divine revelation:

> "- - - Ethiopia has not at any time been without a guardian/guide. - - At first she was guarded/guided by conscience (*həggä ləbbuna*), then by the Torah (*həggä orit*), later by the law of the Gospel (*həggä wängel*), and in modern times by the constitution (*həggä mängəst*) - -." [138]

Abba Yohannəs, who has been educated in the famous Eritrean monastery of Däbrä Bizän, and is head of a main church, delivers a speech to encourage people to contribute to the building of a new school.[139] In his speech, he stresses the official view that all should stand together:

> "And so then, give help, all of you according to your ability, to this school, where our unity is strengthened, where Amhara, Galla, Adal, and Muslim children are taught. - - - What you have given on earth, awaits you in heaven." [140]

But in spite of his appeal to adherents of other beliefs, he on the same occasion asks for contributions to repair the roof of the house where the elements of the Eucharist are prepared.[141] His theme is the unity of all races and creeds, but he says:

> "If the country rejects Christianity ("snaps her Christian neck-

---

[136] *Adäfrəs*, 73:15-22.
[137] *Ib.*, 74:1-3.
[138] *Ib.*, 99:10-12.
[139] *Ib.*, 78:3-7.
[140] *Ib.*, 84:21-24.
[141] *Ib.*, 84:26-30.

cord"), if the faith of the people weakens, the fall of both the country and the people will not be a nice sight - -." [142]

Because he is speaking in a context that is new to him, he is out of his depth and has to qualify many of his statements with "maybe, who knows", and he even forgets the main point of his prepared speech.[143]

A main criticism of some priests is that they become sorcerers. Of one *mämhər* (here used of a priest), a shepherd tells:

"The father of our master, Mämre (what's his name - - I've forgotten it) used to call upon the unmentionable spirits of the sky and of the sea. In addition, they say he was a cheat and a thief.[144] And they tell us that when he was buried, his grave went down to hell, - may God have mercy upon his soul. His grave screams till this very day - - -." [145]

Not in all cases are priests depicted from their weaker sides. Mämhər Täklä Haymanot in *Araya* is a priest who is presented as a moral support for the resistance movement during the Italian occupation.[146] But criticism of some of the clergy is common in much Amharic literature, and priests are often made the butts of ridicule.

The *däbtära*, approximately "cantor", we encounter both as a functionary of the Church, where he is essential for the conducting of Mass,[147] and in his dealings outside church, and then almost exclusively in his dealings on the borderline between Christianity and paganism, where he dabbles in magic, astrology and doubtful medical practices. This is dealt with in chapter II, 3, on syncretism.

A typical attitude people have to the *däbtära* is seen in the freedom fighter Fitawrari Märrəne (in *Ṭälfo bäkise*): he obeys him out of fear, but he also despises him and does not miss an opportunity to vent his spite when he is shown up as a failure and a cheat:

---

[142] *Adäfrəs*, 80:14-16.
[143] *Ib.*, 82:9.10.12, 83:8.9.10, 84:14-16; 84:18-20.
[144] *Dəmbär gäfi sälabi*, literally "pusher of the border, castrator" is probably used figuratively of one who does not respect the property of others, and who can catch people off guard, like one who comes to castrate; the expression thus means "a clever thief".
[145] *Adäfrəs*, 64:26-30.
[146] *Araya*, 275:2-20, 278:21-280:3, 329:5-14.
[147] *Ib.*, 282:5-7.

"There is that uncle of yours, the stupid *däbtära*; he used to make me change your name each time the Evangelist (i.e. the year) changed, saying it is better so. From today on I have had enough; I won't believe a lying sorcerer." [148]

This ambiguous attitude to the *däbtära* seems to be common, but in most cases people take their advice to be on the safe side. There are, however, many who refuse to have dealings with them as sorcerers and astrologers.[149]

The life of a monk or hermit, segregated from the world, is regarded as ideal for the pursuit of holiness and serving God.

When the Emperor Kaleb decides to give up the throne for a monastic life, he prays to God (in the play by Käbbädä Mika'el):

"I have withdrawn from people, from the life of this world to seek righteousness only, from this day on; I have exchanged my kingdom for a monastery, for prayer, I have come to beg at your door: this is my decision." [150]

When one "has had enough" of this world and wants to seek heaven and righteousness, one leaves "the things of the world" and withdraws from people.[151]

When Bäzzabbəh, in *Fəkr əskä mäkabər*, believes he might have angered God because he had tried or desired to violate his mother's vow to God that he should never marry, "he thinks of getting reconciled to God through fasting and prayer, leaving all and renouncing the world".[152]

It seems to be expected that the monastic life should be especially sought by people who have had disappointments, or a surfeit of pleasures, in the world, as they are often designated as "those who have had enough (of the world)", *yäbäkkut*; "those who have had enough, those who have been hidden (from the world)", *yäbäkkut yätäsäwwärut*; "one who has had enough (of), or renounced (the world), and who has awoken (to spiritual realities)"; cf. expressions like "a hermit who has had enough (of the world)", and one renouncing the world is one who says "I have had enough of the

---

[148] *Tälfo bäkise*, 52:23-25.
[149] *Bərr ambar säbbärälləwo*, 38:23-39:18; cf. 15:25ff.
[150] *Kaleb*, 69:1-4.
[151] *Ib.*, 68:18f., 70:12-15.
[152] *Fəkr əskä mäkabər*, 467:2-7.

world", *aläm bäkkañ*.¹⁵³ Ṣiwäne in *Adäfrəs* finds refuge from her disappointments by becoming a nun, and so does Säblä Wängel in *Fəkr əskä mäkabər* when Bäzzabbəh dies, and Guddu Kasa joins her after some years.¹⁵⁴

Monks and nuns can live in communities in a monastery or convent (*gädam, mənnet*), or separate but in the same close vicinity. But to renounce the world can also imply a life in almost absolute seclusion from other people, when a monk or nun lives alone in the forest or a cave.¹⁵⁵ A monk or nun is not known by his or her "worldly" names but is referred to as "father", "mother", "sister", "spiritual poor".¹⁵⁶

Some places are famous for their monastic life, such as Mount Zəkwala, Däbrä Libanos, Gəšän, Lalibäla, Aksum Ṣəyon, Däbrä Bizän, etc., and valued for pilgrimage.¹⁵⁷

A monk or nun is recognized by his or her cap, *kob*, and prayer stick, *mäkwamiya*, skin mantle, *daba*, a gourd or plate for begging, and sometimes the *askema*, "a scapular with twelve crosses".¹⁵⁸

Monasteries and convents are also educational institutions (see the section on church education later in this chapter).

Some monks act as advisers and preachers, and a few deal in magic (see chapter II, 3, on syncretism).

Ethiopian authors often deal with religious questions, but few write about the Mass or other religious activities taking place in church. To go to, or kiss, the church is, however, regarded as an act of piety, and in spite of the low esteem some have of the priesthood, ridicule is not levelled at religion itself or at people who attend church services or functions. One pious person is designated as "one who kisses (i.e. goes to) church, who fasts, who recites the Psalms (i.e. performs the common act of prayer in the Ethiopian

---

- [153] *Adäfrəs*, 220:21, 118:6f., 117:31, 175ult., *Yäkəne azmära*, 25ult.
- [154] *Adäfrəs*, 329:29ff., *Fəkr əskä mäkabər*, 548:30, 552:12ff.
- [155] *Yäləbb hassab*, 150:1.6-8, *Käʾadmas bašagär*, 31:2, *Arrəmuññ*, 76:15-21, 66:11, 67:1f., *Yäkəne azmära*, 145:2.7ff., *Yäfəkər çora*, 145:1-7, 2:10-14, 3:4.
- [156] *Fəkr əskä mäkabər*, 552:6-10, *Arrəmuññ*, 122:3.5, 125:9; 68:1.24; cf. *Yäləbb hassab*, 148:25f.
- [157] *Joro ṭäbi*, 71:10-12, *Adäfrəs*, 78:4.
- [158] *Araya*, 183:5, *Adäfrəs*, 313:9-11. The *askema* is worn only by the most saintly of the monks. There are four parts to the monastic habit, not all visible externally: the cloak of cotton or leather; the leather belt; the cap or headpiece; and the *askema*. (See T. Tamrat, *Church and state...*, pp. 164f.)

Orthodox Church)".[159] "Church kisser", *betä krəstiyan sami*, is the most common way of referring to one who goes to church.[160] At Mass, *ḳəddase*, priests carry censers and crosses in a procession round the holy of holies, dressed in beautiful ecclesiastical attire, chanting the ritual in Ge'ez. As a sign of humility, Mass is listened to with lowered head.[161]

After Mass proper, there are occasionally sermons (*səbkät* or *guba'e*) in Amharic, which can sometimes become decisive factors in the lives of characters described in Amharic literature.[162]

A boy is baptized in church (when the mother's period of impurity, according to Leviticus 12:2-8, is over) on the 40th day after birth and gets a baptismal father, *yäkrəstənna abbat*; a girl is baptised on the 80th day and gets a baptismal mother, *yäkrəstənna ənnat*. The child is given a "baptismal", "apostolic", "biblical" name.[163] A person is commonly known by a name that is different from this baptismal or Christian name.[164] As pointed out earlier, there seems to be a belief that the course of one's life, one's fate, is, partly or fully, decided at baptism; that seems to be implied in the expression "the fate of the 40 days".[165] As a sign of having been baptized, a cord of white and red thread, the *matäb*, is tied around the child's neck.[166]

The day a child is baptized is an occasion for the parents to make a feast.[167]

After, or as part of Mass, Holy Communion, *ḳurban*, is given in the middle section of the church to communicant members, mostly old people and small children, i.e. those without an active sexual life. No food should be eaten before one takes Communion.[168] The

---

[159] *Yalačča gabəčča*, 25:21.
[160] *Fəḵr əskä mäḳabər*, 167:9, *Bälg*, 107:20.
[161] *Fəḵr əskä mäḳabər*, 42:14-19, *Ṭälfo bäkise*, 31:23.
[162] *Arrəmuññ*, 119:10-31, *Fəḵr əskä mäḳabər*, 26:10.
[163] *Yäləbb hassab*, 134:1-4, 139:5-9, *Adäfrəs*, 28:5, 74:17. Cf. J. Doresse, *La vie quotidienne...*, p. 225.
[164] *Arrəmuññ*, 323:18-20, *Bərr ambar säbbärällawo*, 79:14-20, *Yäräggäfu abäboč*, 36:1-3, *Bälg*, 45:9f.
[165] *Kä'admas bašagär*, 61:2, *Bərr ambar säbbärällawo*, 3:9f, *Yähəllina däwäl*, 147:12-14, 165:5f.
[166] *Fəḵr əskä mäḳabər*, 282:28f.
[167] *Yä'ənba däbdabbewoč*, 12:11-25.
[168] *Joro ṭäbi*, 143:7, *Bərr ambar säbbärällawo*, 4:14, *Yäləbb hassab*, 173:3-6, 174:7f., *Yäfəḵər ṭora*, 153:14-16, *Əddəl näw? bädäl?*, 12:11.

elements of the Eucharist, bread and wine, or "His flesh and blood", *səga wädämu*, are prepared in a special house near the church and given to the communicants while candles and incense burn; a deacon sings and a priest gives "the holy things to holy people", *ḳəddusat läḳəddusan*, while intoning, "it is not according to our sins, but according to Your goodness", and saying, "It is the flesh of our Lord Emmanuel", etc.[169]

Church weddings are described together with other kinds of weddings in chapter III, 4, on sex and marriage.

Christian funerals are dealt with later in this chapter, where Ethiopian expressions of grief are taken up.

Religious feasts and fasts go hand in hand, the bigger feasts usually being preceded by days of fasting.

Fasting, *ṣom* or *ṭom*, does not seem to interest Ethiopian authors very much. It is taken as a sign of piety to be fasting,[170] but otherwise fasting seasons may be referred to just to point out the time of year. Of the "seven fasts", *säb'atu aṣwamat*,[171] Lent is the longest and ends in a particularly severe week, lasting from Palm Sunday till Easter morning and called *həmamat*, colloquially, *mamat*, approximately "passion week" (literally "sufferings"), commemorating the "fourteen sufferings" on the way of the cross; there is total fasting from Friday till Sunday, a period called *akfəlät* or *akfəlot*.[172] The severe strain of abstaining from food and drink for long periods is emphasized. At times of total fast, food and drink are forbidden, except for once at night when uncooked food and water can be taken.[173]

KBT defines *ṭomä/ṣomä*, "to fast", as "obeying God's law, to abstain from food, meat, milk, butter, in order to tire the body", and "to deny the desires of one's heart and lust; to keep the eye from seeing evil, the mouth from speaking evil, the ear from hearing

---

[169] *Yäfəḳər ṭora*, 154:6-155:4, 157:4-7, 158:12-15, 159:1-3.
[170] *Yalačča gabəčča*, 25:21.
[171] Cf. KBT and DTW on *ṭom* about the seven kinds of fast. See also F. Heyer, *Die Kirche Äthiopiens*, Berlin, 1971, pp. 79-81. There are discrepancies between Heyer and DTW & KBT on the definitions and dates of the different fasts.
[172] *Yalačča gabəčča*, 93:2f. Cf. DTW on *həmamatä mäsḳäl*, p. 525, and *akfəlät*, p. 666.
[173] *Arrəmuññ*, 76:23; cf. *Yäfəḳər ṭora*, 146:12 and DTW on *hərmät*, p. 527.

evil". DTW calls *ṭom*, "fast", "the bridle of righteousness; the rule decreed in the Holy Book forbidding that one eats or drinks out of time; the brother of prayer". Restraint and self-control are emphasized as the aim of fasting in the expression "the bridle of fasting".[174] The most common fast is the weekly fast called *arb rob*, "Friday (and) Wednesday",[175] observed on those days most of the year. Prostrations, *səgdät*, as a symbolic expression of repentence are common during fasting seasons.[176]

Feast days are days both for religious celebration and for heavy eating and drinking, marking the end of a fast, and they are occasions for general festivities. But, as is the case with fasts, Ethiopian writers of fiction do not take a very great interest in this aspect of the social and cultural life of the country. The main feasts are mentioned, and a few minor or local ones. At New Year, flowers are brought to relatives and friends, with a New Year's greeting, e.g., "I am glad He brought you from the old year to the new", with the reply, "I am glad He brought us both".[177] The *Mäsḳäl* festival celebrating the finding of the True Cross seems to be overshadowed by the feast on the previous day, *dämära*, with bonfires and singing: boys and men go round the burning *dämära* pole singing a "flower-song", frequently repeating "the word of joy" *iyyoha*; girls put *mäsḳäl* flowers in their hair and watch. The following day, both men and women circle the burnt *dämära* pole, walking in the hot ashes and holding branches in their hands.[178]

Christmas is barely referred to. Easter figures more prominently in Amharic literature.[179] The breaking of the Lent fast, the heaviest of all fasts, is marked by specially joyful celebrations:

> "Everywhere they came, many people were seen, carrying *mäsob*-baskets and jars draped in red-ribboned cloths; or carrying flat trays loaded with baked bread and covered with white or mostly red cloths, or carrying drinks (i.e. bottles) wrapped in paper; or according to the requests of each family's protecting

---

[174] *Kä'admas bašagär*, 68:1; cf. *Fəḳr əskä mäḳabər*, 24:24ff.
[175] *Yalačča gabəčča*, 93:2.
[176] *Əddal näw? bädäl?*, 30:1-7.
[177] *Yäšoh aklil*, 23:26-33; *Yäləbb hassab*, 147:3, 160:4.
[178] *Yäləbb hassab*, 162:23-28, 163:16-18, *Fəḳr əskä mäḳabər*, 282ult.; cf. DTW on *iyyoha*, p. 96.
[179] *Yäləbb hassab*, 147:3, *Yalačča, gabəčča*, 65:15f., 88:5, *Kä'admas bašagär*, 63:2.

spirit, dragging an ash-grey, a white-headed, white, or all-black sheep as an Easter gift (*yakfay*)." [180]

But on the whole, there is in Amharic literature little attention paid to these festivals, whether it is the secular *Buhe* in August, with the baking of a special bread: as it occurs during a fasting season, no animal products can be eaten; [181] or when celebrating a saint's day, *tabotun angəsäw*, "crowning or enthroning a saint, or making a saint rule as king" on his special day in the Church calendar; cf. *tabot lämakbär*, "to honour a saint, or *tabot*".[182] The *tabot* is on these occasions taken from the *mäḳdäs*, the holy of holies, and brought outside the church and carried in procession, shaded by colourful umbrellas, *janṭəla* or *dəba/dəbab*, usually to a stream or a place where there is plenty of water, while drums are beaten.[183] Local feasts in honour of a saint can be colourful events, such as the feast for Täklä Alfa in Dima on 10 Tahsas.[184] The clergy spend the night in church from the eve, *wazema*, of a great saint's day, and the feast itself, *zəkəru*, "the memory feast", or the *dəggəs*, "feast, banquet", is celebrated by eating and drinking and other festivities.[185]

Other feasts mentioned, such as Mary's assumption, *fəlsäta*, or the Feast of Täklä Haymanot, are passed over lightly.[186] That the days of rest, holy days and holidays, used to be much more frequent is seen from the use of the phrase *yazäbot ḳän*, which used to designate a saint's day when no work could be done but now is not any longer celebrated as a day of rest but is in fact a week-day, a working day.[187]

Ethiopian authors seem to be more interested in the ethical than in the ritualistic aspects of religion, and in its compatibility with modern knowledge. Little is therefore written about a part of Ethiopian life that seems to be still of importance to the common people.[188]

---

[180] *Kä'admas bašagär*, 54:16-21.
[181] *Arrəmuññ*, 49:1-7; on *Buhe*, see E. Lord, *Queen of Sheba's Heirs*, Washington, D.C., 1970, pp. 56-59.
[182] *Yalačča gabəčča*, 54ult., *Fəḳr əskä mäḳabər*, 135:3f.
[183] *Fəḳr əskä mäḳabər*, 165:27-30, 166:4-6; *Araya*, 315:15-24.
[184] *Fəḳr əskä mäḳabər*, 80:2ff.
[185] *Ib.*, 156:1-4, *Yäləbb hassab*, 178:10f.
[186] *Yäləbb hassab*, 150:15, 151:19.
[187] *Fəḳr əskä mäḳabər*, 155:10, *Kä'admas bašagär*, 45ult., DTW on *azäbot*, p. 914.
[188] On the yearly cycle in Amhara society, see D. Levine, *Wax and Gold*, Chicago, 1965, pp. 61-64, and F. Heyer, *op. cit.*, pp. 82-90.

BELIEFS AND ETHICS 91

A number of books are used as a basis for doctrine or to regulate public and private religious life. "The Book", *mäṣhafu* or *mäṭafu*, i.e. the Bible,[189] is basic and has great authority, with, it seems, equal authority being given to the Old and the New Testaments, but with special emphasis on the Torah, *orit*, and the four Gospels.[190] The Book is regarded as a guide to prevent people from going astray.[191] But, obviously with a reference to the many controversies in the Church over the right interpretation of the Bible, one man observes—and it may not be an isolated view—: "Faith, or religion, and the Book are, as also previously, destroyer and destroyed", i.e. opposites, at logger-heads.[192]

A special place in Ethiopian religious life is held by the Psalms, *Dawit*, which is used both as a textbook in church schools, in religious services, especially at funerals where all the 150 psalms may be read, and as a book for private prayer and devotion, and it may be beautifully bound and decorated as a great treasure.[193] The Psalms must therefore be the most influential book in Ethiopian society, and must have formed the people's mentality and outlook more than any other single source. Often appended to the Psalms for private prayer is a book also much used by Ethiopian Christians, the Praises of Mary, *Wəddase Maryam*, with prayers for each day of the week.[194]

Books containing the stories of saints are read for edification and guidance.[195] Many books are used to cure illness.[196] One book, the Book of *Kedär*, is read when someone has adopted a way of life thought to be incompatible with his Christian faith, and he is at the same time immersed in water.[197]

---

[189] The Ethiopian canonical scriptures are listed in Habtä Maryam Wärkənäh, *Yä'ityopəya ortodoks täwahdo betäkrəstiyan əmnätənna təmhərt*, Addis Ababa, 1970 (?), pp. 42-49. They are not identical with the Canon accepted by any other church.
[190] *Fəkr əskä mäkabər*, 248:21-26, *Addis aläm*, 24:14-19; 20:4ff.
[191] *Adäfrəs*, 41:15f.
[192] *Ib.*, 41:19.
[193] *Adäfrəs*, 327:6-10, *Yalačča gabəčča*, 37:4f., *Yähəllina däwäl*, 115:18, 195:21-23.
[194] *Fəkr əskä mäkabər*, 83:29; cf. DTW sub *Wəddase Maryam*, p. 418.
[195] *Adäfrəs*, 156:9-18; cf. 41:18, 42:29.
[196] *Ib.*, 169:27-29.
[197] *Ib.*, 176:16-177:1. DTW, sub *Kedär*, writes: "When a man has been defiled by denying his Christian faith, snapping his neck-cord (i.e. renouncing Christianity) .... and (i.e. or) contracting syphilis, the priests immerse him while reading this book."

Some books, especially those related to health, astrology, or the signs of the end of the world, are on the borderline between Christianity and paganism; see chapter II, 3, on syncretism.

Individual pious living, apart from attending church, is seen in the exercise of good deeds, mostly in giving alms, in private prayer, and in the making of vows or pledges to God.

Begging for alms is done especially "in the name of, or for the sake of Mary", *mənta* (i.e. *bä'əntä*) *Maryam*, and alms (*məṣwat*) can be given for many reasons: for not attending Mass on Mary's day, one can compensate by giving alms to people sitting by the entrance to the church compound; [198] one who gives for the general benefit of his soul is referred to as "one who gives to the poor, who has lived for his soul", i.e. doing good, or "that good, righteous man who has lived for his soul".[199] Alms giving is a prime virtue, and particularly when a sacrifice or self-sacrifice is involved.[200] Mäkonnən Əndalkaččäw often writes about this, and the whole purpose of *Ṣähay Mäsfən* is to show how a man can atone for his mistakes and failings by a great sacrifice: Ṣähay Mäsfən is an impoverished and widowed daughter of a nobleman, and she dies because of neglect and insulting behaviour from an upstart who loves her but is ashamed of her traditional behaviour and dress; when he discoveres that he has unwittingly caused her death, he gives all his great wealth to her children from her earlier marriage and becomes a hermit; the children go abroad for education and on their return build a resthouse for elderly people with some of the money he left them; he comes there to die and is recognized by the children just before he dies. By his generosity, the old man has atoned for his neglect. And the author adds in a postscript to the reader:

> "As money is a most important thing in life ("the root of life"), and as man's heart is where his money is, it gives the greatest relief of heart to give one's money first to heaven." [201]

In his novel *Yädəhoč kätäma* the same author deals with a similar problem. The main character loses all happiness in life, and then his mind, and finally his life, all owing to his stinginess and greed.[202]

---

[198] *Fəkr əskä mäḵabər*, 102:5f., 360:8-14.
[199] *Yäḵəne azmära*, 25:19, 28:6.
[200] *Ib.*, 11:1ff., *Kä'admas bašagär*, 29:22-25.
[201] *Ṣähay Mäsfən*, 102:17-20.
[202] *Arrəmuňň*, pp. 117ff.

BELIEFS AND ETHICS 93

And to help the reader not to miss the point of the story, the author adds, as is his habit, the moral in the preface: this man's life ended badly because he was not well brought up.[203]

Prayer is important in public and private life. The Church has prescribed hours for prayer in the Horologium, *Mäṣhafä säʾatat* (often referred to only as *satat*, "hours"), and the pious may observe some or all of these, and most frequently the dawn prayer, the dusk prayer, and the prayer of the third hour; a rosary is sometimes used.[204] People can of course pray anywhere at any time, but they seem to prefer prescribed, written prayers said at fixed places, especially the church, or under a tree in the church compound, or a special room in one's own home, or in any case a place where one can find privacy or seclusion (*subaʾe lämägbat*).[205]

Prayers are addressed to God, to Mary, or to any of the saints.[206] Prayers, also when said in private, are regularly set prayers as contained in prayer books, such as the Psalms, Wəddase Maryam, Wəddase Amlak, Arganon, Mälkä Gubaʾe, Dərsanä Mikaʾel, Mälkä Rufaʾel, Bäsälamä Ḳəddus Gäbrʾel, the prayer of Ankəro, i.e. praise of the Creator for the created world, and, very frequently, the Lord's Prayer, *Abunä zäbäsämayat*.[207] As such prayers are repetitions of written prayers, the verb *däggämä*, "to repeat", or the noun *dəgam*, "repetition", are used about the saying of such prayers.[208]

Supplicatory prayer is usually freer in form, and is sometimes very brief; e.g. "while pleading (with God), he said, Have mercy on me (*maräñ*)";[209] a man who woke up after a bad dream "crossed himself in the name of the Trinity", or more precisely, as DTW defines the verb used, *amattäbä*, "he prayed in order to drive away

---

[203] *Arrəmuññ*, 115:31f.
[204] *Fəḳr əskä mäḳabər*, 33:3, 395:29, *Yalačča gabəčča*, 38:9f., *Bərr ambar säbbärälləwo*, 78:20, *Yäfəḳər çora*, 31:3, *Yäləbb hassab*, 159:19.
[205] *Fəḳr əskä mäḳabər*, 154:7-10, 155:5-8, 156:21ff.; 419:5f., *Kaleb*, 69:15, *Adäfrəs*, 175:12.27.
[206] *Araya*, 315:28, 316:1f., *Fəḳr əskä mäḳabər*, 30:19-25, 34:16-18.
[207] *Addis aläm*, 1:17-20, *Yalačča gabəčča*, 69:13, *Bərr ambar säbbärälləwo*, 3:1-3, *Ṭälfo bäkise*, 47:2, *Arrəmuññ*, 73:19f., *Fəḳr əskä mäḳabər*, 103:28, 156:26.
[208] *Yalačča gabəčča*, 38:11, *Fəḳr əskä mäḳabər*, 420:13. DTW defines *dəgam* as "prayer read in a low voice, or in a whisper". The word used for incantation, *dəgəmt*, in pagan rituals, derives from the same root.
[209] *Fəḳr əskä mäḳabər*, 170:10.

the Devil, blessing his face with crossed fingers, saying, "In the name of the Father, and the Son, and the Holy Spirit"".[210] Even spontaneous prayers are full of set phrases, especially in the way of starting each petition, e.g. "Lord (*abetu*), O! my father in heaven", "O Lord! (*əgzi'ota*)", or "In the name of the Father, and the Son, and the Holy Spirit, One God, Amen", as Abunä Petros starts his prayer in prison; or, in times of despair, one just cries *ayadrəs ayadrəs*, "May He not let it arrive or happen".[211]

At the end of a prayer, one can seek a further blessing by spitting on a rosary and wiping one's face with it; or rub one's face with dry soil and dry grass as a sign of humility and repentence.[212]

It is told of Fitawrari Mäšaša, the rich landlord in *Fəkr əskä mäkabər*:

> "Previously, whether he went hunting or to war, he came first to church, and at any time he found the door open; and having gone straight up to the mid-section of the church, having knelt, he rested his forehead on the step of the door of the holy of holies and repeated Our Lord's Prayer and (the prayer) In the Peace of St. Gabriel; standing up, he wets his hand with his spittle and smears his face, and in addition, wiping up the dust on the steps, he rubs it on his face, saying, "My Lord who arrives quickly (i.e. St. George), please be you my shield and protection, embracing and supporting me, and returning me safely home!", and kissing the steps, he takes his leave and goes away - - -." [213]

People pray both for the living and the dead; one man asks a girl who turns out to be his own daughter: "What is your name— so that I can pray for you"; [214] another prays for the soul of his dead parents:

> "O father in heaven, please have mercy on the souls of my father and mother, who bore me in the flesh, who educated me and brought me up. Let them rest with their spiritual forebears, such as Abraham and Moses. You are forgiving, so forgive them. Your mercy lasts forever." [215]

---

[210] DTW p. 964; *Yä'ənba däbdabbewoč*, 129:2f.17f., *Tälfo bäkise*, 46:14f.; cf. *Yäkəne azmära*, 138:3, *Bälg*, 24:10, *Yähəllina däwäl*, 188:7-10.

[211] *Tarikənna məssale*, Book III, 1:5, *Araya*, 275:2, *Arrəmuňň*, 90:17-91:20, *Yäləbb hassab*, 150:26f.

[212] *Yalačča gabəčča*, 51:19-21, *Fəkr əskä mäkabər*, 170:13f.; cf. *Yäkärmo säw*, 23:4f.

[213] *Fəkr əskä mäkabər*, 156:21-32.

[214] *Arrəmuňň*, 323:16f.

[215] *Tarikənna məssale*, Book III, 1:4-8.

BELIEFS AND ETHICS 95

To be "prayerful", (ṣälotäňňa, colloquially ṭolotäňňa) implies also ethical qualities, viz. to be "upright, of good character", and maybe "pious"; it is a characterization used of Ṣiwäne in *Adäfrəs* when the neighbours praise her for her conduct and character, saying she is the best of her family.[216]

A special form of prayer consists of giving a pledge to render a service or gift to a saint in return for the granting of a request. Both the pledge or vow and the thing or service promised are called *səlät*; e.g. *yäsəlät ləjj* is used to mean a child born in answer to a request accompanied by a vow,[217] and of a child who has been given as a gift to serve a saint or saints.[218] Such a vow is binding both on the one who takes the oath, and also on the one on whose behalf it may be taken, as in the case of the child Bäzzabbəh in the last example: his own wish is opposed to his mother's pledge, and this is a conflict he has to live with for the rest of his life.

Almost anything can be promised as a gift if one's wish is granted, but most commonly things of use to the church, such as incense, candles, clerical vestments, umbrellas used both by the clergy and to shelter the *tabot* during processions; or, as it is said of one woman, "she used to make vows on her life".[219]

When the wish or request is fulfilled, the person concerned must go personally to a church dedicated to the saint to whom he or she has made the vow. Wzo Alganäš in *Yalačča gabəčča* would take great pains to come from Addis Ababa to Kulubi near Harar when she had a pledge to fulfil after she had won a court case:

> "I have a vow to fulfil. I have brought incense for the lord of Kulubi (i.e. St. Gabriel). This year the court case that had been going on for twelve years about my land in Ada was finalized in my favour." [220]

Shrines are visited to obtain health and sanctity, especially on the yearly days dedicated to famous saints. From such holy places as Däbrä Libanos, pilgrims may also bring holy water and holy soil to let others share in the beneficial effects of these elements. The water is drunk and the soil is smeared on the body.[221] It is

---

[216] *Adäfrəs*, 133:18.
[217] *Bərr ambar säbbärälləwo*, 9:15, *Yä'ənba däbdabbewoč*, 16:1f.
[218] *Fəḳr əskä mäḳabər*, chapter heading p. 30 and the whole of Ch. 3.
[219] *Ib.*, 241:13-15.
[220] *Yalačča gabəčča*, 55:6-8.
[221] *Yäləbb hassab*, 155:25f., 156:2f., 160:22-25.

not possible to specify whether this serves the purpose of restoring health or of increasing the participant's sanctity or righteousness: as sickness is thought to be caused by evil spirits, sanity and sanctity are two aspects of the same matter, viz. absence of evil influences.[222] The same word, *ṭäbäl*, is used both for holy water, mineral waters, and the beer drunk on a saint's day in a religious gathering,[223] which may all serve the same purpose of union or communion with the saint.

It is convenient here to deal with *Ethiopian expressions of grief*. Although this is not purely religious in all respects, there are so many ritualistic elements related to the Church that it would be artificial to treat "religious" and "secular" expressions of grief separately.

Much of Amharic literature is tragic, and the tragic and sorrowful moments of life loom large in Ethiopian consciousness as well as in fictional writing. Misery and agony occur all through life. Several books deal with the special trials and sorrows that often befall women in Ethiopia.[224] The strongest feelings of grief are related to death, and I treat primarily these aspects here.

A traditional view of life and death is explained thus: a man is a unity of soul and the four elements earth, water, air, and fire, held together by a centre of consciousness. At death, these elements are separated, and the soul is happy to leave the prison of the body; but the fog of the world disappears gradually, as the new world and the new man appear gradually. The soul suffers much in the process of purification, during which it gradually gets used to the new life, and is finally united with God, and the body dissolves; evil-doers, however, will stay in despair and deep darkness.[225]

The announcement of someone's death, the *märdo*, is made carefully and slowly, after cautious preparation of the person it is brought to. When Bäzzabbəh gets a visitor from his own village, he is first told that all is well; then the topic is abruptly changed, so that he senses that something is wrong in his family; only next morning is he told of his parents' death.[226] Mourners meet in a

---

[222] Cf. *Adäfrəs*, 207:22f.
[223] *Ṭälfo bäkise*, 11:25.
[224] E.g. *Kältammawa əhəte* by Abbe Gubäñña, *Ṣähay Mäsfən* by Mäkonnən Əndalkaččäw, *Yä'ənba däbdabbewoč*, by Bərhanu Zärihun, etc.
[225] *Arrəmuññ*, 130:10-133:8; 134:27f., 136:7-11.
[226] *Fəḳr əskä mäḳabər*, 61:5-63:22.28.

"house of sorrow" where they give expression to their grief; mostly they sit without talking, or talking only rarely, or they give vent to their grief by sucking their lips in a characteristic way.[227] One is encouraged to give free and open outlet to one's pent-up feelings of loss and frustration at someone's death, and one is told, *ərməhən awṭa*, approximately "get rid of what is taboo", which is a way of saying that it is not proper to keep one's feelings and tears back at someone's death and funeral;[228] cf. the phrase *ərmun bämmiggäbba awäṭṭa*, "he lamented the dead as it should be done", in this case at a gathering after the burial.[229] Women scratch their faces, tear their clothes, hit their breasts and weep; the men put on (black) mantles and weep.[230] Awwäḳä in *Addis aläm*, educated abroad and copying foreign customs, is blamed and ridiculed for not observing the proper form on such an occasion.[231] Even before a person dies, people start lamenting and moving the body up and down, in anticipation of his death, and they start boasting of the person's character and deeds during his lifetime, saying, e.g. "my arm, my arm, my right hand", and especially the women emit piercing cries; others murmur a kind of subdued song of lament.[232]

Grief is often expressed in cries to God: one may lament and be bitter "towards God", saying words like, "(God,) don't bring what is worse".[233] When the lament seems excessive a mourner can be reproved:

> "Don't think that God is poor in hardships; He can load on you many evil things, many hardships tied and bundled together, and it is better if you do not become bitter against Him." [234]

It is important for the peace of one's soul to have confessed and received absolution before death comes.[235] When someone is dead, the clergy are called with the words, "Come with your censers", and they come and perform the required rituals: prayers, chants,

---

[227] *Ib.*, 445:18-20, *Kä'admas bašagär*, 149:24, 169:5, *Yäbädäl fəṣṣame*, 14:1, 156:9-19, *Əddəl näw? bädäl?*, 110:4.
[228] *Yäšoh aklil*, 43:19.
[229] *Yä'ənba däbdabbewoč*, 136:3-5.
[230] *Addis aläm*, 11:22-26.
[231] *Ib.*, 12:3ff.
[232] *Yägəṭəm guba'e*, 14:2.6.9, *Yäbädäl fəṣṣame*, 157:11, *Ṣähay Mäsfən*, 80:12-81:18, *Yähəllina däwäl*, 234:15, *Əddəl näw? bädäl?*, 109:24f.
[233] *Araya*, 327:24f., *Fəḵr əskä mäḵabər*, 49:16.
[234] *Fəḵr əskä mäḵabər*, 55:7-9.
[235] *Ib.*, 56:26-28.

and binding and shrouding of the body;[236] a *däbtära* recites the Psalms, and the *Mäwas'it*, a book containing chants and prayers for the dead.[237] The ritual to "release" the soul (*fəthat/fətat*, "absolution, funeral ceremony") is short for a poor person and long and elaborate for those who can afford to pay for the whole ceremony.[238] For the very poor, the funeral ceremony consists of a single ritual in the house; then the mourners go to church; after the burial, they return to the house of the dead, bring roasted grain and porridge, and eat and mourn there.[239] When the complete ceremony is used, there are seven stops from the home of the deceased to the grave, with reading of all the 150 Psalms.[240] At burials, lament is also expressed through song and dance, and poems are improvised in praise of the deceased, often by professional hired women.[241] When the corpse is buried, incense is burned, and a priest scatters a handful of soil over the body and says, "O Adam, you are soil, and you shall return to soil"; the mourners also throw a handful of soil over the body and return to the church, where the ceremony is concluded.[242]

The funeral ceremony and lament for the dead can be held also for a person who has vanished and is presumed dead.[243] The *fəthat* in the sense of prayers for the absolution and release of the soul of the dead can be conducted for forty days, i.e. till the first memory feast, *täzkar*, for the dead is held.[244]

One of the greatest misfortunes that can befall a person is to be without someone to look after one in one's old age and to bury one, and to be buried by the people as one of "God's poor or destitute".[245]

---

[236] The thumbs and big toes of the corpse are tied together with a wet rope, and the body is wrapped and shrouded before burial; *Fəkr əskä mäkabər*, 172:14, 57:15.20; cf. DTW on *gännäzä* and *käffänä*; *Yähəllina däwäl*, 152:23.26f., 153:15f., *Əddəl näw? bädäl?*, 12:17f.

[237] *Addis aläm*, 11:28-12:2.

[238] *Ib.*, 24ult.-25:1, *Yä'ənba däbdabbewoč*, 135:23-136:2.

[239] *Adäfrəs*, 74:18-20, *Ṣähay Mäsfən*, 68:7-10. 13-16. Cf. DTW on *zär addam*.

[240] *Adäfrəs*, 327:6-8.

[241] Cf. *ib.*, 326:17-329:11. An example of a dirge is found in *Fəkr əskä mäkabər*, 490:19-491:2, *Yähəllina däwäl*, 153:22-154ult.; cf. 155:5-9, 235:10, *Əddəl näw? bädäl?* 110:19-22, 111:3-8.13-21.

[242] *Arrəmuññ*, 125ult.-126:26; following is a sermon addressed to the deceased.

[243] *Yä'ənba däbdabbewoč*, 14:22.

[244] *Joro ṭäbi*, 10:3-6.

[245] *Yä'ənba däbdabbewoč*, 116:2; 129:21ff.

The purpose and effect of crying and lamenting is supposed to be to make one forget one's grief:

> "Just as all such crying and lamenting causes one to forget everything, his grief began to cool off." [246]

After a person is dead, memory or memorial feasts, *täzkar* or *täskar*,[247] are held several times, but the most important ones, and the ones most often mentioned in Amharic literature are the two held on the fortieth and the eightieth days after a person's death.[248] At such memorial feasts, everyone can come and eat, and especially the poor, the clergy and church school students are fed; there is thus the aspect of alms giving on behalf of and for the good of the soul of the one remembered.[249] The meaning and purpose of such memorial feasts is said to be to rescue the dead person from condemnation.[250]

The frequent references to grief and its expression reflect a life and society where sorrows and tragic experiences are commonplace. The vast majority of Ethiopian fictional books are tragic in content and ending.

Church education has had a profound influence on Ethiopian society and cultural life. Credit is given to the Church for this in Amharic literature, but modern authors also show that it is not always in tune with the times.

Students in church schools, both girls and boys, in the first stages get the same instruction, but girls are of course not given the higher training leading to the priesthood.[251] After reading and writing (based on the first chapter of the First Epistle of St. John), the memorization of the Psalms is stressed; then the students proceed to learn grammar, which includes the study of Geez in a formal way; they may later take up *ḳəne* poetry; other important books studied are Wəddase Maryam, Ṣome Dəggwa, Mälkä Maryam, etc.[252]

---

[246] *Yäfəḳər ṭora*, 50:2-4.

[247] *Adäfrəs*, 71:11f; 10:6, *Fəḳr əskä mäḳabər*, 469:20; 478:3.

[248] *Lelaw mängäd*, 36:11f., *Yäḳəne azmära*, 135:2, *Yäləbb ḥassab*, 180:1, *Amanu'el därso mäls*, 9:2, *Addis aläm*, 16:4.7.16, *Ǝddəl näw? bädäl?*, 15:2f., 5.

[249] *Adäfrəs*, 71:11ff.; drunkenness is not uncommon at a *täzkar*: *Addis aläm*, 14:19ff., 60:28, *Ǝddəl näw? bädäl?* 15:6-8.13f., 16:3-6.11-17, (cf. 17:7-9).

[250] *Addis aläm*, 22:1f.

[251] *Yäləbb ḥassab*, 138:17-22.

[252] *Ib.*, 139:11-20, *Yalačča gabəčča*, 86:8f., *Yä'ənba däbdabbewoč*, 9:5, *Ǝddəl näw? bädäl?*, 58:17-19, *Bərr ambar säbbärälləwo*, 12:4, *Fəḳr əskä mäḳabər*, 39:3-5, 76:6-10, *Adäfrəs*, 27:13f. A survey of Ethiopian church

In some cases, the clergy are shown to be narrow-minded and obstructive to new ideas and influences. One priest objects to the use of the *krar* (a lyre) and to secular music, *zäfän*, because St. Yared said the final word about music:

> "But St. Yared has finalized it, the matter of music. To say there is harmony beyond *gə'əz*, *əzəl*, and *araray* [253] is vain.—Starting with and inspired by *gə'əz*, it is elaborated (or developed) and added to by *əzəl*; and when one is sad, *araray* captures and gladdens the heart; when performed in a refined and beautiful way, there is nothing else beside it." [254]

Another priest is asked to give a speech at a gathering where people are asked to contribute to the building of a school which is for everyone. He tries to speak on behalf of the government on a secular subject, viz. "unity". But throughout he talks in the style of the *andəmta* tradition in the interpretation of the books of the church: [255]

> "- - - Unity is freedom; freedom is unity. Unity is (to be) a nation; a nation is unity. Unity is government; government is unity. Civilization is unity, unity civilization. Life is unity, unity is life. Strength is unity, unity strength." [256]

The study of the Book and books of the Church did have a prestige it does not have today.[257] The same goes for the study of church dance, *akkwakam*.[258]

---

education is given in Habtä Maryam Wärkənäh, *Ṭəntawi yä'ityopəya təmhərt*, Addis Ababa, 1970 (?). Cf. also Paulos Milkias, "Traditional institutions and traditional elites: the role of education in the Ethiopian body-politic", in *The African Studies Review*, Vol. XIX, No. 3 (December 1976), pp. 79-93.

[253] *Gə'əz* is plain chant; *əzəl* is solemn music used during fasts and funerals; *araray* is used on happy occasions. See M. Powne, *Ethiopian Music*, London, 1968, pp. 96f.

[254] *Adäfrəs*, 117:21-25.

[255] Cf. R. W. Cowley, "Preliminary notes on the *baläandem* commentaries", in JES, Vol. X, No. 1 (January 1972), pp. 9-20, and *idem*, "The Beginnings of the *andem* Commentary Tradition", JES, Vol. X, No. 2 (July 1972), pp. 1-16.

[256] *Adäfrəs*, 80:10-13.

[257] *Fəkr əskä mäkabər*, 59:6-8, 66:1f. Cf. Habtä Maryam Wärkənäh, *Ṭəntawi...*, pp. 212-222, on styles of interpretation, the three kinds of interpretation, and the four groups of books studied.

[258] *Fəkr əskä mäkabər*, 61:18; cf. Habtä Maryam Wärkənäh, *ib.*, pp. 108-126. One style of dance was invented by Aläka Gäbrä Hanna and taught secretly to his son, Aläka Täkle, who made it widely known, *ib.*, 110:3ff.; this dance is referred to in *Fəkr əskä mäkabər*, 68:32-69:1, as *əbd täkle*.

BELIEFS AND ETHICS 101

Ethiopian traditional poetry, *kəne*, as taught in church schools seems to have great prestige and to have influenced the thoughts and style of many authors. It is often mentioned, and in *Fəkr əskä mäkabər* there is a long, nostalgic description of the teaching of *kəne* and the life of the *kəne* student.[259] The teaching is given by a revered monk, and some schools have achieved great fame, e.g. Dima in Gojjam. The students with their satchels beg for their upkeep, and get the left-over food from neighbouring houses. The younger students serve the older ones. The study itself is a combination of listening to and interpreting *kəne* poems composed by a teacher, of composing oneself, and of discussing in groups and with one's teachers the students' poems. The head teacher, *mämhər*, who is also head of the monastery, is treated with great respect. The students learn to treat sheep-skins both for clothing and for parchment. Teaching usually takes place in the open air, and starts early in the morning, and the last session is often late at night; the students can be called to class again after they have gone to bed.[260]

The specific forms of *kəne* poetry are rarely referred to, but there is some mention of them, e.g. *guba'e kana* (a poem of two lines), *mäwäddəs* (of 8 lines), *zä'amlakiyya* (of three lines), *səllase* (of six lines), etc.[261] and the better known terms *sämənna wärk*, "wax and gold", *həbər*, "pun", and *wəstä wäyra*, "inside an olive tree".[262]

Many of the better known Ethiopian authors have received education in church schools prior to a modern education, and this has influenced their style and made its mark on Amharic literature.[263]

2. Pagan practices

People are not often referred to as "pagans" in Amharic liter-

---

[259] *Fəkr əskä mäkabər*, esp. ch. 8, pp. 71-76; cf. Mängəstu Lämma, *Mäṣhafä təzzəta zä'aläka Lämma*, ch. 5, pp. 83ff.; Habtä Maryam Wärkənäh, *ib.*, pp. 172-211.

[260] *Fəkr əskä mäkabər*, pp. 71-76; 77:13f.22f., 188:24-26; 384:3ff.

[261] *Ib.*, 75:1-18. Cf. Habtä Maryam Wärkənäh, *ib.*, pp. 176-182, Alämayyähu Mogäs, *Səwasəwä gə'əz*, Addis Ababa, 1950 E.C., pp. 133ff.

[262] *Fəkr əskä mäkabər*, 308:17, 453:1-3, *Čäräka sətwäṭa* 9:1f. "Wax and gold" has several meanings, and there has been much confusion in the use of this term. Cf. Habtä Maryam Wärkənäh, *ib.*, pp. 208f., D. Levine, *Wax and Gold*, pp. 5-9, Mängəstu Lämma, "The Real Meaning of Semenna-Warq", in *Voice of Ethiopia*, January 13, January 20 and February 3, 1967, Alämayyähu Mogäs, *op. cit.*, pp. 120f., DTW p. 887.

[263] This is also stressed by Abbe Gubäñña in several introductory notes to each section of *Mäskot*, a collection of poetry.

ature.[264] Paganism in Ethiopia, as the term is used here, encompasses a wide range of beliefs and practices, covering different forms of divination, beliefs in many evil spirits, and rituals aiming at controlling the activities of these spirits.

The most common and comprehensive term for all kinds of pagan practices, except possession, is *ṭənḳola*, "sorcery". A sorcerer, *ṭänḵway*,[265] deals both in divination and in magic involving spirits. "When we are sick, when we are in trouble", it is said to be customary to go to different kinds of sorcerers and say, "know for us" what to do, or what will happen.[266] The principal purposes of such consultations are to ward off evil, such as ill-health, danger, or someone's love for a partner deemed unsuitable, or to obtain wealth, good health and long life, or favourable outcome in conflicts.

Divination is by its nature fatalistic and tries to interpret a future that is fixed from recognizable signs. These are first and foremost the stars in relation to a person's time of birth. "The secrets of the constellations - - - were written before the creation of the world".[267]

An astrologer is both an interpreter of astrological books and one who calculates the positions of the stars.[268] Not only the future, but also secrets about the present are claimed to be known to astrologers.[269] For their computations, they need a person's name, usually baptismal name, and the name of the mother (and of the father?).[270] Each letter of the name is given a numerical value,

---

[264] They are occasionally referred to as "those without faith or religion". As they sacrifice to pagan deities, they are clearly not atheists. They do not share the faiths of Christians or Muslims and are therefore referred to as "non-believers". (*Adäfrəs*, 77:19, 263:27). The term *arämäne* means "pagan", but connotes also "uncivilized, brute, uncultured". (*Käʾadmas bašagär*, 77:18-20; *Araya*, 52:13).

[265] Other general terms used are: *däbtära, mäläñña, awaḳi, sirak*; see *Fəḳr əskä mäḳabər*, 410:30f., 421:7-13, *Addis aläm*, 41:9f., *Araya*, 256:5, *Yalačča gabəčča*, 75:10f., 77:7f., 122:12f., (cf. DTW sub *sirak*, p. 897); 28:2, *Tarikənna məssale*, Book III, 59:2.6, *Adäfrəs*, 169:24f.

[266] *Adäfrəs*, 72:12-14.

[267] *Yalačča gabəčča*, 152:1f.

[268] *Mäṭaf/mäṣhaf gälaṭ* and *koḳäb ḳoṭari*; *Yalačča gabəčča*, page 16, 150:5f.; cf. 47:20f.

[269] *Ib.*, 48:3-7, 49:5f.

[270] *Bərr ambar säbbärälləwo*, 12ult.-13:9. In *Yalačča gabəčča* 48:9f., the father's name is also mentioned; this seems unusual. Cf. *Hatäta mänafəst wäʾawdä nägäst*, by Zämänfäs Ḳəddus Abrəha, Addis Ababa, 6th ed., 1963, pp. 143f.

BELIEFS AND ETHICS 103

and the nature of the person's star is first calculated. Each person has a sign of the Zodiac with a star of a definite element or character, *bahrəy*, either fire, earth, air or water. To be suitable as friends or marriage partners one must have signs that are in harmony.[271] A person's character is determined by the character of his or her star. A man of the character of fire is told that "a woman of the character of water is no good for you", because "ignorance extinguishes the fire of knowledge, (as) the water of poverty extinguishes the fire of wealth".[272] When a girl's star is said to be "Virgo of the element of earth, Scorpio of the element of water",[273] it shows how much bluff and deceit have entered the practice of astrology: no one can have two stars, but people who consult astrologers are ignorant even of the terms used.[274] Each constellation has its own interpretations or "thoughts" concerning all areas of life.[275] The computation of the facts is not unambiguous. There are possibilities for choice, and one looks for the most satisfactory or gratifying answers. The sum total of the names after the *fidäl* have been given numerical values is divided according to specific rules. To divide a sum by seven, or nine, or twelve is not uncommon, but when Ləzzəbu, in *Yalačča gabəčča*, computes the material prospects ("the thought or prophecy of grain and water") of a couple, he should have divided the sum of their names by nine only, and not by seven or twelve, according to the rules of Ethiopian astrology, and the interpretation he gives of his calculations does not correspond to the one given in astrological textbooks.[276] It is common in Amharic literature to point out the humbug that accompanies the practice of astrology in Ethiopian society.[277] Even people who disclaim any trust in astrology may have secret

---

[271] *Kä'admas bašagär*, 59:3, *Bərr ambar säbbärälləwo*, 16:5-7.
[272] *Yalačča gabəčča*, 151:11-18. The signs of the Zodiac are: *hamäl, säwwər, gäwz, šärṭan, asäd, sänbula, mizan, aḳrab, ḳäwwəs, jädi, däläwi, hut*, "Aries, Taurus, Gemini, Cancer, Leo, Virgo, Libra, Scorpio, Sagittarius, Capricorn, Aquarius, Pisces". Of these, *hamäl, asäd* and *ḳäwwəs* are of the element or character of fire; *säwwər, sänbula* and *jädi* of earth; *gäwz, mizan* and *däläwi* of air; and *šärṭan, aḳrab* and *hut* of water. See Zämänfäs Ḳəddus Abrəha, *op. cit.*, p. 144.
[273] *Yalačča gabəčča*, 49:1.
[274] *Ib.*, 49:2f. Zämänfäs Ḳəddus Abrəha, *op. cit.*, pp. 160-63, 165-67.
[275] *Yalačča gabəčča*, 49:5f. Zämänfäs Ḳəddus Abrəha, *op. cit.*, pp. 144f., 177ff.
[276] *Yalačča gabəčča*, 147:17-20. Zämänfäs Ḳəddus Abrəha, *op. cit.*, pp. 206f.
[277] *Bərr ambar säbbärälləwo*, 15:25-16:13.

doubts that it may be true, after all.²⁷⁸ The basic belief of astrology is that the moon and the stars and the earth are united with each other in some way, and it is the astrologer's job to find and interpret this relationship and how it influences the life of man.²⁷⁹ In practice, the material need or greed of the astrologer often influences the interpretations he gives.²⁸⁰

Other divinatory devices are the interpretation of fat from animals slaughtered for that purpose, of coffee dregs, and the configurations of beads and pebbles thrown by the diviner, in order to find guidance with respect to future actions, to get what one wants, or to get rid of a sickness or other evil.²⁸¹

The "pebble-thrower", *ṭäṭär ṭay*, believes or pretends that he gets his messages through spirits that communicate by placing the pebbles in certain orders. He can therefore speak to a pebble, i.e. the spirit in the pebble, spit on it as a sign of blessing or coaxing, and suggest it could be fed, e.g. with butter made from goats' milk.²⁸² Both the "pebble-thrower" and others associate his art with spirits.²⁸³

Spirits associated particularly with beads are the Galla fertility goddess *atete*, who has been accepted also among other sections of the population,²⁸⁴ and a spirit that possesses the "owner" on one specific day each year and called *təgri* or *təgrit*.²⁸⁵ This spirit is inherited from mother to eldest daughter for generations,²⁸⁶ and an affectionate relationship can develop between the "owner" and the spirit. Ato Wäldu's wife in *Adäfrəs* says she would rather wear the beads and receive the spirit every day than once a year only, and she thinks of the spirit as kindly, protecting her and her family, and providing them with all they need:

> "The *təgri* spirit is the hope of our family - - the *təgri* is migratory - - she is a lady that leads to a land where one can eat honey and where milk flows - - she watches over my husband, my child, my

---

[278] *Fəkr əskä mäḵabər*, 378:26-379:2.
[279] *Yägəṭəm guba'e*, 45:11-13.
[280] *Yalačča gabəčča*, 150:2-6.
[281] *Adäfrəs*, 72:12-14, *Yähəllina däwäl*, 152:11-16.
[282] *Yalačča gabəčča*, 39:14-40:13, 44:19.
[283] *Ib.*, 46:14.17-19, 51:4.
[284] *Yalačča gabəčča*, 41:4-8, 90:9, *Bälg*, 15:5.
[285] *Adäfrəs*, 265:18, 269:5. This spirit is also known as *addo käbäre* or *addo käbir*; cf. DTW, p. 904.
[286] *Ib.*, 265:25-266:2, 267:1-3, 269:5-8.

cattle for me; how I should like to carry her with me every day, instead of only once each year - - -." [287]

" "- - - She is compassionate, she is kind-hearted; in what way has she oppressed me so that I should wish to leave her (or get rid of her) - - -?"

"This custom has, however, come about because of fear - -."

"Fear? You are mistaken, my child! What fear? Does a child fear his mother? What I feel for her is love rather than fear. I love her - - - If all my relatives die, she alone will always remain with me - - -." " [288]

A female house-spirit serving, it seems, similar purposes as *təgrit*, is called *away*.[289]

Associations with evil spirits seem to be of two kinds, (a) the manipulation of spirits through magic, and (b) direct contact with spirits through spirit possession.

An evil spirit can be known as a demon (*ganen*, colloq. *ganel*), *zar*, *kolle*, *säyṭan* or *seṭan*, an evil spirit (*kəfu*, or *ərkus mänfäs*), *wəkabi*, one dressed in flesh (*ləbusä səga*) or an unmentionable or un-namable one.[290] There does not seem to be much distinction between one and the other of these. But among spirits, some are said to live in dirt, others in the sea or in rivers, others again in the air, "and each has its own specific task"; the strongest of all the spirits is said to be the spirit of the air.[291] Spirits are given individual names, but these are kept secret, as one can use them to one's own harm unless a proper ritual is observed.[292]

The sorcerer who deals with spirits is known by many names. Common terms are: *zar färäs*, "horse of a *zar*", i.e. one possessed by a *zar*-spirit, or a *zar*-medium; one can be said to be "in charge of a spirit", *baläwəkabi*; or "one who pulls or drags a demon, a

---

[287] *Adäfrəs*, 265:18-23.
[288] *Ib.*, 266:1-7.
[289] *Fəkr əskä mäkabər*, 417:23.
[290] *Kä'admas bašagär*, 59:5, 109:5, *Yäšoh aklil*, 69:5.11, *Yalačča gabəčča*, 161:7, *Fəkr əskä mäkabər*, 140:21, 282:9, *Adäfrəs*, 61:29, 62:5, 64:22-24, 68:24.31, *Yäkärmo säw*, 64ult., *Bälg*, 26:6, 28:17, 138:12-14; cf. *Säw allä bəyye*, 132:1. See DTW on *ḵurañña*. The poltergeist (*andärəbbe*) is not significant in the literature; cf. DTW, p. 120.
[291] *Adäfrəs*, 64:22-26; the spirit of the sea and of the river is the same, i.e. a water spirit, cf. 64:26f., and 65:26f.
[292] To scare children, one talks about *Abba* (or *Aya*) *Dəbəlbəle, ib.*, 63:25.29-64:6.13f., *Arrəmuñn*, 69ult.-70:1, or the monster or ogre, *ṭərak*, *Arrəmuñn*, 70:4-6. But these are not meant to be the names of real spirits (as e.g. the name *korit* is). See M. Rodinson, *Magie, médecine, possession en Éthiopie*, Paris, 1967, pp. 67-71.

demon-puller", *ganen gottač*.²⁹³ Because magic is used in dealing with spirits, the sorcerer can be called a magician, *məthatäñña*; and because he uses "magic" language, he is also known as *asmatäñña*, "one who uses, or knows how to use, (magic) names (and words), one who casts magic spells"; *mätätäñña* or *azimam*, which are rarer words with more or less the same meaning as *asmatäñña*, point to the use of incantations, *dəgəmt*, and formulas supposed to evoke and communicate with spirits. *Ḳalləčča*, a Galla word that has become common all over the country, is used in about the same meaning as *asmatäñña* and is the preferred term in some areas.²⁹⁴ The rituals of evoking spirits also require sacrifices, *məs*, an important part of which is *rimmiṭo*, dough baked by being put into the fire and ashes, thus getting a dirty, ashen look; animal sacrifices, *č̣ada*, are also common.²⁹⁵ Through the help of magic and by his power over spirits, a man can bring disaster or he can heal, and he is therefore known as *balämädhanit* or *mädhanitäñña*, approximately "medicine-man or -woman", or as *aḳabe səray*, "one who is in charge of (harmful) medicines", or *ṭosäñña* or *mwartäñña*, approximately "one who can put harmful medicine in someone's path and thus bring harm to the person who steps on it".²⁹⁶

The object by means of which harm is caused is called *ṭos*, *səray*, or *dänḳara*; but if it can heal or counteract someone else's harmful magic, it is known as *mädhanit*, "medicine", or *mäftəhe səray*, "medicine of release, solving of charms".²⁹⁷ The release from magic, *mäftəhi* or *mäftəhe*, can also consist of formulas, such as the love antidote, the hate charm, or the jealousy charm.²⁹⁸ Certain "medicines" bring the victim into the power of the "medicine-man" by putting him into a daze or trance: that is the function of *afəz*

---

²⁹³ *Adäfrəs*, 61:17f., 109:18.23, *Yalačča gabəčča*, 46:14 (cf. ll. 17-19), *Yähəllina däwäl*, 22:23, 23:2.

²⁹⁴ *Yäbädäl fəṣṣame*, 105:17, *Yäḳəne azmära*, 35:18, *Yalačča gabəčča*, 165:6.9, 90:7f., *Joro täbi*, 46:8f., *Fəḳr əskä mäḳabər*, 410:30f., 411:3f., cf. *Bälg*, 9:7-9, *Bərr ambar säbbärälləwo*, 39:1, *Yähəllina däwäl*, 22:1, 53:22, 97:1, 135:17-20.

²⁹⁵ *Yalačča gabəčča*, 149:15-150:6, *Ṭälfo bäkise*, 49:25, *Adäfrəs*, 65:25f., 66:1f., *Yägəṭəm guba'e*, 19:1-4.

²⁹⁶ *Adäfrəs*, 149:12, *Fəḳr əskä mäḳabər*, 420:22f., et al.

²⁹⁷ *Addis aläm*, 41:8-14. Cf. *Zämänfäs Ḳəddus Abrəha*, op. cit., p. 247. Other terms for *mädhanit* (e.g. *abənnät, läyəkun, fətun, gäbir, mwal*) hardly occur. Cf. S. Strelcyn, *Prières magique éthiopiennes pour délier les charmes*, Warsaw, 1955.

²⁹⁸ *Yalačča gabəčča*, 111:14-18, 112:3-6.9.

adängəz; the *ṭos* usually transfers sickness from one person to another; the *dänḵara* and the *mwart* may bring harm directly to the victim; such "medicine" is often buried where the victim is expected to pass.[299]

To appease spirits generally, sacrifices are required on special days. A sorcerer beating a drum, *dəbba*, asks for animal sacrifices for the spirits, such as a white chicken with red back, or an ash-grey sheep at the *Mäsḵäl* feast, a spotted goat in the month of *Ṭərr*, etc., or coloured according to the special wishes of the family spirit or guardian angel. This is done to ward off evil influences, especially sickness.[300]

The *ṭəla wägi*, "piercer of the shadow" has the power to harm and kill through the use of a stick with an iron point with which he pierces the shadow of the victim. The belief in the unity of one's personality, "soul", one's shadow and material things (such as the iron-pointed stick) is seen in this form of magic.[301]

Some people, the *buda*, possess the evil eye, *aynä ṭəla*, and can cause harm by looking people in the eye or by staring at them. It involves collusion between one with the evil eye and evil spirits.[302]

There are also charms that protect the wearer against harm, e.g. the *kətab/kitab* or *ašänkətab*, a piece of parchment with writing on it, worn in a leather pouch round the neck; the *ṭälsäm* is a talisman that usually has a picture, and protects against sickness and danger; the *ləfafä ṣədḵ*, "band of righteousness", serves to preserve or restore good health to the wearer, and it is buried with him when he dies.[303]

---

[299] *Yalačča gabəčča*, 111:7, *Fəḵr əskä mäḵabər*, 433:18, *Kä'admas bašagär*, 18:5f., *Yähəllina däwäl*, 139:3f., *Adäfrəs*, 255:15, 276:24; cf. 175:10, 210:11f., 241:11, and DTW sub *dänḵara*.

[300] *Adäfrəs*, 72:14-17, *Kä'admas bašagär*, 26:8-12, 54:16-21, *Yalačča gabəčča*, 128:8-14, 41:4-8, *Yähəllina däwäl*, 31:1-6, 59:21-60:14, 85:10-12, 88:9f., 134:19-22, 158:21, 163:12.16f.; cf. also DTW sub *kalləčča*.

[301] *Fəḵr əskä mäḵabər*, 332:29-333:5; JES, IX, 1 (Jan. 1971), pp. 95-179, Tsahai Berhane Selassie, "An Ethiopian Medical Textbook", esp. note 1, p. 128; Zämänfäs Ḵəddus Abrəha, *op. cit.*, p. 247.

[302] *Kä'admas bašagär*, 141:8f., *Yalačča gabəčča*, 111:7, *Bälg*, 89:15, *Säw allä bəyye*, 114:5, 131:13, *Joro ṭäbi*, 123:9-124:6, *Fəḵr əskä mäḵabər*, 114:27-29, 115:8-11. The expression *yäsäw ayn*, "the eye of man" for "the evil eye" (*Yähəllina däwäl* 136:3), may derive from Arabic 'ayn al-sū'. (I am grateful to Dr. A. Irvine for having pointed out this possible connection.) Cf. R. A. Reminick "The Evil Eye Belief Among the Amhara of Ethiopia", in *Ethnology*, Vol. 13 (1974), No. 3, pp. 279-291.

[303] *Bərr ambar säbbärälləwo*, 39:6-18, *Fəḵr əskä mäḵabər*, 230ult.-231:2, 280:12, 433:20f.

Daňňaččäw Wärku has paid much attention to religious manifestations in Ethiopian society, and he has described scenes where spirits are invoked. One student in *Adäfrəs* recollects an occasion he witnessed as a child:

"..... - It was then I suddenly said to him (i.e. a shepherd), "What is wrong about it if we now see the unmentionable one the master is calling upon." - He looked down and thought for a while. "Wait for me", he said and went out. He returned after a short while. He had two twigs in his blanket. They had just been cut. He gave one to me; one he kept himself. "Follow me", he said. I followed him. Crawling on our stomachs, we arrived at a place where there was an empty grain container with the cover placed on the ground. Standing on a dunghill, the master is reading a book. He, too, is holding a branch in one hand. He is alone. - The shepherd boy touched my hand lightly, "Hold the twig firmly, or they will snatch it from you", he said to me. And later, "Maybe you will see them do something ridiculous, or disgusting and very bad: take care not to laugh; if you laugh, they will slap you", he said. I held my twig firmly and began to look at him (i.e. the master). Close to him, two dark brown and one black persons passed. The master, while stretching out his hand, began to read very loudly in a manner so as to call a name (or using magic words). The three people, individually, placed the things they were holding on top of the dunghill. And suddenly, raising their legs, and sometimes showing indecent hip movements, they began to dance and run about, breaking wind loudly, through their mouths I think. The three persons were naked except for the twigs they held in their hands and what looked like leaves over their private parts ("their shame"). One of them looked like a woman. She was holding between her teeth a big chunk of meat that covered her face. The black man, however, held a curved knife between his teeth. But the main job of the third was only to show different indecent body movements and to change his face into different kinds of grimaces. Suddenly this third man cried loudly. Taking handfuls of soil around him, with stones and pebbles, and with dung, he started to throw it on the house in our direction. And as he finished, the three returned together to where they had come from. - As for the master, he did not interrupt his reading; it was now done at great speed, his reading. - And as he had gone on for a long time, we began to hear a loud voice; it was incomprehensible, roaring, but it seemed to be speaking, too, - it was not possible to know where it came from - even the man's reading was unaudible -. Abruptly, the master fell, holding on to the book. His servant, who had been watching from a distance, lifted him up, and, supporting him, took him into the house. - And the shepherd who came out with me said, "Today I don't think he was successful...."" [304]

---

[304] *Adäfrəs*, 67:2-68:5.

Later, after the master has been brought into the house and put to bed, he explains to one of his tenants what had happened and makes some general remarks on associations with spirits:

"""- - After the spirit of our place had mistreated my father so improperly, I swore I would not again make any connection with evil spirits, and I have kept to this till today", the master says. "- - - But yesterday evening I was not in good health. Also during the night, I was troubled by a nightmare. Therefore, after a bad nightmare, I said, "Come what may", and I broke my oath; all my body was soaked in sweat; I took the book down from where it was hanging and went out without preparing enough food for the spirit. I wouldn't have been so imprudent if it had been the spirit of sea or air. But I did not think the spirit of dirt hated me so much; therefore, when the cock was crowing again and again, I went out, without drying my body, and although I had washed, without cleaning my body properly. I brought it (i.e. the spirit) just what it likes, without leaving out the cajoling. But it, passing beside me like a wind, refused to answer me. Then, finally, I got a pain in my left side; and sweat soaked my body. I could not stand at ease as I wanted - - - After many attempts, when I realized I would not be answered, and as soon as I had finished reading the formulas for its return, I fainted and fell. After that, I think the children (i.e. here: the servants) lifted me up and brought me inside; but as for me, I was unconscious", he says at last".[305]

The most macabre story of association with spirits is told in relation to child sacrifices. One child has disappeared, and later it is found that a weaver has killed it. This leads to the following conversation between Ato Wäldu, Wzo Asäggaš, and Ato Ṭəso:

"""By the way, did he say why he killed the child?" Ato Wäldu asks.
"Oh well, I have forgotten most of it - - As for the blood, it was found in the house, put into a bottle - - -".
"What blood?"
"The child's blood - - -".
"To do what for him, then, did he draw it, the child's blood - - -?"
"- - - What you ask! - It is of course because a false sorcerer has told him: "add the herbs I give you to the blood of a child that has not yet reached puberty - and after you have tattooed your hands, chest, back and loins (with it), you will be rich!" It is in order to be honoured, to be rich - - ! Isn't that what everyone is after these days - -? All who set up a new grain-mill anywhere here, are looking for small children; if possible, they take him to where it (i.e. the mill) is set up and slaughter him; and if that is

---

[305] *Adäfrəs*, 68:23-69:8.

not possible, they bring in a bottle the blood of one slaughtered elsewhere, (thinking that) unless the mill is sprinkled with that blood, they will never find a market (i.e. get customers). - - The children of how many parents do you think do not return at the end of the day? - - - The price even for this blood that comes in bottles is thousands of dollars, they say - - -."

"How do they know it is human blood? It can be the blood of sheep, of goats, for example!", says Ato Ṭəso, who has remained listening -.

"No, they say one must go (i.e. sell it) together with two pieces cut from the ears, as a mark!" " [306]

Ato Wäldu asks how much a living child is sold for, and Wzo Asäggaš answers that the price then is double, and that there is a brisk trade in children "everywhere".[307] Simultaneously with this conversation, the author reports another conversation where Adäfrəs praises the noble character of people in the countryside! [308]

Spirits can also inhabit large trees, and travellers make vows and sacrifices to the spirit of the tree. No one should touch the trunk of such a tree, and it may be wrapped in a piece of cloth.[309]

Spirits can bring disease and cause mental disturbances and take control of a person's mind and actions; there is even an evil spirit that attempts to violate virgins.[310]

One ritual implies the sacrifice of an animal with the purpose of curing a man through transferring the evil spirit causing the disease from the sick man to the animal sacrifice, which is called *boräntəčča*.[311] *Adäfrəs* also contains a description of this ceremony:

"A few people were going towards where the road to Wzo Asäggaš's house, below the house, and the road leading to Mafud meet. Carrying a sick man on a stretcher, pulling along a black sheep. The time is the heavy midday hours when, it is believed, the road is occupied by snakes and incurable diseases. Ato Ṭəso and the people with him appear on the hillock across from there and descend toward the fork in the road. Those who had carried the stretcher lead the black sheep three times round the sick man and slaughter it in the name of the Father, the Son, and the Holy Spirit - as they arrive at the fork in the road. And with the blood, they make

---
[306] *Adäfrəs*, 110:27-111:16.
[307] *Ib.*, 111:20-24.
[308] *Ib.*, 112:6-8.
[309] *Ib.*, 77:1-23.
[310] *Ib.*, 207:22f., 117:28-30, 66:13, 68:26-30; 175:10, 255:15, 276:24; 210:11f., 241:11; 147:8f.12f.
[311] *Ib.*, 102:28, 103:3.

BELIEFS AND ETHICS

the sign of the cross on the forehead of the sick man; and, leaving the place quickly, return to where they came from.

The sheep struggles his last; Ato Ṭəso arrives at the place. "It's our luck!" he says and, pulling a knife out of his pocket, cuts the ear off the sheep - in the name of the Father, the Son, and the Holy Spirit - and, ordering his servant to bring their "luck" (i.e. the sheep) to the house they were going to, continued on his way. Those who had made the sacrifice did not turn back to (see) the sacrificed animal; when they have left the place, the devil begins to help himself to the food. - And they know that if those who invited him (i.e. the devil) to the meal, look back and see him when he is eating, the sickness that left the sick man will catch him again.." [312]

When the meat of this animal is taken to Wzo Asäggaš's compound the workers there, who have found out what happened, try to keep it out, and Wärdofa, the supervisor of her peasants, says: "- - - the meat of the sacrifice does not enter the compound of əmmäbete; the sickness that left him (i.e. the sick man) will finish off both us and the cattle"; and Abba Addise seems equally convinced of the power of the sacrificial animal (i.e. the spirit in it) to cause harm.[313]

The belief in spirits and their influence on human life and the power and reality of magic seems to be strong among practically the whole population, including the clergy and many of the educated.

Medicines to counteract the evil influences of magic are of various kinds. Holy water, ṭäbäl, may cure a tendency to wander.[314] Love can be caused by magic,[315] and different means can be used to get rid of it; food and incense may be used to get the cooperation of spirits in driving out love and causing hate and jealousy to take its place;[316] magic formulas and prayers are also used for similar purposes.[317] As spirits feel the pain of people they possess, some sorcerers prescribe very painful exercises to remove evil spirits.[318]

---

[312] Adäfrəs, 97:18-98:3.
[313] Ib., 102:28f., 105:6-22.
[314] Kä'admas bašagär, 141:25-142:2.
[315] Fəḳr əskä mäḳabər, 410:30f., Yalačča gabačča, 110:8f. 19f., 111:1f., Yäbädäl fəṣṣame, 33:1f. 15f. Cf. Zämänfäs Ḳəddus Abrəha, op. cit., pp. 239-241.
[316] Yalačča gabačča, 115:5-7, 116:3f. 14-16.
[317] The prayer beginning nä'akwətäkä is frequently mentioned in such contexts. Yäbädäl fəṣṣame, 140:15-18, Fəḳr əskä mäḳabər, 415:4.14-17, 416:11f.
[318] Fəḳr əskä mäḳabər, 421:7-13.

Fəkr əskä mäkabər tells of an occasion when a priest was called to exorcise a spirit that had caused Fitawrari Mäšäša's daughter Säblä Wängel to fall in love with Bäzzabbəh:

> "Then, holding the iron cross with his two hands in front of him, he came a little closer to Säblä, and standing with his feet together, he started to recite while looking sometimes towards heaven, sometimes towards the ground. Although his mouth is seen moving, his voice is not heard. He recites and recites, and while puffing, he paddles the air upwards, downwards, to the right, and to the left with the cross. As he thus recites, looking up and down, paddling the air while puffing and reciting again, and again paddling the air for a long time, he finally approached Säblä, and bending down he said,
> "Kiss the cross!" Säblä kissed the cross.
> "Kiss it reverently!"
> Säblä did as she was told. Then he held the cross upside down and said, "Now then, rest your mouth on the cross and your forehead on the handle and be silent for a while and afterwards you will answer what I ask you."
> Now also Säblä did as she was told.
> "Close your eyes!"
> "Yes."
> "What do you see?"
> "I see nothing."
> "What do you hear?"
> "I hear nothing!"
> "Well then, think! and then tell me the first thing that comes to your mind!"
> "Yes."
> "Now what came to your mind?"
> "The reading (text), "Cross, our strength, cross, our redemption, cross, our fortitude, cross, the salvation of our souls" came to my mind!"
> "Fine! Otherwise - - - - nothing came to your mind?"
> "No."
> "All this - - - - the man who brought you all this trouble did not come to your mind?"
> Säblä was silent for a while, and when she said, "N - - -n- - -no!" Abba Täklä Haymanot, holding the cross for her, and while bending forward (looking) as if he felt warm water flowing over his hands, and just as if he were startled, he said - - "Well, then, it is enough; stand up straight!"" [319]

This passage illustrates a situation that is not uncommon, viz., that Christian and pagan practices overlap. This is treated in greater detail in the next section.

---

[319] *Fəkr əskä mäkabər*, 422:2-423:9.

3. *Syncretism in Christianity and paganism*

In the preceding sections, Christianity and pagan practices are dealt with separately,[320] but it is also demonstrated that pagan practices are often perpetrated by Christians. This tendency to mix Christian and non-Christian elements in the practice of religion in Ethiopia is so strong that several authors have made a point of emphasizing this aspect, and it is justified to talk of syncretism or syncretistic tendencies both in Christianity and paganism in Ethiopia. The common people do not seem to draw a clear line between the two types of religion.[321]

A great number of the clergy seems to participate in sorcery and magic of different kinds. Guddu Kasa in *Fəkr əskä mäkabər* discusses with Bäzzabbəh a certain Abba Täklä Haymanot who "speaks magic spells (*asmat*) that have not been known in all of Gojjam, that cannot be solved in all of Gojjam",[322] and then he goes on to comment on the Church and the clergy in general:

> "There you see! Our Church has become a refuge for such rebels, such robbers! There you see! Among our priests, among our apostles,[323] beginning with the head priests, passing through the ranks of the monks, to the common *däbtära* and deacons, many say that they can make magic spells, or release (from) magic spells, one can invoke a demon, another can drive him out, one can bring a scourge, another can bring mercy, - and while thus hiding their lies in their (priests') turbans, in their (monks') caps, in their (church school students') goatskin mantles, they play with the flock that was given them to lead and to teach! Now then, to join in this, and then to call upon the name of God, is not that to mock His holy name? This is what has kept me away from the Church I love!"[324]

The Christians most frequently associated with pagan practices are the *däbtära*, hermits, and occasionally higher clergy.[325] To avert impending disasters they will prescribe remedies that in-

---

[320] Such a distinction can be made on the basis of, e.g. Leviticus 20:27, Deuteronomy 18:10f.14, Jeremiah 27:9, Galatians 5:19-21, Revelation 21:8, 22:15.
[321] Cf. *Yätewodros ənba*, chapter 3.
[322] *Fəkr əskä mäkabər*, 428:5.8f.
[323] This probably refers to itinerant preachers or evangelists.
[324] *Fəkr əskä mäkabər*, 428:13-25.
[325] *Ib.*, 428:3, *Bərr ambar säbbärälləwo*, 10:2, 11:18, *Adäfrəs*, 64:26f. Cf. A. Young, "Magic as a 'Quasi-profession': The Organization of Magic and Magical Healing among Amhara", in *Ethnology*, Vol. 14 (1975), No. 3, pp. 245-265.

clude any religion or god. A *däbtära* in *Yalačča gabəčča* presents his remedy to prevent destruction thus:

> "An unknown, fearful, shocking, disastrous calamity is certain to descend - it is a matter I stake my neck on. It is better if repentance is done, if prayers are held in every church - I have decided to notify *Aläḳa*. And let *Haji* also prostrate himself in (Muslim) prayer (*sälata*) in his mosque, let him (or them) start supplications (*wädaja*).[326] The disaster does not distinguish between Gallas, Amharas, Muslims or Christians." [327]

The same *däbtära* prescribes *adrus*, "incense burnt by Muslims when they drink coffee and pray, "Let our wish be realized"",[328] and sacrifices to pacify the spirits of trees and hills (*adbar* and *awgar*).[329]

An old Christian in *Araya* believes the same prophecy about the war with Italy was revealed to Christians, Muslims and pagans alike, implying that all have access to the same wisdom from above:

> "Do not think it (the prophecy) errs; our country's monks, soothsayers (*wäləy*),[330] sheikhs, hermits, recluses: Christians and Muslims are agreed about this." [331]

A priest, Abba Yohannəs in *Adäfrəs*, accepts Muslim saints almost on an equal footing with Christian saints, probably because saints are regarded largely as miracle workers.[332]

The common people, of whatever belief, can in certain cases take part in the same religious rituals, showing there are several points of similarity between them. It is told in *Adäfrəs* of an *adbar* (in this case a heap of stone, but the word can also refer to a tree supposed to house a spirit) [333] that everyone who passed it performed an act of worship or sacrifice to pacify the spirit dwelling there:

> "They call the heap of stones an *adbar*. The Christian as well as the Muslim, the spirit-medium (*zar färäsu*), the sorcerer and the

---

[326] *Wädaja* can refer to Muslim or pagan night sessions or séances of prayer and meditation; cf. DTW and M. Rodinson, *Magie, médecine, possession en Éthiopie*, pp. 64, 123; see *Yähəllina däwäl*, 201:24, 203:14.

[327] *Yalačča gabəčča*, 127:4-11.

[328] DTW, p. 392.

[329] *Yalačča gabəčča*, 115:6f., 116:16, 117:1-4.10-12, 119:1-8, 120:10.

[330] *Wäləy* is "someone chosen, special; a prophet, sorcerer, soothsayer or magician"; DTW.

[331] *Araya*, 227:29-31.

[332] *Adäfrəs*, 219:26-220:9.

[333] *Yalačča gabəčča*, 117:3f; cf. *Yähəllina däwäl*, 22:24f.

common pagan, if they pass by that road, must put something on top of it when they come (to the place), carrying from afar a piece of wood or a stone, whatever their hands get hold of. They have the belief that it will prevent unexpected accidents from occurring." [334]

This tendency towards syncretism in Ethiopia manifests itself in several ways. Divination and prediction by means of astrology, interpretation of the configurations of pebbles, etc., sacrifices and magic to secure the help or protection of evil spirits, and means to stave off danger from magic spells, such as the *kətab*, are all used together with Christian symbols and rituals, e.g. the cross, holy water, Biblical quotations, etc.

It is told in *Bərr ambar säbbärälləwo* that a *däbtära* who practises astrology visits the mother of a girl about to get married, to tell her what the future holds in store for her daughter. To perform his calculations, he asks for both the girl's and the mother's baptismal names, which the mother hesitates to give because she holds the common belief that anyone who knows that name has power over the person and can use it to cause harm. The *däbtära* adds that special wisdom was given by the God of Israel through a revelation to Aaron and handed down to and preserved by the *däbtära*, but not given to the ordinary clergy.[335]

Aya Ləzzəbu, a *däbtära* in *Yalačča gabəčča*, refers to himself as "the *däbtära*, the priest of God, who is an interpreter of (astrological) books, or one computing (the message of) the stars", thus combining in his own view the functions of priest and astrologer.[336]

To protect themselves against evil spirits, both Christians and non-Christians use the *kətab*, writing on parchment in a small leather bag worn on a neck-cord, as a charm or talisman. The *däbtära* in *Bərr ambar säbbärälləwo* mentioned above offers several kinds of *kətab*, each with a different attribute. He specially recommends a *ləfafä ṣədḳ*, a "band of righteousness", a piece of parchment filled with meaningless words, as long as the human body, and which is buried with a man when he dies.[337] This particular specimen he says "is of universal usefulness", written in Arabic

---

[334] *Adäfrəs*, 77:18-25; cf. *Yähəllina däwäl*, 22:28-23:17, 204:8-10.
[335] *Bərr ambar säbbärälləwo*, 12:7-9, 12:18-13:12.
[336] *Yalačča gabəčča*, 150:2-6.
[337] Cf. DTW, KWK and E. A. Wallis Budge, *The Bandlet of Righteousness*, London, 1929.

on fine cloth, and not by any ordinary *sämonäñña* ³³⁸ either, as he contemptuously calls the priests.³³⁹ He offers several choices of *kətab*, reveals some of the secret names of God they contain, and talks of the usefulness of the *kətab*, astrology and magic concoctions. He then gives advice to the mother of the prospective bride:

> "And this", said the *däbtära*, "this is one (i.e. *kətab*) the God of Israel revealed to Solomon; and after Solomon had written it down in the name of Haha'el Aṣma'el, Ela'el, Lala'el, Amla'el, Məla'el, Hahahahaha'el, Harawa'el, Mamama'el, Mamimä, Adä'el,³⁴⁰ it came to us together with the Tablets of the Law of Moses, for the love of man. However, as for their (i.e. the boy's and the girl's) stars, his is Virgo of the element of earth (*sänbula märet*), which goes out by the entry of the sun, hers is Gemini of the element of air (*gäwz näfas*).³⁴¹ They meet", says the *däbtära*, throwing some roasted grain into his mouth and drinking mouthfuls of beer. "Your child will find honour in foreign parts. But eventually she will get some ailment of the blood. And a magician³⁴² will turn against her, says her star. Now then, I tell you I went down and stayed at Zegamäl³⁴³ to bring the milk of a pregnant leopard, which she must take in conjunction with medicine of the *səndädo*-grass for the blood, and in conjunction with medicine of the *ḵäräṭ*-tree for the spell of the magician." ³⁴⁴

The pious mother finds this explanation quite credible and dares not go against his advice.

In some cases, the whole education and practice of a branch of the Church can turn towards magic, and churches become centres of sorcery and other pagan practices. There are hints in Amharic literature to at least one such place. Aläḵa Kənfu is mentioned in *Fəḵr əskä mäḵabər* as a great teacher, comparable in the field of *ḵəne*-poetry with Täwanäy, the originator of *ḵəne*,³⁴⁵ whose style of

---

[338] A *sämonäñña* is a priest or deacon who does service in one particular church a week at a time; cf. DTW, p. 1186.
[339] *Bərr ambar säbbärälləwo*, 15:15-18.
[340] Cf. *Hatäta mänafəst wä'awdä nägäst*, by Zämänfäs Ḵəddus Abrəha, Addis Ababa, 1945 E.C. (6th ed. 1963 E.C., pp. 145, 250-52).
[341] *Ib.*, pp. 153-55, 160-63. The four triplicities or elements (*bahrəy*) fire, earth, air, and water (*əsat, märet, näfas, may* or *wəha*) "are basic elements in man, recognized by the earliest astrologers"; Mayo, *Astrology*, pp. 47f.
[342] *əjjä säb* can be a magician who brings sickness, or a *buda*, cf. DTW and *Bälg*, 49:11, 61:10f.
[343] Zegamäl is a locality in the vicinity of Däbrä Libanos, or, in the mouth of the local people, Däbrä Libanos itself; see DTW, p. 479.
[344] *Bərr ambar säbbärälləwo*, 15:25-16:13. (*Səndädo* is *pennisetum* sp., *ḵäräṭ* is *osyris abyssinica*.)
[345] *Fəḵr əskä mäḵabər*, 77:7-10.

ḳəne is known as *gonj*, after the place in Gojjam where he taught. His rival for the honour as the father of *ḳəne* is Däḳḳä Əsṭifa, who went abroad and learnt seven arts, six of which are said to be kinds of magic, and he was therefore rejected in his own country; but rumour has it that his magic art "is practised until the present; probably it is secretly passed on from one person to the other". There is a tradition that he taught *ḳəne* to Täwanäy.[346] DTW calls Däḳḳä Əsṭifa "a philosopher, sorcerer, magician who lived at the time of Emperor Iskinder".[347] He is named after his teacher Əsṭifa, who has many of his followers living on islands in Lake Tana, where there are believed to be "many who know magic, sorcery, witchcraft, medicine".[348] In common parlance the islands where they live are known as the islands of Dägga Əsṭifanos.[349]

The ordinary Christian seems firmly convinced of the potency of magic and the truth of divination. Wzo Alganäš, a staunch Christian who has come to visit the shrine of St. Gabriel at Kulubi uses the opportunity of her stay to consult a *däbtära*-astrologer, Aya Ləzzəbu, to find out what the stars say concerning the future prospects of her nephew Bahru and the girl she intends him to marry. Aya Ləzzəbu deals also in magic charms, and when he hears that Bahru is in love with the "wrong" girl, because "someone has read a spell over him", in the opinion of Wzo Alganäš, he speculates about remedies: "the antidote of the love-charm is the hate-charm—and maybe the adultery-charm"; he does not exclude the possibility that someone has cast "the stunning-charm" on him, or "maybe the evil eye", and it is his job to find the countermagic.[350]

Fitawrari Mäšäša, Säblä Wängel's father (in *Fəkr əskä mäḳabər*), believes Bäzzabbəh has won her love through magic powers he has acquired as a church-educated man: "That magician, sorcerer, *däbtära*, that wizzard has put a magic spell on my girl!" [351] He then proceeds to seek someone who knows an antidote and finds an *Abba* who also has church education.[352]

---

[346] Cf. *Ṭəntawi yä'ityopəya təmhərt*, by Habtä Maryam Wärḳənäh, pp. 173:6-12, 174:26f., 175:6.
[347] DTW, p. 380, on Däḳḳä Əsṭifa (2); cf. also his note on Täwane (i.e. Täwanäy), p. 445. The popular view of the Stephanites has no historical basis.
[348] DTW, p. 380, on Däḳḳä Əsṭifa (1); p. 142, on Əsṭifa (2).
[349] *Yä'ənba däbdabbewoč*, 39:13f.
[350] *Yalačča gabəčča*, 110:1f., 111:7f.17f., 112:3-6.
[351] *Fəkr əskä mäḳabər*, 410:30f.
[352] Ib., 417:1-8, 417ult.-418:19.

The ensuing conversation between the *Abba* and the Fitawrari shows how Christian beliefs and magic go hand in hand, without contradicting or excluding each other:

> " "Abba Mogäse has told you about the problem I have!" said Fitawrari as Abba Täklä Haymanot sat with head hanging.
> "Y - yes!"
> "Well then, can you do anything about it!"
> "For God - - - - is anything impossible?"
> "What is impossible for God! You see, I brought you here to make an antidote and release from charms for her! I mean to ask if you have previously done a similar thing!"
> "And I - I don't mean that!"
> "Is it prayer? or what is it that you do to her?" Instead of giving an answer in words, Abba Täklä Haymanot revealed a thing he carried wrapped in an old piece of cloth and showed it to Fitawrari.
> "Oh - - - a cross! Well, what do you do with the cross!"
> "It is not a cross - - - - made by human hands."
> "Well then?"
> "It was given me after I had stood on one leg and prayed for fifteen days and - - - fifteen nights, and it has power over all who use harmful (magical) medicine and all enemies of good."
> "From whom did you receive it?"
> "Who gives except the One prayer is made to?"
> "Is it a cross that came down to you from God?" Abba Täklä Haymanot lowered his head and waited in silence; then, "there is no doubt about it, there is no difficulty; the matter - - - - is easy. Let me find the girl alone on this spot - - - - tomorrow evening!" he said and stood up to go." [353]

When Fitawrari is later told that his daughter is healed, he is in no doubt that it is God who has been at work in the counter-magic and made it effective.[354]

Many people do not seem to find any contradiction between Christian and pagan worship, and they can perform both in the hope that at least one supernatural power, or maybe both in combination, will yield the desired result.

When there is drought and worms spoil the harvest in Illubabor, the farmers complain that God does not hear them, neither has He for a long time - "He is not the God of former times". As the bad conditions must be punishment for some unknown sin they have committed, they pray to God, but to no avail; then they go to

---

[353] *Fəkr əskä mäḳabər*, 420:2-32.
[354] *Ib.*, 424:8-12.

the pagan ritual leader, Abba Ҫäffe, and pray in one of his séances (*wädaja*) and slaughter a black sheep and barley-coloured chickens, but it is no use. As even the pagan rain-maker cannot create rain as before, God cannot be responding to any of the known ways of approaching Him.[355] In the same area, people can sacrifice a white bullock to a local spirit and then pray to God, or take a vow at church after having made a similar sacrifice to the same spirit.[356] Prophecies are pronounced by monks, sorcerers and Muslim sheikhs, and the same future predicted by those who read in the tallow of sacrificial animals and monks who deal in astrology.[357] The *kətab* is used to avert all kinds of magic;[358] and of one young prostitute it is said that there was not one saint she had not prayed to in church, not a sorcerer or a *däbtära* who explains astrological books she had not consulted in order to become pregnant by the man she has fallen in love with.[359]

Christian and pagan symbols are worn together as ornaments, such as the *ṭälsäm*, a charm or talisman made by a sorcerer and which has magical drawings supposed to prevent all sorts of troubles, and put into a leather container like a *kətab*,[360] together with the cross and the neck-cord worn by Christians as a sign of their faith, the *matäb*.[361] The pebble-throwing diviner Abba Mammito in *Yalačča gabəčča* wears the *matäb*, corals and beads and leopard's claws round his neck.[362]

In the last chapter the animal sacrifice called *boräntəčča* was discussed. According to DTW, the custom originates in Borana in south Ethiopia and is thus of pagan origin. Those who perform the ceremony in Christian northern Shoa (as told in *Adäfrəs*) believe in the possibility of curing a sick man by slaughtering a black sheep at the midday hour—both associated with evil spirits—and by performing the correct ritual: to walk the sheep three times round the sick man, slaughter it in the name of the Father and the Son and the Holy Spirit, and with its blood make the sign of the cross

---

[355] *Yähəllina däwäl*, 59:21-60:14; cf. 81:12-20.
[356] *Ib.*, 134:19-22, 166:15-22.
[357] *Ib.*, 135:17ff., 152:11-16.
[358] *Ib.*, 139:2-11; cf. 138:21-25.
[359] *Ib.*, 96:10-12.
[360] Cf. DTW; it can also mean a gold or silver ornament worn by Muslims, similar in form to the *ašän kətab* (on which, see DTW, p. 690).
[361] *Fəkr əskä mäḵabər*, 280:11-14, 282:22-283:2.
[362] *Yalačča gabəčča*, 38:21f.

on the sick man's forehead, and leave quickly without looking back.[363]

Some of the more warlike Ethiopians brought up in the old warrior tradition, although Christians, seem to have a secret admiration for the Devil who ventured to rise against and challenge God. When Fitawrari Märrəne, an old-style *arbäñña* in *Ṭälfo bäkise*, hears that Bäzzabbəh Tori, a friend of his son, has organized the abduction of, and plans to marry, a girl from Addis Ababa, just as he himself had abducted his wife to marry her, he cannot hide his admiration for this young man who defies modern customs, only fit for weaklings, as he thinks:

> "Where is Bäzzabbəh Tori, that cursed devil - hey? For it was the Devil who quarrelled with God. The demon! Call him! Let me kiss him on his cheeks." [364]

And when the man he wants enters, he says:

> "The devil, Bäzzabbəh Tori! - - he is cursed, you see! - He who quarrelled with God! - - The demon, Bäzzabbəh Tori." [365]

Ethiopian authors show how much dishonesty prevails in these magic practices and how sorcerers use religious beliefs and superstition to fleece simple, gullible people, sometimes through cajoling, saying the money is for the poor, other times through scaring and threatening words. Although everything depends on the will of God, as one *däbtära* puts it, "He has permitted us to think, to examine, to take care, and also to do what is best"; and as those who deal with magic maintain they know what is best, they expect to be generously rewarded.[366] The authors find it necessary, though, to point out that the magic is of no avail and frequently leads to unhappiness. A girl the *däbtära* said he would benefit with his magic in *Bərr ambar säbbärällǝwo*, encounters much trouble and is soon divorced, just because she wore signs of his machinations, something the bridegroom's family did not approve of.[367] The magic supposed to influence Säblä Wängel in *Fəkr əskä mäḳabər* and Bällätäč in *Yalačča gabəčča* is shown to be just a waste of time.

---

[363] See *Adäfrəs*, 97:18-98:3; cf. 102:28f., 105:6-22.
[364] *Ṭälfo bäkise*, 57:20-22.
[365] *Ib.*, 67:18f.
[366] *Bərr ambar säbbärällǝwo*, 11:8ff.16ff., 12:15f., 17:1ff.
[367] *Ib.*, 39:6ff.

But most Ethiopians seem to take the advice of sorcerers to be on the safe side.

Common to adherents of all kinds of faiths in Ethiopia is a strong awareness of supernatural influences on daily affairs. "The Ethiopian people, whether Muslim, Christian or pagan, are all godfearing", says Ato Təso,[368] and this opinion is shared by a French priest who talks to Araya about the Ethiopians' strong "fear of God".[369] This faith is generous and tolerant, and in practice it seems as if people expect God to respond and reveal Himself in many unexpected and mysterious ways, and Christian, Muslim or pagan ritual specialists may know only part of the truth and how to meet the divine requirements on man. Therefore they are not averse to giving all options a fair trial, and magic may, in the view of many, work where Christian (or Muslim) rituals prove ineffective.

4. *Ethics*

Ethical norms are of two kinds, the laws of religion and the requirements of convention and decency.

The religious norm is the will of God, expressed in the Bible ("the Book"), and primarily the Ten Commandments, or "Ten Words" of the Torah.[370] To discourage an action, one can say, "God does not like it!"[371] The neck-cord worn by Christians implies a commitment to follow Christian rules, and to ask someone to "snap your neck-cord" is equal to asking him to commit a sin.[372] The best commendation a man can receive in Christian Ethiopia is that he is a person "of straight conduct, of strong faith", who fears God and honours man;[373] thereby he finds "righteousness",

---

[368] *Adäfrəs*, 263:26-28.
[369] *Araya*, 41:10.
[370] *Fəkr əskä mäkabər*, 14:13f., 15:1f., *Yäkəne azmära*, 54:10, *Yähəllina däwäl*, 174:16. The Ten Commandments do not quite follow *Exodus* 20:1-17. They are: (1) Do not worship a foreign God; (2) Do not use your God's name vainly; (3) Honour your God's Sabbath; (4) Honour your father and your mother; (5) Do not kill; (6) Do not commit adultery; (7) Do not steal; (8) Do not witness falsely; (9) Do not desire your companion's property; (10) Love your companion as yourself. (See Habtä Maryam Wärkənäh, *Təntawi...*, pp. 44f.) Together with the Six Words of the Gospel (based on *Matthew* 5:21-43 or 25:35f., according to two different traditions), the Ten Commandments form the basis of the Church's ethics. (*Ib.*, pp. 45f.). The tenth Commandment in the Ethiopian tradition is taken from *Leviticus* 19:18.
[371] *Yalačča gabəčča*, 157:9f.
[372] *Ib.*, 91:10.13f.
[373] *Yäləbb hassab*, 153:13, 170:22f.

implying a full and complete life.³⁷⁴ When justice seems not to be done, one prays that "God may see for" the wrongdoer, i.e. that the latter may see his error and repent.³⁷⁵

A priest in *Fəkr əskä mäkabər* says that what distinguishes man from animals is his capacity for self-control and to live in accordance with God's commands:

> "What distinguishes man from an animal is not that he can walk on two legs; chickens also walk on two legs. So then, is it because he has a language? No; animals also have a language that is understandable among themselves. The special characteristic that distinguishes man from animals is the fact that he can govern himself. What distinguishes him from an animal is the fact that he can control the characteristics he has in common with an animal: hunger, greed, sexual lust, and the like. If he, driven by hunger, must eat everything he desires, if he, driven by greed, must have everything he sees, if he, driven by lust, fulfils the act of adultery with every woman he desires, he has stopped being a man and becomes an animal walking on two legs. Man, to the extent that he is created as a unity of flesh and spirit, is a battlefield on which worldly and spiritual feelings continuously join forces, wrestle and fight. In case the spirit should be the victor in such a battle, it means it will check, it will govern the flesh and the desires of the flesh. And if man's spirit, being strengthened, conquers the flesh, and if he can keep the desires of the flesh in check, it means that man, purified and cleansed from bodily dirt and misery, can approach God in heaven and in the conversation of prayer be the associate of the saints. It was for this purpose that the ordinance of fasting was made, (it was) the main reason. Fasting was made to strengthen the soul and weaken the flesh, to check the bodily wishes and desires that change man into an animal, or, in short, in order that man shall be able to govern himself." ³⁷⁶

But in popular attitudes, faith in God is not necessarily combined with a moral commitment to "do good". There are cases where people invoke God's help for evil: "He begs Him for (success in) an evil undertaking", it is said of one man; a thief makes a vow to St. George before he goes out stealing; and a go-between prays for success in her mission to get a wife away from her husband and into the hands of a seducer.³⁷⁷

---

[374] *Yalačča gabəčča*, 122:2, *Adäfrəs*, 198:19 (cf. DTW on *ṣədk*, p. 1016).
[375] *Fəkr əskä mäkabər*, 135:5.24f.
[376] *Fəkr əskä mäkabər*, 24:24-25:14, cf. the continuation of his speech, 25:15-26:7.
[377] *Yä'ənba däbdabbewoč*, 53:1-11; cf. *Säw allä bəyye*, 38:21f.

BELIEFS AND ETHICS

Another normative force in forming people's conduct is "fear of what people will say", yəluñta or yəluññəta, which prevents one from doing "what is shameful, a scandal", näwr, or "indecent behaviour, bad manners", bəlgənna.[378] One fears to have one's "shame", gudd, revealed, and begs "for the sake of shame" (məntä əfrät), i.e. do not bring shame upon yourself by refusing.[379] The "fear of what people will say" can also lead to cowardice, weakness, or evil, and be a negative quality:

> "Pulled by the ties of relationship and of concern for what people would say, they came to do the evil thing they hated, together with the evil-doer." [380]

Ethiopian authors are much more preoccupied with vices in man than with his virtues. Besides self-control, which is in itself little more than suppression of evil tendencies, the two main virtues referred to again and again are self-sacrifice, mäswa'ətənnät,[381] and humility or modesty, with the implication of politeness, təhtənna.[382] But there is also some emphasis on diligence, patience, the giving of alms and sacrifice, kindness, helpfulness, generosity, hard work, etc.[383] "The sole jewel of a man is, having worked, to feed (his family)".[384] In other respects, what is counted as virtuous conduct is often little more than to avoid vices.

In Amharic literature there is a strong preoccupation with vices and human frailty. A vice can be regarded as a mistake, an error, səhtät,[385] or given a religious interpretation and classified as a sin, haṭi'at.[386]

It might be difficult to grade vices or sins according to their

---

[378] Kä'admas bašagär, 31ult.-32:1, Fəkr əskä mäkabər, 184:13, 104:2, 137: 16.18, 187:12f.; 35:28: Yalačča gabəčča, 40:3, 53:2f., Adäfrəs, 24:2.21-25, 143:6, 150:1, 176:11f., Yäräggäfu abäboč, 56:4, 152:1f., 171:19, 173:3, Säw allä bəyye, 27:10, 75:23, 98:8.18.
[379] Fəkr əskä mäkabər, 353:26, Yähəllina däwäl, 205:23.
[380] Fəkr əskä mäkabər, 288:19-21; cf. 511:5f.
[381] Ṭälfo bäkise, 31:2, Yä'ənb adäbdabbewoč, 16:2f., Ṣähay Mäsfən, 3:7-11, 19-21, 72:7.21.24 (this is the theme of this book), Adäfrəs, 225:30, 268:17.
[382] Ṭälfo bäkise, 47:6, Araya, 19:14, 188:13, 195:14, Adäfrəs, 10:13.
[383] Araya, 19:8; 191:1.2, 346:12f., 348:7. Yä'ənba däbdabbewoč, 97:4, Adäfrəs, 10:22-24, 12:3-13, 26:8-10; 8:4; 143:3; 11:23 Yähəllina däwäl, 6:22.
[384] Adäfrəs, 205:23.
[385] Ib., 118:6f.
[386] Ib., 79:26, Araya, 191:15.

"seriousness", but the ones most frequently written about seem to be sexual sins, greed, and deceit.

Sexual sins are common and are regarded as serious. Sex itself can make people unclean; the word *haṭi'at*, "sin" also means "sperm", and the Geez word for "sperm", *rəshat*, literally means "dirt";[387] a woman is unclean during menstruation, and the sex organs are often referred to as one's "shame".[388] A girl's virginity is her "honour", and to break her virginity before marriage is "to dirty her".[389] Even the term for girl, *ləjagäräd*, is only used of a virgin; as soon as virginity is lost, at whatever age, a "girl" becomes a "woman", *set*. How serious a matter it is to lose one's virginity is seen by the fact that Wzo Asäggaš rejects her daughter when she says she is not a virgin; and her father confessor is in great fear of the "demon of fornication" and objects to secular music because it leads to sexual sins.[390] See also chapter III, 4, on sex and marriage.

Sexual desires lead to unfaithfulness and many divorces, and to prostitution, all of which are becoming more common.[391] It designates the lowest level of moral failure to be promiscuous, particularly when it is done out of lust and not poverty; such a promiscuous person is called *šärmuṭa*, which designates any person, male or female, who has the urge to and habit of being with many sex partners, and money need not be involved. But the word is frequently used for a prostitute, in the same sense as a *setäñña adari*, "a woman who earns her keep by providing womanly, i.e. sexual, services".[392] A "life of vulgarity and pleasure"[393] is a life of promiscuity and drunkenness;[394] and it is a great insult to be called "frivolous".[395]

Greed is the subject of entire books in Amharic. *Yädəhoč kätäma*[396] deals with the tragic life and death of a man who was consumed with greed. Out of greed a woman leaves her husband and child to

---

[387] *Adäfrəs*, 220:21f.
[388] *Ib.*, 67:22, 205:19.
[389] *Ib.*, 307:11.13.24f., 305:7, 304:1-3.
[390] *Ib.*, 308:20-31; 171:19-172:3.
[391] *Ib.*, 39:23f., 40:7-12, 194:15f.
[392] *Kä'admas bašagär*, 97:22-25. Cf. *Yalačča gabəčča*, 154:18 (*ləkəskəs səra*, "wanton behaviour, loose conduct, promiscuity").
[393] *Amanu'el därso mäls*, 31:20.
[394] *Ib.*, 30:17-32:10.
[395] *Araya*, 240:15, 297:11.
[396] *Arrəmuñň*, pp. 105-185.

become the mistress of a rich playboy from Addis Ababa—and when he is tired of her, she ends up as a prostitute and dies of misery and venereal disease: that is the story told in *Yä'ənba däbdabbewoč*. In *Almotkum bəyye alwašəm* [397] we are told of a woman who out of convenience agrees to live with an Italian officer when she hears false rumours that her husband has died in battle against the Italian invaders. The literature just after the war often returns to the motif of women who lived with the conquerors in order to have an easy and luxurious life. Greed is serious in itself,[398] but it also often leads to theft—another sin strongly condemned in Ethiopian ethics.[399]

Deceit is employed for gain, real or imaginary, and is thus connected with greed and theft. "To deceive", or to be "deceitful" are common terms,[400] but most frequently deceit is described as *tänkol*, "devious ways, subterfuge, malice"; [401] or as *bəlṭät*, "cunning"; [402] and related to this is "hypocrisy".[403] The purpose of deceit is to get power over another person, and it thus often leads to "oppression".[404] The motive power behind it all is often envy, a vice particularly odious to Araya.[405] People do not keep faith or trust, they take bribes, become proud or puffed up, and want to show off.[406]

There are of course many other vices mentioned, but they are often not dwelt on; e.g., laziness, flattery, vanity, lying, gossip-mongering, back-biting, drunkenness, usury, killing, and being "for sale" for the sake of survival or out of greed ("one who says, I shall eat", *əbäla bay*).[407] Cowardice is a vice with religious connotations, as God does not accept or "justify" a coward.[408]

---

[397] *Arrəmuňň*, pp. 273-338.
[398] *Fəkr əskä mäkabər*, 26:18-20.
[399] *Adäfrəs*, 33:8f.12f.
[400] *Amanu'el därso mäls*, 39:10, *Yalačča gabəčča*, 156:19f., 164:8, *Araya*, 240:16.
[401] *Yalačča gabəčča*, 72:8, *Joro ṭäbi*, 19:2, *Araya*, 192:9.12f., 194:5f., 240:15, *Fəkr əskä mäkabər*, 136:25, *Ṭälfo bäkise*, 55:5, *Bälg*, 93:11, *Yähəllina däwäl*, 66:9.19, 67:23, 247ult., cf. *Yäkärmo säw*, 73:19.
[402] *Joro ṭäbi*, 19:2, *Araya*, 270:10f.
[403] *Araya*, 193:14.
[404] *Araya*, 194:5, 197:7.21, 270:10f., 296:19, *Ṭälfo bäkise*, 47:17. *Arrəmuňň*, 320:24f.
[405] *Araya*, 191:22-195:3.
[406] *Fəkr əskä mäkabər*, 410:3, *Yalačča gabəčča*, 156:16, *Araya*, 191:22, 195:10, 291:29, 292:9.15.
[407] *Araya*, 191:3, 197:14.23, 198:15, 240:14-16, *Säw allä bəyye*, 31:22, *Adäfrəs*, 7:10-12, 79:21, 11:15, 313:5-7, 88:30f., 89:6f.
[408] *Adäfrəs*, 198:19.

Virtues are encouraged by prospects of wealth and high position, and sins are punished with disasters, humiliation and hard toil.[409] There is always the prospect of forgiveness if one repents, an act sometimes symbolized by wearing a black stone on one's head.[410] But because of the predominance of vices, particularly among the young, the world will certainly soon perish: we live in the eighth millennium.[411] This is partly due to the weakness and evil inclination of human nature: by nature man is selfish and worse than an animal or an ogre [412] and is led astray by evil spirits, so much so that man is to some extent exempt from responsibility for his moral failings, and the way to overcome his vice would be to get rid of the evil spirit that leads him to fail.[413]

As the world is full of sin and temptation, the best way to escape from sin and achieve holiness and the highest virtue is to renounce the world, and in particular to sever all sexual relationships and become a monk; or to fast and to pray.[414]

It is a particularity of some of Mäkonnən Ǝndalkaččäw's characters that those who have the greatest moral flaws are at the same time fervent Christians. This is the case of the main characters in *Yädəhoč kätäma, Yäfəkər čora*, et al. In *Ṣähay Mäsfən* a man atones for the offence that led to Ṣähay Mäsfən's death by a huge sacrifice: he gives all his wealth to Ṣähay Mäsfən's children by a previous marriage and withdraws from the world and lives as a recluse in a forest till the end of his days is near, when he returns to Addis Ababa and dies just as he is recognized by Ṣähay Mäsfən's children many years later.

A moral dilemma is posed by Bäzzabbəh in *Fəkr əskä mäḳabər*: should he follow his inclination to marry, or is his mother's vow that he should live in celibacy binding on him for life? [415] There is no final solution to this question, although he does marry Säblä Wängel on his death-bed, and as it is a *ḳurban* marriage, Säblä Wängel lives in celibacy, as a nun, for the rest of her life.[416]

---

[409] *Adäfrəs*, 7:28-31, 8:28-31; 7:11-13.15-17.31-33.
[410] *Ṭälfo bäkise*, 44:18f.
[411] *Ib.*, 63:25-30.
[412] *Adäfrəs*, 9:22f, 49:16f., 79:26, 84:6, 118:10, *Yä'ənba däbdabbewoč*, 23:1, *Bälg*, 95:10, *Yäräggäfu abäboč*, 174:1ff., 192:18.
[413] *Adäfrəs*, 171:19-26, 263:25f.; 28:1-11, 40:23-25, 165:14-17; cf. *Bälg*, 111:11f., *Säw allä bəyye*, 63:23, 67:21, 122:2.
[414] *Adäfrəs*, 221:25; 40:18-21, etc.
[415] *Fəkr əskä mäḳabər*, 462:12-14, 463:13-26.
[416] *Fəkr əskä mäḳabər*, last chapter (chapter 34).

BELIEFS AND ETHICS 127

It is a striking feature of Amharic literature that so many stories end tragically, especially for the best characters in them. Bad people often prosper for a time, and then disaster overtakes them, too. This may reflect the author's view of life, or it may be a commentary on the times in which they live.

5. *Some traditional beliefs, ideals, and customs*

Among Ethiopians, as reflected in Amharic literature, there are beliefs that are not clearly religious, although some of them may have religious origins; and there are ideals that are not easily classified as good or bad in an ethical sense.

Much of the traditional wisdom has been formulated in proverbs and folk-tales. Mäkonnən Ǝndalkaččäw frequently intersperses his stories with proverbs. Daññaččäw Wärku, in *Adäfrəs*, puts proverbs into the mouths of the traditionalists, mostly the conservative landowner Wzo Asäggaš. In these cases proverbs express the wisdom of the ages but they are not always relevant to our times.[417] Modern authors use them sparingly on the whole.

Folk-tales are not often included in modern fictional works.[418] As is the case with proverbs, they often express contradictory values, as when the kindhearted Ṣiwäne tells a story to illustrate the point that one should share with one's kin, followed by the brave and sturdy Gorfu's story which illustrates the point he wants to make, namely that the brave and strong always get an advantage and the lion's share.[419]

To analyse Ethiopian attitudes and ideals on the basis of such material would require an independent study not limited to a few works of fiction.[420]

There seems to be an ideal of the correct body, mind and behaviour, with an appropriate insult for every deviation from the norm. Beggars ask for alms "for the sake of (your) whole body".[421] One author writing in English has said, probably not quite sincerely,

---

[417] A good collection of proverbs is Mahtämä Səllase Wäldä Mäskäl, *Yabbatoč kərs*, 3rd ed., Addis Ababa, 1961 E.C.

[418] Haddis Alämayyähu's *Tärät tärät yämäsärät* is a collection of tales written as folk-tales.

[419] *Adäfrəs*, 195:28-197:23, 198:9-199:25.

[420] Some such attempts have been made, on proverbs by J. Faitlovitch, *Proverbes abyssins, traduits, expliqués et annotés*, Paris 1907, and on folk-tales by D. C. Korten, *Planned Change in a Traditional Society*, New York, 1972, pp. 115-141.

[421] *Yähəllina däwäl*, 177:20-23.

that Ethiopian faces are "too well-proportioned, too refined to hold interest more than fleetingly",[422] but the well-proportioned, refined face is the ideal. Insults belong of course to colloquial speech, but there are a few reflections in books too, e.g., one character is called *wäsfe*, "awl", because of the shape of his face and the sharpness of his voice;[423] an *ašara bis* (literally "fontanelle-less", but referring to one who has this soft membrane in front of, or behind the top of the head) is one who is believed to bring bad luck, misfortune and death to his family and friends.[424] Psychologically, it may relate to the Ethiopian ideal of the perfect body, because a person with physical defects may become "revengeful".

There exists a belief that the earth is encircled by two serpents,[425] and that some people, especially blacksmiths, can change into hyenas during the night and devour people—one aspect of the myths about the *buda*, "someone with the evil eye".[426] These stories have their origins in religion, but, like expressions such as "it is my fate" and "it is my lot",[427] they have become detached from their religious origin. So also the saying *sänenna sänño* (literally, "Säne and Monday", referring to the belief that if the month of *Säne* begins on a Monday, a bad harvest will follow) is probably based on astrological myths but is now mentioned as a belief seemingly independent of astrology and in fact as a general statement of bad luck that has causes beyond human control.[428] Astrology may also have given rise to expressions like, "I who was created during an incomplete night", i.e. approximately like our "born under an unlucky star".[429] It is interpreted as a bad sign, auguring disaster, when a jackal crosses the road in front of someone, or when it howls.[430] Wednesdays and Fridays are bad days to start a campaign or go hunting—this probably has religious reasons, as these are fasting days.[431] Many believe that dreams give portents of future events.[432]

---

[422] Solomon Deressa, "Opaque Shadows", in C. R. Larson (ed.), *More Modern African Stories*, London, 1975, p. 134.
[423] *Kä'admas bašagär*, 159:15-20.
[424] *Yäšoh aklil*, 92:25; cf. DTW, p. 145.
[425] *Yalačča gabəčča*, 126:4-6.
[426] *Mäskäräm*, 15:4-8, 16:5-12 (the whole of the first story in this collection deals with this belief); *Joro ṭäbi*, 123:9-124:6.
[427] *Yalačča gabəčča*, 134:9.
[428] *Adäfrəs*, 9:18, 328:11.
[429] *Fəkr əskä mäkabər*, 13:3, 47:10. (Cf. *Job*, ch. 3.)
[430] *Ib.*, 158:21-159:21, 164:12f., 296:9f.
[431] *Ib.*, 276:18-20; cf. 276:26-277:2.
[432] *Kä'admas bašagär*, 96:1ff.

That the umbilical cord is buried where one is born [433] may have a purely symbolic meaning: a boy's umbilical cord is buried in the house, signifying that he will stay at home, whereas a girl's is buried outside the house, signifying that she will leave the house at marriage. The characteristic Ethiopian ululation (əlǝlta) and clapping of hands on happy occasions [434] are also used differently when a child is born: five (or seven) times for a boy, two or three times for a girl.[435]

Among ideals mentioned are, for example: manliness and bravery, independence and self-reliance; [436] maturity and wisdom, and respect for age and authority; [437] hospitality and mutual help, especially as such help is organized in mutual help associations (such as əddər, wänfäl, giso, däbo, mahbär; see chapter III, 1); [438] respect for people's property and rights.[439]

There are many ideals of a more superficial kind, relating to correct behaviour, such as the correct way of greeting people, of eating, of sitting (men and women separately; women can sit with legs wide apart, but not girls), of dressing (men throw a corner of the näṭäla over the left shoulder, women over the right, etc.), of walking, of laughing, weeping, yawning, sneezing (and to say "grow!" when a child sneezes, and "May He have mercy on you!" when a grown-up person sneezes), of holding and using a stick, of dancing and playing of music, of painting, etc.[440]

The importance of ideals and customs is to give people an identity and a feeling of responsibility, in the opinion of Ato Ṭəso, an educated, but rather conservative judge:

> "What makes one say, "I have a country and a nation" are habits, traditions, heritage - and other customs we mentioned that stay with people, when their harmony brings beauty and authority

---

[433] Fəkr əskä mäḵabər, 53:16f., Yähəllina däwäl, 194:8ff., Tarikənna məssale, Book III, page following list of contents, ll. 9f. Cf. J. Doresse, La vie quotidienne...., p. 223.
[434] Fəkr əskä mäḵabər, 170ult.-171:1.
[435] C. H. Walker, The Abyssinian at Home, London, 1933, p. 1, J. Doresse, La vie quotidienne...., p. 222.
[436] Ṭälfo bäkise, 42:29, Mäskäräm, 102:16f., Fəkr əskä mäḵabər, 102:9, Käʾadmas bašagär, 143:20, Adäfrəs, 36:7f., 54:28-30, 78:8-16, Yähəllina däwäl, 58:1-3, Bälg, 69:21, Säw allä bəyye, 17:19f.
[437] Fəkr əskä mäḵabər, 111:29-32, Adäfrəs, 75:2-9.
[438] Yägəṭəm gubaʾe, 15:22-16:1, Adäfrəs, 10:22-24, 12:3-13, 74:11-15, Käʾadmas bašagär, 48:18, Joro ṭäbi, 6:6-12.
[439] Adäfrəs, 72:22-73:9.
[440] Adäfrəs, 65:17-20, 74:21-75:3, 75:14f.

- but otherwise you are without a country, without a guiding spirit you are not one who has a country or a nation." [441]

6. *Views on sickness and health*

The natural causes of ailments, with corresponding natural or "scientific" attempts at cures, are referred to only a few times in Amharic literature, except when modern Western medicine is concerned. A healer who deals with minor injuries, but also cases such as broken bones, is called *wägeša*.[442] Herbs, leaves, or roots are often used in combination with magic.[443] One of the commonest ways of seeking relief from any kind of suffering is to use "mineral waters", *ṭäbäl*, either for drinking or for bathing; but this water is regularly blessed by the church, and as "holy water" it is thought of as healing through driving out evil spirits who are regarded as the real cause of the ailment.[444] The *ṭäbäl* is said to be good for one who has gone mad, and it is supposed to purify the blood, polish the complexion, and cure illness.[445]

As people think that evil spirits cause illness, healing is a question of combating these spirits. The *däbtära* is consulted to find cures through the interpretation of his books, which often means books of astrology; and he frequently prescribes the wearing of a *kətab* covered with magic formulas.[446] Satan is thought to possess people sexually and give them epileptic fits, and epilepsy is called "Satan's infection", or, as slaves are believed to be particularly prone to attacks of this kind, the "slave's disease".[447] An epileptic should not be touched when he is having a fit to prevent others from being infected; likewise, people should not look at a sacrifice into which a disease-carrying spirit has been transferred, so as to prevent the spirit from attacking them.[448] Sickness is often regarded as a punishment by God because a person has done something wrong or neglected a religious duty.[449]

The different views on sickness and suffering, both causes and

---

[441] *Adäfrəs*, 76:12-16.
[442] *Yä'ənba däbdabbewoč*, 119:15, *Yäləbb hassab*, 172:10-12.
[443] *Bərr ambar säbbärälləwo*, 16:11f., *Adäfrəs*, 111:2, 126:6-10.
[444] *Adäfrəs*, 177:15-17, 179:1, cf. 209:24f.
[445] *Addis aläm*, 7:13, *Yalačča gabəčča*, 89:2-9, *Yähəllina däwäl*, 187:18-21, 188:7-10, 189:4f. 17-26.
[446] *Addis aläm*, 8:9ff., *Yäləbb hassab*, 172:10-173:3.
[447] *Yä'ənba däbdabbewoč*, 116:3, *Yäšoh aklil*, 38:9.
[448] *Adäfrəs*, 97ult.-98:3 (cf. the context, 97:18ff.).
[449] *Ib.*, 170:2f.11-19.

BELIEFS AND ETHICS 131

methods of relief are described in a scene where the suffering, but very religious Wzo Asäggaš discusses her illness with Gorfu, who asks her:

""And you, as for this rheumatic leg of yours - - what relief did you find for it - - - ?"
"What have I found for it? There is (i.e. I trust in and pray to) the Archangel [450] - - it gives me relief when I rub it with ashes of incense [451] burnt for him."
"There are so many healers, and still sickness is not eradicated - - -".[452]
"It is better not to raise the matter of the wise men, if you please - - All the kinds of writing that I have girded around my waist have passed over my shoulder [453] - - - how can one sort them out - - the *səmä amlak*,[454] the *təmərtä boʾat*,[455] the *asmatä Sälomon*,[456] the *čäbčäbe*,[457] the *gərma mogäs*,[458] that kind of writing on parchment as long as my body [459] - - - but what shall I tell you - - There is not a medicine said to exist that I have not tried - - -."
"Maybe it is because he (Michael) did not order the means of relief - - -."
"He did not order it - - - he did not order it - - - It is because he did not order it - - The Archangel (i.e. Michael) is displeased with me - - Maybe you remember last year, on his day, I had his day commemorated by slaughtering three head of cattle [460] - - inviting the clergy and *däbtära* of three churches. - How many influential people, secular and ecclesiastical, my beer and mead

---

[450] Here it refers to Michael, cf. 174:7-12.

[451] *əmmät* is (a) ashes of incense burnt in church and used as a cure by rubbing on the ailing part of the body, or (b) soil touched by the blood or the bones of saints, used in the same way.

[452] Literally "The wise man (healer) as his plenty (i.e. as there are so many of them), the non-disappearance of sickness (is surprising)—."

[453] This refers to the custom of covering parts of the body with parchment filled with sacred or magic texts to obtain a cure.

[454] Literally "The Name of God", a "book or written text sorcerers write according to their own thoughts" (DTW).

[455] Also *təmhərtä həbuʾat*, "The Teaching of Secrets", "a small book or text hung on the chest like a *kətab* and read during mass, containing portions of the Book of the Covenant" (DTW).

[456] Literally, "The magic of Solomon". Solomon is known, among other things, as "a capable magician, *awaḳi*" (DTW).

[457] *Čäbčäbe* stands probably for *čärčäbe*, which DTW calls a "*kətab* or magic text sorcerers write, as long as the human body".

[458] "A magic text, or *kətab*, high officials wear on their chest and forearms in order to obtain the king's favour and induce respect among the people; a means of obtaining favour, or becoming a favourite" (DTW).

[459] This may refer to the *ləfafä ṣədḳ*; cf. earlier.

[460] Literally "old head of cattle", the only cattle normally slaughtered in Ethiopia; it does not mean they are of inferior quality.

made shaky! - - You may remember, even the tent was pulled down on the third day.⁴⁶¹ - - I just cannot understand in what I have offended him (i.e. Michael). - Now, when I travel on my mule, in whatever direction he (i.e. a Michael's church) appears to me, I jump down without the help of a servant to greet him. - What Abba Addise says is also that "you have done nothing wrong, my child; it is his (Michael's) habit to repeatedly test those he loves - -". Well then, but what makes me wonder is that he does not desist when he knows I am his after having tested me again and again - - and what is more, it is even so that it is each Sunday (i.e. when I go to church) and each time that I prepare food and drink to celebrate a feast in his honour ⁴⁶² that the rheumatism is worst - - when I get up in the night and go to church and when I work hard from morning till evening, every time I make ready the beer and bread (for his feast) - - -. What does he tell me to contribute, then! At each of his yearly feasts - if they tell me (to give) wheat, (I give) wheat; if they tell me (to give) firewood,⁴⁶³ (I give) firewood; if they tell me (to give) candles, (I give) candles; if they tell me (to give) incense, (I give) incense; if they tell me (to give) a vestment, (I give) a vestment, - - Oh, even he (i.e. Michael himself) now does not know what he wants - -.""" ⁴⁶⁴

How the Christian religion and paganism try to solve the problems of sickness and health is dealt with in the discussion on religion.

Modern medical help is often difficult to find in the countryside, and many countrypeople have even been hostile to modern methods of treatment.⁴⁶⁵

---

⁴⁶¹ "Three head of cattle", "three churches" (above) and "the third day" are mentioned because three is a holy number.

⁴⁶² *Ṭäbäl ṭädik̯* refers to the beer and bread used on religious occasions, saints' days, at burials and memory feasts, at baptism and the Eucharist, and at *mahbär* gatherings. (Cf. DTW)

⁴⁶³ *Gad* or *mugad* is firewood for the church kitchen where the bread for the Eucharist is prepared.

⁴⁶⁴ *Adäfrəs*, 169:20-170:19.

⁴⁶⁵ *Adäfrəs*, 192:4, 202:24f., *Addis aläm*, 8:7f.

CHAPTER THREE

PRIVATE RELATIONSHIPS AND INDIVIDUAL LIFE

1. *Forms of social intercourse in the local community*

People of different ethnic and religious backgrounds mix fairly freely with each other on the local level of Ethiopian life.[1] In the family, however, the members usually form a closely-knit and frequently exclusive unit,[2] although it is both a custom and a duty to show hospitality to strangers, especially to travellers who have nowhere else to go, "God's travellers", or "black, i.e. unexpected, guests".[3] When a family is thrown out of their house to make room for an officer during the Italian occupation, Mäkonnən Ǝndalkaččäw (in *Almotkum bəyye alwašəm*) tells how they are received and accepted as members of the family by their neighbours.[4] Neighbours visit each other often, especially the women, to drink coffee and gossip about local events.[5] Abäba, in *Yä'ənba däbdabbewoč*, who has left her husband and child to live with a lover, is beginning to long for her home and remembers the good times there, such as the gatherings of the women of the neighbourhood to drink coffee:

> "She remembered the chats and the gossip of the coffee table, when neighbours were gathered, the snacks being munched, and the coffee being drunk from the first cup till the third, - what form and ceremony it had! ! As these coffee-gatherings made the village women pass their leisure happily, it cannot be denied that it sometimes meant their leaving their homes for too long."[6]

The men usually meet in the local bar, called "drinking houses", (*mäṭäṭṭ bet* or *mäšäta bet*), "beer house" (*ṭälla bet*) (with a tin on a stick outside to signify that beer is available), "mead house" (*ṭäj bet*) or, most commonly, "coffee house" (*bunna bet*), to drink, talk,

---

[1] *Adäfrəs*, 84:21f.
[2] *Fəḳr əskä mäḳabər*, 288:4-21.
[3] *Araya*, 317:26-30, *Yägəṭəm guba'e*, 15:22-16:1, *Bərr ambar säbbärälləwo*, 10:9, 13:23; *Bälg*, 118:2f.7f., 121:5.
[4] *Arrəmuññ*, 324:15-20.
[5] *Kä'admas bašagär*, 14:3-7, *Adäfrəs*, 70:20-26, 71:2.
[6] *Yä'ənba däbdabbewoč*, 78:11-17.

or visit the prostitutes,[7] or they meet more formally to discuss local affairs in the council, *šängo* or *mäjlis*.[8]

Bərhanu Zärihun gives a brief description of life in a bar:

> "It cannot be doubted that hostesses or workers in bars are often expert conversationalists and raconteurs. A bar-visitor needs to be adept at making assessments, jokes, and at flirting in order to be an appreciated habitué. The principal aim [9] of the drinking house is the animation of its entertainment. One can venture to say that a man who only gulps down his drink and goes away, as if he is muzzled, does not get a taste of it (i.e. the atmosphere of the bar). A hostess, however, on her part, has as her principal obligation to see to it that old customers do not flee, and also that new ones are added, and to please all the customers as much as she can. As she listens to gossip and jokes, is compassionate with those who tell of misfortunes, and is amused by those who tell jokes, she has to be deceitful, a flatterer, and compliant. It cannot be hidden that her one main duty is to provide (viz. sex) whenever it is desired." [10]

On Sundays, people go to church also for the purpose of meeting friends and relatives, and the young girls and boys to get a chance to look each other over, and after Mass they can partake in a gathering and meal outside the church, called the *sänbäte*; people who come to church festivals from afar can be fed at gatherings called *mərfak*.[11]

It is popular to have parties and invite many guests, with much food and drink. Earlier big banquets, *gəbər*, were given by the king and the nobility,[12] but this custom did not last very long after the Italian occupation. Parties, *dəggəs* or *gəbža*, are held on all national holidays, saints' days, at weddings, etc., and the more there is to eat and drink, the grander it is; singing and dancing are part of the entertainment and fun, sometimes with hired professional entertainers.[13]

---

[7] *Käʾadmas bašagär*, 95:7, 46:5-17, *Fəkr əskä mäkabər*, 394:4f., *Säw allä bəyye*, 64:22, *Yähəllina däwäl*, 83:13f., 95:10, *Yäšoh aklil*, 31:1f.
[8] *Adäfrəs*, 74:12, *Ṭälfo bäkise*, 48:23.
[9] *Alämu*, "the world", is probably a misprint for *alama*, "aim".
[10] *Yäʾənba däbdabbewoč*, 52:6-20.
[11] *Adäfrəs*, 168:22, *Fəkr əskä mäkabər*, 13:17, 42:4-7, 43:15ff., 87:14ff., 156:5-7., *Käʾadmas bašagär*, 56:23. See Habtä Maryam Wärkənäh, *Mahbärawi nuro bäʾityopəya*, pp. 20-28.
[12] *Araya*, 155:3-158:13, *Fəkr əskä mäkabər*, 81:2ff., 442:8ff.
[13] *Bərr ambar säbbärällawo*, 91:3ff., 98:12f., 102:1ff., etc., etc., *Adäfrəs*, 27:2ff., *Fəkr əskä mäkabər*, 81:5ff. See also the chapter on food and drink.

People organize themselves for mutual help during harvesting or when help is needed to build a house, etc.,[14] or in groups established both for social purposes and to help during times of trouble. Of these, the *mahbär* has a religious character, is dedicated to a saint, etc., and assists members particularly at burials and at times of privation.[15] The *əddər* serves also a social function of a less formal and non-religious kind and it assists its members when needed.[16]

It is regarded as important and a great virtue to be on good terms socially. A priest says it is "the wages of sin" when people "remain estranged and at loggerheads".[17]

2. Family life

In traditional society it is taken for granted that people want to marry, have their own place and have children.[18] The family come together and discuss their problems, especially questions of the family honour and when someone is to get married.

> "As it is said, "However thin, however weak family ties become, no blade can sever them", - however much Fitawrari separates himself from his relatives, having gone against their advice, and seeming to have made enemies and broken relations with them, - in the end, those family ties took his relatives, both near and distant, pulling them where he went!" [19]

The man is normally in control of his family and can beat his wife if it is necessary to remind her of that point or even to express his love for her;[20] but a widow can have great authority over her family, as for example Wzo Asäggaš in *Adäfrəs*, or Wzo Alganaš in *Yalačča gabəčča*.

In writing about family life, Ethiopian authors stress the im-

---

[14] *Adäfrəs*, 74:13, *Yähəllina däwäl*, 18oult.-181:3. See Korten, *Planned Change in a Traditional Society*, pp. 86ff.
[15] *Joro ṭäbi*, 6:6-12, *Adäfrəs*, 175:24-26, 178:3f., 198:5. Cf. Walker, *op. cit.*, pp. 121-129; Habtä Maryam Wärḳənäh, *Mahbärawi....*, p. 28-33.
[16] *Käʾadmas bašagär*, 48:18, 56:24, 73:19-23, *Yähəllina däwäl*, 29:16, *Bälg*, 64:18. Cf. Alemayehu Seifu, "Eder in Addis Ababa: a Sociological Study", in *Ethiopia Observer*, Vol. XII, No. 1, pp. 8-18 and 31-33, Habtä Maryam Wärḳənäh, *Mahbärawi...*, pp. 79-81, Korten, *op. cit.*, pp. 94ff., D. Levine, *Wax and Gold*, Chicago, 1965, pp. 277ff.
[17] *Adäfrəs*, 79:26f.
[18] *Fəḳr əskä mäḳabər*, 35:21f., cf. *Yäləbb hassab*, 131:19-24.
[19] *Fəḳr əskä mäḳabər*, 288: 4-10.
[20] *Joro ṭäbi*, 48:3-8; *Adäfrəs*, 73:4-7, *Yalačča gabəčča*, 135:7f., cf. 136:1-16. Cf. *Yäkärmo säw*, 42:8f.

portance of children. Boys are more appreciated than girls,[21] but the greatest misfortune is to have no children at all,[22] or to have children that do not perform their filial duties: parents of such children are called "those who have given birth and are (still as if they were) barren", *yäwälad mäkanoč*.[23] It is said with pride of a girl that "she is of a fertile family".[24] A child is the fruit and remembrance of love and happiness, a helper in old age, the one who buries the parents and inherits their property.[25] A childless mother will pray to God for a child, and may visit holy places to pray and make vows and drink holy water that is supposed to help barren women.[26] Children carry on one's name and are securities against problems of old age and sickness:[27]

"My child, my support, that will care for me and help me when my strength declines, when my eyes darken."[28]

The future of the children is mostly decided by the parents, and a child can, for example, be given to serve the Church, another to become a government official, some to inherit and carry on the work on the land of a landowner, etc.[29] During childhood, before a child "knows his soul", i.e. reaches maturity,[30] it stays close to the mother or a nurse, who in the first years carries it under her arm or on her back when working or travelling.[31] Children are first of all brought up to be obedient; they are frequently punished and must then promise not to make the same mistake again ("get used to it a second time").[32] A child that has not been punished and instructed becomes useless to its parents,[33] and it implies strong disapproval and reproach of someone's behaviour to say (in this case about a girl):

---

[21] *Arrəmuññ*, 283:26f.
[22] *Tarikənna məssale*, Book III, 1:1f. 9f.
[23] *Fəkr əskä mäkabər*, 37:31, chapter heading p. 47, *Kä'admas bašagär*, 22:19.
[24] *Yalačča gabəčča*, 42:1f.
[25] *Yä'ənba däbdabbewoč*, 11:14-17, *Yähəllina däwäl*, 56ult.-57:1, 57:6-9, 86:14.23.
[26] *Yä'ənba däbdabbewoč*, 11:18-20.
[27] *Fəkr əskä mäkabər*, 41:23, 48:1, 49:8f.
[28] *Ib.*, 31:11f.
[29] *Joro ṭäbi*, 5:2-5.
[30] *Fəkr əskä mäkabər*, 241:8, cf. 289:25.
[31] *Ib.*, 27:15-18, *Yäləbb hassab*, 172:2-4, 174:23ff.
[32] *Kä'admas bašagär*, 67:7-9, *Yalačča gabəčča*, 64ult., *Joro ṭäbi*, 49:3f., cf. 62:4f.
[33] *Tarikənna məssale*, Book III, 18:19-20:15.

"The one who brought her up has done her harm; she has gone unpunished, unpinched." [34]

A child should not talk too much, not look people straight in the eyes, but be shy, serious, careful and truthful.[35]

Children of course have their games and spend their time playing, although this is not considered a valuable part of a child's upbringing.[36] But early on they learn to take responsibility, for example as shepherds,[37] and at least one ideal is seen fulfilled in Araya's character because he as a child showed marks of the grown youth or man:

> "Araya was a child who by nature was full of straightforwardness and in whom already in childhood were seen diligence and ability. He had the desire to work hard to know and understand the cause of all he saw, which is mostly found in the minds of grown up people. Together with his mother's plan of upbringing to make his character serious and careful, it made him love truth." [38]

Meals are very much social affairs in the family, and children are both taught their subordinate position by being fed the leftovers after the others have eaten, and also love through often being fed by the hands of their parents; but some of these customs are dying out.[39]

Divorce has become more frequent in modern times [40] (cf. chapter III, 4, on sex and marriage).

Step-children are usually accepted by their "bread-father" or "bread-mother" as the step-parents are called,[41] but in some cases the plight of a step-child can be miserable, and some children escape from home for this reason; the story of *Kältammawa əhəte* is about such a child.

Servants are common in all households [42] (see chapter I, 1, on classes).

Blattengeta Həruy wrote *Yäləbb hassab* at least partly to lay the foundation for good marriages in the education of both husband

---
[34] *Țälfo bäkise*, 15:18.
[35] *Tarikənna məssale*, Book III, 10:12f., 16:22f., *Yä'ənba däbdabbewoč*, 19:17f., *Araya*, 16:9-11.
[36] *Kä'admas bašagär*, 66:21, 89:14f., *Adäfrəs*, 191:27f.
[37] *Tarikənna məssale*, Book III, 50:1-5.
[38] *Araya*, 16:5-11.
[39] *Adäfrəs*, 61:9-18.
[40] *Ib.*, 40:7-16.
[41] *Ib.*, 96:21-24, 199:4.
[42] *Ib.*, 61:23f., etc.

and wife and in the use of modern methods of child-care and upbringing. After the Italian occupation, the stability of the family was shaken, particularly as a result of urbanization and the increased use and temptation of money. This is a theme Bərhanu Zärihun is concerned with, for example, in *Yä'ənba däbdabbewoč* and *Amanu'el därso mäls*. It is also touched upon in one way or another by most Ethiopian authors, primarily as an aspect of life in the capital (see Part II of this book).

3. *Food and drink*

In an agricultural country like Ethiopia it is natural that much attention is paid to food, not only as a means of survival, but also for social and cultural reasons. The men spend most of their time producing food, the women in preparing it, and social life is largely spent eating and drinking, both at home and in public "food houses" or "drinking houses". The three stones where food is made signify the "home, hearth" (*sost guləčča*).[43]

Both *Araya* and *Adäfrəs* point out in several places the variety of Ethiopia's agricultural produce and potential. Otherwise, food is discussed and written about on many occasions and is probably the most important factor in all social and private life, as well as in the religious life of the people. The poor dream of food, especially fat food, such as butter, a sign of affluence.[44] In particular coffee drinking serves the social function of showing hospitality to neighbours at all times, and while one has to sit till the third cup is emptied, the local news and gossip can be shared.[45] Although one may refuse politely at the first offer to have something to eat or drink, it is impolite to persist in refusing.[46] It is a social obligation to give food to the poor and hungry, especially to "God's travellers" or "God's guests" who have no friends or relatives in a locality.[47] The basic food and drink, "grain and water", signify food and drink in general.[48] It is a question of prestige to supply an abundance of food and drink at a party or at any time when guests come.[49]

---

[43] *Lelaw mängäd*, 27:26, *Yähəllina däwäl*, 156:2.
[44] *Yalačča gabəčča*, 151:14f.
[45] *Mäskäräm*, 116:11f., *Yä'ənba däbdabbewoč*, 54:23ff., *Yalačča gabəčča*, 115:4ff.
[46] *Adäfrəs*, 273:22-274:16.
[47] *Fəkr əshä mäḳabər*, 509:7ff., 216:30, 536:5.
[48] *Fəkr əshä mäḳabər*, 22:5, 302ult., *Tarikənna məssale*, Book III, 52:15.
[49] *Yä'ənba däbdabbewoč*, 12:11-25, *Bərr ambar säbbärälläwo*, 25:2ff., *Araya*, 189:4-11.

When one has had one's fill, one can refuse to eat more by a polite phrase, e.g. "my appearance is enough to me",[50] but even then one is often fed by others who express concern, friendship or love through putting food into one's mouth.[51] The idea behind the great banquets practised in earlier times was that the rich should share with and provide for the poor and thus make them one big family, at least in the opinion of some nobles.[52] At the main meals (breakfast, lunch and dinner, and the odd coffee-break, maybe with something to eat) [53] different kinds of food and drink are served, but the greatest variety is provided on festive occasions. The fasting season has of course its special food, when no animal products are consumed by most of the people. The heaviest eating and drinking occur at annual holidays, weddings, and memorial celebrations for the dead,[54] and previously when the peasants brought in their tax or tribute in kind.[55]

The staple foods and drinks are stews (*wäṭ*), bread (*ənjära* or *dabbo*), coffee, beer (*ṭälla*) and mead (*ṭäj*); [56] but these are made in many forms and with many different ingredients for different purposes. The stew can be made with meat of different kinds, or with vegetables, or cereals, according to one's means or as the occasion requires, and with many or few spices.[57] During a fast, one can eat *kəkk wäṭ*, stew of coarsely ground split peas or beans, or *säljo*, stew of beans, mustard seed and garlic, *šəro wäṭ*, a mash of peas or beans, etc.[58] The poor may have to eat such stews out of necessity most of the time, together with other inferior kinds of stew, such as the *doyyo*, which is made without butter and spices, or *dokke*, which is a diluted variety of the *doyyo*, both made of beans or peas.[59] The stew is scooped up with the *ənjära*, which is mostly made of *ṭef*, a millet-like cereal (Poa abyssinica) which

---

[50] *Ṭälfo bäkise*, 18:24.
[51] *Kä'admas bašagär*, 59:19f.
[52] *Araya*, 158:10-13.
[53] *Fəḵr əskä mäḵabər*, 152:8, 83:17, *Amanu'el därso mäls*, 32:10, *Yäbädäl fəṣṣame*, 146:7f.
[54] *Yä'ənba däbdabbewoč*, 18:11-13, *Bərr ambar säbbärälläwo*, 25:2-36:20, *Joro ṭäbi*, 86:14-87:4, *Yalačča gabəčča*, 100:10-13, *Kä'admas bašagär*, 50:5f.
[55] *Fəḵr əskä mäḵabər*, 443:2-450:17.
[56] *Yäləbb hassab*, 134:13f.
[57] *Adäfrəs*, 95:22f.
[58] *Yäbädäl fəṣṣame*, 11:12, *Kä'admas bašagär*, 68:20, *Fəḵr əskä mäḵabər*, 210:10.
[59] *Yalačča gabəčča*, 88:18, *Adäfrəs*, 232:22, *Kä'admas bašagär*, 48:19, 148ult.

occurs in a number of varieties, and the lighter the *ənjära* is in weight and appearance, the better.[60] But poorer, darker kinds are common, and servants and poor people eat the *garre*, made of red sorghum and barley, or the *kəyyət*, which is made of a mixture of leftover ground grain from the mill.[61] The *ənjära* can be cut up and mixed with spiced stew (*fətfət* or *ənfərfər*); a small *ənjära* called *əngočča* is often used as provision on travels, and so is *çəbbəṭo*, made from *bässo*, a dough of ground roasted cereals (*ḳollo*) soaked in water, sometimes mixed with honey; the *bässo* is itself eaten by travellers and shepherds.[62] Dried strips of meat, *ḳwanṭa*, are also often used as provisions on journeys, and so is *ḳiṭṭa*, unfermented bread, and *dərḳoš*, dried and pounded *ənjära*.[63]

Some foods are used mostly at specific times, such as *ḳənče*, boiled cereals, mostly wheat or barley, and butter, for breakfast, and roasted cereals, *ḳollo*, or small roasted dough balls, *dabbo ḳollo*, which are often eaten (thrown into the mouth or slowly crushed after having been placed between the teeth) while one is waiting for the main dish or meal to be ready.[64]

On festive occasions, special kinds of chickens, sheep, goats, etc., may be required, the colouring depending on the season or the advice of "witch-doctors".[65] The festival of *buhe* occurs during a fast, so special bread is made, the *mulmul*, a small variety of the *ṭəbəñña*, a round bread.[66] Those who can afford it buy for example a bullock for a holiday, or several people buy one together and share the meat; a great amount of spices is also desirable to make the feast a memorable occasion.[67]

Besides coffee, the commonest drink is local beer, *ṭälla*, made mostly of barley, but also of sorghum or wheat.[68] It can be drunk unfiltered (then called *guš*), and also unfermented (*əmbušbuš ṭälla*);

---

[60] *Araya*, 157:13.
[61] *Yalačča gabəčča*, 88:18, *Adäfrəs*, 61:13.
[62] *Yalačča gabəčča*, 89:12, 126:17, *Yäbädäl fəṣṣame*, 75:1, *Bərr ambar säbbärälləwo*, 18:7, 23:1, *Fəḳr əskä mäḳabər*, 375:12.19, 502:3-10, *Yägəṭəm guba'e*, 37:19, *Arrəmuñň*, 289:1.
[63] *Yäbädäl fəṣṣame*, 53:1, *Fəḳr əskä mäḳabər*, 375:10-12, *Mäskäräm*, 39:20, *Adäfrəs*, 210:14.
[64] *Amanu'el därso mäls*, 76:5f., *Yalačča gabəčča*, 92:18, 115:5, *Fəḳr əskä mäḳabər*, 27:19ff., 375:9.19, *Bərr ambar säbbärälləwo*, 16:7f., 84:18f.
[65] *Kä'admas bašagär*, 54:16-21, *Adäfrəs*, 72:14-17; cf. DTW on *ḳallačča*.
[66] *Kä'admas bašagär*, 69:18f., *Mäskäräm*, 30:8.
[67] *Fəḳr əskä mäḳabər*, 290:6-8, *Kä'admas bašagär*, 78:11f., 94:8f., *Araya*, 157:17.
[68] *Yalačča gabəčča*, 128:13, *Adäfrəs*, 95:13, *Fəḳr əskä mäḳabər*, 348:24.

on the leftover dregs one pours water three times before they are thrown away; this drink is called ḳərrari.[69] More appreciated, as a drink for those who can afford it, is the honey wine or mead, ṭäj, especially when made from "white honey", i.e. very pure honey, and used on most festive occasions, sometimes unfermented, and then called bərz.[70] Distilled alcohol or arrack, aräḳe/aräḳi, is often made locally, and known as katikala or katikala aräḳe.[71] Some drinks are common at breakfast, such as the abəš, made from fenugreek seed, and the tälba, made from flax seed and sometimes mixed with honey; aṭmit and muḵ are hot soup-like drinks made from cereals, drunk mostly by sick people; but all can of course also be consumed at other times.[72]

Fruit, although plentiful, is not an important ingredient in the Ethiopian diet. The strict laws regulating what can be eaten and what not, or clean and unclean foods, are not subjects of concern to Ethiopian authors. But there occurs mention of the fact that Christians will only eat meat of animals slaughtered in a Christian way, i.e. in the name of the Father and the Son and the Holy Spirit, by a ritually pure man.[73] The food is normally eaten from a round basket-table (mäsob, ərbo, sädiḳ or lemat), and the ṭäj is drunk from a decanter-like glass called bərəlle, and the ṭälla ideally served in a horn cup, wanča, preferably the horn of a buffalo or ox, i.e. a kolba.[74] In the countryside mostly, the woman who serves the food may taste of it and pour some of the drink into her hand and drink it before she serves it up, to show that it is good and not poisoned.[75] Before and after a meal, water is brought so the participants can wash their hands.[76]

At the grand banquets, hundreds of guests used to be invited,

---

[69] Bərr ambar säbbärälləwo, 14:9.18, Yalačča gabəčča, 128:12, Fəḳr əskä mäḳabər, 262:28, 534:25, Əddəl näw? bädäl?, 54:24.

[70] Araya, 157:18, Adäfrəs, 12:18, 93:4, Yäbädäl fəṣṣame, 53:1, Yalačča gabəčča, 53:17, 128:12.

[71] Yä'ənba däbdabbewoč, 69:11, Yalačča gabəčča, 129:2, Əddəl näw? bädäl?, 43:5, 50:13.

[72] Yalačča gabəčča, 20:18, 92:18, Fəḳr əskä mäḳabər, 375:9, Ṭälfo bäkise, 45:4-7, Yäšoh aklil, 95:22.

[73] Adäfrəs, 103:4.

[74] Ṭälfo bäkise, 18:26, 58:29, Fəḳr əskä mäḳabər, 21:25, 150:28, 348:25, Adäfrəs, 30:29-31, 61:9, 95:5-7, Araya, 157:23, Bərr ambar säbbärälləwo, 15:21.

[75] Fəḳr əskä mäḳabər, 28:1f., 332:14-18.

[76] Araya, 157:10-12.

and the large tent or dining hall would be filled with guests several times.[77]

A banquet described in *Araya* is typical of a rich feast, although on a scale that has been reduced in recent years:

> "The hall was partly carpeted with different kinds of carpets, but towards the further end it was covered with grass and straw. Here and there were placed basket-tables covered in red (cloths). But down at the bottom, wickerwork tables lined up in a row and covered with white cloths were waiting. At the top, above the floor, a level place was screened off by a high curtain. Here and there along the walls of the hall, young servants were standing. Maids carrying saucepans and *ənjära* were passing in great haste. The usher called Araya, led him up to the curtain and saying to him, "Wait for me a moment", he entered inside the curtain. And immediately he heard the hoarse voice of the old man. While he spoke, saying, "But where is he? Let him in!" he opened the curtain for him. And when he entered, he saw many lords and ladies eating, sitting round basket-tables in groups of four and five. And the host was eating seated on a big pillow on a beautiful carpet, supported around him by red cushions. At his side, a fat, light brown ("red") lady was sitting. At his feet, facing the basket-table, a maid was standing with arms crossed in front of her. At her feet, about ten saucepans and dishes were lined up. Now and then she bends down and scoops up stew and places it on the basket-table in front of her master. And also the *ənjära* she selects and takes out of the basket-table in front of her and places it in front of each of them. And sometimes when her mistress orders her, not by words but by signs, she scoops stew into a bowl and, passing by the basket-tables near her, she distributes stew. A ten year old boy with hair cut like a tonsure holds a long white fly-whisk, and standing far to the side of the master, keeps the flies away. Also (groups of) two and three young boys stand watching, leaning against the wall in readiness. When they (i.e. the guests) eat, except for the sound of chewing and the swish of the fly-whisk and also the hoarse speech of the host, no other noise was heard." [78]

The greatest health problem with Ethiopian food, especially because of the custom of eating raw meat, is the common occurrence of tapeworm; the painful way of getting rid of it is by drinking *kosso*, a purgative drink made from the *kosso* tree (Hagenia abyssinica). One is encouraged to drink it by promises of good food later, in words like, "(You will get) chicken tonight", and after the bitter medicine is drunk, friends bring tasty food, "*kosso*

---

[77] *Fəkr əskä mäkabər*, 443:2-450:27, *Araya*, 157:22-158:2.
[78] *Araya*, 156:3-157:5.

supper".[79] The euphemism used to signify that someone has drunk *kosso* is the expression, "I have said goodbye to you", implying, "Don't be offended if I rush off without saying goodbye properly".[80]

The variety of food in Ethiopia has only been alluded to here. The social and cultural importance of food and drink takes precedence over most other aspects of the people's life. Even religious life is to a large extent a question of food (feasts and fasts). A semi-religious institution like the *mahbär* ends with the leader ("the Moses") saying to the one who will host their next meeting: "Who is in charge of the next gathering (literally "week")? May He cause eighteen (oxen) to be yoked up for you", i.e. may you have plenty of food and drink to offer us.[81] Similarly, most gatherings are judged successful or not in relation to the amount of the food and drink provided, and to how well it is prepared.

4. *Sex and Marriage*

In Ethiopian society everyone is expected to marry, and marriages are matters of concern to the whole community;[82] the idea that a man does not want to marry is, except for religious reasons, a novelty among some sophisticated people in the capital.[83]

Parents traditionally choose marriage partners for their children, but already in the 1930's Blattengeta Həruy advocated that the boy and the girl themselves should be allowed to choose and decide whom they want to marry.[84] It has also become customary that the young people themselves, especially the boys, suggest their views to their parents, and these then work out the formal arrangements for marriage.[85] Boys and girls have their meeting-places, such as the pond or river from which the girls fetch water, or "under (the protection of) the fence", close to the home of the girl.[86] A boy shows his feelings by courting the favour of the girl, by patiently waiting before the house or, if necessary, by abducting the girl, sometimes with the connivance of her parents.[87] Feasts,

---

[79] *Țälfo bäkise*, 29:29-31, *Adäfrəs*, 14:21-30, *Yätewodros ənba*, 48:22f.
[80] *Adäfrəs*, 14:23.
[81] *Ib.*, 175:24.26, 178:3f.
[82] *Bərr ambar säbbärälləwo*, 92:10f., *Yä'ənba däbdabbewoč*, 18:24-19:3.
[83] *Adäfrəs*, 146:1f.; cf. 40:13-17.
[84] *Yäləbb hassab*, 166:21-29.
[85] *Ib.*, 140:3ff., 141:14ff.
[86] *Adäfrəs*, 166:2-4, 171:19f.; 17:1-23:16.
[87] *Ib.*, 14:10-13, 275ult.-276:4.23, 277:1-3, *Fəkr əskä mäkabər*, 84:27-31, 87:5ff., 338:11ff., 383:22ff., *Yäbädäl fəṣṣame*, 33:1f. The whole play *Țälfo bäkise* is built round the idea of abduction.

especially weddings, are occasions for choosing partners and flirting with each other; often the girls take the initiative by showing their preference through signs:

> "At each wedding and each holiday celebration, when he was about fourteen years old, small girls used to look stealthily at him, and while faintly smiling at him when they passed him, they stepped slightly on his foot as if inadvertently, or pinched him lightly in passing; when they came and arrived in front of him, they dropped a lemon or a flower they had brought from afar, pretending to lose it, - when they showed him similar signs that were expressions of their choice, at that time Bäzzabbəh suddenly changed." [88]

A girl often throws a lemon to the boy of her choice, and if he catches it before it falls to the ground, or at least tries to, it is a sign that he responds favourably.[89] Ostentatious flirtations are frowned upon,[90] but there are ways of being "shy" in a flirtatious and still acceptable manner.[91] Sometimes love will be declared through a letter, occasionally in poetic form, and it may be handed personally to the girl, the written communication of love being preferred to the oral one.[92]

But even when a boy and a girl have made their own choices and become "lip friends", the parents may decide otherwise and marry the girl to someone else:

> "When we were together as lip friends, her parents suddenly married her off." [93]

The principle behind parents' choice is that their child should marry a partner of equal or better social standing:

> """...I thought it would make you happy that my thoughts turned towards marriage..."
> "Of course! Surely it makes me happy. But marriage, to make one happy, must be with an equal."
> "I don't understand..."
> "She is not your equal either by family or by upbringing. I have heard she is of poor family ("of broken bones")...".." [94]

---

[88] *Fəkr əskä mäḳabər*, 45:18-26.
[89] *Ṭälfo bäkise*, 59:31.
[90] *Araya*, 291:29-292:2.
[91] *Ib.*, 313:4.
[92] *Adäfrəs*, 78:20ff.; cf. *Yäfəḳər ṭora*, 25:9-27:5.
[93] *Kä'admas bašagär*, 174:9f.
[94] *Ib.*, 112:23-113:3.

PRIVATE RELATIONSHIPS AND INDIVIDUAL LIFE 145

The equality sought is one of family, wealth, and sometimes, in a modern context, education; love is not always asked for or possible where the partners do not know each other.[95]

"Wise men" (i.e. a sorcerer or a *däbtära*, or both) may be consulted before a partner is decided on.[96]

For Säblä Wängel's parents, it would be better if she remained unmarried than to marry someone inferior to her:

> "Rather than spoiling her family by marrying someone not her equal, it will not subtract from but rather add to her honour if she is called "one who remained unmarried because she could not find someone similar to her"."[97]

The age of marriage could be very young, as young as ten in some cases, but it has increased gradually. Blattengeta Həruy fought for raising the age of marriage for girls.[98] When a boy or girl is ready for marriage, he or she is said to have "arrived".[99]

A common prerequisite of marriage for a girl is that she is a virgin.[100] Bərhanu Zärihun has written a short story [101] about a girl who was returned to her parents because "the sign of honour, the red colour which is the sign of the way of the cross, of absolution (i.e. virginity) was not found in her".[102]

If a man violates a virgin it is equal to

> "putting her below humanity, having satisfied what his feelings demanded, having snapped the thread of her bread (i.e. the hymen whereby she could find a husband and be supported)".[103]

When Säblä Wängel reaches the age of twenty four, suitors refuse to marry her "by the ceremony of a virgin (i.e. of a first marriage)", which is expensive, and want to marry her by "the ceremony of divorce (i.e. of a second marriage)", which is comparatively inexpensive.[104]

---

[95] *Bərr ambar säbbärälləwo*, 19:13ff., 53:10f., *Yalačča gabəčča* 67:11-18; 48:6f., 49:11f.
[96] *Yalačča gabəčča*, 45:15f.
[97] *Fəkr əskä mäḳabər*, 86:29-87:1; cf. 85:4-87:2.
[98] *Yäləbb hassab*, 143:1-31; cf. *Yä'ənba däbdabbewoč*, 31:3, *Lelaw mängäd*, 33:26-28, *Əddəl näw? bädäl?* 31:20-25.
[99] *Fəkr əskä mäḳabər*, 89ult., *Yähəllina däwäl*, 57:3f.
[100] *Fəkr əskä mäḳabər*, 410:4f.
[101] *Bərr ambar säbbärälləwo*, pp. 94-108, esp. pp. 102ff.
[102] *Ib.*, 103:22-24.
[103] *Adäfrəs*, 54:11f.
[104] *Fəkr əskä mäḳabər*, 87:3-11, 88:4f., 99:20-100:2, 101:6, 138:10-22.

A proposal can come from the boy or young man directly: Araya proposes to Sərgutä without a go-between and rather abruptly;[105] Ṣähay Mäsfən gets a proposal of marriage the first day she meets Ləjj Alämu, and she responds by showing interest but asks for some time to think it over;[106] Gorfu proposes to Ṣiwäne, and she refuses him, without intermediaries,[107] etc.[108] But marriage agreements between boys and girls who have not seen each other are common; promises of marriage can even be made between families before the birth of any children.[109] Formal proposals of marriage are usually made through middlemen or go-betweens, *ammalaj* (or *gälagay*),[110] and the father confessor of one of the persons involved is often used in this capacity, together with a group of "elders", *šəmagəlle*; the main go-between is called *yänägär abbat*, meaning both "father of negotiations" and "father of troubles", i.e. peace-maker, and the couple can call on him to solve problems that may occur when they are married.[111] These middlemen are also used when the boy and girl have first agreed among themselves that they will marry.[112] After the families have agreed, they conclude a marriage contract, if possible in writing, including a stipulation of the dowry.[113] Another boy is not supposed to talk to or be friendly with a girl who is engaged to be married.[114]

To arrange a marriage is an involved process that proceeds through several steps, carefully spaced out. Such an arrangement is described in detail by Bərhanu Zärihun, and some extracts from his story will give an impression of how this process evolves. It may require three meetings between the families before agreement is reached and the contract is drawn up. Three men, including a priest, come to Balambaras Kənfu's compound to ask for his

---

[105] *Araya*, 311:3-13.
[106] *Ṣähay Mäsfən*, 20:5-9.
[107] *Yä'ənba däbdabbewoč*, 25:25-26:2, etc.
[108] *Adäfrəs*, 238:24f. ("Adäfrəs" in l. 25 must be a misprint for Gorfu), 241:14ff.
[109] *Ib.*, 121:29-122:1, *Bərr ambar säbbäralləwo*, 95:3-96:7.
[110] *Fəḳr əskä mäḳabər*, 85:25, 100:17 (cf. l. 11 and 278:6: *gälagay*).
[111] *Ib.*, 11:22-24, *Yalačča gabəčča*, 100:14ff., *Adäfrəs*, 124:22, 299:22, chapter 54 (pp. 298f.); cf. *Yä'ənba däbdabbewoč*, 10:23, 26:10 (*amač rämač*, "middleman, one who arranges a marriage, go-between").
[112] *Araya*, 312:20-30.
[113] *Ib.*, 312:32, *Bərr ambar säbbäralləwo*, 23:10f., 100:19ff., 101:24f., *Adäfrəs*, 304:16f., 306:1; cf. 46:23, 166:6f., *Fəḳr əskä mäḳabər*, 544:9.
[114] *Adäfrəs*, 150:5-7.

daughter in marriage.[115] He invites them into the house, and gradually they come to the point. He inquires about their business and the priest replies:

> "'To you we come on good business; whenever can it be said that a bad matter brought us, Balambaras? Even your cattle have never been impounded for straying!" When Ķes Wäldarägay got up, the two men also stood up with him.
> "Now then, by the Quick to help (i.e. St. George or God), sit down! What is the good of standing!" said the Balambaras, standing up from where he was sitting.
> "Ķäňňazmač Adäfrəsäw in Mwahit has a splendid son", said Ķes Wäldarägay.
> "I don't know the son, but as to the Ķäňňazmač, we grew up together", the Balambaras said, exaggerating.
> "He also does not ever separate you from his mouth (i.e. he always talks of you). Well then, he has sent us to beg, if it is not too bold, that you will give you child to be his child, seeking to be your relative, having chosen your to be father to his child", said Ķes Wäldarägay, combing his fly-whisk with his fingers. The Balambaras lowered his head and seemed to be thinking for a while. "As for this matter, now, who could be better for me than he? Who is closer to me than the house of Däjjazmač Ṭasäw? However, she is still a very small child. How can I separate her from the bosom of her mother?" he said, answering in the form of a question.
> "Now then, Balambaras! Even if she is your child, still that also will be her home! It is her mother's bosom (i.e. in the new place, too)", said the priest, waving his fly-whisk.
> "Well, that is so", said the Balambaras in a tired voice.
> "Well then! Ləjj Däggəfe, speak then, you too!" he (the priest) said, turning to the two men.
> "We think you are putting it well, Father", the first one replied.
> "Say, Balambaras. Tell us one thing (i.e. decide one way or the other) and then see us off. (Don't you realize) I am standing before you pleading as if to a *tabot*?" said Ķes Wäldarägay as if he was a bit angry.
> "Now then, may your enemy stand (pleading), Abba! But give me time to think of it all! Let her mother also hear about the matter", said the Balambaras.
> "But of course! May He honour you as you have honoured us. A great man is always great. As for us, we did not say it had to be finalized now. We did not fail to understand this! Well then, is it not better if we go after we have just today fixed a date when we can come back to know the decision?" he asked, turning towards the two men.
> "When is it convenient for you?"

---

[115] *Bərr ambar säbbärälləwo*, 3:17ff.

> "I have been thinking of going to Addis Abäba one of these days", said the Balambaras.
> "What about Abbo's day (i.e. the 5th) of the month after next, then?"
> After they had agreed about this, Ḵes Wäldaragay prayed, saying the Paternoster and ənnəbäl asra hulätt. . . . .".[116]

As Balambaras Kənfu is an impoverished nobleman, this is an extremely good offer; but decency and custom demand that he does not show himself too eager to conclude the matter. A couple of months later, on the day agreed upon, the middlemen, now increased to four, return. The Balambaras pretends still to hesitate because he has not had time to consult the rest of the family, and the priest takes him to task.[117] But the Balambaras finally agrees to give his daughter in marriage, and the priest again says some prayers; the day for signing the marriage contract is then agreed upon.[118]

For the third meeting, the bridegroom's father arrives with witnesses, in addition to the four middlemen of the last meeting:

> "On the Day of her (i.e. Mary's) entry (into the Temple) (i.e. on the 3rd) of the month of Nähase, when Ḵäññazmač Adäfrəsäw came, having added two men to the previous elders, seven men including himself, Balambaras Kənfu received them with five men including himself. After having come inside, they sat in silence, the bridegroom's party on one side, the bride's party on another side. Without anyone saying, "Let us rise", everyone rose again and stood up.
> "Get on with it, then!" the priest said to the Balambaras.
> "I give (literally "have given") my child Hamälmal to Ḵäññazmač Adäfrəsäw's son, to Ləjj Gobäna. And to this, Grazmač Ašäbbər and Ato Ǝndaylallu are my witnesses", said the Balambaras.
> "I receive (literally "have received") Balambaras Kənfu's daughter Hamälmal for my son, for Gobäna. And to this, Ḵäññazmač Säyfä and Ato Däggəfe are my witnesses", said Ḵäññazmač Adäfrəsäw, replying with the appropriate response (aṣäfa). Father Wäldaragay was made family arbitrator (yäzämäd dañña). Ḵäññazmač Adäfrəsäw took out a silver ring hanging from a silken neckcord and gave it to the Balambaras.
> Wäyzäro Ǝlfənäš gave a moderate feast to celebrate the engagement. It was not more than a big jar of beer, a wineskin of mead, a sheep and three chickens. She saved up for the main feast.

---

[116] Bərr ambar säbbärälləwo, 6:1-7:25. (ənnəbäl asra hulätt is a prayer said in the name of a number of saints.)
[117] Bərr ambar säbbärälləwo, 19:24-22:3.
[118] Ib., 22:4-23:13.

PRIVATE RELATIONSHIPS AND INDIVIDUAL LIFE 149

The wedding was fixed for the day when the feast of Cana of Galilee fell on a Thursday." [119]

The "decree of marriage" or "marriage contract" [120] can be of several kinds. As engagements can be "by custom, by ceremony, by elders", [121] marriages can be by "coronet and communion", "by eighty", or "by (temporary) contracts". [122]

The kind of wedding that takes place in church is fairly rare, though often referred to in Amharic literature. It is called to be married by "coronet", *täklil*, or "the ceremony of coronet", and the Eucharist is usually taken by the bride and groom during this ceremony (*ḳal kidan bäḳurban*) in which case the marriage is indissoluble.[123] Impressions of the ceremony celebrating this church wedding are sketched both by Blattengeta Həruy and by Bərhanu Zärihun,[124] and most fully by the latter in his book about different marriage customs in Ethiopia, *Bərr ambar säbbärällawo*.[125] The couple are dressed in a heavy cape (*mänṭola'ṭ*),[126] and the ceremony starts at dawn:

> "As dull rays began to penetrate through the panes of the windows and the roof, the priest entered, holding a censer, having tucked a book under his arm, and accompanied by two deacons, one holding a cross, the other a candle. Then he said a blessing, making the sign of the cross in the four directions in the name of the Father and of the Son and of the Holy Spirit, and opened the Book of the church wedding, decorated by a covering of brocade, on top of the lectern. After he had read two or three pages, he spread out a school register and asking their baptismal names, began to note them down."....[127]
>
> ... "The priest at one time prays in a whisper, at other times he reads in Geez in a loud voice, then he mumbles in Amharic, then suddenly he bursts into chant, then the deacons join in, and while the head deacon, who is holding a cross, is leading the chant and the priest is swinging the censer, they go round the sanctuary and return......".[128]

---

[119] *Bərr ambar säbbärällawo*, 23:20-24:18.
[120] *Adäfras*, 46:23, *Yä'ənba däbdabbewoč*, 72:6.
[121] *Yä'ənba däbdabbewoč*, 72:7f.
[122] *Ib.*, 79:11, 72:11f.
[123] *Araya*, 291:28, 312:31, *Bərr ambar säbbärällawo*, 78:22, *Yäləbb hassab*, 168:5.10.12, *Fəḳr əskä mäḳabər*, 548:3-549:13, *Adäfras*, 74:18, 46:30-32, 50:20.
[124] *Yäləbb hassab*, 168:12-28, *Yä'ənba däbdabbewoč*, 31:26-32:8.
[125] *Bərr ambar säbbärällawo*, 79:7-82:18.
[126] *Ib.*, 81:10.
[127] *Ib.*, 79:7-16.
[128] *Ib.*, 79:20-25.

"......after a long time, their rings were blessed, and both stood before the priest, having been crowned with coronets that could break the neck because of their weight.

"Do you want this man to be your husband according to the rite of the Ethiopian Monophysite Orthodox Church?" she was asked.

"I do", she replied.

"Do you want this woman to be your wife according to the rite of the Ethiopian Monophysite Orthodox Church?"

"I do", said Həruy without hesitating.

"When you say she is old, she is weak, or if she is in want, if she is grey ("white"), you must not leave her", he said, continuing the threat of excommunication; and when he said, "if her eyes run (i.e. if she becomes blind), if her arm is broken (i.e. if she is maimed)", Həruy cringed." [129]

"After that, they placed one hand over the other and took the oath not to separate one from the other, neither in body nor spirit, until death separated them. He put the ring on her finger. She put the ring on his finger." [130]

Then they attend Mass, a final "prayer of blessing" is read, and they kiss the cross and leave the church, with the priest accompanying them with his blessing: "May He bless you. May He multiply your seed as the stars in the sky, as the sand of the sea. May He make your house rich as the house of Abraham", and then he asks for alms; this priest also becomes the father confessor of the couple.[131] If communion is taken, it is at the end of Mass; after Mass the couple and the clergy may go round the church.[132]

This ceremony probably continues an old Semitic tradition that is similar to the one described in the Song of Solomon, where the couple also are "king" and "queen" for the duration of the wedding celebrations.[133]

Civil marriage agreements, although more common, are mentioned more briefly. One kind specifies that husband and wife shall have all their property in common; it is called "your property by my property", *kabtəš bäkabte* or *habtəš bähabte*, and it means that "if you obtain anything by means of my property, and if I obtain anything by means of your property, what we obtain we have in

---

[129] *Bərr ambar säbbärällawo*, 80:9-23.
[130] *Ib.*, 81:1-3.
[131] *Ib.*, 81:7f., 82:1-6.13, cf. *Addis aläm*, 35:18-22.
[132] *Yäləbb hassab*, 168:22-28.
[133] Cf. B. B. Trawick, *The Bible as Literature: The Old Testament and the Apocrypha*, New York, 2nd ed., 1970, p. 289.

common, between us there is no private property".[134] It is an oath taken in front of a local judge,[135] and the man and woman declare, "You are my wife" and "you are my husband", and he says, "By your property, by my property", and she says, "by your shield, by my spindle" (i.e. what we get, we have together), and they become man and wife.[136]

The marriage by "eighty", sämanya, is the most common form of civil marriage.[137] In this case, the husband and wife keep what they bring into the marriage as their private property, and the contract is usually concluded in the name of the king. [138]

Short-term salaried marriages are also common. A woman is hired as a servant and is paid for her work, while being also sexually available to her master. Such an arrangement can be referred to as a "marriage" contract "by hire", bäkəṭər, or for a salary, dämoz; or a girl is hired to be "maid of the thigh", yäčən gäräd, with the same implications.[139] Especially among the poor, very free sexual relationships are common.[140]

These temporary "marriages" are often contracted by men who stay away from home for some time, and the temporary "wives" can be taken in addition to the wife they may have at home. Therefore the "wives" in such marriages are sometimes referred to as "mistresses" or "concubines".[141] Concubinage is not uncommon, but as it costs money, it is particularly common among the wealthy and the nobility.[142] Fitawrari Mäšäša maintains it is "the custom of nobles" to "place concubines in several houses", and one of his relatives replies that "I know that it is a fact that all nobles do this".[143] The Fitawrari himself, although he is about seventy years old, has several "concubines" or "maids of the thigh", and his wife is called "the main wife"; but he has also a favourite among

---

[134] DTW, p. 402.
[135] Ṣähay Mäsfən, 7:7f.
[136] Ṭälfo bäkise, 60:10f.
[137] Yä'ənba däbdabbewoč, 72:11, Arrəmuññ, 111:15, Yähəllina däwäl, 156:1.
[138] Cf. Laketch Dirasse, Survival Techniques of female migrants in Ethiopian urban centres, paper submitted to the International Congress of Africanists, 3rd session, Addis Ababa, December 1973, p. 11; see also DTW, p. 1186.
[139] Yä'ənba däbdabbewoč, 72:11, Laketch Dirasse, op. cit., ibid., Yalačča gabəčča, 96:1f., Fəkr əskä mäkabər, 277:30-278:14.
[140] Fəkr əskä mäkabər, 309:28-310:10.
[141] Ib., 277:30-278:14.
[142] Ib., 113:5-15.
[143] Ib., 113:16-23.26-29.

his concubines.[144] Marital unfaithfulness is not only committed by men: Fitawrari Mäšäša's wife has as a lover, "equal to a husband", a "head of the *däbtära*", and her love is ascribed to "her vulgar love, her lust", or to "her addiction".[145]

A *ḵubat/əḵubat*, "mistress, concubine", or a *ṭawənt* or *gobban*, "lover of a married person",[146] can have a respectable position, but the mistress who is hired only to supply sexual services with no rights except to be paid a stipulated regular fee, the *wəšəmma*, is looked down upon.[147]

The wedding feast takes place after the church wedding, but when the marriage is civil or secular the couple are married as part of the festivities. It is usual that the bride shows her sadness at leaving her parents' house, and she often weeps on her wedding day, and she will thus suppress manifest signs of joy and happiness.[148]

Before the wedding day, much work is needed to prepare the food and drink, the tent, and the house for the bride and groom. For the couple's mothers in particular this is a busy time, but the whole family joins in the preparations.[149] Relatives, far and near, and all friends and neighbours will normally be invited to, and expected to attend the wedding, and weddings thus often become very expensive, a custom Blattengeta Həruy tried to change.[150] Both the tent, *das*, where the feast is held and the couple's new house, *ǯagula bet*, are strewn with fresh-smelling grass or reeds, *ḵeṭäma*.[151] The main helpers during a wedding are the bridegroom's three best men, the "head" or "main" best man, the "foot" or "junior" best man, and one other.[152] The size of the dowry is stipulated before the wedding day, but as it is unknown except to a few, and because it may be added to on the wedding day, the giving

---

[144] *Fəḵr əskä mäḵabər*, 277:28-278:23.

[145] *Ib.*, 312:15-17, 320:18-20.

[146] *Ib.*, 401:24, *Bälg*, 116:3, *Yähəllina däwäl*, 21:9, *Čäräḵa sətwäṭa*, 56:3, 57:1.

[147] *Arrəmuññ*, 176:14-16, *Yä'ənba däbdabbewoč*, 58:16.

[148] *Ṭälfo bäkise*, 25:22-24.

[149] *Bərr ambar säbbärälləwo*, 24:24-25ult., *Adäfrəs*, 292:2-5, 298:20-23, *Fəḵr əskä mäḵabər*, 477:8-478:2.

[150] *Fəḵr əskä mäḵabər*, 478:6-13, *Bərr ambar säbbärälləwo*, 25:2-36:20, *Yäləbb hassab*, 166:14-16, *Kä'admas bašagär*, 21:4-7, *Yähəllina däwäl*, 100:8-113ult.

[151] *Yäləbb hassab*, 169:8-10, *Ṭälfo bäkise*, 8:15f.

[152] *Ṭälfo bäkise*, 11:21f., *Bərr ambar säbbärälləwo*, 65:25-27, 71:22, 72:2, 73:1, 102:20, *Yä'ənba däbdabbewoč*, 36:6f.

of the dowry is a moment of excitement and reflects social status and sometimes the "value" attached to the bride and the family connection.[153] The bride is fetched from her house and brought to the bridegroom's house, and the main meal is given in a tent erected for the occasion.[154] There is heavy eating and drinking, singing and dancing. The songs are composed and sung by guests and hired minstrels, and they are often lewd.[155] Ethiopian love songs and music are mostly nostalgic, called "murmurings" and "memories".[156] Towards the end of the celebrations, the test of the bride's virginity comes, and if the sheet is coloured red by her blood, the guests sing a song to the bride's parents, beginning, "He (i.e. the bridegroom) broke a silver bracelet (i.e. an unbroken hymen) for you", acknowledging the validity of the marriage;[157] in cases where the bride does not show signs of virginity, she may be returned to her parents.[158] After the wedding, the newly-weds spend a few days in their new home,[159] and then, a few days or about a month later, a "return" party, *mäls* or *məllaš*, is given by the girl's parents. This party is ideally on the same scale as the wedding party, but is often a more modest affair.[160] Bərhanu Zärihun gives full descriptions of both a wedding feast and a "return" party, although the second is a subdued affair, because the girl is about to be left with her parents because she was not found to be a virgin.[161]

Married life as such is not much described, and the glimpses we get are dealt with in chapter III, 2, on family life.

Divorce seems to be easy for those who have married according to a "secular" marriage ceremony, and it is on the increase,[162] but

---

[153] *Bərr ambar säbbärälləwo*, 30:1-32:17, *Adäfrəs*, 124:28f.; cf. 104:26, *Fəkr əskä mäkabər*, 401:4-10, *Yä'ənba däbdabbewoč*, 33:4.

[154] *Yä'ənba däbdabbewoč*, 32:14-16.

[155] *Addis aläm*, 35ult.-38:22, *Yäləbb hassab*, 170:1-4, *Bərr ambar säbbärälləwo*, 26:14f., 27:10-14.16-21, 32ult.-33:12, 34:10-16.23f., *Yähəllina däwäl*, 83:11-13; cf. Taddäsä Mulat, "Bäsärg zäfänoč wəst yämmittayyu yamarəñña gətəmoč, in JES Vol. VIII, No. 2 (July 1970), pp. 155-170.

[156] *Adäfrəs*, 45:30f., 79:14.

[157] *Bərr ambar säbbärälləwo*, title of story, p. 71, song quoted p. 93:22-26, cf. *Yä'ənba däbdabbewoč*, 34:4-7.

[158] *Bərr ambar säbbärälləwo*, 102:1-108ult.

[159] *Yäləbb hassab*, 170:11-13.

[160] *Yä'ənba däbdabbewoč*, 31:15f., *Bərr ambar säbbärälləwo*, 36:21ff., 37:2, *Fəkr əskä mäkabər*, 480:12f., *Yähəllina däwäl*, 71ult.

[161] *Bərr ambar säbbärälləwo*, 25:2-37:2, *Yä'ənba däbdabbewoč*, 32:14-34:10.

[162] *Yalačča gabəčča*, 99:13-15, *Arrəmuññ*, 111:15f., *Adäfrəs*, 40:7-12, 107:1-4, 107:23-108:3.

many, especially women, stay with their marriage partners out of necessity, as there are not many alternatives to marriage or prostitution for women in Ethiopia. The result for a woman is often that

> "her heart being overcome by (her need for) bread (i.e. support), she remains (with her husband) while she is being mistreated." [163]

Sexual relationships between unmarried people are not expected to take place, so when a girl is not a virgin, there are rumours of "demons" and "baboons" who violate virgins, or possibly rape by "shepherds and farmers".[164] If girls have sexual experience before marriage, they regularly end up as prostitutes; this is dealt with in the next section, on the position of women in Ethiopian society. In towns, and especially Addis Ababa, sexual mores are more relaxed, and there are also greater opportunities for women; cf. Part II of this book. Men have always had greater freedom than women in this respect.

5. *The position of women*

Ethiopian women can be independent, achieve high position and regard, and be honoured for their personal contribution to the family and to society; but on the whole they are at a disadvantage when compared with men.

The news of the birth of a girl is normally not received with so much joy as the birth of a boy.[165] Not so much is normally invested in the education of girls as in the education of boys, but when they are sent to school, they are as a rule taught the same as boys, but in addition also some handicrafts.[166] The "value" of a woman is thought to increase with her ability, and she is encouraged to learn to work.[167] A home without a woman is not regarded as a proper home at all, as the proverb says, "*Ǝnjära* without *wäṭ* (is like) a home without a woman (or) a cattleshed without cattle".[168] A great compliment is paid to the work and skill of women in the proverb, "When no rain comes, everywhere is a house; when no guest comes, everyone is a woman", which means, "During the

---

[163] *Adäfrəs*, 52:20f.
[164] *Ib.*, 147:8-29, 171:24f.
[165] *Arrəmuññ*, 283:26f.; cf. *Adäfrəs*, 49:3.
[166] *Yäləbb hassab*, 136:25ff., 138:17-22 (cf. 139:11-18).
[167] *Tarikənna məssale*, Book III, pp. 13-15, esp. p. 15:16-18.
[168] *Ib.*, 15:20f.

dry season, one can stay and sleep everywhere, even in the open; when no guest comes, no special skill is needed, but when guests come, women get a chance to show their superior skill in making food and looking after the guests".[169]

Girls may in some cases influence the choice of husbands for themselves, but usually this is done by the parents without consulting the children, and the girls least of all.[170] Widows and divorced women, on the other hand, mostly make their own choices whether they will marry or not, when a man proposes.[171] Girls may develop a high degree of independence and may refuse to accept what their parents or guardians decide for them and may even flee from home. In that case, they have few options in their fight for survival. A few may choose to become nuns,[172] but mostly they end up as prostitutes, the luckier ones after a stay with a "husband" who asks them to stay with him without marriage. After some time, these latter women are usually thrown out by their lovers and start the process of decay and further degradation, which for example is the story of Abäba in *Yä'ənba däbdabbewoč*.[173]

Wives are often listened to and respected by their husbands, both for their contribution to the family and the home, and for their opinions.[174] A husband who went through a lot of difficulties, says of his wife, "The one who saved me from destruction and decay was Ṣəggenäš (i.e. his wife)".[175] *Amanu'el därso mäls* tells of a man who left his wife and home and spent a fortune on drink and women and ends up in a mental hospital. When he finally gets out and returns to a normal life, it is with the help of his wife.

Wives can keep as their own the property they bring into the marriage [176] and can inherit from their fathers and their husbands and be trustees of their children till they come of age,[177] and can manage their affairs capably and with authority.[178]

---

[169] *Adäfrəs*, 8:16f.
[170] Cf. previous section on sex and marriage.
[171] *Adäfrəs*, 36:2-20.
[172] *Ib.*, 301:7, 302:19f., 307:24-27, 311:5, 329:29-31; cf. *Arrəmuñ̃*, 71:6ff., 72:26-73:2, 74:9-13.
[173] Cf. also *Adäfrəs*, 292:10-12, 322:17f.
[174] *Yäləbb hassab*, 134:11-17.
[175] *Yäbädäl fəṣṣame*, 89:11f.
[176] Cf. previous chapter, on the marriage by *sämanya*, "eighty".
[177] *Addis aläm*, 11:13-16, *Adäfrəs*, 177:4-7; 93:1-15; 36:32-37:6.
[178] *Adäfrəs*, 29:1-8, 93:1-94:10, 104:10f.; cf. 8:16f. Wzo Alganäš in *Yalačča gabəčča* is a lady of the same kind as Wzo Asäggäš in *Adäfrəs*.

Divorce is rather easy for men,[179] but women, although they can divorce, often stay with their husbands even when they would like to leave, because they have nowhere to go, or because they need their husbands simply to survive:

> "I cannot drop everything (literally "my cloth") and go, because I have nowhere to go. I have no education. My poor parents have passed away." [180]

Wealthy women have of course much greater freedom of action and choice, and many women therefore regard wealth and good family a much more important asset than love in their choice of husbands; security is what they seem to seek in the first place.[181]

A woman who chooses to live alone, without a husband or lover, is often slandered, as such a situation is not usual:

> "As for me ..... and I ..... that you live in purity, sleeping alone, embracing your own knees here in this empty house ..... that I know, but what good is it that I alone know this? The cure for all this, what will stop the mouths of the back-biters, what will restore your broken heart, what will do all this is just what I told you now, it is to get married. You see, Əmmät Wəddənäš, what can conquer the grief of (the loss of) one husband, is to marry (another) husband." [182]

Poor widows or divorcees, and girls who lose their virginity without marrying, most often become prostitutes unless they can find a husband [183] (although modern towns of course offer other alternatives; cf. Part II of this book).

Towns in particular develop their areas where prostitutes are plentiful: [184]

> "He continued his search with great diligence. He went round the whole area, (all the places) one by one. He went through Wəbe Bäräha in detail. He searched Gädam Säfär carefully. He asked everywhere in Doro Manäkiya. Särratäñña Säfär, Ǝrri Bäkäntu, Hakim Bora, Addis Kätäma, Churchill Road, - he did not leave out a single area said to be a living area for prostitutes." [185]

---

[179] *Addis aläm*, 30:1-3, *Yalačča gabəčča*, 99:13-15.
[180] *Kä'admas bašagär*, 6oult-61:2. Cf. *Adäfrəs*, 52:12-27.
[181] *Yalačča gabəčča*, 48:3-7, 49:11f., *Adäfrəs*, 36:9-11.
[182] *Fəkr əskä mäḳabər*, 12:16-23.
[183] Cf. *Adäfrəs*, 54:11f., *Yähəllina däwäl*, 24:5-7, 58:4-9, 87:8, 94:3, 95:4, 99:14.
[184] *Amanu'el därso mäls*, 32:4-7.
[185] *Yä'ənba däbdabbewoč*, 126:12-18.

They have areas where they walk about trying to attract customers;[186] and they develop their own styles:

> "However, this characteristic of hers that did not agree with the policy of the modern prostitutes did not harm her much. A few men who preferred the shy to the sophisticated, the bashful to the brazen, used to visit her. Except for a few, many were generous to her. She had the gift to be liked by men."[187]

Women may choose to become prostitutes in the hope of finding an easy, affluent life,[188] but in most cases they have little choice. The luckier or prettier ones may become mistresses of different kinds: "concubines", a maid-mistress or "maid of the thigh", or a paid mistress that is available on agreed days.[189] Those who have some money, which they might have accumulated as successful prostitutes, may open their own bars and hire barmaid-prostitutes to work for them.[190]

Kältammawa əhəte by Abbe Gubäñña tells the story of a girl who runs away from home because she is mistreated by her stepmother. She finds a man to live with, and when he is tired of her, she goes to others, and finally she ends up at the lowest level of prostitution, living alone in a poor shack and a poor area, getting few customers at low prices, suffering from mistreatment and illness.

Bä'alu Gərma gives us in one of his novels an impression of how women in a brothel are treated:

> "When Abärra had chosen a quiet house and entered quickly, Haylämaryam entered after him, holding the whisky bottle by the neck.
>
> As Abärra had expected, there was nobody except four women. It was difficult to distinguish one from the other in the red light. Two were dressed in national dress, the others were dressed in very short skirts that fitted tightly around the body. Abärra chose a woman whose hips were broad and who did not seem as listless as the others when he entered, and while saying, "One who hesitates gets nothing", he took her hand and dragged her inside (to the bedroom). The others skinned her out of envy. The other three

---

[186] *Yä'ənba däbdabbewoč*, 97:10-99:16.
[187] *Ib.*, 98:21-27; cf. 95:17-23.
[188] *Adäfrəs*, 39:23-25.
[189] *Fəḵr əskä mäḵabər*, 113:8.16-23.26-32, 277:30-278:14, *Yäšoh aklil*, 74:24-29; *Yalačča gabačča*, 96:1f., *Arrəmuññ*, 176:15, *Yä'ənba däbdabbewoč*, 58:16.
[190] *Amanu'el därso mäls*, 25:10-17, *Čäräḵa sətwäṭa*, 87:11.

women surrounded Haylämaryam and attacked him; "Elder brother (gašše), you ..... what can we offer to you then?" they started saying to him....."[191]

Women usually go to a place where they are unknown if they want to start as prostitutes; that is why one suggestion for reducing prostitution is to return the women to the places where they came from.[192]

The impression we get from much Amharic literature is that Ethiopian women are often confronted by situations and choices that force them into denigration and humiliation, and abuse by men, especially by men with wealth.[193]

In some cases authors prefer to write about girls and women who are very much in charge of themselves and, as it seems, their own destiny. This is for instance the case in Mängəstu Lämma's two plays. Taffäsäč, the "heroine" of *Ṭälfo bäkise*, does not submit to the plan of some young men but makes up her own mind; so does Bällätäč, the girl Bahru has secretly married, in *Yalačča gabəčča*, and Bahru's strongwilled aunt, Wzo Alaganäš, yields in admiration to Bällätäč, who wins in the end. But Wzo Alganäš herself is a woman clearly used to being in command and to managing most situation. Bərhanu Zärihun describes women that fall far when they do fall; but also women of the highest character who are stronger than their husbands and help them out of their direst predicaments, the latter kind in *Amanu'el därso mäls* and *Yäbädäl fəṣṣame*, the former in *Yä'ənba däbdabbewoč*.

---

[191] *Kä'admas bašagär*, 46:5-17.
[192] *Adäfrəs*, 40:2-5.
[193] E.g. *Yä'ənba däbdabbewoč*, 62:1-20, *Bälg*, 57ult.-58:1, 73:12. Cf. Laketch Diressa, *op. cit.*, pp. 1-14, R. Pankhurst, "The history of prostitution in Ethiopia", in JES, Vol. XII, No. 1 (January 1974), pp. 159-178. See also Ǝnanu Agonafər, *Setäñña adari*, Addis Ababa, 1956 E.C.

CHAPTER FOUR

NATIONAL CHARACTERISTICS: HOW ETHIOPIANS SEE THEMSELVES

No attempt will be made here to draw conclusions or make generalizations concerning the national characteristics of Ethiopians on the basis of a general review of Amharic literature. Such generalizations are hardly ever correct, and of little value. But it is of some interest to note what image some Ethiopians have of themselves and of the Ethiopian national character.

Not many statements of this nature have been made by Ethiopian authors, and when made, are regularly expressed by some character in their fictional work and may not necessarily be the view of the author. As could be expected, such remarks occur mostly in *Araya* and in *Adäfrəs*, as these novels deal with questions that relate to the whole Ethiopian nation.

It seems that the Ethiopians are *a religious people* and regard themselves as a chosen nation. The quotation from Psalm 68:31 occurs frequently and reads in Ethiopian versions: "Ethiopia stretches, or shall stretch, her hands out to God".[1] A priest talks about Ethiopia as "our holy land",[2] and the author of *Araya*, Gərmaččäw Täklä Hawaryat, seems to express as his opinion:

> "Until today Ethiopia has put her trust in her prayers and in God, but has she ever boasted of her power? Whenever did her enemies leave her in peace? No, all this time God has not abandoned her but kept her all along, placed her by herself, given her honour among the peoples of Africa and Asia. This is certain, this is the unshakable faith of all Ethiopians."[3]

Ato Ṭəso says that "the Ethiopian people, whether they are Muslims, Christians or pagans, are all God-fearing";[4] and Ato Wäldu says that "most Ethiopians" live by maxims such as, "having done good, having fulfilled all God's commands, having

---

[1] *Araya*, 346:1, 348:11; *Adäfrəs*, 100:16, *Yähəllina däwäl*, 18:10f., 173:22, 178:18
[2] *Araya*, 275:11.
[3] *Araya*, 231:16-22; cf. 229:3-6, 232:24f.
[4] *Adäfrəs*, 263:26-28; cf. *Araya*, 41:10.

entered the kingdom of the heavens, I shall live (forever)",[5] and that "the Ethiopian people believe more in miracles than in logic (the intellect)".[6]

The views Ato Ṭəso and Ato Wäldu express are not shared by them, but they believe their statements are valid for the majority of the Ethiopian people.

The Ethiopians are also a very *patriotic nation*. They refuse to be ruled by foreigners [7] and take great pride in their history of freedom.[8] Gərmaččäw Täklä Hawaryat quotes with approval from De Lamartine that "he who keeps silent when he sees permanent (or fundamental) interests suffering (or in abeyance) or in danger betrays not only the truth, but also his country".[9] Araya observes his people's patriotic fervour with great admiration.[10]

Ato Ṭəso says to Adäfrəs:

> "I must not forget the spirit of the people, although it maybe seems rather misguided to me, that when they know their goal, they will pursue it with determination. Tell them that "someone has come to attack your religion - your property - your land", - they will rise up, taking up their shields, shaking their spears - : they have an aim. Tell them that "someone who poisons the water you drink, who destroys the grain you sow - a civilization that will not let you sleep when you come tired to your house has come against you" - they will rise up, grasping their guns with blood-shot eyes - : they have an aim." [11]

The Ethiopians have great respect for authority, and their society is *a patriarchal society*.

Ato Ṭəso again gives his views on the character of the people: they show respect for other people, especially for the authorities and superiors "who protect our rights", comprising the father in the family, the clergy in the church, and government officials who "serve as guarantee for a peaceful life".[12]

This respect for and obedience of authority is first of all directed towards the Emperor, whom the people trust to protect their country and lead them in war and peace.[13]

---

[5] *Adäfrəs*, 157:25-28.
[6] *Ib.*, 156:10f.
[7] *Araya*, 317:22.
[8] *Ib.*, 319:8-25.
[9] *Ib.*, 45:1ff.
[10] *Ib.*, 231:27-232:13.
[11] *Adäfrəs*, 89:20-27.
[12] *Ib.*, 72ult.-73:9; cf. 153:1-12.
[13] *Araya*, 168:1f.10-21, *Yähəllina däwäl*, 177:24-27, *Adäfrəs*, 112:15f.

Ato Ṭəso, who seems to have the inclination to interpret the Ethiopian national spirit, says that the people have a strong *desire for justice*:

> "What the Ethiopian people want is true justice. - Without it, land, property, religion are of no interest to them - -. If the land is overgrown with weeds, if friend or enemy tramples their property, even if they enter the fire of hell - Sheol - because of their faith - they don't care. - But from the time they believe they have failed to obtain truth (i.e. justice), till the day they get it ("till the day is filled in their favour"), they will be waiting while their life is no life. - But the day they find truth, even if it is (or has been) by killing the man who has been withholding the truth - even if they lose their life right away, they do not care. - They count true justice as eternal life, and false judgement - as life-long hell-fire." [14]

In Amharic literature there are few generalizations about the Ethiopian people of the nature of the quotations and references given above. A few are casual remarks, e.g. about "the Habäša's hypocrisy",[15] or the abundance of "pride and strength (or endurance)" in the hearts of the people.[16] The different views are summed up in a passage in *Araya*:

> "The Ethiopian people live in love, solicitous about their religion, their faith. What friends have sought and obtained together, they divide among themselves; having told each other about their misfortunes, they help each other. Keeping their word, their honour, their religion, all loving each other, they strive to serve their king and their country with a pure heart, and to obtain position, honour and wealth through skill and bravery." [17]

This romanticized image of the Ethiopian probably represents ideals commonly found among the people.

---

[14] *Adäfrəs*, 251:8-17.
[15] *Čäräḵa sətwäṭa*, 62:6.
[16] *Araya*, 28:6f.
[17] *Araya*, 162:12-17; cf. *Yäräggäfu abäboč*, 118:7f.

PART TWO

CHANGING ETHIOPIA

CHAPTER FIVE

INFLUENCES FOR CHANGE

1. *Indigenous influences*

Ethiopian authors realize that they live in a time of deep and far-reaching change for their country, and they seem to welcome this fact. But they also want to influence the development and shape the future of Ethiopia. They do not only look abroad for models to follow but find inspiration in the great periods of Ethiopian history and in the proudest cultural achievements of the past.

Some of the works of fiction attempt to set out aspects of what has made Ethiopia great. Käbbädä Mika'el's *Yätənbit ḳäṭäro* is set in an indeterminate past, when Christianity first came to the country, and is only vaguely historical. But it makes the point that Ethiopia is specially chosen by God and that there are prophecies relating to the country that must come true.[1] The author has also found inspiration in the story of Kaleb and has written a play by that name, dealing with the Ethiopian victory over Dhu Nuwas. Emphasis is put on the Christian faith of Kaleb and his countrymen as a main cause of their victory, whereas the Byzantine Empire is said to have been defeated because it had succumbed to Islam. A Roman captain in the play praises the old imperial Aksum as a power almost on a par with Rome, and Dhu Nuwas foresees his defeat as soon as he hears the Ethiopian king has come against him. Kaleb is presented as a staunch defender of the Christian faith.[2]

Mäkonnən Əndalkaččäw in *Salsawi Dawit*[3] and Abbe Gubäñña in *Yädäkamoč wäṭmäd* have written about the Era of the Judges, *Zämänä Mäsafənt*, but to both of them history is of only secondary importance; they use the background of history to express favourite moral views and endeavour to give advice that is of relevance to

---

[1] *Ṭobbiya*, by Afäwärḳ Gäbrä Iyäsus, can be allegorically taken to be about Ethiopia ("Ṭobbiya" is a colloquial form of "Ethiopia"). As the girl by that name becomes instrumental in converting a pagan country, so Ethiopia is God's chosen country to bring light to the world.

[2] *Kaleb*, 5:1-8, 6:3ff., 7:1ff. 7ff., 10:4-12, 32:20-35:2, 57:21-23, 64:8-19, 67:7f.

[3] *Arrəmuññ*, pp. 193-245.

the present. This was not a heroic period in Ethiopian history, and it serves as a warning against repeating the errors of that era if Ethiopia is to progress properly.

Tewodros II has come to represent vision, reform, and nationalism in Amharic literature. His individual excesses and acts of cruelty are not considered important, but his attempts at unifying the country by breaking the power of the local princes, and at modernizing the country are significant aspects of what modern authors want for Ethiopia. Also Mäkonnən Ǝndalkaččäw, whose play *Ṭaytu Bəṭul* does not present Tewodros as a great man, states towards the end of the play that he did much good to unify the country and died like a hero and a patriot. Gərmaččäw Täklä Hawaryat has written a play about Tewodros, and Bərhanu Zärihun and Abbe Gubäñña have written novels about him; Käbbädä Mika'el and Ṣäggaye Gäbrä Mädhən have written poems about him, and there are also numerous other references to Tewodros in Amharic literature.[4] All these authors, except Mäkonnən Ǝndalkaččäw, are highly laudatory about Tewodros and see him as a great Ethiopian leader. Undoubtedly they have used their writings about this Emperor to express views they hoped would be accepted and acted on by the government of their own time, with the aim of recreating the country in its former greatness and glory as they saw it. Blattengeta Həruy has also written on Ethiopian history, and particularly on Yohannes IV, whom he admired, as well as on other periods of Ethiopia's past, but his works in this field are not fictional and are, therefore, not discussed here.

The defeat of the Italians at Adwa and at Dogali are remembered;[5] but the last armed encounter with the Italians is a particularly important motif in Amharic literature. The brave resistance and battles at Mayčäw and elsewhere are occasions for pride, even if they ended in defeat, as described in *Araya*, in *Almotkum bəyye alwašəm*, and elsewhere.[6] A special reason for pride by the Ethiopi-

---

[4] *Tewodros*, by Gərmaččäw Täklä Hawaryat; *Yätewodros ənba*, by Bərhanu Zärihun; *And lännatu*, by Abbe Gubäñña; *Aṣe Tewodrosənna hulätt yäwəčč agär säwoč*, by Käbbädä Mika'el, is printed in *Yäkəne azmära*, pp. 111-114; and Ṣäggaye Gäbrä Mädhən's poem *Yätewodros sənbət kämäkdäla* is found in *Ǝsat wäy abäba*, pp. 204-208. Ṣäggaye has also written a play about Tewodros in English, called *Tewodros*, and printed in *Ethiopia Observer*, Vol. IX, No. 3, Part Two, pp. 209-226.

[5] *Ǝsat wäy abäba*, pp. 54-59, 159.

[6] *Araya*, pp. 226ff., *Arrəmuññ*, pp. 273ff., 339ff., *Ǝsat wäy abäba*, p. 184f.

ans is the *arbäñña*, "patriots", who never gave up the fight against the occupying enemy. A large part of *Araya* is dedicated to this struggle.[7] Abunä Petros is remembered for his heroic defiance of the enemy.[8]

This retrospective admiration for Ethiopia's past is not used as an argument for resisting change, rather on the contrary. Ethiopia at one time, in the Axumite period, had a leading position among the nations of Africa and the world, and modern Ethiopians would like to see her regain that prominence. By studying the past, they also try to understand what made Ethiopia great then. The same old values may give the country new strength.

Some authors, such as Mäkonnən Əndalkaččäw, Käbbädä Mika'el, Bərhanu Zärihun, and Mängəstu Lämma, stress the faith, the morals, the bravery of the old Ethiopians. Others fight to preserve Ethiopia's cultural heritage. Especially Abbe Gubäñña wants modern authors to imitate traditional Ethiopian forms of writing poetry and finds them adequate for the expression of modern thoughts as he states, for example, in his collections of poetry, *Mäskot* and *Ǝretənna mar*. He thinks that the best of Ethiopian poetic tradition is as great as anything that has been imported from the West. In *Adäfrəs*, too, there are many expressions of genuine admiration for Ethiopia's greatness and rich cultural heritage. Young intellectuals find much to inspire them in the past of their country.[9]

Ethiopian self-confidence is expressed by Käbbädä Mika'el in poems about the Italians in Ethiopia during their occupation of the country. Here we encounter some very early notions of what has been termed black consciousness, or *négritude*. Instead of an angry riposte, the author can afford to make fun of Italian superciliousness and feelings of superiority. In one poem, *Ṭəkuroččəm əndä säw*,[10] he tells of one Italian who is surprised that Ethiopians were eating and drinking "like human beings", contrary to what he had been led to expect. In a poem about the prisoners at Asinara in Sardinia, *Yä'azinara əsräñña*,[11] he is more contemptuous of European civilization and correspondingly proud of Ethiopian

---

[7] *Araya*, pp. 274ff.
[8] *Yädäm dəmṣ*, in *Arrəmuññ*, pp. 80-104.
[9] *Adäfrəs*, 6:21f., 74:6f., 75:4-20, 134:2f., 216:21-26.
[10] *Yäḳəne azmära*, pp. 68-70.
[11] *Ib.*, pp. 52-57.

civilization which the Italians treated like a pagan culture. His possibly most famous and influential poem, in which he ridicules Fascist ideas and extols Ethiopian values, is *Ǝroro*.[12] This may be the proudest expression of the Ethiopian personality and of Ethiopian values in the Amharic language. There is a total rejection of the Fascist propaganda of racial superiority, or indeed superiority of their ideology or culture, which is rejected as something evil and to be resisted by every Ethiopian proud of his country. The author calls his countrymen to vigilance against such ideas, to a refusal to be anyone's servants or submit to a foreign power.

2. Foreign influences

Contacts with foreigners have alerted Ethiopian national consciousness and awareness and have caused Ethiopians to emphasize their own values and characteristics—as shown at the end of the last section in the case of Fascist ideology. But in spite of the conflicts caused, influences from abroad have provided a powerful impetus for change in Ethiopia. Much may have been resisted, but many concepts and ideas have been accepted almost without a fight or serious objection.[13]

Strong foreign influences have, of course, been exerted in Ethiopia from the beginning of historical times. The legend of the serpent (or dragon) killer who is rewarded with kingship (and not punished for hubris or driven out of Paradise for trying to compete with divine powers),[14] Judaic beliefs and practices,[15] Christianity,[16] and Islam[17] derive from the Middle East, and these contacts and influences have persisted throughout Ethiopian history, although obviously not always to the same degree. The country's isolation at other periods should not be exaggerated either.[18]

But the influence for change that is of the greatest importance for Amharic literature in this century is embodied in the new ideas, technology, and life-style of the modern West, i.e. Europe and the United States. Käbbädä Mika'el has written with admiration about

---
[12] *Yäḳəne azmära*, pp. 58-68.
[13] Cf. E. Cerulli, *La letteratura etiopica*, 3rd ed., Milano, 1968, pp. 11-13.
[14] D. F. McCall, "Dragon-Slayers and Kingship", in *Ethiopian Observer*, Vol. XII, No. 1, pp. 34-43.
[15] E. Ullendorff, *Ethiopia and the Bible*, London, 1968.
[16] F. Heyer, *Die Kirche Äthiopiens*, Berlin, 1971.
[17] J. S. Trimingham, *Islam in Ethiopia*, London, 1952.
[18] E. Haberland, *Altes Christentum in Süd-Äthiopien*, Wiesbaden, 1976, pp. 1f.

Japan for its progress—but along Western lines.[19] He also admires the spirituality of Eastern people like Gandhi.[20] Araya, too, praises the Eastern mentality and appreciation of spiritual values.[21] But these Eastern influences seem small compared with the massive and enduring influence and adoption of European culture and civilization. Imports from the East, such as the fine leather called *bahr aräb*, or the eucalyptus tree, *bahr zaf*, or the trousers and shirt called *märdufa*, brought to Ethiopia during Menelik's time,[22] etc., seem rather insignificant as against the total amount of recent imports from the West.

Most authors are generally favourable to Western influences in Ethiopia, although some voice a note of caution against the wholesale importation of European civilization. Awwäḳä in *Addis aläm* and Araya in the novel by that name have been to France for education,[23] and the basis of all their ideas for reform and change are taken from their stay abroad. The authors are evidently favourably inclined towards these influences, as hardly any criticism of such ideas is expressed. Araya is admittedly a bit sceptical of some aspects of Western morality, but he does not see these as necessary consequences of Western culture and of a European kind of economic development. He therefore wants to imitate Europeans in almost every field except their lax morality.[24] Blattengeta Həruy sees many advantages in learning from the West and in correcting some of what he regards as excesses or harmful practices in Ethiopian society. He defends such reforms in both private and public life in his two novels, *Yäləbb hassab* and *Addis aläm*; and he shows the beneficial results of accepting new ideas in terms of improved health, greater personal happiness and better use of economic resources. Gərmaččäw Täklä Hawaryat seems equally favourable towards the ideas Araya has brought with him from the West, but he appears less optimistic that Ethiopians will accept them quickly or willingly. Araya sees the most suitable model for Ethiopia's progress in the French bourgeoisie.

---

[19] Käbbädä Mika'el, *Japan əndämən säläṭṭänäč?*; cf. *Araya*, 44:1-10, 91:18-24.
[20] Käbbädä Mika'el, *Sələṭṭane malät məndənäč?* pp. 49ff., 135ff., 199ff.. 209ff.
[21] *Araya*, 89:25ff.
[22] *Fəḳr əskä mäḳabər*, 39:18, *Yähəllina däwäl*, 244:4, *Adäfrəs*, 257:7,
[23] *Addis aläm*, 4:1-6.19, 5:19, *Araya*, chapters 3-5.
[24] *Araya*, 26:1-5.11f., 27:5f. (cf. 26:23f.); 147:26-149ult.

Other authors have also stressed the importance of France as a source of inspiration for Ethiopian intellectuals. Many of Mäkonnən Ǝndalkaččäw's characters go to France and admire French culture, as seen for example in his books *Ṣähay Mäsfən, Yädəhoč kätäma*, and *Yäfəkər ṭora*. In *Adäfrəs*, Daňňaččäw Wärku has introduced two characters who have been to France for education: Ato Wäldu, who has resigned from government service and become a merchant in Däbrä Sina and who, although disillusioned, still harbours some liberal and enlightened ideas; and Kəbrät, a painter and friend of Adäfrəs, who has had his whole artistic outlook and concepts shaped by French art.[25]

The few students who have returned from the United States are not depicted as very eager for reform but are often cast in rather sombre colours. Ləjj Alämu Dästa, in *Ṣähay Mäsfən*, goes into business and adopts methods that are rather exploitative. He tries to profit from making deals with people in trouble and builds a fortune through doubtful deals, even forms of usury. Abärra Wärku, the main character in *Kä'admas bašagär*, becomes a rather purposeless bureaucrat and does not give much thought to what is good for his country. Both of them have received their higher education in America.[26]

Bahru, in Mängəstu Lämma's play *Yalačča gabəčča*, has been to England [27] and he is not so much a man of revolutionary words as a practical man with reforming ideas who goes to the countryside to teach, thus hoping to bring a better life and more enlightenment to the people there. The author's own experiences in England are reflected in his collection of poetry, *Yägəṭəm guba'e*.[28]

Strong foreign influence in Ethiopia is also noticeable in Amharic literary forms. Modern authors have absorbed ideas from the West, and the forms they have adopted to express these ideas are largely Western: Amharic novels, plays, short stories, essays and poetry are all shaped much like their Western counterparts. Educated people in Ethiopia are further influenced by the introduction of an educational system into the country that is almost totally copied from Europe and the United States—and the language of instruction in higher education is English. This wide contact with the West, and

---

[25] *Adäfrəs*, 50:27-51:7, 52:3-12, 53:24-29, 57:24-33, 58:1-12.
[26] *Ṣähay Mäsfən*, 20:11-13, *Kä'admas bašagär*, 20:8f.
[27] *Yalačča gabəčča*, 23:14f.
[28] *Yägəṭəm guba'e*, pp. 15-22.

the East for that matter, has made the whole range of literary, philosophical, political and economic ideas accessible to the younger generation of Ethiopians.[29] Not even people who are opposed to, or sceptical of, Western ideas or who regret their uncritical acceptance without adaptation to the Ethiopian situation [30] are able to ignore this influence. This is the case with those who criticize reformers like Awwäḵä or Araya. Some may be affected only superficially, but the amount of goods, such as clothes, cars, utensils in daily life, or weapons, and cultural influences, such as Western music and films, in addition to education,[31] make it increasingly difficult to escape this influence. The task of the people is to decide how to react to these influences and how to shape their own society. Both old traditions and new ideas are strong, and the symbiosis of such influences, often in conflict with each other, is one of the main themes of this book.

[29] *Yähəllina däwäl*, 180:10f.
[30] E.g., *Adäfrəs*, 44:1-8, 177:8-13, 294:7f., 295:2-296:25, *Yägəṭəm guba'e*, 38:13f.
[31] E.g., *Adäfrəs*, 14:8f., 30:5-7, 89:22-27, 110:1, 127:7, 168:3, 197:8, 229:6, 247:1f.; 35:10, 114:16f.; 27:29-31; 25:9f.21f.; 58:24, 228:26, etc., etc.

CHAPTER SIX

ATTITUDES TO CHANGE

1. *Conservatives*

Conservative attitudes may be limited to a small field or they can be more comprehensive. Mäkonnən Əndalkaččäw, for example, shows generally a conservative attitude to change, but still he wants the country to progress. Bərhanu Zärihun, on the other hand, shows concern for the preservation of traditional moral values and may be regarded as a conservative in this field, but nothing can be deduced about his general attitude to social change on that basis.

Most of the conservatives we meet in Amharic literature are, of course, people who benefit economically from keeping the old system, primarily members of the nobility. Many authors have stressed this point, and conservative nobles figure prominently in several works. Araya has long discussions with a nobleman from Gondar, and the latter fears the new development in Ethiopia, namely that people imitate Europeans, because this will destroy the martial tradition and the faith of the country. He believes inequality is willed by God and that the government is above the people; modern attitudes have created selfishness and competitiveness and have destroyed cooperation. Thus troubles increase and people refuse to obey, not accepting their proper place with praise to God, and therefore there is no peace; as people despise each other, there is no unity and love, no peace and happiness, only riots and problems, he argues.[1]

This nobleman, who lives in Addis Ababa, says that "in Shoa we do not attach much value to the matter of birth and family", and that it is more important to show ability and to be noticed by the king.[2] Although this refers to the period before the Italian occupation, it probably is a reflection of the Emperor's general policy of giving appointments to people who are not of noble birth;[3] it would therefore apply primarily, but not exclusively, to

---

[1] *Araya*, 138:4-20, 139:7-24, 159:6-15, 160:7-18, 161:29-162:3.
[2] *Araya*, 162:5-11.
[3] *Adäfrəs*, 100, 19-23, 172:19-23.

people living in and around the capital. Though nobility was not necessarily hereditary, there was a tendency to ennoble sons of nobles, and noble families could develop great jealousy about their rights and privileges and the purity of their line. In *Fəkr əskä mäḳabər*, Fitawrari Mäšäša in Gojjam is the principal spokesman of traditional, conservative attitudes; several of his relatives try to modify his viewpoints, but in the main they go along with him. In conflicts with peasants who become defiant when too much tribute and tax are demanded of them, many nobles insist that an attitude of weakness or compromise on their side would lead to a weakening of their authority and that nothing should be conceded; only a few advocate moderation because they realize that if the peasants were to unite and rise against them, they could not be resisted.[4] Guddu Kasa, who has rejected the views and attitudes of his relatives, gives his view of the conservative elements of the nobility to Bäzzabbəh:

> "You see, there are many beliefs that have been a trusted custom for a long time, that make a man go only where he is led, without looking to the left or to the right, like a bridled mule. These customary beliefs - God knows who their apostles were - have divided people into different categories of classes called the class of master, the class of poor people, the class of artisans, the class of slaves. Not only this, on (the basis of) these customary beliefs it has been defined what is proper for (each of) these classes to do, what is not proper for them, how they (can or should) live, who can marry whom, who shall honour (or give preference to) whom, without forgetting who can scorn whom. It has been specified that slaves can be sold and exchanged, artisans can be scorned and humiliated, the poor can be ordered about and trodden on by a master. It has been established that a tradition going back to time immemorial shall be maintained, namely that a member of the master class is to be addressed as "you" (polite form), and a poor old man dies being addressed (i.e. is addressed to his death) as "thou" (familiar form). It has been specified that one who idly speaks his idle thoughts is called modern and becomes an admired ruler, and one who thinks and does worthwhile things becomes a despised underling. You'll be surprised! If you consider this useless custom, this evil custom founded on injustice, and in case you say it is not right (or proper) to preserve such a system, even that it is intolerable, that its demise would not be bad, and that it is better to make slow changes, you will be counted as a traitor and a rope with which you will be hanged will be prepared for you! Also in case you are a sad, silent spectator

---

[4] *Fəkr əskä mäḳabər*, 214:30-215:9, 217:4-8, 217:28-218:7; 217:23ff., 218:8ff.

> - they will call you a madman, a fool (or freak) like me, taking away your peace, ostracizing you from society, and make you live like a stranger in your own family, as an outsider in the country (or place) you were born and grew up. But now, if they who do all this to you, who say they are aristocrats, who sit on top, having crushed everyone, are (i.e. had been) alone, you (might) say it is (i.e. they do it) in order that their privileges shall not suffer. But what do you say when all the slaves, the artisans, the poor, all those who suffer injustices are in league with those who perpetrate injustices and condemn you? You can only keep silent, thinking of the worthless proverb that says, "Truth that does not agree with custom (or tradition) is always false"! There you see! All of us are prisoners of (this) custom (or tradition).
>
> Now then, if we start from this general custom and go into details, if the relationship between me and Ǝnkopa (i.e. his wife) goes beyond what it should be, unless it is a servant-master relationship, in case it passes this and becomes a husband-wife relationship, they deride her, saying she does not know her proper place (literally, "her strength"); me they despise, calling me a knave; the children we bear they hate, and what they have come to hate you know they (will) kill", said Guddu Kasa. . . ." [5]

Fitawrari Mäšäša calls the times "this corrupting era", and he says he is not "a man of this time" but "a man of that past good time".[6]

Wzo Asäggaš in *Adäfrəs* does not want to accept that the changes taking place in education and in manners (especially as seen in towns) are better than her traditional way of life; on the contrary, she wants people to understand that she is familiar with these new things and that she has rejected them because she despises them, not because of ignorance or lack of opportunity.[7] In particular, she cannot stomach the young people's lack of respect for authority, as she shows when Gorfu, a nobleman's son, tells her what he has heard:

> "These people, also what is said about them in town is not nice. - - I heard it said yesterday on the Thursday market that just recently one father killed his son, a university student - - -."
> "What did he accuse him of - - -?
> "It was said that they had used the expression, We will not obey the king - - -."
> "We will not obey the king! We will not obey the king -. "Just as a rat is being born, it squeaks (i.e. like a grown up rat) as soon

---

[5] *Fəkr əskä mäkabər*, 334:2-335:14.
[6] Ib., 142:2-10.
[7] *Adäfrəs*, 119:25-28, 141:19-21.

as its tail is out" - - -. Whom will they obey then! It is just because he gathers any poor man's child about him that this king sees his troubles -. One who is of poor descent is of similarly poor character - (even) if he (the king) gives them appointments or honours - -. Now, if he decorates a donkey, what grandeur does it find - -? He (i.e. the father who killed his son) was too kind - - even death was not enough for him (i.e. the son) - - -." [8]

Wzo Alganäš in *Yalačča gabəčča* is another conservative landowner, but maybe not to the same degree as Wzo Asäggaš, as she has at least accepted many of the gadgets of modern life, e.g. she wears a watch and uses a land-rover and lives in Addis Ababa; yet she is happy that the girl she has chosen for her nephew's wife has become westernized, as a result of her stay abroad, "only on the surface", in dress, hair style, speech and the way she walks, but deep down she has remained faithful to her old traditions and obeys her parents in important matters.[9]

Ayyalew's father in *Yäšoh aklil* is also a traditionalist, and he says ironically:

"I don't want any change done in the world. If everything remains as it is, it will be the most exciting. Unless some are rich, others poor, some oppressors, others oppressed, this world will be boring. No change is needed." [10]

It is said that the common people in the countryside are indifferent to change, and that modernization does not actually make any difference to them:

"- - You had better understand, Adäfrəs - - - to them (i.e. country people) your idea does not mean anything. - What they drink, what they eat, what they see, what they touch - - - these are the things that are truth to them! The hope you gave them, they count like having a cow in the sky - -. Whether it happens or not, they do not even care - - -." [11]

In *Addis aläm* the people are equally resistant to new ideas and suggestions to abandon the old traditions.[12]

But this conservative attitude should not be overemphasized. Both Guddu Kasa, a nobleman, and the peasants who oppose

---

[8] *Adäfrəs*, 172:12-14.
[9] *Yalačča gabəčča*, 40:21-41:2, 54:4ff., 68:1-5.
[10] *Yäšoh aklil*, 18:17-21.
[11] *Adäfrəs*, 150:22-26 (cf. line 4).
[12] *Addis aläm*, 8:7f.18f., 6:1ff., 7:12ff., 10:8ff., 14:19ff., 29:19ff.; cf. 2:15f.

Fitawrari Mäšäša in *Fəkr əskä mäkabər* want change and progress, and Fitawrari Täkka in *Yähəllina däwäl* is progressive and helpful to peasants and poor people who come to him for aid and advice,[13] but when some tenants complain that they have been evicted, he cannot do anything about it: "it is a problem brought about by the times", he says.[14]

An old nobleman whom Araya meets in the palace compound does see some value in an education abroad, especially in a subject related to modern technology, such as engineering, medicine, the art of making cannons, guns, or cars; but when Araya tells him he has been to France to study agriculture, the noble can show only contempt: nobody needs to go abroad or to go to school to learn how to cultivate the land.[15]

Conservatives usually want some kind of change, but not in the social system itself. Without major disturbances or structural upheavals, education, freedom, and charitable institutions, like homes for orphans and old people, are suggested as beneficial for the country.[16]

The clergy are, as already pointed out, usually conservative and support the established authorities and the *status quo*. Abba Addise in *Adäfrəs* despises modern youth and believes the end of the world has come because of the moral decline; he feels sorry about the freedom children have and finds that young people are arrogant, crooked, and critical of well-established values; he opposes change and believes it is sinful to trust reason, because people are selfish and use their intelligence only for evil purposes.[17] But among the clergy there are also some who try to adapt to modern times, like Abba Yohannəs in the same novel.[18]

We do not read much about other (i.e. non-Christian) religious leaders in Amharic literature, but when they are mentioned they are mostly seen to be opposed to change and to modern civilization. This is the case with Abba Čäffe, a sorcerer, and Abba Märga, a pagan rainmaker, in *Yähəllina däwäl*, who both oppose the building of a school because it puts them out of business.[19] A similar situation

---

[13] *Yähəllina däwäl*, 36:15-26, 57:11-20, 61:6-17, 62:19.
[14] *Ib.*, 62:6-17.
[15] *Araya*, 171:8-172:1, 173:1ff.
[16] *Yäfəkər çora*, 175:9-13, 187:10-15, 189:1-6, 192:6-194:12.
[17] *Adäfrəs*, 101:16-19, 102:7, 104:1-4, 156:8. 12-18.22-24, 157:19f.
[18] *Ib.*, chapter 12.
[19] *Yähəllina däwäl*, 59:21-60:14, 81:12-82:8.

occurs in *Yalačča gabəčča*: the wise old men, astrologers and pebble-throwing diviners, are driven out of their job because Bahru has opened an elementary school in the village;[20] and the Haji is strongly opposed to modern civilization because it makes people soft and weak:

> "May civilization that kills ardour and makes people lose their courage get out of my nose."[21]

This point, that modern civilization makes people weak, is also stressed by Mängəstu Lämma in his poem *Yäwänd ləjj yalläh*,[22] part of which he has placed at the beginning of his play *Ṭälfo bäkise* which deals with the same problem. The play is about a group of young people who want to demonstrate their courage and resoluteness by abducting an unknown girl and marrying her to one of the young men, the son of an *arbäñña*, a freedom fighter, who had got his wife the same way. Somehow the times are not right for this kind of resourcefulness and bravery. The poem sums up the nostalgic regret that things are changing, and in some respects for the worse:

> "My goodness, civilization: to cross seas (for it)!
> Will (possibly) men who have put on trousers (i.e. real men) disappear in (i.e. from) the land?
> Oh civilization that turns (everything) upside down;
> (Our) women have put on trousers while (our) men flee...."[23]

With respect to certain traditional values, Bərhanu Zärihun can also be classified as a conservative. He has seen that urbanization and rapid change occasioned by the accessibility of money, sometimes obtained too easily and in too large amounts for many to handle responsibly, have led to moral decay, particularly in sexual relations. Husbands leave their wives, and wives leave their husbands, and children are neglected, because of money or the allurements of money. He writes tragic stories about such changes in *Yä'ənba däbdabbewoč* and *Amanu'el därso mäls*. In *Čäräka sətwäṭa* he tells the story of a man who falls deeply in love with a girl he trusts; but she makes love to and marries a friend of his. He then goes to a prostitute and "having been infected with gonorrhea[24]

---

[20] *Yalačča gabəčča*, 80:9-12.18-21.
[21] *Ib.*, 138:4f. (cf. 137:15ff., 139:2f.).
[22] *Yägəṭəm guba'e*, pp. 37-40.
[23] *Yägəṭəm guba'e*, 38:13-16. Cf. *Ṭälfo bäkise*, 54:1f., 56:7f.
[24] *Jəgəl* is a variety of gonorrhea, *ṭäbṭ*, according to DTW.

he became a man like everyone else".[25] *Yäbädäl fəṣṣame* shows how money easily leads to deceit and crimes. Like many other authors, he is concerned with the preservation of the moral values of the past.

Mildly conservative attitudes are shown by some who have found their place in government service and have become part of the bureaucracy. This is the case with Ato Ṭəso in *Adäfrəs*, who is almost liberal in some respects and a conservative in others; he does not believe in "bad (i.e. disruptive) jumps" forward, but in slow, orderly change.[26] *Araya* cites the views of an Ethiopian consul in Djibouti: he believes in change, but it would be a mistake to change everything at once. He advocates slow and gradual change, and he seems to be expressing the general view of the government in Addis Ababa at that time. He may not be opposed to change, although Araya calls him conservative when he defends his views with the question, "What is the good of hurrying to destroy the customs of the country?"[27]

Yähəllina däwäl tells of a school director who excuses his inertia by saying he has written repeatedly to the government in Addis Ababa about necessary improvements to his school but has only received the negative reply that there is not enough money. Haddis, one of his young teachers, does not accept this as a valid reason for letting things remain as they are, and he organizes the local people to build their own school. At this juncture the school director turns fiercely on him, and with the help of the police and religious leaders he tries to prevent the building of the new school. Bureaucrats who pay lip-service to progress, but when it comes to doing something are opposed to change, are met elsewhere too. In *Yäbädäl fəṣṣame*, those who make public statements in favour of development are depicted as corrupt officials and thieves who are not interested in the country.[28] *Adäfrəs* has a chapter [29] about *afaddašoč* and their policy of *fəddäsa*, words invented by the author: an *afaddaš* or *af addaš* (literally, "mouth renewer"), is a person who talks about reforms, but, it is clear from the context, does nothing to bring them about; *fəddäsa*, i.e. *af əddäsa*, is, then, "talk of reforms, oral reforms" but no real work of reform. The chapter is

---

[25] *Čäräka sətwäṭa*, 93:7f.
[26] *Adäfrəs*, 89:10ff.
[27] *Araya*, 113:1-18, 113:29-114:6.
[28] *Yäbädäl fəṣṣame*, 70:7-71:22.
[29] *Adäfrəs*, chapter 13, pp. 86ff.

intentionally obscure, but it transpires that it is directed mainly at the government and national leaders. They have formed a closed circle and are only concerned to preserve their self-interests.

One of the most conservative authors in Ethiopia is Mäkonnən Əndalkaččäw. He has written about the evil that often befalls those who become fond of money (*Yädəhoč kätäma*); those who make compromises in their moral standards for the sake of convenience (*Almotkum bəyye alwašəm*); and those who are so strongly prejudiced against what is not counted as modern that they do not show feelings of kindness and love when they think it may bring them shame (*Ṣähay Mäsfən*). But his strongest attack on progress is delivered by taking up an old biblical motif: the story of Cain and Abel which has been slightly dramatized in *Yäḳayäl dəngay*.[30] Cain kills Abel out of envy, and "he invented the stone as a new weapon. Therefore - - Cain's stone has become the prototype ("father") of all weapons to attack one's enemy..."[31] "Cain thus became the originator of death, envy, malice, selfishness, adultery, pride, perfidy, in short, all sins".[32] Because "human nature is inclined to evil rather than good", "all the arts/skills created for the benefit of man, went, together with man's nature, in an evil, and not a useful direction; and as it is said, a bad tree does not bear good fruit: so man's evil made Cain's bitter fruits—all created to be useful (in various ways) to man, and following upon Cain's stone and gunpowder—to become weapons with which to harm his brothers".[33] The objection that competition may stimulate progress and improvement is brushed aside.[34] "Man has not even excepted bread (food) from becoming a weapon against his brother; he has made it a weapon with which to kill his brother".[35] Peace cannot be found on earth,[36] and the story ends on a sad note.

Few authors share Mäkonnən Əndalkaččäw's pessimism about development and progress.

A mocking attitude to radical socialists is probably expressed in one of Mängəstu Lämma's poems, *Mänor mäla agäññä*, approximately, "Life has got a new meaning;"[37] it says:

---

[30] *Arrəmuññ*, pp. 33-42.
[31] *Ib.*, 33:5-9.
[32] *Ib.*, 33:12-18.
[33] *Ib.*, 36:13-20.
[34] *Ib.*, 37:16ff., 38:4ff.
[35] *Ib.*, 39:12-14.
[36] *Ib.*, 39:19ff.
[37] *Yägəṭəm guba'e*, p. 34.

"Living has found a way (i.e. to be meaningful) - even once again.
Even if one dies (literally, "they die"), no matter - as one lies in the meadow;
As he had nightmares thinking you (fem.) would not come,
Dreaming of your (fem.) coming - even if one dies, no matter."

In this poem, "the meadow", *mäsku*, is very likely a pun on Moscow, and the author could well be making fun of revolutionaries like Gərmame Nəway, who dreamt of the coming of a socialist revolution, "resting (their hopes) on Moscow", which may stand for the Marxist-Leninist ideology.

2. *Radicals*

There are, of course, many forms and degrees of radicalism, and in Amharic literature we meet people who want to change customs and attitudes, or to speed up progress without altering the social structure; and there are others who want a more fundamental change in society, new attitudes and an acceleration of economic growth.

The use of fiction to advocate change in Ethiopia goes back to Blattengeta Həruy, and he also started the tradition of letting a character who has gone abroad and absorbed new ideas become the protagonist of change in the country. Awwäķä in *Addis aläm* has been to France, and on his return he wants to have things his own way. He refuses to follow the old customs in mourning the dead, and he will not pay for an expensive *täzkar* ("memorial feast for the dead"), nor be too extravagant at his own wedding. He even insists on choosing his own wife and forbids lewd songs and such abundance of alcohol that people get drunk. Gradually the conflict widens from his own family to involve the local priest who does not accept a *täzkar* where people do not get drunk, and in the end the conflicts he stirs up lead to a programme of reform involving the whole Church and much of social life. Ten proposals are finally accepted and promulgated by the leaders of the Church, including the əçäge and the Patriarch, viz., to reduce drunkenness at weddings and *täzkar*; that priests should not divorce their wives; that no one should be ordained to the priesthood unless he can read and explain the Scriptures; that an *aläķa* should know Geez; that ordination to the priesthood should not be a matter of money; that funeral ceremonies should be the same for rich and poor; that priests should not administer the last rites to dying people for money; that priests should marry in church by *täklil* wedding; that priests should not give their blessings only for money; that priests should interpret the Gospel in such a way that the congregation can hear and understand them.[38] Other reforms relating to private life are also suggested, especially to end such wastefulness at weddings that the bridegroom is in debt for many years thereafter.

In another novel, *Yäləbb hassab*, the same author strongly advocates education for girls and a higher age of marriage; and when the young couple in the book have children, he goes into great detail about how to bring up children and what to do when they are taken ill. The help of a local medical practitioner (*wägeša*), a sorcerer or a *däbtära* is rejected,[39] and when the child is taken to a modern hospital in the capital, the doctor's advice on how to feed and treat babies is repeated in the book;[40] and, it is added, children can get sick if they are carried in cloths (*ankälba*) on their mother's back.[41]

In *Araya*, Gərmaččäw Täklä Hawaryat also makes the main character go to France, and on his return he is full of enthusiasm for reforming Ethiopia. Araya sees the agricultural potential of his country and believes there is great scope for economic growth. He enters government service but finds that there are many obstacles to implementing his ideas. The reader is left with only a vague impression of what he actually wants to do. There is much general talk of progress but no concrete plans or suggestions. When Araya finds it impossible to work in the government, he withdraws to his farm in Hararge and starts organizing his land like a gentleman farmer, paying much attention to the aesthetic aspects of his surroundings. But even here, we do not know how he envisages that economic progress should take place. On his way back from France, Araya meets different people with whom he exchanges ideas. One of them has the appearance of a bourgeois, and this observation gives rise to a description of the French bourgeoisie and the changes that took place in France after the revolution (of 1789).[42] The pre-revolution nobility has striking

---

[38] Cf. *Addis aläm*, 60:26ff.
[39] *Yäləbb hassab*, 172:10ff.
[40] *Ib.*, 175:29-176ult.
[41] *Ib.*, 172:1-4, 174:23ff.
[42] *Araya*, 48:31ff.

similarities to Ethiopian nobles, prizing highest of all martial skill and government appointments, or titles, and despising the common people. In this situation the bourgeoisie was able to increase their power, and Araya seems to admire especially their thrift and hard work, their appreciation of knowledge, education and skill. The nobles finally had to accept them and intermarry with them and the kings started appointing them to high positions. The country came, in the end, to be controlled by the bourgeoisie who had republican sentiments and supported the basic principles of the revolution, "liberty, equality, fraternity", and fought for "human rights" and "democracy". It seems clear that Araya had great sympathy for the French bourgeoisie and would like to implant the philosophy that inspired them in Ethiopia as well. They were serious and determined people who put their money in the bank, bore few children whom they educated well, worked from an early age with no time for frivolity and could retire in comfort, knowing they had been a great success. This kind of life seems to harmonize with Araya's character who had had the inclinations of grown-ups already as a child. Araya seems to want to change "everything at once" and believes that only a few determined and enthusiastic leaders are needed to bring about radical change in Ethiopia.[43] He seems to admire Japan and her quick progress, and the word gəsəggase, "rapid advance", is used about her development.[44]

Araya is also full of sympathy for the principles underlying the establishment of the Commune (i.e. the Paris commune). If copied in Ethiopia, it would, he thinks, reduce the powers of the nobility and give people the right to govern themselves, which would accelerate progress; people could choose their own officials, and would thus not go in fear of them and could not be oppressed by them, and they could control their own finance, and this would be of great benefit to the morale of the community, and it would encourage competition; cooperation between local communities and the central government would also be smooth.[45] He is disappointed

---

[43] *Araya*, 113:29-114:4.

[44] *Ib.*, 44:9. The most common term for change is *läwṭ*, "change". Common terms related to development are: *ərməjja*, "progress", *ləmat*, "growth, development", *ədgät*, "growth"; *səlləṭṭane* is used of development according to a Western pattern; *zəllay*, "jump" has a slightly negative connotation; *Adäfrəs*, 89:10, 99:22, 100:2, 250:7, *Kä'admas bašagär*, 72:8, *Yähəllina däwäl*, 87:11f., 91:4.

[45] *Araya*, 143:22ff.

with Ethiopia's backwardness and is fearful that even such measures of progress that have taken place will be lost and that the country will go to sleep again after the war with Italy, which had alerted the people;[46] but he thinks that any progress within Ethiopia must come through the people's own efforts:

> "- - If you don't help yourself, who will come and help you? Now we must become strong, helping each other. Our spirit must be strong; we have started our journey and there is no stopping before we reach our goal." [47]

He does not want purely material progress for Ethiopia and finds it difficult to accept Europe's example in all respects:

> "Civilization has two aspects. One is improvement in efficient living, in wealth, in planning, in technology. And the second is to grow strong and mature in spiritual culture, in morality. What is conspicuous in present-day European civilization is the improvement of life (in living standards) and the rapid technological advance, but with respect to spiritual culture it is difficult to say they (i.e. the Europeans) excel." [48]

Gərmaččäw Täklä Hawaryat makes use of the Emperor in support of the views on progress which he has expressed through Araya, by quoting from a speech Haile Sellassie delivered immediately upon his return to Ethiopia after the end of the Italian occupation in 1941. The Emperor said "this day is the opening of a new era in the history of a new Ethiopia", and that new work in which all must participate is to begin;[49] and, he goes on,

> "in the new Ethiopia we want from now on that you shall be people who indiscriminately have freedom and equality before the law.
> To be perfect, you must add your effort in the work we strive to do, having changed the administration of the country according to the new civilization by which the country will develop, the people will become rich, agriculture, trade, education and technology will expand, and by which our people's lives and wealth will profit, and so on." [50]

Few authors would dare, or indeed wish, to draw the Emperor's views into their works, but there seems to be a desire among earlier

---

[46] *Araya*, 96:6, 17:9, 26:23f.; 349:8-350:6.
[47] *Ib.*, 152:26-29.
[48] *Ib.*, 147:26-148:1.
[49] *Ib.*, 341:9-12.
[50] *Ib.*, 346:20-27.

authors to identify with the Emperor's attempts to change the country. Blattengeta Həruy has an *aläka* in *Addis aläm* say that there is no harm in changing customs according to the times, as long as they do not harm the king, the government, or the people.[51]

Käbbädä Mika'el wrote, in all likelihood, much of his nonfiction to encourage and guide the Emperor in his programme of reforms; and in his fictional work he sometimes has, like some other authors, introductory prefaces addressed to the Emperor, e.g. in *Yätənbit ḳäṭäro*; in *Tarikənna məssale*, Book III, there is a laudatory passage about the "king" preceding the text of the book itself. Gərmaččäw's *Araya* also opens with a "letter" from the author to the Emperor.

Later authors generally have pictures of the Emperor at the beginning of their works, but there are few references to the Emperor in the main text of the books, and one should hardly look for the Emperor's views in such places. Many authors, beginning with Gərmaččäw Täklä Hawaryat, use Emperor Tewodros as a mouthpiece to express views on the country and how it should develop. It is, of course, easier to adapt and to make use of the words and alleged views of a dead emperor than those of a living one, and that may be one reason for writing more about Tewodros than about Haile Sellassie. But there was a diminution of enthusiasm about Ethiopia's actual development during the latter stages of the reign of the last emperor, and it is likely that some criticism of him and his government was implied in writing about Tewodros. In any case, Tewodros came to symbolize vision and progress, and many authors write about him as if they idealize him and look for a leader of his calibre to advance the country further. Tewodros was used to represent both the revolutionary leader and the head of a strong central government.

In *Fəḳr əskä mäḳabər*, Haddis Alämayyähu gives a rather vague impression of a radical peasants' leader who leads them in determined, even violent, opposition to oppressive landlords. This leader, Abäjjä Bäläw, has been a *šəfta*, "rebel, outlaw" (and has thus something in common with Tewodros), who has received a pardon (*bawaj gäbba*) and has become a popular hero to whom the peasants look for guidance and about whom both men and women make poems.[52] He is a man of action who leads the peasants to victory

---

[51] *Addis aläm*, 50:26-30.
[52] *Fəḳr əskä mäḳabər*, 228:22ff., 232:6ff.

over their master, Fitawrari Mäšäša, both in the field of battle and in court.[53]

Guddu Kasa is a rebel against the views of his noble relations. He does not express this in action so much as in words, although he has married his maid against the will of his family and helps Bäzzabbəh and Säblä Wängel to elope together. In words, he expresses his views courageously and is in opposition to the family on numerous occasions, although he must pay the price of being called "an idiot, a fool (or freak)".[54] When nobody dares speak out frankly to Fitawrari Mäšäša, Guddu Kasa openly voices his opposition to one of the Fitawrari's wilder schemes:

> "Whether I am asked (for my opinion) or not, what I have said is true: Fitawrari, because you are a man who lives above other people and in another world, you need a good leader. For example, you are as if you lived together with and in the world of people like Aṣe Zär'a Ya'ḳob and Aṣe Ləbnä Dəngəl who died four or five hundred years ago, and as if they, long after their bones had turned to earth and the earth to stone, were to refuse to stay in their graves and be alive again, and as if they had given birth to you (directly), as you call them all "my fathers"; you think that they are pleased when your wishes come true, and that they are grieved and offended when they do not come true. If there is blood inherited from Aṣe Zär'a Ya'ḳob, it has been distributed and diluted in so many people's veins during these four or five hundred years that it has vanished. In the five hundred years since Aṣe Zär'a Ya'ḳob died, how many poor farmers, how many poor merchants, how many poor priests, including me, too—how many do you think there are who have him as forefather if one had added them together as you do—if he is your (fore)father! This, however, is by way of explaining your vanity, but it has no connection with the problem we now have on our hands. - - - - In case you go and force the peasants to pay tribute, they will fight back and arrest you."[55]

Although this is phrased carefully and does not sound too radical, it would be taken as a warning to landowners and nobility not to go to excessive lengths in exercising their rights under the law or

---

[53] E. J. Hobsbawm (in *Bandits*, London 1969, Penguin ed. 1972, pp. 26f.) writes on social bandits among the peasantry that they do not have any other programme of reform than to restore the traditional order of the "good old days". This is in line with the demands of the peasants in *Fəkr əskä mäḳabər*, 213:15-23, 213ult.-214:29.

[54] *Fəkr əskä mäḳabər*, 334:26f. Cf. Olga Kapeliouk, "Un roman éthiopien qui annonçait la révolution", in *Le Monde Diplomatique*, April 1976.

[55] *Fəkr əskä mäḳabər*, 221:6-31.

in insisting too much on old customs, or to be unreasonable in their demands and in the use of power: force would be met with force, and the peasantry would win the day.

With *Adäfrəs*, Daññaččäw Wärku introduces us to the student world. Adäfrəs spends a year in northern Shoa on "National Service", for the time between the third and the final years of study students at the university of Addis Ababa had to work for the government, frequently as teachers. He vociferously expresses his views and is always ready to meet a challenge to his opinions and arguments.

Adäfrəs is optimistic about the nature and capabilities of man. Traditional views tend to be rather pessimistic and maybe fatalistic about man and society. Adäfrəs believes this attitude has kept Ethiopia back. Ethiopia should not fold her hands or stretch them out (hinting at Psalm 68:31), but she should work hard to progress quickly.[56] He believes ignorance is the main cause of backwardness, and education could both improve the good qualities of the people and help it to move forward fast.[57] If people are sceptical about the possibility of changing, he maintains that such doubts lead to indifference, so that they will do nothing for the development of the country; people must, he says, be brought to a better life, if necessary by force, and the first requirement is to spread literacy and to write and distribute literature about a better life:

> " - What I say is that the people, willy-nilly, even if it is by compulsion, have to learn to know a better life. - - One must open schools everywhere - - if not stone and wooden houses, then at any rate to build many mud houses - - employ teachers who have received either a modern or a traditional education, so that the people at the very least can read and write." [58]

Adäfrəs would like to see the common people wake up from their inertia and submissiveness and become assertive and defiant. To a farmer who passes singing, "Say "yes" to all they tell you, you man", Adäfrəs shouts, "Say "no" you man!" [59] and explains to Ṣiwäne:

> "The words that make me happiest are these: - - No! I refuse! No, I refuse! Of all words these seem to me to be (most) alive - -." [60]

---

[56] *Adäfrəs*, 99:25-100:3 (cf. 100:16ff.).
[57] *Ib.*, 44:26f., 112:6-10.15-18.
[58] *Ib.*, 159:12-17 (cf. the context, ll.5-20).
[59] *Ib.*, 105ult.-106:1.
[60] *Ib.*, 106:9-11.

He supports this defiant attitude when it is expressed, for example, through a "peaceful demonstration", which was not an uncommon way for students to make their views and grievances known. Students could be incited to the point of civil disobedience directed against the Emperor and the government. All these forms of protest seem to be disapproved of by the common people. Sometimes violence breaks out, and Adäfrəs is himself fatally injured by a stone thrown during a students' demonstration.[61]

Several people try to calm some of Adäfrəs's enthusiasm and to make him see other points of view as well. Ato Wäldu tells him that people who have received a modern, Western, education return to their former attitudes when they are out-numbered by people who do not have such education, and most people forget about their high ideals once the question of jobs and positions and property arises. Then most idealists adapt themselves to the system and become like all the others.[62]

Ato Wäldu has probably assessed Adäfrəs correctly. He is more radical in words than in action. By his free talk of how Ṣiwäne and Roman, the daughter and the adopted daughter of Wzo Asäggaš, can make their own way in life, and by indicating that he will personally help them, he becomes the cause of their running away from home. But when he is confronted with his own words and empty promises, he becomes evasive and does not give them any assistance at all. Roman ends up as a barmaid and a prostitute; Ṣiwäne becomes a nun. Roman he later makes his mistress—probably not exactly what she had in mind when she looked to him for help in the first place.

Mängəstu Lämma's books are not characterized by radical rhetoric, but Bahru in *Yalačča gabəčča* is in some respects radical, although in a way that is in almost direct contrast to Adäfrəs. Bahru does not talk much about change and how the country should develop. Instead, he is a man of action, and in fact he possibly contributes more to bring about change than Adäfrəs does. After he has finished his education, he does not seek government service in the capital, which seems to be the fashion among educated Ethiopians, but he goes to a small village in Hararge to teach. He marries a simple girl and lives an uncomplicated but contented and happy life. He prevails over the will of his powerful tradi-

[61] *Adäfrəs*, 38:6-11, 172:12-14, 293:9f., 325:1-21.
[62] *Ib.*, 231:26-232:6.

tionalist aunt and gets his way without too much radical or defiant talk. One could say that he is a more unusual intellectual than Adäfrəs, and he does not inspire hopes in people that he is not able to fulfil—as Adäfrəs does.

Abbe Gubäňňa is mostly concerned and preoccupied with material growth. In two of his novels, *Məlkam säyfä näbälbal* and *Aləwwällädəm*, the main characters bring about fantastic material progress and national growth within a few years. He does not seem to find change in the social system necessary, but incorruptible people can, within the existing structures, transform the country into an economically advanced nation by expanding industry, intensifying agricultural development, and by introducing all the West has to offer in the way of technical and scientific knowhow. His aim seems to be economic growth first of all, but with the preservation and strengthening of Ethiopia's traditional ethical values. There is no indication in his books how this economic miracle will or can be brought about, but his words, by being simple and by avoiding all complicating details—pointing to a bright and prosperous future—, are capable of raising great, if possibly unrealistic hopes. He does not go into problems of the cost to the people of such rapid growth, nor does he deal with the influence it will of necessity have on the customs and attitudes of people. The country that emerges in his books after such a transformation is basically old Ethiopia, but without sickness or poverty, and where the people are educated and enlightened. There are very few nuances in his characters, and the simplicity of his message might have made it more persuasive and influential and may have raised unrealistic expectations among many young people.

Bä'alu Gərma's second novel, *Yəhəllina däwäl*, sees the solution of Ethiopia's problems of progress in a new way. Haddis is a student who wants to teach and he goes to a small place in Illubabor. The school where he works is too small, the classes are too crowded, and there are too few textbooks, etc. In his frustration he goes to the headmaster to discuss possible solutions to their predicament. The director shares his worries and shows him the large correspondence between him and the government in Addis Ababa; the ministry cannot afford to expand, the school has to wait, is the recurrent theme in all answers to his complaints and his pleas for more money. Haddis is satisfied with this answer only for a short while. Then he suggests they must do something on their own. This leads to a sharp conflict between him and his boss; because the initiative and leadership come from this young man, the school director interprets this as a direct affront. The police and the religious establishment join the side of the director, while Haddis is encouraged and helped by his students and many of the students' parents and, unexpectedly, by the most powerful nobleman and landowner in the area, Fitawrari Täkka, who is among the few progressive nobles we meet in Amharic literature.

After a number of serious clashes, both with weapons and in court, all parties are reconciled, and the people join hands in a common effort to help themselves and build their own school when there is no other way.

The thrust of the argument in the story is to make people more independent of help from the central government in solving their problems and to show that a community can manage to be self-sufficient and to handle their own affairs if they cooperate and show good will.

Authors can in some cases give the strongest expression of radical criticism of existing conditions in indirect ways. Taddäsä Libän in *Mäskäräm* and *Lelaw mängäd,* and Bərhanu Zärihun in *Yä'ənba däbdabbewoč* and other books portray people, especially women, who succumb to the temptations of a changing society and founder and sink in the tumultuous maelstrom modern city life is, compared to the rather uneventful situations they, and particularly their parents, were born into. A society and a culture that crushes so many people gives rise to many objections or at least questions. Bäzzabbəh in *Fəkr əskä mäkabər* is a rather colourless figure who has things happen to him without any decisive attempts to shape events on his part. He wonders about what he sees and experiences without passing any judgment; but his innocent wondering has a radicalizing effect on the reader:

> "Now he realizes that what has happened to him is tied up with the system of social life man in general is living in. He realizes it is a system which is based on injustice, favouritism and oppression between people, between master and slave, between rulers and ruled, whether secular or spiritual. In the king's court he previously used to assume the weak would find support, those who had suffered an injustice find restitution, and a man's rights and freedom would be honoured; but he remembers what he saw one day in a royal banquet and realizes the fact that it is a place where the weak,

instead of being supported, are trodden on when they have fallen, and even those who have suffered an injustice, thinking they will find restitution for the injustice there, will not find freedom to boast of. Then he realizes clearly that among those who claim to be spiritual leaders and teachers there is no less corruption, bribes, abuse of power, injustice and foul play than the secular leaders practise.

"Oh yes, the world is a mix-up like beggar's grain; it is made like an assembly of vulgar people, so that only those who have a loud voice are heard there, and so that only those who have strong muscles win there! As for me, I am one of those who have neither an audible voice nor strong muscles! But who is it who made all this to be as it is? Is it God? Or is it custom, as Gudda Kasa always puts it?" says Bäzzabbəh, fixing his staring, non-seeing eyes in front of him. "Has the wise ("truth-knowing"), just, good, great God made this whole system based on favouritism that has neither eyes nor ears (i.e. no compassion)? And if He is not the cause of it, why does He remain silent to (i.e. does not reprove or punish) those who have made it and, while making it, live (in or by) it? I don't know! - - -"."[63]

Careful in his criticism, Haddis Alämayyähu does not let Bäzzabbəh arrive at any definite conclusion about the cause of his plight nor that of society, but the reader is not likely to blame it all on God. Social criticism is often voiced in such indirect ways, not least in the literature about life in the capital.

3. *Escapists*

In Amharic literature we meet another important group of people who can be described as escapists when it comes to getting personally involved either in preserving the old system or in creating a new one. It is possible to distinguish between escapists who do not work in or fit into any established political structure, and those who have adapted themselves to the existing system and have usually become rather faceless, purposeless members of the bureaucracy, and who are mainly found in Addis Ababa.[64]

The lonely, individual outsiders seem to have become disillusioned with society and withdrawn into themselves; frequently these have previously expressed radical views. The first character of this kind we meet is Araya. He returned to Ethiopia with strong enthusiasm and many radical ideas for changing the country into

---

[63] *Fəkr əskä mäkabər*, 462:23-463:16.
[64] E.g. *Yäkärmo säw*, 47:3-15.

a modern nation in a short time. After a brief spell as an employee of the Ministry of Agriculture, he finds that he cannot continue in government service and withdraws to a farm in Hararge and becomes a gentleman farmer till the Italians attack the country. During the war he finds some purpose, living and fighting as a freedom fighter, *arbäñña*. After the war, he is afraid the Ethiopians who have been stirred by patriotism to give all their best efforts for their country, again may fall asleep. He is offered government jobs but refuses them all at first, although his hesitation seems eventually to be overcome by his sense of duty. He has realized that his people can give their best during opposition and hardship, such as the war, and he may have a feeling that religious beliefs may be a retarding influence on Ethiopia's progress. He hardly ever voices any religious enthusiasm himself, and he obviously enjoys witnessing how a French priest is ridiculed and cornered in discussions with another Frenchman whom he characterizes as bourgeois, a category of people he likes and admires. Ethiopians are strongly attached to the Bible, and especially biblical references to themselves are cherished, first of all Psalm 68:31, "Ethiopia stretches, or shall stretch out her hands to God" (in Ethiopian versions). The Emperor also refers to this saying in a speech on his entry into the capital after the Italian occupation.[65] Araya is a man who trusts reason and hard work more than faith and divine intervention, and after he seems to have given up hope that he or his generation can achieve the reforms he had been hoping for, he looks with hope at his child as it stretches its hands, not towards God, but towards Araya, who in the novel has come to represent a rational, progressive attitude: when Ethiopia accepts his attitude, there is hope for the country; it will prosper and have a great future —this seems to be the concluding thought the author of the novel wants to convey.[66]

Ato Wäldu in *Adäfrəs* has several traits in common with Araya. He has been to France for training, been in government service in the capital, but he could not work within the bureaucracy, so he left his job and started as a merchant in Däbrä Sina. He is the

---

[65] *Araya*, 346:1-3, 348:11f.
[66] *Ib.*, 350:7-16. Both Adäfrəs, in *Adäfrəs*, 99:25-100:2 (cf. 100:16f.), and Haddis in *Yähəllina däwäl*, 178:19-21, 223:12ff., think that to progress Ethiopia should work, and not only leave it all to God, referring to Psalm 68:31.

brother of Wzo Asäggaš, who keeps and runs the farm they should have inherited together. As he does not care too much about the farm, and as he is a kindly, perhaps rather weak personality, he lives a simple life, marries an illiterate woman with traditional, pagan beliefs, and he does not interfere with politics or anything outside his business. Adäfrəs, with his pronounced views, draws Ato Wäldu into many discussions on politics, development and reform.

Like others in similar positions, Ato Wäldu tries to rationalize and justify his escapism and does his best to modify Adäfrəs's views and his provocative way of airing them. What it amounts to is practically a defence of passivity. He does not try to lead his wife away from her trust in pagan spirits and their manifestation through or by means of beads, because he is sceptical about people's capacity for or willingness to change; Ethiopians do not use or trust their intellect, and they prefer to keep their children as shepherds rather than send them to school, and they prefer to spend their money on *ṭäj* rather than on books that could improve their lives.[67] Ato Wäldu's son Bälay also believes Adäfrəs is wasting his efforts when he tries to change people.[68] When Ato Wäldu senses the direction of Adäfrəs's thought, that he advocates wide-ranging, almost revolutionary reforms and changes, he goes into details about similar developments in Austria during the reign of Maria Theresa's heir, and how disastrous the outcome was. Although the example is taken from Europe, it is meant to apply to Ethiopia and serve as a warning to Adäfrəs, and since it is one of the most detailed discussions in Amharic literature of a radical, revolutionary programme for a country, it is worth noting. This is how Ato Wäldu tells it, slightly shortened:

> This Austrian king, successor of Maria Theresa, believed, as so many of his contemporaries, in human rights, expressed in the words liberty, equality and fraternity. His mother, who lived till she was ninety-nine years old, had experience of many kinds of government. She made peerages hereditary, so that a nobleman's son became a nobleman and the sons of the poor remained poor. The people were content, the inferior obeying their superiors, and the superiors imbuing their inferiors with proper respect. The king, in the spirit of equality, decided to do away with this stratification of inferiors and superiors and make all one. As soon as his

---

[67] *Adäfrəs*, 156:25f.29-31, 159:5-9.21-26.
[68] *Ib.*, 43:28ff.

mother was dead, he invited the nobles and high officials to the palace, and after the banquet he shut them in the palace so they should not return home and distributed their lands and wealth to those who were living or working under them. It is said he called them "my mother's hangers-on" when he invited them. And what was the outcome of his actions? Human rights: equality, fraternity, liberty indeed! Because there was no justice or equality anywhere, "small" and "big" were created. The "big" people he created became worse than those created by his mother. They fleeced and tormented the people. The people came to the palace to complain, asking for their former masters to be released. The king could not understand this. He asked them why they preferred a class-society to equality. They replied that it was because they were poor and used to poverty, affliction, hunger, thirst, being whipped and arrested and did not feel anything from it, but their masters felt it because they were caught in an unusual situation and the people did not want to see them suffer. The king said they were not able to value and appreciate equality because they lacked education, so he would send them teachers and build schools. But they countered that they only wanted their masters back, and neither teachers nor schools. The king had been deluded by ideas of equality and would not accept the petition of the people. The outcome was that the peasants came one night and broke into the palace where the nobles were kept. The guards killed many of the peasants, but some of the nobles were able to escape. Under the leadership of these nobles, the countrymen rose against the king, who was unable to resist or defeat them and was forced to release the remaining prisoners from among the nobles and officials. The king had to flee and died in exile. And this, adds Ato Wäldu, was his reward for thinking and working for illiterate, ignorant people.[69]

When Adäfrəs challenges him to give his view on the Ethiopian situation, Ato Wäldu says the Ethiopian people may choose a class society, but their first concern is to be left in peace, with stability, so that they can live without worry and do what they like. They will have "security" rather than "liberty"; freedom without stability means nothing to the Ethiopian people. Their symbols of stability are their wives, property and religion, just as liberty, equality and fraternity symbolized freedom for the French. Perhaps Ethiopians would accept the idea of "fraternity" if it were not presented as a new-fangled thing, but presented in the context of traditional values, such as showing hospitality to strangers. And they may accept "equality" too if it is presented in the context of their religion, because man was created in the image of God and

---

[69] *Adäfrəs*, 151:1-152ult.

is equal before his Creator. And also "liberty" they may accept if one does not present it as a novelty but says it means to respect a man's private property and not to expand one's land at the expense of someone else's, in which case one would be called an enemy of liberty. It is therefore not to be wondered at, says Ato Wäldu, if people do not accept the ideas of modern youth but regard them as mad and want to exclude them from their society if the modern generation talks of liberty and pretends it is something that has never existed or been seen before, because "one is not homesick for an unseen land". Even the youth of today should understand that limitless freedom is no freedom but an unrealizable illusion or fixation of the mind, he concludes.[70] Although he adds later that he has been to France and therefore can understand and sympathize with the aspirations and views of the younger generation of students,[71] one gets the impression that not much would be changed if his attitude were shared by all the people, including the educated. He can "sympathize" but counsels moderation and tries to calm and cool Adäfrəs's enthusiasm as much as he can. He is not a man who wants too much responsibility, and he withdraws easily within himself.

Guddu Kasa in *Fəkr əskä mäḳabər* has already been mentioned as a person who expresses radical views, but there may be aspects of his "madness" that are expressions of escapism. He takes recourse to his reputation for being "mad" or "a fool" to express unpleasant views, but he uses this soubriquet also as a refuge to avoid too sharp a rejoinder and rebuke for expressing his thoughts.[72] He even says he has been given his nickname because he has kept silent and wants to live his own life in peace.[73] He is, in other words, not called "madman" or "fool" only for voicing his views but also for withdrawing and not wanting to have anything to do with his family's affairs. In his wish to avoid conflicts and troubles he has been driven out of his inheritance and left with only a small piece of land. He is educated in the traditional wisdom of his country as the son of a nobleman and has spent several years in church schools. He has turned radical in many ways, but he is also a philosophical man who believes in sticking to himself, except

---

[70] *Adäfrəs*, 153:1-30.
[71] *Ib.*, 154:12-18.
[72] *Fəkr əskä mäḳabər*, 116:19-26, 118:21-30, 123:2-13.
[73] *Ib.*, 334:25-29.

when he sees a chance of rescuing Säblä Wängel from the stifling influence of her family and surroundings. Towards the end of his life, Guddu Kasa escapes from society by living like a monk together with Säblä Wängel, his niece, till he dies.[74]

Madness is an excuse for saying what could not otherwise be said that has been resorted to in many societies through the ages, and it seems to be prevalent during times of crises and social change. The "mad fool" is often the sanest of all, as Guddu Kasa is in *Fəkr əskä mäkabər*, and his "madness" is at the same time a form of protest against society and against the norms most people live by.[75] In a sense Emperor Tewodros may also have exaggerated his reputation for madness to find excuses for some of his ideas and excesses. He was given the nickname *əbd gäbrä kidan*, "Gäbrä Kidan the fool, or madman".[76] Ethiopian authors have been aware of this kind of "madness", and Afäwärk Yohannəs has written a poem with the title, "Even madness has its uses".[77]

Another group of people that can be termed escapists have accommodated themselves within the bureaucracy and are in government employ. We have already met the Ethiopian consul in Djibouti, as described in *Araya*, and both he and a secretary at the consulate advocate slow, carefully prepared change and progress, so that the old order is not unnecessarily upset. This view seems to be an excuse for doing as little as possible, and Araya calls it conservative. He maybe censures the two men too severely, and it is probably closer to the truth to say that they have to voice government policy and that there is not much they can do on their own. To be on the safe side, they defend the "official" view; but it may still be called escapism. The consul even hopes Araya's zeal may not cool off after he has entered Ethiopia, a thing that had happened to many young people after they returned home, as he observes.[78]

Ato Ṭəso in *Adäfrəs* is a government judge who is in favour of change, but when it comes to actual proposals of how this should be done, he gets entangled in contradictions and sees so many objections to concrete steps to be taken that his attitude amounts to one of leaving things much as they are.

[74] *Fəkr əskä mäkabər*, 552:3-25.
[75] Cf. Chr. Hill, *The World turned Upside Down*, London, 1972, chapter 13.
[76] Cf. DTW, p. 74.
[77] Afäwärk Yohannəs, *And afta*, Addis Ababa, 1972-73, p. 50.
[78] *Araya*, 110:6-116:11, 121:19ff.

Sudden, disruptive changes he believes are harmful and must be avoided. What the country needs is change based on true knowledge of the people, not theoretical knowledge that is obtained "only at the university or in an office" (an argument often used to reject the legitimacy of other views, as the speaker usually claims to be the sole possessor of a true knowledge of the people). Social change, he says, must take account of the spirit of the people and what they will fight for. If they feel threatened, they will rise in defence of their religion, property, or land. This is the kind of aim and purpose the people must be given in order to be alerted and give of their energy and fighting spirit, and "any change must avail itself of such spiritual aspirations"; otherwise it is of no use to try and introduce changes and reforms.[79] The kind of change he envisages is the spreading of "light" through education by building schools, but one should not ask for the impossible, "so that you are not compared to the biased judge who asks for the hump of a chicken".[80] But when it comes to doing something, he defends the kind of leader he calls *afaddaš*, those who only talk of reforms but do nothing to implement them.[81] If they actually did anything, it would lead to massive, unbridled demands for change that could not be stemmed, and this would be harmful and destroy the traditional values of the common people.[82] Such demands for change would hardly be any threat if there were no need for them, so he is left with the ideal of preserving as much as possible of the "Ethiopian personality", at least as much as is compatible with modern life. One should not give up any of the national character if it is found to be better than the imported Western culture.[83] In practice, he comes back repeatedly to his main idea, that change should be slow, after careful consideration of all the pros and cons, although this in reality amounts to little or nothing. His escapism is seen in his admission that he does not have any firm views at all:

"I did not say that my way is the best".[84]
"I want that each man should investigate for himself, but not that he should follow my way." [85]

---

[79] *Adäfrəs*, 89:10-30.
[80] *Ib.*, 91:8-12.
[81] *Ib.*, 86:1-89:7.
[82] *Ib.*, 87:25-88:6.
[83] *Adäfrəs*, 230:1-14. Chapter 37 contains a discussion of what to change and what to preserve unchanged.
[84] *Ib.*, 284:11.
[85] *Ib.*, 284:12f.

> "If we had wanted to choose everything that is compatible with our times, it means we would have destroyed (all) trace of our identity. Moreover, how can we only say the past is past and forget it? How can it be denied that everything that was true in the past is also true today? Truth does not become old and vanish, Adäfrəs; truth is eternal." [86]

For a man who does not say his idea is right or want others to follow his path, it seems peculiar that he has so many objections to concrete proposals for change. In fact, he talks like a man who seeks ways to escape from the responsibility of taking the consequences of his own views, which are sometimes arch-conservative, at other times almost radical, as for example his support of more education, which would eventually undermine and lead to the loss of many of the old values. He does not want to commit himself either way.

The Ethiopian consul in Djibouti thought Araya's vigour and enthusiasm might one day wane, as had happened to other returning students of a similar frame of mind:

> "And, truly, because so many youths,—when they returned after having stayed abroad, after they initially had shown a strong eagerness concerning service of their country and concerning love of work,—as they stayed for a short while, their spirits gradually cooled off and were defeated, he grived (thinking) that this youth too might become like this." [87]

In a way, one can say that the consul's fear was justified: Araya's zeal did abate.

A similar prediction was made by Ato Wäldu concerning Adäfrəs: when those with Western education were outnumbered by those lacking such education in a place of work, the westernized youths would forget about their former ideas and ideals and return to more traditional values and behaviour. Adäfrəs does withdraw from responsibility when it comes to taking the consequences of his reformist ideas, and had he lived, it seems likely he would have become like so many of Ato Wäldu's contemporaries who had been absorbed by the system when they obtained wealth and position and achieved greatness.[88]

The majority of the educated we meet in literature about life

---
[86] *Adäfrəs*, 284:19-24.
[87] *Araya*, 116:6-11.
[88] *Adäfrəs*, 231:26-232:2.

in Addis Ababa are working in government jobs. Mostly they are faceless, purposeless young men who are only preoccupied with the pursuit of pleasure. When this is satisfied, they get involved in philosophical questions of the kind, "Who are we?", and go in search of their own "identity".

Office talk among young men, especially on Monday mornings, mostly concerns their successes with women during the weekend.[89] Many authors have written about these restless, aimless people. Ṣäggaye Gäbrä Mädhən sets the scene of *Yäšoh aklil* among "young Ethiopians of today", living in a different world from that of previous generations, where traditions have been mixed up with modern civilization and ideas, unsteady, undecided, confused about who they are and where they are going.[90] The problems are much the same in *Bälg* and *Yäkärmo säw*. Bərhanu Zärihun lets the main character in *Amanuʾel därso mäls* characterize himself as "one of the lost generation".[91] Taddäsä Libän writes often about the same kind of young townspeople in both his collections of short stories, *Mäskäräm* and *Lelaw mängäd*. Abbe Gubäñña's characters in *Yäräggäfu abäboč* travel from bar to bar, seeking enjoyment and discussing social problems. The question of "knowing oneself" often recurs in this literature set in the capital, and it is an important theme in *Käʾadmas bašagär* and in *Adäfrəs* (which is not set in Addis Ababa but deals with people who have come from there).[92] In the former book, Bäʾalu Gərma tells the story of many mixed-up people, and particularly of Abärra and Lulit, the two main characters in the book. Abärra is a well-educated man, but he cannot settle down to anything for long. He goes from job to job but wants to be an artist. Like many of his friends, he leaves his work half-finished. His mind "gallops from one thought to another" without being able to keep to one line of thought or to one plan, so he has to drop "his hopes of becoming a poet or a writer or a painter"; he concludes that it is useless to think as "thinking leads nowhere; the important thing is to live, to know the taste of living".[93] People come to hate themselves, dependent as they are "on the shoulder of the government", unable to stand

---

[89] *Čäräḵa sətwäṭa*, 16:21-17:10; cf. *Käʾadmas bašagär*, 15:6-8.
[90] *Yäšoh aklil*, 5:1-7.
[91] *Amanuʾel därso mäls*, 5:8-11.
[92] Cf. *Adäfrəs*, 40:28, 41:1-3, etc.
[93] *Käʾadmas bašagär*, 6:1-11.

on their own two feet. "So what do you suggest that we can do? Let us rather drink!" [94] But if they are asked to make even a small sacrifice for the development of the country, without waiting for the government to take the initiative and do everything alone, these same people are the first to complain. "We are afraid to stand on our two feet. We have no faith in ourselves. We do not know ourselves (our identity) - - -".[95] Lulit has been sexually assaulted and abused as a child and now enjoys taking revenge on men she can gain power over and humiliate. Both she and Abärra find hope "beyond the horizon" (the title of the book) when they fall deeply in love with each other. But by that time Abärra is in prison, having killed a man with whom he believed Lulit had been unfaithful to him, and Lulit falls in love with him when she realizes the strength of his love when he would go to the extent of killing for her sake. When they both seem to have found hope and some kind of meaning to their lives, they are in a rather hopeless situation.

The last categories of escapists worth noting are not very prominent in Amharic literature but might be socially more important than the literature gives impression of. These are simple people who are caught up in events they cannot handle and seek a way out.

Roman in *Adäfrəs* cannot stand the isolated, restricted life of the countryside, nor the thought of marrying a man she does not know, so she runs away to town, although she has no choice but to become a prostitute. With the abundance of whores we encounter in Amharic literature, it is a likely inference that many have chosen the same way as Roman, and for similar reasons. Abbe Gubäñña tells of such a girl in *Kältammawa əhəte*.

Gorfu, also in *Adäfrəs*, does not succeed in his plans for his private life, to marry Şiwäne and take over his father's land, so he leaves it all behind and joins the army. Of many who must have taken the same way, he is one of the few we find described in Amharic literature.

More authors have depicted flight to a convent, or the life of a solitary nun, as the way out for girls and young women who have met with situations or problems which seem to have no straightforward solutions. A mistreated servant girl in *Aläm wärätäñña* runs away to a convent, is reunited with her mother and lives in

---

[94] *Kä'admas bašagär*, 32:23-33:8.
[95] *Ib.*, 72:8-13.

peace for the rest of her life.[96] Haddis Alämayyähu finds a similar solution for Säblä Wängel in *Fəkr əskä mäḵabər*: after she has fled home and believes Bäzzabbəh is dead, she starts living a solitary life; and after they are actually reunited for a few days and are married shortly before Bäzzabbəh dies, she lives the life of a nun "till the grave", as the title of the novel alludes to. In *Adäfrəs*, too, the problems overwhelm Ṣiwäne, and Daňňaččäw Wärḵu finds the same way out for her: she escapes to a convent. There seems to be no other way in which she can keep her sanity and dignity, as she cannot return home, and neither does she want to become a prostitute, nor has her education prepared her for an independent, professional life.

---

[96] *Arrəmuňň*, pp. 43-77.

CHAPTER SEVEN

MAIN AREAS OF CHANGE

1. *Progress*

a) *Education*

When Ethiopian authors write about the need and benefits of education for a modern society, they normally mean Western-type education. Blattengeta Həruy does stress the value of church education for the spiritual development of Ṣəyon Mogäsa in *Yäləbb hassab*, and Araya also realizes there are certain benefits of such an education.[1] But in both these books the emphasis is on a modern secular education, as in most Amharic literature.

Araya wants "to learn Western education" because he thinks Ethiopians have "remained in ignorance", "stayed behind or backward", and are split on ethnic and religious grounds because of "lack of education". Education is needed for progress, for material and moral growth, and to obtain equality.[2] He says:

> "In their talents and natures all people are different. But this is not a difference between the common people and the nobility, between master and poor. Because all people are of one nature, they are equal. Only education and competition have produced differences. If the country's wealth is properly distributed to everyone according to his knowledge, ability or responsibility, and each one takes his proper place, the benefit he will give to the country will be immeasurable. From the time the people of Europe gained their rights, even if it was by revolution, the progress in civilization flowing from this revolution has been beneficial to all mankind." [3]

Emphasis on education is one of the points Araya notices in favour of the French bourgeoisie, whereas the French nobility had lost power and influence by neglecting education and valuing, instead, government appointments or titles and martial arts.[4]

Mäkonnən Ǝndalkaččäw envisages a time and a society with

---

[1] *Yäləbb hassab*, 147:17-23, *Araya*, 16:15-30.
[2] *Araya*, 17:7-13, 26:23f., 96:6f., 147:26-29, 302:7-16.
[3] *Ib.*, 139:28-140:30.
[4] *Ib.*, 50:7-14; 49:2ff.

freedom for all and sees education as necessary to make good use of one's freedom and to gain spiritual freedom.[5] In *Adäfrəs*, schools are seen as a melting pot of all ethnic groups and languages. Adäfrəs thinks school wakes people up and that students are "lights" in the country. Education, he says, ought to be compulsory up to the sixth grade and could prevent the ill effects of rapid change, i.e. revolution.[6] Education is spreading, not only through schools but through radio and newspapers.[7] Most educational facilities are found in towns, and it seems to be an allegorical reference to this situation when Daňňaččäw Wärku describes the Ṭarmabär mountain range covered in dark clouds that move and form chaotic patterns. Beneath, a thin milky fog is hanging over the forests and mountain slopes, all the way down to the towns. A strong, dry wind blows relentlessly, carrying with it a strong smell of fire.[8] This probably alludes to the effect enlightenment is likely to have on the rest of the country: it will be like a wind that sweeps the darkness away and causes a conflagration in the land. This is in line with the characterization of students as "lights", already referred to.[9] Adäfrəs sees crime as a result of ignorance, and instead of hanging a murderer, society should remove the cause of his crime which, he believes, is ignorance: instead it should educate him, so that he can become a useful member of society and avoid criminal deeds.[10] Evil and backwardness are overcome, and all good qualities are encouraged and strengthened through education, he thinks. The result of it will be a better life.[11] In *Addis aläm*, proposals for higher moral standards for the clergy are linked to suggestions for enhancing their level of education.[12] When people are educated, they are likely to stop trusting sorcerers, and the conditions of life and the health of the people begin to improve.[13] Also traditionalists can say that "there is no greater wealth than knowledge" and that "education has no end" but stress that "the most important thing is not to learn much: the most important

---

[5] *Yäfəkər ṭora*, 192:6-194:12.
[6] *Adäfrəs*, 84:21f., 91:10-14, 165:5-7, 108:4-6.
[7] *Ib.*, 164:22f.
[8] *Ib.*, 92:1-5.
[9] Cf. also *ib.*, 91:3-12.
[10] *Ib.*, 252:10-24, 263:25-264:6, 264:11-15.
[11] *Ib.*, 112:6-18, 159:12-20.
[12] *Addis aläm*, 24:3ff.
[13] *Yäläbb hassab*, 172:24-174:2 (cf. 175:29ff.); *Yähəllina däwäl*, 97:1-13.

thing is to practise what you have learned".[14] Haddis, a university student in *Yähəllina däwäl*, almost makes a religion out of education. "Love is God, God is love", he says; and people who love do not distinguish between people's race, colour or religion, between rich or poor, big or small, but regard all as equal. And "the ladder of love is knowledge—and the basis of knowledge is the school. Therefore I say school is the new church (or house of God)".[15]

Käbbädä Mika'el has done much in his writing to promote education. His views on the benefits of education are briefly stated in a short poem he calls "The gleam of knowledge", which reads in prose translation:

> "When the child studies diligently and the scholar works night and day to strengthen the spirit, and when the ray of light that was a gleam of knowledge expands and becomes the light of dawn, and when the light of wisdom shines and warms like the midday sun, and steadily grows - then one can say the country has become civilized.
> If knowledge does not spread, if wisdom is not heightened, if the child is not crowned with the crown of education, and if the wise man does not develop (proper) laws of procedure, wanting to attain greatness seeking another kind of way, that is a vain dream, that is a great deception; believe me, it is in vain, it is to chase the wind." [16]

Araya showed early on a spirit of enquiry—he wanted to know, to understand—which was in many respects perceived as a new thing; and by observing Europeans he acquired a spirit of competitiveness, hoping to do something for his country that could eventually lead Ethiopia to reach the same level of development as the West.[17]

Several authors have seen Western Europe as a model for Ethiopia's progress. Blattengeta Həruy presents his ideas for reforming the Church and aspects of society through the character of Awwäḳä in *Addis aläm*. Awwäḳä comes soon upon his return from France into conflict with those around him through objecting to honouring customs of long standing in Ethiopia. Not only does he object to ruining himself through giving expensive feasts, but he rejects a girl his family has chosen for him as a wife; he will

---

[14] *Yähəllina däwäl*, 144:9-15.
[15] *Yähəllina däwäl*, 144:15-145:18; cf. 147:15-19.
[16] *Yäḳəne azmära*, 7:1-14.
[17] *Araya*, 16:7-9, 17:11-13.

not express his grief in the traditional manner, and he even insists on dressing like a European. Mockery of his behaviour soon leads to more serious clashes, but in the end he gets his way, and many reforms are introduced.

Araya also goes to France to acquire a modern European education before he starts his attempts at reforming his country. He has studied agriculture, but his desire is to stimulate comprehensive changes in the whole of society and that such changes should happen quickly. He tries to work for change within the government and also to convince others, including government officials, members of the nobility, and his own illiterate mother, of the benefits of such reforms. Unlike Awwäḳä, Araya cannot be said to be successful in his attempts at reforming society. But the book *Araya* has had a profound influence on a whole generation of Ethiopian students, as it has been used as a school textbook in secondary schools for many years.[18]

In a less conspicuous way, Mängəstu Lämma has used a similar character, Bahru in *Yalačča gabəčča*, who has been abroad for education and then quietly takes up the work of a teacher in a remote village in Hararge and finds satisfaction in his work. Slowly, the people catch on to his ideas, and even the local astrologer finds some school education useful for his calculations.

Adäfrəs has not been abroad, but he wants to go abroad one day, and so does the less educated Ṣiwäne in the same novel.[19] In the literature of more recent years, ideas are often seen to be spread by university students. Both Adäfrəs in the book of that name and Haddis in *Yähəllina däwäl* go into the countryside and communicate new ideas, which are also spread by the daily habits of educated youth, such as eating at the same table as their servants.[20]

Modern education is not always very deep, causing not only enlightenment but also confusion. People who share the old beliefs and superstitions of the country, although realizing certain benefits in the building of schools, become hostile, in *Yähəllina däwäl*, when there seems to be a conflict between new ideas and their old religious

---

[18] Cf. Asfaw Melaku, "Language teaching materials: Amharic". (in M. L. Bender *et al.*, (eds.) *Language in Ethiopia*, London, 1976, pp. 400-414), p. 411.
[19] *Adäfrəs*, 23:1-4.
[20] *Yalačča gabəčča*, 61:1-65:4.

practices. During a time of drought, the local people want to destroy a school built at a place where they used to sacrifice, as they suspect the natural catastrophe may be caused by the cessation of sacrifices at the accustomed spot. "Shall we perish for the sake of one school?" they ask.[21]

Superficial education may also have its cause in teachers who are not really interested in their job but have taken it because they cannot find anything better; as soon as an opportunity comes, they will leave for better paid jobs.[22] Modern education is confusing because of the many aspects and choices it offers the student, especially the student going abroad; therefore many become westernized "only on the surface".[23]

Taddäsä Libän's story *Jəbb näč* [24] tells of a secondary school pupil who rejects the old belief that a girl who has the evil eye (a *buda*) can turn into a hyena by night, because he thinks such a view is contradicted both by the Bible and by science. But when he spends a night with a girl rumoured to be a *buda* and she is not found in bed when he wakes up, but her hair is in the room, his biblical and scientific arguments fail to convince him and he reverts to the belief that she may be a *buda* after all. Only after the girl returns and tells her story that she lost her hair in an accident when she was young, and only after inspecting her head does he accept that she is a normal girl wearing a wig. The story points to the shallowness of many recently acquired views and beliefs and how easy it is to relapse into traditional, "unscientific" ways of thinking.

There is also some scepticism of education among students themselves; Bälay, a twelfth grader, tells Adäfrəs that he does not think "too much" education is good.[25] Purely theoretical knowledge is not much good,[26] and Gorfu, a farmer and a nobleman's son who has been to a government school for six years, is critical of an education that is copied from Western countries without being adapted to Ethiopia's needs and tested under local conditions. He finds, for example, the traditional classification of animals into useful, harmful, poisonous, useless and bothersome

---

[21] *Yähəllina däwäl*, 85:10-17, 86:8.
[22] *Ib.*, 141:11-142:26.
[23] *Yägəṭəm guba'e*, 20:22-21:3, *Yalačča gabəčča*, 40:21-41:2, 54:4ff., 68:1-5.
[24] *Mäskäräm*, pp. 11-28.
[25] *Adäfrəs*, 58:21.
[26] *Ib.*, 89:10-14.

ones more relevant for farmers than the academic classification of animals according to whether they are vertebrate or not, as this does not help anyone to get a good harvest or to shoot straight. Instead of envying educated people, Gorfu pities them: if they should not find employment in government offices but had to live among the people and help themselves, they would be completely helpless.[27] He extends his criticism to other fields also: imported agricultural machinery is not suited to the Ethiopian uneven landscape and soil; foreign pesticides do not kill all pests but only the weaker ones, whereas the stronger ones become resistant and flood the land; some medicines that have an effect abroad may not work in Ethiopia.[28] His views, although somewhat naïvely expressed, are sensible and more relevant to Ethiopia than the views expressed by many students. On the whole, there is much emphasis on the value of education in Amharic literature, but there is very little discussion of what should be taught and for what specific purpose or purposes. "Western education" and a knowledge of foreign languages and science may have much prestige,[29] but the direct use to which they are or could be put is hardly considered at all. Even a novel like *Yähəllina däwäl*, which has the building of a school and the promotion of education as the leading thought, does not go beyond generalities when it comes to stating what schools and education are for. Haddis, the main character, sees the schools of western Ethiopia as a source of new ideas, a meeting point for parents and children, a "sanctuary of love, the basis of unity and a big market of knowledge".[30]

Much of the discussion of the value of education lacks precision and direction. Probably Blattengeta Həruy is the most specific in *Yäləbb hassab* and *Addis aläm* where he relates education to improved health and childcare and to a number of concrete reforms and changed customs. Ethiopian authors do, however, strongly urge better education, which in most cases means Western education.

b) *Urbanization*

Urbanization is related to changes in the economic structure of society, with increased opportunities for the enterprising or for

---

[27] *Adäfrəs*, 200:1-201:28.
[28] *Ib.*, 202:4-203:4.
[29] *Ib.*, 25:20-22, 27:29-31.
[30] *Yähəllina däwäl*, 147:15-19.

those who feel oppressed or too restricted by the traditional way of life; and it is related to changes in the administration of the country, to education, and to improved communications. In all these fields towns have benefited more than the countryside, and new ideas from abroad and new patterns of behaviour in personal and social relationships occur first in towns.

When signs of a new lifestyle, new affluence and new ideas of freedom reach the countryside, the temptation to move to town—first the nearest, than the bigger, and especially Addis Ababa—becomes great.

People seem prepared and eager to accept at least some changes, so many of the new influences are readily accepted.[31] Young people flood to towns, and both uneducated people, young and old, and others who have been to school, long to go to Addis Ababa or some other town.[32] Education seems to have whetted young people's appetites for more changes, and the older generation, in particular those who need their children's help on the land or to look after them in their old age, complain of being deserted by their young children who have been to school. An old man says:

> "What I feel sorry about is that at this hour I lack someone to look after me in my old age, and a helper (in my work). My eldest son said, "I have learned the European alphabet and (therefore) I will not live here", and he ran away. Also my daughter, visiting some relatives who had spent the rainy season (or some time) in Addis Ababa and were glittering with ornaments, and seeing some friends who came (from there), she also ran away from home, saying, "Why shouldn't I too be like them". Since this gravel road came here to Supe, everyone has gone away. Only old women and old men stayed at home—without anyone to look after them in their old age, without helpers." [33]

Both education (with the new opportunities for employment and earning money), luxury and roads are here mentioned as reasons for young people's flight to the towns. The educated are particularly blamed for not wanting to work with their hands but to look only for "wealth" in Addis Ababa.[34] The motivation for this migration is primarily the pursuit of luxury and the easy life, and this often changes the character of young people:

---

[31] *Adäfrəs*, 28:11-14.
[32] *Ib.*, 108:21f., 122:13f., 123:3f.; 23:2f.
[33] *Yähəllina däwäl*, 86:23-87:2; cf. 57:1-6.
[34] *Ib.*, 107:6-17.

"But many who were born in these valleys emigrated to town in pursuit of a comfortable life, and when they started a new life, they got a completely different character, and became either like Taddäsä (i.e. a degenerated man he had met in Dire Dawa), or they became extremely selfish, devious and crafty and give civilization (or Western culture) a bad name." [35]

Obviously people are streaming to towns faster than they can be properly absorbed. Therefore large numbers of beggars, streetboys and thieves are found, and prostitutes are so numerous— 50,000 prostitutes and 20,000 bars in Addis Ababa are mentioned in a novel by Bərhanu Zärihun—that many have to beg to survive; drunkenness is rife and many live in poor conditions.[36]

The urban style of living has often made only a superficial impression, "cut into only on the edges" (ṭraz näṭṭäḵ), and people who have been slightly affected by such changes in appearance are said to have "parted their hair", not a particularly useful or convenient custom to take over from the West.[37] Town life has come with so fast and sweeping changes that many have been confused by it. One man in Addis Ababa with roots in the countryside says, "I and my equals do not know what we want".[38] Ṣäggaye Gäbrä Mädhən's play Yäkärmo säw is largely about this conflict between the town and the country, and one young man in the play who goes to prison sees his future life as more meaningful if he can go back to his father's land and cultivate the soil and leave the town behind.

A girl like Frewa (Ato Ṭəso's daughter) in Adäfrəs, who has grown up in Addis Ababa, is depicted as restless and full of pretence and artificial behaviour (and strongly contrasted to Ṣiwäne who has grown up in the countryside).[39] Townspeople, especially the young, dress differently, neglect religious customs, are careless about outward appearances, how they dress and behave; children have greater freedom from parental authority and interference, and they develop faster. But in towns there are also great problems: marital problems increase, divorce and unfaithfulness are more frequent, etc.[40]

---

[35] *Araya*, 181:28-32.
[36] *Čäräka sətwäṭa*, 29:19-22; 5:10-6:2, *Kä'admas bašagär*, 56:8f., 100:21f., *Amanu'el därso mäls*, 31:1ff.
[37] *Yalaččä gabəččä*, 68:1-5, 81:3-5, *Araya*, 135:8, *Adäfrəs*, 58:24f., 108:4-6.
[38] *Yäkärmo säw*, 41:8f., cf. 47:3-8.
[39] *Adäfrəs*, 35:1-13 (cf. 26:14-21, 27:2-12.22-26).
[40] *Ib.*, 36:6f., 37:19-28, 104:1-4.17f., 107:23-108:3, 108:8-11.

MAIN AREAS OF CHANGE 209

In Amharic literature we meet different views of urbanization in Ethiopia, and several authors are critical of the development, especially in the form it has taken in some of the bigger towns.

When Araya arrives in Dire Dawa, coming from abroad, he pays compliments to the "foreign" section of the town for being orderly, clean and well regulated. But he is severe in his criticism of the "native" part of the town.[41] He meets Taddäsä, the son of a man he had known as a child, and describes him as a man who has accepted the worst parts of urban "culture". His clothes are half European, half Ethiopian, his hair is cut without style or taste; his speech and behaviour do not please Araya, because it is neither Ethiopian nor foreign but a tasteless mixture of the worst elements of both.[42] Taddäsä's drinking habits Araya finds particularly objectionable, because he finds they take the place of more valuable, "spiritual" interests.[43]

When Araya comes to Addis Ababa he is not much more favourably impressed. There is no plan or style or organization in the way houses are built, and all kinds of houses are erected side by side; this gives the town an ugly look, and the visitor notices the poverty and lack of cleanliness. Pedestrians have to find their way among cars and cattle, and this causes great confusion. Armed riders with their retinues can be seen in the streets, and merchants —mostly foreigners—display their goods—mostly clothes and arrack—to the passers-by.[44] During the Italian occupation, Addis Ababa changed much.[45]

When Bäzzabbəh, in *Fəkr əskä mäkabər*, travels towards Addis Ababa in the company of some merchants from Gojjam, he is being prepared for what to expect by the views of these merchants:

> ""If people who know how to work walk till the skin peels off their legs, don't think they will find a place like Addis Ababa!" one of them tells him.
> "Addis Ababa is a place for thieves but not a place for people who work and live (normally)! Do you think the thieves of Addis Ababa are like the thieves of your place who steal under cover of darkness? No, they take your money out of your pocket while your

---

[41] *Araya*, 126:23ff., 129:1-27.
[42] *Ib.*, 131:1-22, 135:7-20.
[43] *Ib.*, 131:23-135:6.
[44] *Ib.*, 151:15-152:9.
[45] *Ib.*, 334:26-335:4.

eyes look at them! How, I don't know, I believe they hypnotize you!", another one tells him.

"Oh - - - -! And one who can write can get bags of money for writing *ləfafä ṣədḳ* and *kətab* (i.e. pieces of parchment with magic formulas to keep evil away) in Addis Ababa!" the first one tells him.

"Now, today the educated (i.e. church educated) man has become of little value, he is of no use! Previously, if you wrote a life of a saint and gave it to a noble, you would get a strong slave or fifty to sixty dollars; but today - - - it is better to be ignorant like me than to be a scholar; one who carries wood or stone or water will live with a full stomach!" the other one tells him." [46]

Later Bäzzabbəh nearly gets beaten up for doing what good manners require in the countryside: he greets everyone he meets in the street. In Addis Ababa, he is told, this is done only by thieves and other criminals.[47]

In Addis Ababa the big open-air market called Mercato is the centre of much activity and the place where most people go to make their purchases or to sell; others come to steal. Ṣäggaye Gäbrä Mädhən has written a poem he calls "Oh, Mercato", in a collection of poetry.[48] This market is a mirror of the teeming life in the capital. He describes the Mercato as a crowded place where people bring all kinds of goods to sell, and where one has to wind in and out among people and things to get anywhere. There everyone is trying to buy cheap or sell with a high profit, and people move about with feelings of hope or worry, not knowing what the day will bring. Some make a fortune out of the market transactions, others are ruined; one man's profit is the other man's loss, and fortune frequently smiles on one who is clever at bargaining. Noisy discussions and squabbles are commonplace here where people from the countryside bring their goods for the townsman or the "worldly monk or priest" to buy. Merchants find rich profits and labourers earn their daily bread here—everyone can gain something. But all the business of trading is accompanied by plenty of insults and fighting that sometimes end in someone getting hurt; at other times, agreement is reached and the parties separate while blessing each other (which may take the concrete form of the merchant adding a small quantity of his merchandise as a free extra, i.e. a "blessing"). A multitude of different languages are heard, and

---

[46] *Fəḵr əskä mäḳabər*, 433:11-434:3.
[47] *Ib.*, 435:8-438:5.
[48] *Ḥsat wäy abäba*, pp. 30-33.

some gain in popularity whereas others wane, and words from one language are mixed into another language, and sometimes new words and argots are created. Everything must be done in a hurry, causing a flurry of life, activities, words, altercations; and there one's sweat flows. Brokers, small traders and thieves are all active, trying to get what they can from prospective customers. When traders return home with their profits, they are often attacked by robbers "who hit the nape of the neck". The Mercato is a place of commotion, full of all kinds of noises and bad smells, that fills many people's needs, and many profit from it; it has become "all-embracing".

What this poem says of the Mercato applies in many respects to the town as well. It is a place of transactions where people of many tribes and languages assemble from the rest of the country. It is not primarily productive, but goods from everywhere arrive there. Many try to find work and make a profit from its existence, without being productive of much except services. Crimes increase in towns, and people seek profit and pleasure without always wanting to work for them.

The town is important in Amharic literature and for the intellectual and cultural life of Ethiopia. Of the books used as primary sources for this study, most are related to urban life in one way or another, either describing life in a town, or by using characters born and bred in town who then go to the countryside. The work and behaviour of the latter group often start off a new development and serve to put traditional Ethiopia in relief, where the impulses from town can serve to create something new in the rural community, usually on the whole beneficial, but not exclusively so. The result seems always to bring people out of their lethargy and customary thinking and life, and the point the authors make is that change is coming and it is inevitable, and in most cases it is for the good. The new culture is born in town, first of all the capital, and then brought to the rest of the country by students and others who have been to town.

A further indication of the importance of the town is the fact that all the authors whose writings this study is based on have spent much or most of their lives in Addis Ababa.

c) *Economic development*

There are many signs of affluence in many families in Amharic literature, but from early on Ethiopian authors have criticized the way this wealth is used, or wasted.

The most ostentatious way of displaying one's standing and affluence, often by means of incurring debts, has in the traditional society always been to give lavish feasts.

Awwäḳä in *Addis aläm* had great difficulties with his relatives and the clergy because he wanted to keep expenses down when his father died, for his memory feast, *täzkar*, and, later, for his own wedding.[49] Araya is severe with the sumptuous banquets of the nobility,[50] but he also finds that this wastefulness with food and drink is a common feature at parties he is invited to by his friends, and he makes mental observations about the custom, relating it to Ethiopia's economy generally:

> "What amazed him most of all in every party and feast was the great squandering of both food and drink. And truly, the abundance of food and the selection of drinks were very amazing. When one considered the reason for this being so, it was because the people did not know thrift and a life of moderation. Also at the present time the organization of life was to have one European foot and one Ethiopian foot without yet being able to find the balance. But in future, when life becomes gradually more expensive and the need to save money is felt, this over-abundance and wastefulness will certainly end." [51]

Wealthy people in modern Addis Ababa spend money in similar ways, and the time of "thrift" that Araya envisaged has not been quick in coming. A man who gets engaged to a rich man's daughter, Taddäsä Libän tells in one of his stories in *Lelaw mängäd*, spent hundreds of dollars on her clothes and jewellery, hundreds on himself, and further hundreds for the feast.[52] And those were only the engagement celebrations. A grand wedding in Addis Ababa is also expected to contain a great number of cars. Wzo Alganäš in *Yalačča gabəčča* envisages a cortege, at her nephew's wedding, of three hundred cars, "without counting the Volkswagens", that will stop the traffic in Churchill Road, one of the main thoroughfares of Addis Ababa.[53]

In *Ǝddəl näw? bädäl?* Abbe Gubäňňa tells the story of a man whose

---
[49] *Addis aläm*, 14:2-15:22, 35:15-22, 35:26-36:4.
[50] *Araya*, 158:3-160:6.
[51] *Araya*, 189:4-14.
[52] *Lelaw mängäd*, 27:12-19.
[53] *Yalačča gabəčča*, 85:17-19, 143:16-22.

life was totally ruined because of the demands upon his resources after his wife died. The local priest, his father confessor, reminds him that matters relating to the soul are not to be taken lightly, and obediently he sells or slaughters his cattle to pay for *täzkar* and prayers for her soul. From then on, he is not able to look after his farm and children.

Towns have an affluence unknown among the wealthy in the countryside, and the contrast between rich and poor is also greater in towns.

In the story by Taddäsä Libän already referred to in this chapter, we read about a rich man who gets 50 to 60 thousand dollars a year from his land and in addition the income from renting out several houses he has in town. When his daughter asks for money, he always gives her much more than she asks for, without enquiring what she wants it for.[54] The man his daughter gets engaged to has had to advance through hard work and seeking the help and protection of the powerful. But when he has got some money, he advances fast through speculation in land, which is particularly profitable in towns that are being developed.[55]

A man who suddenly comes by a fortune in one of Bərhanu Zärihun's novels, *Amanu'el därso mäls*, displays the common tastes of many young people in Addis Ababa who want to live a modern life of ease and luxury: he wants a car, women, and alcohol.[56] In this story, we are told how money can change people.[57] To get some part in this wealth, people from the countryside can travel far. We are told in *Fəkr əskä mäḳabər* how merchants bring their goods on mules to Addis Ababa all the way from Gojjam.[58] Townspeople have often little understanding of the poverty of the farmers. Adäfrəs causes amazement among the countrypeople when he wastes many bullets after some wild fowl. The value of these bullets represents several days' wages for a peasant.[59]

The change from barter and living on the fruit of the land to a money economy is noticed most strongly in towns, where most people do not have land but are dependent on finding work. The towns are not able to absorb properly and make good use of all

---

[54] *Lelaw mängäd*, 16:1-14.
[55] *Ib.*, 16:21-18:6.
[56] *Amanu'el därso mäls*, 17:13ff.; 11:1ff.; 18:10ff.; 23:1-24:11.
[57] *Ib.*, 11:17-20, and the whole of this novel.
[58] *Fəkr əskä mäḳabər*, 433:5-8.
[59] *Adäfrəs*, 132:8-10, 133:5f., 203:10-13.19f., 204:17.

who seek their fortune there. Therefore nepotism and other forms of selective criteria exist, not always giving a man an opportunity to prove his abilities. Taddäsä Libän tells a story of a boy who leaves school to help his poor family by starting work. He goes from office to office and applies for one job after another. Even when he meets employers who approve of his qualifications and could use a boy like him, he fails to get a job because he has no "big man" to recommend him, and he is not of "good family". He develops into a cynic about his chances. When he finally gets a job, and a fairly good one, it is through a "big man" whom his sister has married.[60]

In the same book he tells another story of a beautiful woman who gets married and bears two children. Then her husband dies, and she tries to manage on her own. She can only make food and tries to sell *ənjära* in the small local market, *gullət*, but cannot compete with the other, more practised women. When both she and her children are practically starved, she chooses the only way left to her: she becomes a prostitute.[61]

Women may become prostitutes or mistresses of rich men out of necessity, as a means of survival, but others choose this kind of life to try to get their share of the wealth and luxury of modern times. Some leave husbands and children for such an easy life, but they are usually depicted as tragic women who come to a bad end.[62] In the cases where women choose this career, they may sometimes be motivated by a desire for greater freedom and emancipation from the domination of men, which can be a harsh experience for some of them. (Cf. chapter III, 5.)

The abundance of both prostitutes and beggars in towns shows how the economic life there lags behind in making use of the available labour force.[63]

There is in Ethiopia a new spirit of competitiveness,[64] and the times favour those who are not too particular about the ways they obtain wealth, which may well be deceit and cunning.[65] Money has

---

[60] *Lelaw mängäd*, pp. 43-53, esp. 46:21-47:9, 48:1-4, 53:1-12.
[61] *Ib.*, pp. 33-41.
[62] E. g. *Arrəmuññ*, 324:23-325:6, 334:4, 337:3; *Yäʾənba däbdabbewoč*, 5:13-17 and the whole of this novel.
[63] *Käʾadmas bašagär*, 56:8f., 100:21f., *Yähəllina däwäl*, 177:1-3. 20-23, 178:10-13, 179:9-13.
[64] *Araya*, 17:13.
[65] *Yäfəkər çora*, 189:14-190:1.

become more important than honour, as one noble complains; "second (only) to God, the other great power is money. Money has a mouth—it speaks. Money has ears—it hears".[66] Money has a strong attraction among the poor in the countryside, and the phenomenon of migrant workers is connected with the season for the picking of coffee beans, etc.[67] Times have changed so that "the happiness of the time is to obtain land and collect much money".[68] An old noble like Ṣahay Mäsfən's father could not adapt to the new ideas and regarded it as a shame to seek to get money. But that led also to hardships for his daughter, who is left with small means when he dies.[69] Ṣahay Mäfən finds some of the new methods of getting rich objectionable, especially the practice of *wälläd aggəd*, that has brought wealth to Ləjj Alämu Dästa, who is in love with her. The custom of *wälläd aggəd* consists of giving a loan to a person without interest, but some property, usually a house, is put up as guarantee for the loan, and this property is at the lender's disposal for the specified period, usually two or three years, until which the loan is to be repaid. During all this time, the lender can live in or rent out a house, etc., given as guarantee, and the value of this use, the "usufructure", is vastly more than any bank would pay as interest. If the loan is not repaid on the specified date, the whole property goes to the lender, and it is usually worth several times the sum borrowed. In all cases this practice favours people with capital. The legal name for this practice is, euphemistically, *wälläd aggəd*, "stop interest", but is in fact a form of usury. That is why Ṣahay Mäsfən finds it objectionable.[70] This way of obtaining wealth fast seems to have been common in towns, as was speculation in land properties, as already mentioned.[71]

Economic growth and development seem on the whole to be erratic. One coffee farmer criticizes the country's heavy dependence on one crop, coffee. This has made both coffee farmers and the national economy vulnerable and dependent on weather, pests and fluctuating prices, and it can easily ruin a man during an unlucky year. An economy based on a great variety of crops and other

---

[66] *Yähəllina däwäl*, 73:15-22.
[67] *Ib.*, 65:14-26.
[68] *Ṣahay Mäsfən*, 16:24-17:1.
[69] *Ib.*, 17:1-5.
[70] *Ib.*, 36:12-38:16.
[71] *Käʾadmas bašagär*, 114:6f., *Bälg*, 58:4, *Lelaw mängäd*, 17:22-18:6.

sources, not only agricultural, could alter that, it is argued.[72] Araya believes great efforts should be made to improve Ethiopia's economy, in cultivation and animal husbandry, with inspection of the animals' health and experimental stations to develop new crops and to cross-breed cattle. Agricultural banks would help the farmers, and more exports, better roads, and trade treaties with neighbouring countries could bring wealth and development to the country.[73]

But the situation remained rather haphazard, with some very rich people and a multitude of poor, but neither Mäkonnən Əndalkaččäw, who makes this observation,[74] nor other authors have much to suggest to change the situation in very concrete terms. Much was left to a vague idea of "luck".[75] Käbbädä Mika'el attacks this attitude of trusting in luck, because it is so unreliable:

> "Mrs. "Good Luck", of a capricious nature, -
> her unpredictable acts are very astonishing,
> her scheme is unknown (as is) her character, her style;
> suddenly she departs, just the way she came." [76]

"Tomorrow is a big unknown, a hidden lot", the author writes in another poem.[77] The point he tries to make in both contexts is that people should rely on their work, not on uncertain good luck or fortune, or idly dream that a brighter tomorrow will come by chance. A similar thought is expressed in *Yähəllina däwäl*, where Bä'alu Gərma strongly emphasizes the importance of work, and work with one's hands first of all. The main character in this novel once says:

> "I would say a little work is better than much thinking. One of the great tools God gave man was his hand. But in our country a man who works with his hands has been regarded with contempt. It is this kind of attitude that has kept Ethiopia backward. What Ethiopia needs now is a hand that works (or working people)." [78]

The uncertainty in the economy that people have had to live with has given rise to some voluntary organizations that are set

---

[72] *Yäräggäfu abäboč*, 136:11-147:10.
[73] *Araya*, 221:24-222:12.
[74] *Yäfəḳər ṭora*, 189:10-13.
[75] *Ib.*, 189:1-6.
[76] *Yäḳəne azmära*, 102:11-14.
[77] *Ib.*, 107:19.
[78] *Yähəllina däwäl*, 104:16-21.

up to cater for the most basic needs of their members in times of crises, *viz.*, mutual help organizations, called *mahbär* or *əddər*, etc. Often people from the same areas join together and form such organizations when they move to town.⁷⁹

Some authors have stated or implied that progress has been slow in the country, and especially in outlying places. Araya is surprised that so little has changed in the small towns where the train stops on his way back to Addis Ababa after an absence of fifteen years.⁸⁰ A man who returns to Dessie, where he was born, after many years, wonders at the minute changes that have taken place.⁸¹ The adjective "minute" (*ṭəkakən*) implies more criticism of than praise for the speed of development in the town. Several authors make references to the difficulties of obtaining medical aid in the countryside. No doctors are available there, and sometimes a patient has to be carried a long way to town.⁸² But Adäfrəs also points out that the progress Ethiopia has made in the twentieth century is without precedent in the nation's history.⁸³

2. Decay

a) *Relaxation of traditional ties and mores*

That manners and customs change is of course in itself no indication of decay, but Ethiopian authors give more prominence to the degenerative rather than the beneficial effects of this relaxation of traditional ties and manners. Thus the freedom to choose one's own marriage partner might have created as many good marriages as when the custom of letting the parents decide for their children was prevalent; but the authors write more about the crises that ensue from free choice and easy relationships and show that they often result in divorces and increased prostitution.

An old man in *Yähəllina däwäl* is sceptical of modern civilization because those who strive most eagerly to reap the benefits of it end up, more often than not, as loafers and prostitutes, and he says it leads to decay or degeneration and destruction of the family; although people call it civilization, not decay, he sees it as a manifes-

---

[79] *Yäbädäl fəṣṣame*, 68:9f., *Bälg*, 64:18.
[80] *Araya*, 123:22-29.
[81] *Yäšoh aklil*, 12:15.
[82] *Yäləbb hassab*, 173:5-174:2, *Adäfrəs*, 194:4, 202:24f., *Araya*, 185ult.-186:1, *Yähəllina däwäl*, 225:23-226:1.
[83] *Adäfrəs*, 99:21-25.

tation of the wrath of God with the object of castigating man.[84]

Käbbädä Mika'el has written a poem he calls "Father and son",[85] where the son expresses the unusual idea that he does not want to have children. The father talks strictly and sadly to his son, saying that in his youth having children was the greatest desire of a young man. But now, in this last age of the world, the eighth millennium, people are changing for the worse, seeking bad things and fleeing the good; still they call their stupidity knowledge or insight, a new philosophy. All this the older generation can only despise.

The young do not follow in the footsteps of their parents, and even those who accept this fact want to retard the development so that the bad can be sifted out and only the good changes adopted.[86]

Taddäsä Libän has written a story that is bitingly critical of members of the modern generation who have been abroad and who fail to assimilate to an Ethiopian context on their return.[87] A family has been able through great sacrifices to send a daughter abroad and keep her there for eight years. When she is due to come back, her parents and other relatives and friends prepare a big feast to welcome her. But when she arrives at the airport she hardly wants to show she recognizes her poor family, and they have difficulties in finding out who she is, all made up as she is according to the latest fashion. After having reluctantly greeted her family, she says she wants to go and stay with some friends rather than come to her poor parents' home. Later she hardly ever visits or associates with her parents or others of her family. She pretends to have difficulties in understanding plain Amharic, and herself speaks an artificial kind of Amharic mixed with English words and phrases.[88] She despises all things Ethiopian and prefers everything that comes from the West, which she accepts uncritically. This kind of attitude, even in much milder forms, naturally aggravates the antagonisms between old and new customs, and between the old and the new generations.

The custom of choosing one's own wife was advocated by Awwäḵä in *Addis aläm* and practised by Bərhane and Ṣəyon Mogäsa, the couple who are the main characters in *Yäləbb hassab*, and by Araya

---

[84] *Yähəllina däwäl*, 87:1-17.
[85] *Yäḵəne azmära*, pp. 90f.
[86] *Adäfrəs*, 42:25f., 104:17-19, 230:1-14, 284:11-26.
[87] *Mäskäräm*, pp. 29-66.
[88] This phenomenon is discussed by Getaččäw Hayle, "Sənä ṣəhufənna ḵwanḵwa", in *Mänän*, Vol. I, No. 3 (January 1965 E.C.), pp. 14-24.

as well.[89] Bahru in *Yalačča gabəčča* has secretly married his maid. All these people seem to have been happy enough, but the idea of making one's own choice in this matter was new and caused conflicts and incredulity among older people, especially in the countryside. When even girls insist on choosing their own husbands, they go beyond what decency would require.[90] Such a proposal of marriage can be very spontaneous and does not always leave much time for the boy and the girl, or the man and the woman, to become properly acquainted. In *Ṣähay Mäsfən*, Ləjj Alämu Dästa meets Ṣähay Mäsfən by chance and starts talking to her. After only a short conversation, he tells her, "My friend, don't think me audacious, but I have fallen deeply in love with you, (so) let us marry". She replies, "I should have been very happy to marry you. But it is not proper of me to give my word at once, the same day we have met". Although she has been educated in France and he in the United States, this sudden proposal of marriage does not seem improper to them. On their second meeting, he invites her to his home to meet his mother and to make plans for their marriage.[91] Araya is also quick to propose; and a boy in a story by Taddäsä Libän gives a love-letter to a girl he has seen only one day, and they soon become "lip-friends".[92]

The question of finding the right marriage partner poses agonizing problems for young people. This is a problem for the main characters of several books, e.g. *Yäšoh aklil*, *Kä'admas bašagär*, *Bälg*, some stories in *Mäskäräm* and *Lelaw mängäd*, and many others. In *Bälg*, a married couple learn to love and accept each other only after much suffering and after their romantic illusions have been shattered. In *Kä'admas bašagär*, a girl comes to understand love when her lover has committed a crime in a fit of jealousy.

A story in *Mäskäräm* shows how easily these freer relationships between boys and girls can lead to abuse of each other's emotions and trust. Käbbädä meets a girl, Aṣädä, and they become friends. When she refuses to go to bed with him before marriage, he accuses her of not trusting him and not being willing to do what any girl would do for her friend if she really loved him. She then considers his many gifts, and how selfless he has been in not asking anything

---

[89] *Addis aläm*, chapter 7, *Yäləbb hassab*, chapter 3, *Araya*, chapter 25.
[90] *Addis aläm*, 29:19ff., *Yalačča gabəčča*, 67:19-22.
[91] *Ṣähay Mäsfən*, 20:5-9, 34:13-16; 10:16-21, 20:11-13.
[92] *Lelaw mängäd*, 19:11-17.

for himself in return, so she agrees to be a bit more intimate with him, and then finally she gives in to his demands for full sexual union. After she has surrendered to his wishes, he announces that he intends to go abroad for further education, so they cannot marry after all, and it is better if they break their relationship immediately. Later she finds out that, far from going abroad, he has started the same process over again of seducing another virgin.[93]

Even the modern young people in Addis Ababa who choose partners for themselves compromise with tradition to some extent and send elders in the usual way to negotiate the marriage, after the boy and the girl have agreed between themselves.[94] Townspeople may even choose not to marry in some cases,[95] and if they do marry, they do not seem to care whether a girl is a virgin, much to the surprise of people of a more conservative bend, who, moreover, believe marriage can help people grow up properly.[96]

Another manifestation of the relaxation of traditional ties is seen in the weakening of the bonds that keep the family together and the reduced respect for parents and other people in authority among the young. Children have greater freedom and the young are independent.[97] As a result they often leave their parents to fend for themselves in their old age, without fulfilling what used to be thought of as their filial obligations, and the parents are left as if they had no children, since their children are no use to them. The young who get good jobs and earn salaries are least willing to support their families.[98]

In extreme cases, this lack of respect for authority may even lead some people, especially students, to acts of civil disobedience, and the parents, if the conflict is brought to a head, may turn against their own children and in some cases resolve the matter by causing their death.[99] But such fierce collisions between old and young are rare.

In many fields the barriers between people are being broken down and some complain of this, saying the tribute-paying peasant or the tenant does not respect his landlord, nor the servant his

---

[93] *Mäskäräm*, 95:1-25, 97:11-25, 98:22-99:24, 102:5ff., 104:12-17.
[94] *Lelaw mängäd*, 27:10-12, *Čäräḵa sətwäṭa*, 70:13f.
[95] *Yäšoh aklil*, 21:4f.
[96] *Käʾadmas bašagär*, 21:4-7, 23:4.
[97] *Adäfrəs*, 104:1-4.17f.
[98] *Käʾadmas bašagär*, 21:9-13, *Yähəllina däwäl*, 86:23-87:2.
[99] *Adäfrəs*, 172:12-24.

master.¹⁰⁰ The nobility do not easily adapt to the novel idea that their will is not law, but that they have to respect the law of the land.¹⁰¹ A rich old lady is horrified by her nephew's opinion that all men are equal, and his habit of eating at the same table as his servant she finds offensive.¹⁰²

Breakdown of old beliefs and customs is seen in conflicts that lead to refusal to use old medicine men to cure sick people and to preferring modern medicine instead. The use of the telephone, which was feared to be a trick of some evil spirit, or the adoption of new, mostly European ways of dressing, introducing new fashions, and being careless about one's appearance in more recent times could also be symptoms of a lessening respect for tradition.¹⁰³

But the greatest break with the past is seen in the attitude to religion and the Church. Early demands for reform aimed only at some external customs, such as reducing the expenses of memory feasts for the dead, but without attacking or showing indifference to the Christian faith.¹⁰⁴ But the younger generation soon showed they were not interested in religious customs or observances. They stopped fasting and maintained religion was a private matter. They did not love God but rather money and pleasure. Instead of going to church on religious holidays, they spent their time dancing and drinking.¹⁰⁵ In some cases also older people can be critical of some aspects of religious life, especially in relation to the more deceitful practices of the *däbtära*.¹⁰⁶ Rarely is religion directly mocked, but it does happen. One man excuses his acts by saying he is God's creation, so he cannot be criticized or held responsible for what he does; it is rather God who should be held responsible and criticized since He created him.¹⁰⁷ Bahru in *Yalačča gabäčča* shows a modern unconcerned attitude by humorously mocking a Muslim by greeting him in a Christian manner, and a Christian by greeting him in the Muslim manner.¹⁰⁸ Maybe he is most typical of many young Ethiopians we meet in Amharic

---

[100] *Yähəllina däwäl*, 118:16-20, *Kä'admas bašagär*, 94:8-95:3.
[101] *Yähəllina däwäl*, 134:3-7.
[102] *Yalačča gabəčča*, 62:1-65:4, 72:4-6.
[103] *Addis aläm*, 6:1ff., 7:12ff., 8:7f.18f., 10:8ff., *Adäfrəs*, 36:6f., 37:19-28.
[104] *Addis aläm*, 14:19ff., 18:1ff.
[105] *Araya*, 302:18f., 306:5-10, *Kä'admas bašagär*, 25:4-16, 32:4-7, 95:7f., *Yalačča gabəčča*, 54:4ff.
[106] *Yähəllina däwäl*, 121:7-13.
[107] *Yäšoh aklil*, 33:1-3.
[108] *Yalačča gabəčča*, 76:6-8.

literature: he does not give much thought or importance to religious questions, but he does not show any open hostility to the Church either.

Relaxation of traditional ties and manners has led to both good and bad things, but the authors often concentrate on the moral decay and the increase in deceit and crime that can be the result of such changes.

b) *Moral decay*

Many Ethiopian authors write about the educated young who have got more money and leisure than they know how to use properly or profitably. Even work is not a very serious matter for many, and a main concern of the young is how to fight and overcome their boredom. Mäkonnən Əndalkaččäw, in *Yädəhoč kätäma*,[109] attacked a main cause of the change in attitudes to traditional norms and the decay of morals by trying to fight a new kind of pursuit of money and luxury. He tries to show that insatiable greed can lead to confusion and madness.

The characteristic of modern times is a restless pursuit of pleasure, and the ways to find satisfaction for one's desires are limited to few things, first of all alcohol and sex. In *Yäräggäfu abäboč*, Abbe Gubänña describes a group of young people rushing in cars from one drinking house to another, both to drink and to find female company, to discuss any subject that comes up and to dance. The same author has written another book, *Yä'amäṣ nuzaze*, about a man who has exhausted his strength "in alcohol and adultery".[110] Bərhanu Zärihun has also written a novel, *Čäräḵa sətwäṭa*, about young people's pursuit of pleasure. The talk in the office at the beginning of the week is of who slept with whom during the weekend. The car is a bait to pick up girls more than a necessary means of transportation for these young people; and the secretaries, to get jobs and stay popular, are expected to be sexually available to the male staff, mainly the bosses. Professionally it seems no advantage for a woman to be "hard to get".[111] The author also writes how life in Addis Ababa, especially on a Sunday afternoon, is marked by drunkenness, scuffles, squabbles and

---

[109] *Arrəmuňň*, pp. 105-185; cf. *Amanu'el därso mäls*, 11:17-20.
[110] *Yä'amäṣ nuzaze*, 10:7ff.
[111] *Čäräḵa sətwäṭa*, 33:3-7.

fighting.¹¹² The main temptations for a man who can afford it are to have a car and to obtain women and drinks, the author shows in another of his novels, *Amanu'el därso mäls*.¹¹³

Mängəstu Lämma has written about the weakening of modern people; his play *Ṭälfo bäkise* revolves around this theme, as do some of his poems, such as *Yäwänd ləjj yalläh*.¹¹⁴ Some of his characters blame the new, Western civilization for this development; and Araya also warns against accepting everything from the West indiscriminately without distinguishing between what is good and what is bad.¹¹⁵ In Abbe Gubäñña's novel *Əddəl näw? bädäl?*, the main character wonders if it is a sign of civilization that bad things increase and good things like love, compassion, trust and faithfulness are disappearing.¹¹⁶

The description of the rather lurid aspects of people's sex life in modern Ethiopia, and especially in Addis Ababa, takes up much space in Amharic fiction, and the theme has become somewhat overworked and tends to be repetitive and monotonous. Some examples can stand for many similar cases.

Well-educated young people like Abärra and his friends, in *Kä'admas bašagär*, think and talk about their women friends most of the time, and the girl friends they often make love to they refer to as their "mistresses" or "concubines"; and one of them says, to illustrate how much of their leisure is spent, "For a change I didn't sleep with a whore yesterday, I'm getting bored with their smell. For a change I spent the night with an Italian maid".¹¹⁷ Taddäsä Liban's story *Wəššawənna mängädoččU* ¹¹⁸ tells about a man who spends his time in the pursuit of young girls, only to discard them when he has satisfied his desire with them.

Several authors have pointed out that this desire for pleasure is a strain on married life. The "I" of the novel *Amanu'el därso mäls* leaves his wife when he gets enough money to live as he pleases, drinking and being in the company of other women, mostly whores, and their marriage is just salvaged, after much suffering by both

---

[112] *Čäräḳa sətwäṭa*, 5:13-6:2.
[113] *Amanu'el därso mäls*, 17:13ff., 18:1ff. 10ff., 23:1-24:11, 31:1ff., 39:10ff.
[114] *Yägəṭam guba'e*, pp. 37-40.
[115] *Ṭälfo bäkise*, 54:1f., 56:7f., *Araya*, 148:1-5.
[116] *Əddəl näw? bädäl?* 89:7-20.
[117] *Kä'admas bašagär*, 15:1.6-8.
[118] *Mäskäräm*, pp. 81-109.

husband and wife, by the great generosity of the wife. She gets him out of Amanu'el, the lunatic asylum. *Yäʾənba däbdabbewoč* is the story of a wife who leaves her home to be with a man of better means than her husband. The man who seduces her is well educated and has also been abroad for education. He has a good job in Addis Ababa but is weak in his spiritual and religious life and lives to enjoy the present. He has "a vulgar character strengthened by modern civilization".[119] Mäkonnən Indalkaččäw writes in *Yäfəkər čora* about a man and a woman who are both married, but not to each other, who fall in love and have to find excuses to go to Europe separately, and when they meet there, they are able to spend some time together, travelling around in Europe. But when they have to return, they separate and go to their own spouses. Other authors write that unfaithfulness is common and divorce frequent and easily obtained in our time.[120] Friendships are broken and friends become enemies when they want the same woman: this is the conclusion of Daňňaččäw Wärḳu's play *Säw allä bəyye*.

With increased demand for sexual pleasure, there has also been a corresponding growth of prostitution. Some authors just state the fact that prostitution is common and growing, without commenting too much about it; others give the problem more detailed treatment. The main characters in Bä'alu Gərma's novels, *Käʾadmas bašagär* and *Yähəllina däwäl*, visit prostitutes as a normal part of life and may even have a close relationship and friendship with a whore, as the latter book shows. Roman in *Adäfrəs* becomes a prostitute because she is left with no other choice when she runs away from home. *Kältammawa əhəte* tells of another girl who escapes from a harsh step-mother and ends up as a prostitute after having lived with a series of temporary lovers. This is also the fate of Abäba in *Yäʾənba däbdabbewoč*. Towns are full of whores, some having chosen this occupation voluntarily, others having been driven into it because they could do nothing else. Some operate from their own little house, others work as "sales girls" (*aššašač*) in bars. Whole areas in towns can be known as prostitutes' areas.[121]

Araya shows the corrupting influence the pursuit of luxury and

---

[119] *Yäʾənba däbdabbewoč*, 40:22-41:7.
[120] *Adäfrəs*, 40:7, 107:23-108:3, 108:8-11, *Yalačča gabačča*, 99:14f., *Čäräḳa sətwäṭa*, 6:7f., *Amanuʾel därso mäls*, 19:14ff., 27:6ff., 29:13ff.
[121] *Adäfrəs*, 39:23f., 108:10f., *Čäräḳa sətwäṭa*, 12ult., 36:20, *Bälg*, 43:11f., *Yäʾənba däbdabbewoč*, 126:12-18, *Käʾadmas bašagär*, 39:23, 45:19, 56:8f.

an easy life had on Ethiopian women who fraternized with the Italians during their occupation of the country.[122] *Almotkum bəyye alwašəm* [123] describes the tragic outcome of a relationship when a woman consents to live as the mistress of an Italian officer. The force of economic circumstance can be the main reason why a woman becomes a prostitute in many cases. In his story *Abbonäš*,[124] Taddäsä Libän tells of a widow for whom all attempts at earning a decent living fail, and in the end she is driven by hunger to put some bottles on a table, leave the door to her house ajar, and when a man knocks and asks leave to enter, she invites him in. She has made the beginning of her new career as a prostitute.

Many authors clearly show they are worried by the direction the development in the country has taken, and particularly the weakening of moral principles has given them much concern. The remedies proposed can be of different kinds, and some see no way out of the situation. One man thinks that changes should go hand in hand with better education, otherwise the outcome will be bad, a "sickness".[125] As shown in the last section, many people blame the decay in morals on the indifference of young people to religion and old traditions and customs.

c) *Increase of crime and deceit*

Although the moral standards of the people have been lowered, most people respect the law and oppose criminal activities. Also the modernized sections of the population can express great displeasure and moral indignation when people contravene the law of the land. But Amharic literature still gives the impression that crime has been vastly on the increase, and so has deceit, in words and action, for unlawful or dishonest gain.

Ethiopian authors are not so interested in petty crimes by the ordinary thief (*leba*), robber (*majrat mäči*, "hitter of the nape of the neck") or streetboy (*durəyye*)—their existence is noted more or less in passing [126]—as they are in those who misuse their positions of power to break the law to enrich themselves on a grand scale, often by giving the appearance of being strict upholders of the

---
[122] *Araya*, 290:30-294:12.
[123] *Arrəmuňň*, pp. 273-338.
[124] *Lelaw mängäd*, pp. 33-41.
[125] *Adäfrəs*, 108:4-6.
[126] *Čäräka sətwäṭa*, 5:12, *Əsat wäy ababa*, 32:15, 33:6, *Säw allä bəyye*, 41ult.

law. Deceit occurs of course in many ways, as for example in order to seduce, as Täčan seduced Abäba in *Yä'ənba däbdabbewoč*, or as Käbbädä persuaded Aṣädä to relinquish her state of virginity by insincere promises of marriage, in the story *Wəššawənna mängädoččǔ* in *Mäskäräm*. But in this chapter the main interest is deceit in connection with criminal activities, deceit to by-pass the law and thus obtain one's aim, usually economic gain.

It is often people in high position with good connections that are able to use their influence to enrich themselves. Therefore they fight for position, appointment in government service; and one natural consequence of the competition this implies is envy of others who are appointed to positions of power or influence. Araya felt this very strongly, and in *Araya* there is a long passage on envy and its harmful effects.[127] Araya noticed later that the Italians during their occupation of Ethiopia tried to set tribes and adherents of different religions against each other and to maintain their rule through splitting and deceiving the people.[128] This was, however, also the effect of suspicion and envy in the closed circle of people in positions of power. Jealous of their own privileges, they guard their own interests and are thus not concerned about the state of the country except as far as it benefits them. This argument is developed in *Adäfrəs*.[129] The main character in Abbe Gubäňňa's *Əddəl näw? bädäl?* makes a comparison between the rule of the Fascists in Ethiopia and the present state of the country and finds that misrule, exploitation and injustice after the Italians left have become worse, at least in some cases.[130] A new problem for some officials and noblemen has arisen with the introduction of written statutory laws. They used to think that their will was the law, that justice was invested in their positions, and that they could act more or less as they wanted, and that nobody could judge or touch them. This has changed the situation for many.[131] Thus Fitawrari Mäšäša acts arbitrarily and ruthlessly against peasants who are unable because of a bad year to pay all the tribute he demands.

---

[127] *Araya*, 191:22-195:3. Abbe Gubäňňa writes much on envy, e.g., in *Yähamet susäňňoč, Gobland ačbärbariw ṭoṭa, Məlkam säyfä näbälbal*, but as this seems to reflect a private controversy, it will not be considered here.
[128] *Araya*, 296:10-12, 299:27-30, 314:26-315:1.
[129] *Adäfrəs*, 86:1-91:12.
[130] *Əddəl näw? bädäl?*, 77:12-78:16.
[131] *Yähəllina däwäl*, 118:16-20.

When he is defeated in a confrontation with the peasants and taken to court, he is defeated there, too, and finds there is no more justice in the land because there is no respect for the nobility.[132]

Power and position are for many not enough to obtain what they want, and a new kind of criminal has developed, the thief who specializes in the finer points of law and, under cover of observing the law strictly, robs other people;[133] a new concept has been coined for this kind of person: he is a "legal robber".[134]

One of Mäkonnən Ǝndalkaččäw's characters makes the observation that when some get too rich, it must increase the number of poor people, and that excessive wealth is obtained through devious ways and means and through cunning and deceit,[135] and Bäzzabbəh in *Fəkr əskä mäḳabər* sees oppression, favouritism, bribery, injustice and foul play both in church and state affairs.[136] The author of the latter book, Haddis Alämayyähu, has also written a collection of stories in the style of traditional folk tales under the title *Tärät tärät yämäsärät*. Particularly the first three and the last of these stories are, as is much of *Fəkr əskä mäḳabər*, a warning to people in power against misusing their power: they are the ones who will suffer in the end. In the first of these tales, an antelope has been caught in a trap but then freed by two jackals. The antelope praises the jackals, saying she much prefers to be eaten by jackals rather than by men, as she feels greater affinity to jackals, but throws in the question how they intend to divide her among themselves, as they are of unequal size. This starts off a quarrel that leads to serious fighting between the jackals, in the course of which the antelope escapes. The second tale is the story of two hyenas who get married and get along well as long as they have plenty to eat. But when scarcity and hunger come, the male hyena says his "wife" looks a bit like a sheep, and when he gets her to cover herself with a sheepskin, he says she smells like a sheep, too, and devours her while she giggles, thinking his bites are caresses. The third story is about two donkeys. One is lazy and is able to cause her loads to fall off her back and is therefore not used for carrying loads. As she grows fat, she is praised for her beauty and fed well

---

[132] *Fəkr əskä mäḳabər*, 392:1-400:16.
[133] *Ǝddəl näw? bädäl?*, 60:14-61:4.
[134] *Ib.*, 61:5.
[135] *Yäfəkər ḍora*, 189:10-190:1.
[136] *Fəkr əskä mäḳabər*, 462:23-463:4.

and used as a breeder. The other donkey loves her master and works hard all day to please him, but she is fed bad food because it is believed to give strength, and she is beaten so as not to become indolent. Thus the lazy and crafty one is rewarded, and the hardworking and kind one suffers hardships. When the latter one seeks advice on how to get out of her miserable plight, she is told there is only one who can help here, and he is called death; otherwise there is no escape. The last story tells of a serpent who tricks many animals to their death; but finally he also meets an adversary that defeats him. In many stories the author thus points a moral, that evil people may prosper for a time, but justice one day catches up with most of them. But one of the stories seems to say that there is no hope for the oppressed, at least not for the kindhearted among them. That is in one sense also the conclusion of his novel, *Fəkr əskä mäḵabər*, where the main characters, and the best people in the book, find a kind of peace in escaping from the affairs of this world. The author, as well as others who stress the tragic aspects of life, may well be saying in this way that society is turning into an unjust and violent society, where evil thrives and good suffers; but justice, or nemesis, may also catch up with those who perpetrate evil, although this is not always made explicit. The reader, however, may be left with a desire for a better world.

Bərhanu Zärihun's novel *Yäbädäl fəṣṣame* may be described as Ethiopia's first detective story. The "I" of the story is an auditor, and when checking an account he finds that a large sum of government money has been embezzled. He sends a report about it and then receives a number of anonymous warnings not to pursue the matter further; and when he is persistent, he is sacked from his job. The attitude of people around him is that he is to blame for being over-zealous and for poking his nose into what is none of his business, also called "political affairs", and for showing too much idealism and patriotism.[137] There is strong criticism of corruption among people in high places, and reflection on the fact that common people in the final analysis will have to pay for the money that is misappropriated. In the bureaucracy there are people who pay lip service to the development and welfare of the country but are in actual fact no better than thieves.[138] The devices

---

[137] *Yäbädäl fəṣṣame*, 17:4ff., 23:16-26:22, 43:13f., 45:3ff., 53:16-18, 54:7ff., 55:1ff.
[138] *Yäbädäl fəṣṣame*, 24:20ff., 70:7-71:22.

established to prevent detection are almost watertight, and since many people are corrupt, they protect each other. The "I" of this story finds it very difficult to prove the guilt of his deadly adversary, and has to pursue the matter patiently in rather subtle ways. In the end he finds proof that he had been a *banda*, a collaborator with the enemy during the Italian occupation, and had denounced and caused the death of several Ethiopian freedom fighters. This evidence is damning, and it is not improved by his attempt to show that he had been a "freedom fighter on the inside" (*yäwəst arbäñña*), pretending to work for the Italians but in reality being on the side of his countrymen. He had in fact sold bullets to them at exorbitant prices and later denounced them. When the Italians seemed to be losing, he tried to switch sides towards the end of the war; but justice finally catches up with him, and he has to pay. The embezzlement becomes an aggravating circumstance.[139] Greed also here leads to all kinds of crimes, including persecution and betrayal of his own countrymen.

Abbe Gubäñña often writes about corrupt people in influential positions. In *Əddəl näw? bädäl?*, an impoverished peasant tries to obtain justice after his only ox has been stolen and killed. The thieves are caught and sign a written confession in front of several witnesses, including a "neighbourhood judge". But the case goes from one judge to another, and through delays, subterfuge, and taking of bribes by the judges, the poor peasant is confused, obtains no justice, and when he becomes too insistent, is accused of contempt of court and is the one who ends up in jail. In this novel, there is severe criticism of the perversion of justice that has taken place. Bribes are said to have become more common, and justice cannot be obtained without bribes, that are also increasing in size. Actually there is no real justice, and no rule of law; officials are oppressive and use the law to pervert justice; some are even worse than the Italian Fascists. Officials have become the helpers and co-conspirators of thieves, are often incompetent, and have become promoters and defenders of injustice.[140]

The same theme is also treated by the author in other books. In *Aləwwällädəm* a group of people clear and cultivate a large tract of land in the wilderness that the government has permitted them

---

[139] *Yäbädäl fəṣṣame*, 96:21-97:3, 97:7, 124:4, etc.
[140] *Əddəl näw? bädäl?*, 52:5-16, 52:23-53:8, 58:3-5, 59:12-15, 60:14-61:5, 77:12-78:16, 89:14-20, 94:4, 96:15-21, 132:14-17, 134:25-135:13.

to develop. After it has been planted and the value of the land is vastly increased, there come people of influence who claim the land as their own. In another book, *Məlkam säyfä näbälbal*, the author tells of a prime minister who does much to develop the country, and is then poisoned by his envious enemies.

In *Yähəllina däwäl*, Bä'alu Gərma presents a corrupt policeman who is frank enough to admit: "I used to think I could change the world. However, the matter was turned upside down and the world changed me". As for corruption, he adds: "It is the road everyone takes"; and he says his friends and colleagues have been able to proceed much further in their careers because they are more corrupt and were corrupted earlier than him.[141]

Attempts had also been made to legalize ways of gaining vast riches. One has already been referred to and appears as "interest-free" loans (*wälläd aggəd*) for which a guarantee must be put up, the usufructure of which far exceeds normal interests on loans. It is a kind of lawful usury. If the loan is not repaid in time, the borrower forfeits the guarantee, and the lender has made a neat profit.[142]

Ethiopian authors take less interest in other forms of crime. But Daññaččäw Wärku, in his play *Säw allä bəyye*, has dealt with a case of a faithless friend, Gizew, who turns criminal. Gizew has been helped by a friend, Biləllañ, who is driven away from home because he refuses to leave Gizew to himself in his troubles. They go to Däbrä Bərhan together and live on the money Biləllañ has brought with him; but when that is exhausted, Gizew comes by money, and then their friendship starts to deteriorate. Biləllañ has fallen in love with a girl, but later Gizew falls in love with the same girl and tries to poison Biləllañ. Instead, someone else drinks the poison, and when Gizew sees he has failed in his scheme, he kills himself. The play concludes by saying no true friend can be found. All through, a rather low estimate of human nature transpires.[143]

Such crimes of passion, or crimes committed for the sake of survival, do not have the same appeal to Ethiopian authors as the acts of criminals who run amok in their pursuit of excessive wealth, how they infiltrate the government and become oppressors of the common people and are a scourge to the country.

---

[141] *Yähəllina däwäl*, 91:22-25, 91ult.-92:3, 92:7-23.
[142] *Ṣähay Mäsfən*, 36:13-38:16, *Kä'admas bašagär*, 114:6f., *Bälg*, 58:4.
[143] *Säw allä bəyye*, 28:4-22, 72:5-7, 122:5-10, etc.

CHAPTER EIGHT

BUILDING A NEW SOCIETY: VISIONS OF CHANGE

1. *New aspirations*

That Ethiopian society is changing, for better or worse, is realized by all Ethiopian authors and strongly reflected in their writing. But they do not see this so much as a new era as a "transitional period",[1] when the country is underway to a new, and most Ethiopian authors would say better time. It is a legitimate question to ask: transition to what? Ethiopians do not want to give up all of their traditional culture, and neither do they want to accept all that is new, or all that comes from abroad, particularly the West.[2] That it is a time for reforms and quick, sometimes fundamental or radical change is obvious.[3] Bä'alu Gərma puts these words into the mouth of one of his characters:

> "Now is a time for running. We must run before we (learn to) crawl." [4]
> "Yes, it is a time for running. When you run, you will make mistakes. But one cannot sit down (doing nothing) for fear of (making) mistakes. Change follows upon change." [5]

We can very well ask where they are going. Why all the hurry? If one seeks specific indications of the direction Ethiopian authors want their country to take in future, what sort of change and what kind of society they want, one will find that few of them commit themselves to any programme or to any precise answers.

Araya takes a favourable view of the French revolution (of 1789) and believes the French bourgeoisie are the preservers of the heritage of the revolution.[6] Ato Wäldu tries to cool Adäfrəs's enthusiasm about social change a bit by referring to ideas originating in the French revolution, and by citing an example of how these ideas can lead to disaster. He says that people had ideas about liberty, equality and fraternity, and about human rights,

---
[1] *Araya*, 11:12, 42:7, *Adäfrəs*, 108:8-11.
[2] *Araya*, 148:1ff.
[3] *Ib.*, 26.1ff, 30:24ff., 127:23-128:5, etc.
[4] *Yähəllina däwäl*, 109:3f.
[5] *Ib.*, 109:9-11.
[6] *Araya*, 48:31ff.

"like you, like the children of this time", thus indicating that such ideas are common among young Ethiopian intellectuals today.[7]

Abbe Gubäñña's characters express ideas that are of a socialist kind in both *Məlkam säyfä näbälbal* and *Aləwwällädəm*, and one of his protagonists who expresses strong views about quick progress and a different Ethiopia in the future states that he has Marxist views.[8] If my interpretation of Mängəstu Lämma's poem *Mänor mäla agäñña*[9] is right (VI, I), the word *mäsku*, "the meadow" is a pun on Moscow, and he refers to a person who dreams of the coming of a revolution of the Russian kind, or at least with support from Moscow.

There is a passage in *Yähəllina däwäl* describing the meeting of two students who spend a year working in Illubabur. One had been given the nickname Mao, obviously for his Maoist views.[10] He had been a student leader, heading "peaceful demonstrations" to demand that land be given to the tiller, property to the workers, and education become available to all. Such ideas are shown to be common among students.[11] But Haddis, his schoolmate, blames his thoughts and attitude for being only theoretical, and in practice these revolutionary students do not care about the common people, but only themselves.[12] Instead, he thinks, they should work, and particularly with their hands; and as a student he used to talk so much about manual work that his companions used to mock him for always "saying hand, hand", which is an Amharic idiom for "nagging".[13] Ethiopia's salvation is a working hand, not hands that stretch out to God in prayer, but hands that do useful work.[14] This reference to Psalm 68:31 occurs also in *Adäfrəs*, with the same implication that work is better than prayer;[15] and most likely the scene at the end of *Araya* is meant in the same way: Araya's child stretches its hands towards him, and he sees hope for his country in his child. Araya was not able to realize his hopes, but the next generation can perhaps implement the progressive,

---

[7] *Adäfrəs*, 151:11f., cf. context, 151:1-152ult.
[8] *Yäräggäfu abäboč*, 193:12.
[9] *Yägətəm guba'e*, p. 34.
[10] *Yähəllina däwäl*, 176:25.
[11] Ib., 176:18ff., 177:7ff.
[12] Ib., 177:12ff.
[13] Ib., 178:3-8.
[14] Ib., 178:1f.17-26; 54:13f., 83:21-26, 84:27f.
[15] *Adäfrəs*, 99:25f., cf. 100:16-18.

enlightened ideas Araya has advocated but usually to little avail. The references in the book to Psalm 68:31 are not made by Araya.[16]

The radical view that blood must flow to change the country, and that all talk of patience is harmful to the progress of the country,[17] is not often expressed. Haddis, the main character in *Yähəllina däwäl*, represents a more moderate view. He believes in change through education. He would like to see the school as the central meeting place for the whole community, so that it will be a new church, relating to all of life, and be, for both children and grown-ups, a place where everyone can join hands as Ethiopians without being divided because of tribal or religious differences.[18] And he believes equally strongly in the need for hard work to build a better nation and is nicknamed "the philosopher of the hand" by his fellow students.[19] True improvement, he says, must start in the mind; but it is equally important that one's faith and convictions are followed by work and actions proceeding from that faith; otherwise one's theories will be empty, false words and lead to self-seeking and the worship of ease and luxury. He finds such attitudes socially destructive.[20]

Yähəllina däwäl presents a student who becomes a leader of a social group in its efforts to achieve a brighter future. Haddis starts building a school himself when he realizes no public funds are forthcoming. Gradually he is able to overcome opposition to his project and to unite everyone behind him. A student is thus a leader, one of the elite, the vanguard that will show the way for the rest of the Ethiopians. Although the people also must wake up, and the educated can do little without favourable response from the masses, the masses can do little without someone to show them the way. Fitawrari Täkka, who supports Haddis in his undertaking, understands this, and says that the people's enthusiasm to help and rule themselves must be given direction or it will lead to chaos.[21]

The question of guidance and leadership is often approached in Amharic literature, but an answer is not always given, at least not a clear one. Students or educated people as guides of the people

---

[16] *Araya*, 346:1f., 348:11f.; 350:14-16.
[17] *Yähəllina däwäl*, 179:16-24, 182:1-17.
[18] *Ib.*, 179:25-181:17; 142:15-25, 229:21-25, 244:19f., 244ult.-245:1, 245:3-6.
[19] *Ib.*, 197:18-20.
[20] *Ib.*, 198ult.-199:21.
[21] *Ib.*, 208:13-27.

we meet frequently (in *Addis aläm, Araya, Adäfrəs, Yähəllina däwäl*, etc.); but the question of leadership on a national level is also taken up, and here the answer is given in two ways. Abbe Gubäñña has presented national leaders who transform the country economically in the course of a few years. He has also written a long historical novel on Tewodros. Both his and many other authors' preoccupation with Tewodros is a search for solutions to Ethiopia's development and national questions through a strong leader who can unite all parts of the country and at the same time speed up economic development. Tewodros's zeal for reforms and his nationalistic spirit are seen as being a good basis for establishing a society of a kind many authors would favour. A strong, prosperous Ethiopia is thus envisaged as evolving through the inspiration and guidance of one strong national leader. But this is not the only answer given. Some stress the importance of self-help on the local level, without waiting for initiatives from a central government. This is one of the arguments of Haddis in *Yähəllina däwäl*, who says that education is the business and obligation of the local community.[22] Self-help among the peasantry is also urged by the suggestion to establish and become members of peasants' associations to solve the problem of failing harvests (instead of trusting chance, or God, or government aid).[23]

Although most authors see a brighter future for the country through orderly development under the direction of a strong leader and a progressive central government, some see justice and progress for the poor as growing out of resistance against the authorities. Araya had seen that Ethiopians yielded of their best and were most alert during times of hardship and when encountering a certain amount of opposition, and he was therefore worried that his countrymen would go to sleep again after the Italian occupation, which they had been resisting, was over.[24] Haddis Alämayyähu quotes a popular song about a rebel leader to the effect that people believed rebellion could be a necessary and effective means to promote the good of the people:

"Although he has no title that is inherited in the flesh like syphilis, to appoint him would be a remedy for this oppressed

---

[22] *Yähəllina däwäl*, 11:26-12:11.
[23] *Ib.*, 60:18-22, cf. 63:4f., 65:4-6, 78:1-4.
[24] *Araya*, 349:8-10.

country, (he could) give true justice, lead the people, cause the right of each poor man to be honoured." [25]

The thought that the country must always change to preserve justice is expressed; [26] but the ideal most authors seem to find attractive as a solution to Ethiopia's problems appears to be a strong, progressive leader to guide the country forwards. At the same time, writing about Tewodros would serve as a means to express to Haile Sellassie and his government how the authors would like to see the country develop, without necessarily expecting one man to embody all their ideals.

It should be stressed that Ethiopian authors are not unanimous in their views on the question of leadership; and many of them have not expressed any views on the matter.

2. *A changed society envisaged*

A strong motif in practically all Amharic literature is a desire for change, progress and development, but few authors are very precise in stating what kind of society they want. This chapter will therefore rely to some extent on inferences from attitudes and aspirations expressed for a new society, and it is not possible to give any exact picture of what kind of future Ethiopians aspire to. In a general way, however, several aspects of it can be inferred, both in a positive and a negative way, i.e. things they want and other things they do not want to see occurring in their country.

It seems possible to summarize the hopes for a future society under four headings, as follows:

a) *Education*

One of the most persistent themes in Amharic literature is the great importance attached to education. The authors may not be specific in stating what they want education for, or what results they expect it to lead to, but there seems to be a belief or a hunch that if only people are educated, they will find their own way to a better society, maybe on the model of Western countries.

Blattengeta Həruy shows in *Yäləbb hassab* how education can lead to better marriages, healthier and happier children, and improved health. In *Addis aläm* he lets an educated man, Awwäḳä,

---

[25] *Fəkr əskä mäḳabər*, 235:22-27.
[26] *Yähəllina däwäl*, 211:5-9.

be a protagonist of social and church reforms, and presents the results as beneficial both for the community, the church, and the individual, not least in economic respects. Gərmaččäw Täklä Hawaryat continues this argument and presents Araya as a man who could give shape to a better society if his ideas, acquired in French schools, were implemented in Ethiopia. Käbbädä Mika'el has supported education through his non-fictional as well as his fictional work, e.g. *Tarikənna məssale*, Book III, and several poems; Mängəstu Lämma has demonstrated the value of education in *Yalačča gabəčča*, and so has Daňňaččäw Wärku in *Adäfrəs* and Bä'alu Gərma in *Yähəllina däwäl*. The most attractive characters Haddis Alämayyähu has presented in *Fəkr əskä mäkabər*, namely Bäzzabbəh, Säblä Wängel and Guddu Kasa, are also the best educated people in his novel, although they have only received a traditional church education. Abbe Gubäňňa's heroes in *Məlkam säyfä näbälbäl* and *Aləwwällädəm* do much for education and build many schools. Mäkonnən Əndalkaččäw has written less about education, but he sees it as valuable and necessary in a modern society, and he has voiced this view in, for example, *Yäfəkər ҫora*,[27] and all main characters in *Ṣähay Mäsfən* are educated. At least when knowledge is united with high moral standards, it is described as beneficial. This view, that knowledge and morals should go together, has been expressed also by Käbbädä Mika'el,[28] and particularly Bərhanu Zärihun is worried lest education should be used for evil purposes and lead to a worsening situation for the country. The seducer in *Yä'ənba däbdabbewoč* is well-educated, and so are others of his "bad" characters. But this is not an objection to education as such, but only to the misuse of it, showing that education does not automatically create better people. Other authors, such as Bä'alu Gərma in *Kä'admas bašagär*, Taddäsä Libän in his short stories and Ṣäggaye Gäbrä Mädhən in his plays, have dealt with this question, too. This note is sounded most strongly in more recent Amharic literature to point out that Ethiopia should respect her heritage, too, especially in the areas of morality and interpersonal relationships.

The emphasis on promoting education and destroying what keeps Ethiopia backward seems to be unanimous in Amharic

---

[27] *Yäfəkər ҫora*, 192:6-194:12.
[28] *Yäkəne azmära*, p. 141, etc.

literature, and an educated people appears unambiguously to be an aim for a future society.

b) *Patriotism*

Ethiopian authors are all patriotic and nationalistic and want a strong, independent country. Especially the confrontation with the Italians in 1935-41 caused a mighty upsurge of the nationalist spirit, but also other times of threat or pressure from outside have served to stimulate nationalism. Some of these are celebrated in poems by Ṣäggaye Gäbrä Mädhən, viz. Tewodros at Mäkdäla, and the battles of Adwa, Dogali and Mayčäw.[29] The heroism of Abunä Peṭros he has also remembered in a poem,[30] and a play by Mäkonnən Əndalkaččäw, *Yädäm dəmṣ*, is dedicated to the same topic.[31] This latter author has also written a novel from the time of the occupation, *Almotkum bəyye alwašəm*,[32] and a historical essay on the battle of Mayčäw in relation to global politics.[33] Gərmaččäw Täklä Hawaryat has dedicated a large portion of *Araya* to the resistance against the Italians during all the years of their occupation of the country. Käbbädä Mika'el has remembered these years in several of his poems.[34]

With the passing of the years, when a generation of writers who had no clear personal memories of the years of occupation came into prominence, other nationalistic themes came to the fore, and first of all the figure of Tewodros. As mentioned already, many authors have written about Tewodros with admiration and see in him the prototype of the true, patriotic Ethiopian. Even Mäkonnən Əndalkaččäw, who finds much to criticize in Tewodros, gives him credit for being a true patriot who preferred to die rather than to bring shame upon Ethiopia by surrendering to the enemy. His bravery, his attempts at uniting the country and his nationalism are all praised, and Ethiopian authors seem to identify themselves with most of his plans and aspirations. Typical of this use of Tewodros to express contemporary feelings is a poem by Käbbädä Mika'el, *Aṣe Tewodrosənna hulätt yäwəčč agär säwoč*.[35] It relates

---

[29] *Əsat wäy abäba*, pp. 54-56, 159, 184f., 204-208.
[30] *Ib.*, pp. 126-130.
[31] *Arrəmuññ*, pp. 79-104.
[32] *Ib.*, pp. 273-338.
[33] *Ib.*, pp. 339-360.
[34] *Yäkəne azmära*, pp. 44-47, 52-70.
[35] *Ib.*, pp. 111-114.

the story of two foreigners who visited Ethiopia, and in spite of the fact that they were known to be spies, they were shown all hospitality and given freedom to travel anywhere in the country. At their departure they were given rich gifts; but before they entered the ship that was to take them home, their shoes were washed. Inquiring the reason for this, the king told them that he could afford to give them gifts of gold and precious stones, but Ethiopia's soil was so valuable that he could not part with even a small part of it. This symbolic action was meant as a warning against any plans the foreigners, or their government, might have of conquering any part of the country.

Mängəstu Lämma regrets the weakening of the Ethiopian spirit that has resulted from the westernization of the country. He would be glad to see a revival of the strong patriotic spirit of the *arbäñña* and has written a play, *Ṭälfo bäkise*, and poems on this theme.[36]

Araya considers the situation of his country and believes there is no way ahead unless Ethiopia can stand on her own feet, help herself and solve her own problems.[37] This seems to be the general attitude among Ethiopian authors.

c) *Moral values*

Ethiopian authors want the Ethiopian people to preserve high moral standards and to reject outside influences that tend to corrupt them. Early enthusiasm for much that came from the West was soon tempered by hesitation and doubt when people saw some of the bad results of such influences.

In *Araya* we get glimpses of life in Dire Dawa and Addis Ababa that Araya disapproves of, and he ascribes the ugly aspects of life there to the superficiality of the new influences from abroad. But other authors do not accept this as a satisfactory, or at least complete explanation. A businessman who loses his sanity in his pursuit of profit in *Yädəhoč kätäma* by Mäkonnən Əndalkaččäw [38] is in many respects a highly cultured man. Bä'alu Gərma writes about well-educated people who are without purpose or direction in *Kä'admas bašagär*; so, too, Bərhanu Zärihun in *Čäräḳa sətwäṭa*, etc. It is clear that many authors write about the dissolution of

---

[36] *Yägəṭəm guba'e*, pp. 17-21, 37-44.
[37] *Araya*, 152:26-29.
[38] *Arrəmuññ*, pp. 105-185.

social relationships and the decay of morals with much concern, and some of them might be described as moralists.

Practically all the writing of Mäkonnən Ǝndalkaččäw and Bərhanu Zärihun have a strong moral tone, and they demonstrate the tragic unhappiness modern civilization can lead to. Abbe Gubäñña's characters tend to be thoroughly good or total villains. In a simple, but effective way he uses people who are almost perfect to convey his thoughts. Käbbädä Mika'el, who strongly stresses the value of knowledge, writes forcefully about the importance of high morals, of being and doing good.[39] Taddäsä Libän shows in his stories from Addis Ababa sadness about the immorality of urban life, but he has also much understanding and compassion for the victims who are tempted and taken in by the attractions of modern life, those who end up reaping a harvest of disappointment and sorrow. In *Araya*, Gərmaččäw Täklä Hawaryat stresses primarily the need for modernization and westernization in Ethiopia; but when it comes to moral growth, which he believes is of equal importance when it comes to being a civilized country, he does not think the West has much to offer. Here Ethiopia must preserve and develop her own principles, so that she does not accept a materialist philosophy.[40]

Some authors show a moral concern without pointing a finger too obviously. The most attractive people in *Fəkr əskä mäkabər* are Bäzzabbəh, Säblä Wängel and Guddu Kasa. They are all of high moral character, and in some way they either are or become attached to the Church; the first has been educated for many years in church schools and himself later becomes a teacher in subjects he studied there; the other two have also some traditional education and end their lives in monastic seclusion. In *Adäfrəs*, the most sympathetic and fine personality is Şiwäne, of whom the author draws an almost ideal picture. She also ends up as a nun. As her resolution matures, the author uses the device of beginning or ending several chapters with increasing or diminishing dotted lines, until chapter 63 has such lines both at the beginning and end, and it occupies exactly one page. The outline of this chapter, including the dotted lines, forms an Ethiopian cross. It might be that in these ways both Haddis Alämayyähu and Daňňaččäw Wärku want to hint that true spirituality and the best people in Ethiopia

---

[39] E.g. *Yäkəne azmära*, pp. 9-44, 71-73, 99-101, 103-106, 137f., 147-155.
[40] *Araya*, 147:26-148ult.

are found in the Church and that a moral regeneration of the country would originate from within the Church. It might also be more than a coincidence that the best people in these books come from noble families. Gorfu is another character in *Adäfrəs* who shows healthy views and a straightforward and independent way of acting and is depicted with sympathy. He is the son of a nobleman and ends up in the army. Against the background of severe criticism of the nobility and the clergy in other parts of Amharic literature, this positive view of other aspects of the two groups is worth noting. On the whole, it seems as if Ethiopian authors find the best basis for preserving high moral standards in the Ethiopian Orthodox Church and in the best Ethiopian families.

d) *Prosperity*

Most Ethiopian authors want to see increasing prosperity in their country. A few are more concerned with the corrupting influence of wealth and write little about economic growth from other viewpoints. Clearly they would reject prosperity at the cost of destroying moral and nationalistic values.

Blattengeta Həruy was not so much writing about increased prosperity as a better use of available wealth in *Addis aläm*. That is behind several of Awwäkä's proposals for reforms. Araya (in *Araya*) observes Europeans and believes Ethiopians should be able to do the same things as them. He believes economic growth is necessary for a modern country and that Ethiopia should be self-sufficient.[41]

Käbbädä Mika'el expresses his views on material development in praising manual work, and his poem *Sǝlä tägbarä əd*[42] states his belief in how Ethiopia can prosper. Laziness must be overcome and work regarded as an honourable activity, factories built and people educated and "civilized" with all speed. Full stature and maturity are reached only through work. The country has a wealth of raw materials, and if others are better off economically, it is only due to the Ethiopians' laziness. If people work, the country can reach greatness. Now is the time to learn, to work and to compete.

Bä'alu Gərma equally strongly stresses the importance of work if Ethiopia is to prosper. Haddis in *Yähəllina däwäl* says people must leave old habits that are harmful to the country and start

---

[41] *Araya*, 16:18f., 17:4-6, 147:26ff., 152:26-29.
[42] *Yäkəne azmära*, pp. 47-52.

working with their hands. This is not a time for words but for work. The brave warrior of the past should now be replaced by the worker as the Ethiopian ideal.[43] Fitawrari Täkka sees the cooperation of the people in building their own school, and he comments:

> "It seems to me as if they are aroused to build their own future with their own hands. It seems to me as if they have realized the fact that their future does not fall from heaven like manna. It seems to me as if it has been revealed to them that to sit still, putting all their hope in their Creator and their leaders is unprofitable. If they do not help (i.e. themselves), God does not help. It is the same with the leaders. It seems to me as if they have begun to incline towards ruling themselves rather than being ruled. A people which has begun to rule itself is a great people." [44]

Most specific in his demand for quick material development is Abbe Gubäñña in *Aləwwällädəm* and *Məlkam säyfä näbälbal*. In the former book, the main character develops the country within a few years on a scale never equalled in any country before. Even more successful in such work is the hero of the latter book. Məlkam is prime minister of his country, and in the book, which is for the most part a collection of speeches he gives at the inauguration of factories, schools, etc., his main achievements are listed.[45] He establishes a very modern parliament and has fantastic development plans. He reduces the number of holidays so people can work more, he redistributes land, he expands education and health care, creates a magnificent army, eradicates idleness, unemployment, and prostitution; he promotes science and religion. He creates, in other words, the ideal state more or less single-handed. Although the author's recipe for future Ethiopia may be simplistic, and his dreams seem utopian, he may express wishes for rather quick economic growth that are not uncommon among some of the school population. But most of the intellectuals would probably agree that a slower progress is a matter of necessity, and for many a matter of preference.

Ethiopians are more or less agreed that they would like to see the ideals listed above implemented in the country in future. The

---
[43] *Yähəllina däwäl*, III:7-19, 247ult.-248:6.
[44] *Yähəllina däwäl*, 208:13-22.
[45] The book does not state that it deals with Ethiopia, but the contents make it impossible to place it anywhere else.

picture that emerges is rather vague, and the authors appear hesitant to commit themselves to specific solutions of their country's problems. With the traditional attitude of resignation and possibly fatalism, with acceptance of the Old Testament view that "all is vanity" still strong, one should perhaps not expect Ethiopian authors to have broken totally with this viewpoint. What all Ethiopians seem agreed on is that the country is inevitably changing, and changing fast, and most are glad of this happening. The disagreement starts in evaluating the changes that have taken place and in agreeing on the future course of the country. In all its vagueness, Bäzzabbəh Tori's wish in *Ṭälfo bäkise* could probably get the approval of most young Ethiopians, namely to accept the best of Western civilization and the best of the country's own customs and practices, unite both and thus create a new kind of civilization from what is best in both of these.[46]

[46] *Ṭälfo bäkise*, 12:12-14.

CONCLUSIONS

Amharic literature gives a broad and many-faceted view of social and cultural phenomena in modern Ethiopia. Not only does this literature mirror the life of the society by which it is created, but it is itself a social and cultural phenomenon which, through the authors' observations and critical analyses, tries to influence and shape other social and cultural phenomena.

As the readership lives within the milieu the authors write about, the descriptions given are unselfconscious and direct, without too didactic a tone. But when the discussion moves into the field of moral and cultural values, or problems of development, Ethiopian writers often become didactic and patronising. They obviously regard themselves as guides and teachers of their people and write both as guardians of their national heritage and pathfinders to a better future, envisaged not simply in materialistic terms.

The society we meet in Amharic literature is steeped in age-old traditions and cultural values. This is reflected in the much richer material in the first part of this book, compared with part two where questions of change and new values are discussed. Ethiopia was, during 1930-74, largely a traditional society in the process of accepting a new outlook and a different way of life, and much of Amharic fiction reflects the birthpangs associated with this process. Many authors seem caught between opposing, rival desires of preserving what is good of the old society and of accepting ideas and social structures that can bring great material advantages. Often their writing is inconclusive, not committing the authors one way or the other in stating what is most important, the losses or the gains, in the transition to a society that is more like western societies.

Without rejecting traditional values, Ethiopian intellectuals want to weed out superstition, to reform and improve old institutions, and to revive values that time may have corrupted. Thus the ignorance and bigotry of many priests and the misuse of power and the moral degeneration in the Church are attacked and criticized with arguments and values borrowed from the teachings of the same Church. "Bad" Christianity is attacked with "good" Christianity, but rarely are ethical values in such a dispute taken from outside the Church, and even more rarely are arguments used to denounce the Church or refute Christianity.

In a similar way, other institutions are criticized for not measuring up to the authors' ideals of the same institutions. Few authors have attacked the existing system of government, the nobility, or the imperial throne, but assaults on misuse of power and incompetent administration are frequent. The remedy for corrupt officials is to replace them with upright ones, and nobles who do not oppress and exploit poor peasants or tenants are described with approval, as a model for those members of the nobility who place too heavy a burden on the peasantry. When people were not satisfied with the performance of the government and blamed the Emperor for their unfulfilled expectations, they did not attack the throne itself but expressed their criticism through putting up a leader they approved of. The literary expression of this sentiment is primarily found in the many works giving an idealized picture of Tewodros II.

Many educated people were dissatisfied with the existing relationships between different social groups in Ethiopia, but what they wanted were readjustments rather than basic change, as the intellectual climate is reflected in Amharic literature. Some authors express strong attachments to institutions strongly attacked by other writers. The warmhearted descriptions of the best among the nobles or of cherished aspects of Church life and education testify that many want to preserve these institutions in a purified form, although they may have doubted that essential reforms will actually take place. The nostalgic way in which the life of some nobles or churchmen is described seems to indicate that the authors did not have much faith in the resurrection of past traditions. Misuses had made the survival of even the valuable aspects of some institutions questionable.

Ethiopian authors have realized that their country is undergoing a period of rapid transformation, and this has created feelings both of anxiety and great expectation. In their attempts to halt the deterioration of what they value and to indicate the path Ethiopia ought to follow, Ethiopian writers are outstandingly repetitive and vague. Vices monotonously decried are greed, envy, lasciviousness and inebriety. A bright future will come if people are educated and behave well. In their evaluations of society, many writers of fiction are more critical than constructive. They want Ethiopia to advance beyond the old society but they are sceptical of much of what is new, particularly western importations, which they tend to reject on moral grounds. They may be seeking to build something unique, proceeding from their people's own creativity and expressing their own national values; but the steps in this direction seem to be only tentatively indicated and formulated with a goodly amount of reticence. We do not get a clear impression of how it is expected that the desired social rebirth and new prosperity will be brought about. The existing political institutions are found wanting, and the politicians are deemed incapable and unwilling to promote undertakings that might threaten their position. The Church, even though the custodian of many cherished values, is shown to be out of touch with the times and opposed to views that may undermine its credibility. Students and other intellectuals, though perhaps harbingers of new times, are weak and easily corrupted and are best at verbal skirmishes when they do not have to act on their own arguments.

There emerges, however, a desire for a society where people of the highest character, such as the best of the nobility, of sincere faith, such as the truly pious, and of integrity and courage among the well-educated will join hands to shape a community that meets with approval from Ethiopian authors. In spite of differences in emphasis, and sometimes more fundamental disagreements, Ethiopian writers have much in common, and they have views and aspirations that can appear contradictory but are still capable of being harmonized. They find much common ground in the ethical heritage preserved in the Church, and this heritage is reflected in writers of the most dissimilar views of and approaches to social and cultural issues. Moral values are more important than material gain in Amharic literature, and both old traditions and new ideas and customs are given ethical evaluations and accepted or found wanting on the basis of the authors' sets of values, deeply rooted in Ethiopia's history.

ALPHABETICAL LIST OF THE PRIMARY SOURCES FOR THIS STUDY

Adäfrəs, Daňňaččäw Wärḳu
Addis aläm (also *Haddis aläm*; sub-title: *YäḳənoČənna yädägg adragiwoČ mänorya*), Həruy Wäldä Səllase
Aläm wärätäňňa—see *Arrəmuňň*
Aləwwällädəm, Abbe Gubäňňa
Almotkum bəyye alwašəm—see *Arrəmuňň*
Amanu'el därso mäls, Bərhanu Zärihun
And lännatu, Abbe Gubäňňa
Araya, Gərmaččäw Täklä Hawaryat
Arrəmuňň, Mäkonnən Əndalkaččäw
    This collection contains:
    Yäḳayäl dəngay
    Aläm wärätäňňa
    Yädäm dəmṣ
    YädəhoČ kätäma
    Salsawi Dawit
    Assabənna säw
    Almotkum bəyye alwašəm
    Yä-May Čäw ṭorənnätənna baČČəru yä'aläm polätika
Assabənna säw—see *Arrəmuňň*
Bälg, Ṣäggaye Gäbrä Mädhən
Bərr ambar säbbärälləwo, Bərhanu Zärihun
Čäräḳa sətwäṭa, Bərhanu Zärihun
Dəll kämot bähwala, Bərhanu Zärihun
Əddəl näw? bädäl?, Abbe Gubäňňa
Əretənna mar, Abbe Gubäňňa
Əsat wäy abäba, Ṣäggaye Gäbrä Mädhən
Fəḳr əskä mäḳabər, Haddis Alämayyähu
Gobland aČbärbariw ṭoṭa, Abbe Gubäňňa
Haddis aläm—see *Addis aläm*
Joro ṭäbi, Mäkonnən Əndalkaččäw
Kaleb, Käbbädä Mika'el
Kä'admas bašagär, Bä'alu Gərma
Kältammawa əhəte, Abbe Gubäňňa
Lelaw mängäd, Taddäsä Libän

ALPHABETICAL LIST OF THE PRIMARY SOURCES 247

Mäskäräm, Taddäsä Libän
Mäskot, Abbe Gubäňňa
Məlkam säyfä näbälbal, Abbe Gubäňňa
Salsawi Dawit—see *Arrəmuňň*
Säw allä bəyye, Daňňaččäw Wärḵu
Ṣähay Mäsfən, Mäkonnən Ǝndalkaččäw
Tarikənna məssale, Book III, Käbbädä Mika'el
Tärät tärät yämäsärät, Haddis Alämayyähu
Tewodros, Gərmaččäw Täklä Hawaryat
Ṭaytu Bəṭul, Mäkonnən Ǝndalkaččäw
Ṭälfo bäkise, Mängəstu Lämma
Yalačča gabəčča, Mängəstu Lämma
Yä'amäṣ nuzaze, Abbe Gubäňňa
Yäbädäl fəṣṣame, Bərhanu Zärihun
Yädäkamoč wäṭmäd, Abbe Gubäňňa
Yädäm dəmṣ—see *Arrəmuňň*
Yädəhoč kätäma—see *Arrəmuňň*
Yä'ənba däbdabbewoč, Bərhanu Zärihun
Yäfəkər ċora, Mäkonnən Ǝndalkaččäw
Yägəṭəm guba'e, Mängəstu Lämma
Yähamet susäňňoč, Abbe Gubäňňa
Yähəllina däwäl, Bä'alu Gərma
Yäkärmo säw, Ṣäggaye Gäbrä Mädhən
Yäḵayäl dəngay—see *Arrəmuňň*
Yäḵəne azmära, Käbbädä Mika'el
Yäləbb hassab (sub-title: *Yäbərhanenna yäṣəyon mogäsa gabəčča*), Həruy Wäldä Səllase
Yä-May Čäw ṭorənnätənna baččəru yä'aläm polätika—see *Arrəmuňň*
Yäräggäfu abäboč, Abbe Gubäňňa
Yäšoh aklil, Ṣäggaye Gäbrä Mädhən
Yätewodros ənba, Bərhanu Zärihun
Yätənbit ḵäṭäro, Käbbädä Mika'el

BIBLIOGRAPHY

A. PRIMARY SOURCES

(All works listed under A. are published in Addis Ababa, except Gərmaččäw Täklä Hawaryat, *Araya*, which was first published in Asmara.)

Abbe Gubäñña:	*Yä'amäṣ nuzaze*, 1955 E.C. (A.D. 1962-63)
	Aləwwällädəm, 1955 E.C. (1962-63)
	Məlkam säyfä näbälbal, 1956 E.C. (1963-64)
	Kältammawa əhəte, 1957 E.C. (1964-65)
	Yähamet susäññoč,[1]
	And lännatu, 1961 E.C. (1968-69)
	Ǝddəl näw? bädäl?, 1962 E.C. (1969-70)
	Mäskot, A.D. 1971 [2]
	Gobland ačbärbariw ṭoṭa, A.D. 1971 [2]
	Yäräggäfu abäboč, 1964 E.C. (1971-72)
	Ǝretənna mar, 1965 E.C. (1972-73)
	Yädäkamoč wäṭmäd, 1965 E.C. (1972-73)
Bä'alu Gərma:	*Kä'admas bašagär*, 1962 E.C. (1969-70)
	Yähəllina däwäl, 1966 E.C. (1974)
Bərhanu Zärihun:[3]	*Yä'ənba däbdabbewoč*,[4] 1952 E.C. (1959-60)
	Dəll kämot bähwala, 1955 E.C. (1962-63)
	Amanu'el därso mäls, 1956 E.C. (1963-64)
	Yäbädäl fəṣṣame, 1956 E.C. (1963-64)
	Čäräka sətwäṭa, No date
	Yätewodros ənba, 1958 E.C. (1965-66)
	Bərr ambar säbbärälləwo, 1960 E.C. (1967-68)
Daññaččäw Wärḳu:	*Säw allä bəyye*, 1950 E.C. (1957-58)
	Adäfrəs, 1962 E.C. (1969-70)
Gərmaččäw Täklä Hawaryat:	*Araya*, 1941 E.C. (1948-49)
	Tewodros, 1950 E.C. (1957-58)
Haddis Alämayyähu:	*Tärät tärät yämäsärät*, 1948 E.C. (1955-56)
	Fəḳr əskä mäḳabər, 1958 E.C. (1965-66)
Həruy Wäldä Səllase:	*Yäləbb hassab* (sub-title: *Yäbərhanenna yäṣ-əyon mogäsa gabäčča*), 1923 E.C. (1930-31)
	Addis aläm (also *Haddis aläm*; sub-title: *Yäḳənočənna yädägg adragiwoč mänorya*), 1925 E.C. (1932-33)
Käbbädä Mika'el:	*Tarikənna məssale*, Book III, 1934 E.C. (1941-42)
	Yäḳəne azmära, 1956 E.C. (1963-64)
	Kaleb, 1958 E.C. (1965-66)
	Yätənbit ḳäṭäro, 1959 E.C. (1966-67)

---

[1] The page with the date is missing in the only copy I have been able to consult.
[2] The book is published in the 41st year of Haile Sellassie's reign.
[3] Also Züryəhun.
[4] Alternative title on an inside page: *Hulätt yä'ənba däbdabbewoč*.

Mäkonnən Əndalkaččäw: *Arrəmuññ*, 1947 E.C. (1954-55)
This collection contains:
Yäḳayäl dəngay
Aläm wärätäñña
Yädäm dəmṣ
Yädəhoč kätäma
Salsawi Dawit
Assabənna säw
Almotkum bəyye alwašəm
Yä-May Čäw ṭorənnätənna baččəru yä'-aläm polätika
Yäfəḳər čora, 1949 E.C. (1956-57)
Ṣähay Mäsfən, 1949 E.C. (1956-57)
Ṭaytu Bəṭul, 1950 E.C. (1957-58)
Joro ṭäbi, 1951 E.C. (1958-59)

Mängəstu Lämma: *Yägəṭəm guba'e*, 1955 E.C. (1962-63)
Yalačča gabəčča, 1957 E.C. (1964-65)
Ṭälfo bäkise, 1961 E.C. (1968-69)

Ṣäggaye Gäbrä Mädhən: *Yäšoh aklil*, 1952 E.C. (1959-60)
Bälg, 1958 E.C. (1965-66)
Yäkärmo säw, 1958 E.C. (1965-66)
Əsat wäy abäba, 1966 E.C. (1973-74)

Taddäsä Libän: *Mäskäräm*, 1949 E.C. (1956-57)
Lelaw mängäd, 1952 E.C. (1959-60)

B. LITERARY CRITICISM

Beer, D. F., "Ethiopian literature and literary criticism in English: an annotated bibliography." *Research In African Literatures*, Vol. VI, No. 1, (Spring 1975), pp. 44-57.

Cerulli, E., "Nuovi libri pubblicati in Etiopia." *Oriente Moderno*, Vol. XII (1932), pp. 170-175.

——, "Nuove pubblicazioni in lingua amarica." *Ib.*, Vol. XII (1932), pp. 306-310.

——, "Rassegna periodica di pubblicazioni in lingue etiopiche fatte in Etiopia." *Ib.*, Vol. XIII (1933), pp. 58-64.

——, *La letteratura etiopica*, 3rd ed. Milan, 1968.

Comba, P., "Une année de publications en langue amharique." *Annales d'Éthiopie*, Vol. I (1955), pp. 151-152; Vol. II (1957), pp. 263-264; Vol. III (1959), pp. 301-312.

——, "Bref aperçu sur les débuts de la littérature de langue amharique et sur ses tendences actuelles." *Ethiopia Observer*, Vol. II (1958), No. 3, pp. 125-128.

——, "Le roman dans la littérature éthiopienne de langue amharique." *Journal of Semitic Studies*, Vol. IX (1964), No. 1, pp. 173-186.

Donzel, E. van, "De Amhaarse literatuur in Ethiopië." *Kroniek van Afrika*, No. 2, 1973, pp. 119-132.

Fusella, L., "Recenti pubblicazioni amariche in Abissinia." *Rassegna di studi etiopici*, Vol. V (1946), pp. 93-102.

Gérard, A., "Amharic Creative Literature: The Early Phase". JES, Vol. VI, No. 2 (July 1968), pp. 39-55.

——, *Four African Literatures*, Berkeley, 1971.

Getaččäw Hayle, "Sənä ṣəhufənna ḳwanḳwa." *Mänän*, Vol. I, No. 3 (January 1965 E.C.), pp. 14-24.

Guidi, I., *Storia della letteratura etiopica*, Rome, 1932.
Kane, T. L., *Ethiopian literature in Amharic*, Wiesbaden, 1975.
Kapeliouk, O., "Un roman éthiopien qui annonçait la révolution." *Le Monde diplomatique*, April 1976.
Mängəstu Lämma, "From Traditional to Modern Literature in Ethiopia." *Zeitschrift für Kulturaustausch*, Sonderausgabe, 1973, pp. 81-83.
Moreno, M. M., "Notizia su uno scritto modernista abissino." *Oriente Moderno*, Vol. XIII (1933), pp. 486-489.
——, "Letterature dell'Etiopia". *Le civiltà dell'Oriente*, ed. G. Tucci, Rome, 1957, Vol. II, pp. 25-58.
Pankhurst, R., "Abuna Petros: an Ethiopian Patriot Martyr in the Modern Amharic Theatre." *Ethiopia Observer*, Vol. XVI (1973), No. 2, pp. 118-124.
Ricci, L., "Pubblicazioni in amarico di questi ultimi anni." *Oriente Moderno*, Vol. XX (1950), pp. 186-198.
——, "Romanzo e novella: due esperimenti della letteratura amarica attuale." *Journal of Semitic Studies*, Vol. IX (1964) No. 1, pp. 144-172.
——, "Storia delle letterature d'Etiopia." *Storia delle letterature d'Oriente*, ed. O. Botto, Como, 1969, Vol. I, pp. 801-911.
Sengal, E., "Note sulla letteratura moderna amarica." *Annali dell'Istituto universitario orientale di Napoli*, Nuova seria, Vol. II (1943), pp. 291-302.
Solomon Deressa, "The Amharic Dime-Novel." *Addis Reporter*, Vol. I, No. 1, (3 January 1969), pp. 17-22.
Tsegaye Gabre-Medhin, "Literature and the African Public." *Ethiopia Observer*, Vol. XI (1967), No. 1, pp. 63-67.
——, "Die darstellende Kunst und die literarische Verantwortung gegenüber der afrikanischen Mentalität" (übersetzt und bearbeitet von E. J. Tetsch), *Zeitschrift für Kulturaustausch*, Sonderausgabe, 1973, pp. 141-143.
Ullendorff, E., *An Amharic Chrestomathy*, London, 1965.
Wright, S., "Amharic Literature." *Something*, Vol. I (1963), No. 1, pp. 11-23.

C. OTHER WORKS

Abbie Gubegna, *The Savage Girl*, Addis Ababa, 1964.
——, *Defiance*, Addis Ababa, 1975.
Afäwärḵ Gäbrä Iyäsus, *Ləbb wälläd tarik*, Rome, 1908. (Later editions also called *Ṭobbiya*.)
Afäwärḵ Yohannəs, *And afta*, Addis Ababa, 1972? (42nd year of Haile Sellassie's reign).
Alämayyähu Mogäs, *Säwasəwä gəʾəz*, Addis Ababa, 1950 E.C.
Alemayehu Seifu, "Eder in Addis Ababa: a Sociological Study." *Ethiopia Observer*, Vol. XII (1969), No. 1, pp. 8-18 and 31-33.
Amarä Mammo, *Yäləbb-wälläd aṣṣaṣaf*, Addis Ababa, 1968 E.C.
Asfaw Melaku, "Language-teaching Materials: Amharic." *Language in Ethiopia*, eds. M. L. Bender, J. D. Bowen, R. L. Cooper, C. A. Ferguson; London, 1976, pp. 400-414.
Ayala Takla-Haymanot, *La chiesa etiopica e la sua dottrina cristologica*, 2nd ed. Rome, 1974.
Budge, W. A. Wallis, *The Bandlet of Righteousness*, London, 1929.
Clapham, C., *Haile Selassie's Government*, London, 1969.
Cohen, J. M., and Weintraub, D., *Land and Peasant in Imperial Ethiopia*, Assen, 1975.

Cowley, R. W., "Preliminary notes on the *baläandem* commentaries." JES, Vol. X, No. 1 (January 1972), pp. 9-20.
——, "The Beginnings of the *andem* Commentary Tradition." JES, Vol. X, No. 2 (July 1972), pp. 1-16.
Daniachew Worku, *The Thirteenth Sun*, London, 1973.
Dästa Täklä Wäld, *Addis yamarəñña mäzgäbä ḳalat*, Addis Ababa, 1962 E.C. (A.D. 1970).
Del Boca, A., *La guerra d'Abissinia, 1935-1941*, Milan, 1965. (English translation, *The Ethiopian War 1935-1941*, Chicago, 1969).
Doresse, J., *Au Pays de la Reine de Saba. L'Éthiopie Antique et Moderne*, Paris, 1956. (English translation, *Ethiopia*, London, 1959.)
——, *La vie quotidienne des Éthiopiens chrétiens (aux XVIIe et XVIIIe siècles)*, Paris, 1972.
Ǝnanu Agonafər (pseudonym for Nägaš Gäbrä Maryam), *Setäñña adari*, Addis Ababa, 1956, E.C.
Faitlovitch, J., *Proverbes abyssins, traduits, expliqués et annotés*, Paris, 1907.
Farago, L., *Abyssinia on the Eve*, London, 1935.
Gedamu Abraha, "Wax and Gold." *Ethiopia Observer*, Vol. XI (1967), No. 3, pp. 226-243.
Greenfield, R., *Ethiopia, A New political History*, London, 1965.
Haberland, E., *Altes Christentum in Süd-Äthiopien*, Wiesbaden, 1976.
Habtä Maryam Wärḳənäh, *Mahbärawi nuro bä'ityopəya*, Addis Ababa, 1966? (36th year of Haile Sellassie's reign).
——, *Ṭəntawi yä'ityopəya təmhərt*, Addis Ababa, 1970 (40th year of Haile Sellassie's reign).
——, *Yä'ityopəya ortodoks täwahdo betäkrəstiyan əmnätənna təmhərt*, Addis Ababa, 1970 (40th year of Haile Sellassie's reign).
Hess, R. L., *Ethiopia, The Modernization of Autocracy*, Ithaca and London, 1970.
Heyer, Fr., *Die Kirche Äthiopiens*, Berlin, 1971.
Hill, Chr., *The World turned Upside Down*, London, 1972.
Hoben, A., *Land Tenure among the Amhara of Ethiopia*, Chicago and London, 1973.
——, "Family, Land, and Class in Northwest Europe and Northern Highland Ethiopia." *Proceedings of the First United States Conference on Ethiopian Studies, 1973*, ed. H. G. Marcus, Michigan, 1975, pp. 157-170.
Hoben, S. J., "The Meaning of the Second-person Pronouns in Amharic", *Language in Ethiopia*, eds. M. L. Bender, J. D. Bowen, R. L. Cooper, C. A. Ferguson, London, 1976, pp. 281-288.
Hobsbawm, E. J., *Bandits*, London, 1969.
Ješman, C., *The Ethiopian Paradox*, London, 1963.
Kaplan, I. (ed.), *Area Handbook for Ethiopia*, 2nd edition, Washington, 1971.
Käbbädä Mika'el, *Japan əndämən sälättänäč?* Addis Ababa, 1946 E.C.
——, *Səlattane malät məndənäč?* Asmara, no date.
Kidanä Wäld Kəfle, *Mäṣḥafä säwasəw wägəss wämäzgäbä ḳalat haddis*, Addis Ababa, 1948, E.C.
Korten, D. C., *Planned Change in a Traditional Society*, New York, 1972.
Kriss, R., and Kriss-Heinrich, H., *Volkskundliche Anteile in Kult und Legende äthiopischer Heiliger*, Wiesbaden, 1975.
Laketch Dirasse, "Survival Techniques of female migrants in Ethiopian urban centres." Mimeographed paper submitted to the International Congress of Africanists, 3rd session, Addis Ababa, December 1973.
Leiris, M., *La possession et ses aspects théâtraux chez les Éthiopiens de Gondar*, Paris, 1958.

Leroy, J., *La pittura etiopica*, Milan, 1964. (English edition, *Ethiopian painting*, London, 1967.)
Levine, D., *Wax and Gold. Tradition and Innovation in Ethiopian Culture*, Chicago, 1965.
——, *Greater Ethiopia*, Chicago and London, 1974.
Lewis, I. M., *Social Anthropology in Perspective*, (Penguin), 1976.
Lifchitz, D., *Textes éthiopiens magico-réligieux*, Paris, 1940.
Lipsky, G. (ed.), *Ethiopia, Its People, Its Society, Its Culture*, New Haven, 1962.
Lord, Ed., *Queen of Sheba's Heirs*, Washington, 1970.
Mahtämä Səllase Wäldä Mäskäl, *Yabbatoč kərs*, 3rd edition, Addis Ababa, 1961 E.C.
——, *Če bäläw (yäfäräs səm)*, Addis Ababa, 1961 E.C. (Also JES, Vol. VII, No. 2 (July 1969), pp. 195-303.)
——, "Portrait retrospectif d'un gentilhomme éthiopien." *Proceedings of the Third International Conference of Ethiopian Studies*, Addis Ababa, 1970, Vol. III, pp. 60-68.
Markakis, J., *Ethiopia, Anatomy of a traditional polity*, Oxford, 1974.
Mathew, D., *Ethiopia*, London, 1947.
Mayo, J., *Astrology*, London, 1964.
Mängəstu Lämma, "Muggət." *New Times and Ethiopia News*, February 9, 1952.
——, *Mäṣhafä təzzəta zä'aläka Lämma Haylu*, Addis Ababa, 1959 E.C.
——, "The Real Meaning of Semenna-Warq." *Voice of Ethiopia*, January 13, 20, and February 3, 1967.
McCall, D. F., "Dragon-Slayers and Kingship." *Ethiopia Observer*, Vol. XII (1969), No. 1, pp. 34-43.
Mesfin Wolde Mariam, *An Introductory Geography of Ethiopia*, Addis Ababa, 1972.
Pankhurst, R., "The Foundations of Education, Printing, Newspapers, Book Production, Libraries and Literacy in Ethiopia." *Ethiopia Observer*, Vol. VI (1962), No. 3, pp. 241-290.
——, *Economic History of Ethiopia, 1800-1935*, Addis Ababa, 1968.
——, "The history of prostitution in Ethiopia." JES, Vol. XII, No. 1 (January 1974), pp. 159-178.
Parkyns, M., *Life in Abyssinia*, London, 1853, 2nd edition, 1868.
Paulos Milkias, "Traditional institutions and traditional elites: the role of education in the Ethiopian body-politic." *The African Studies Review*, Vol. XIX, No. 3, (December 1976), pp. 79-93.
Pausewang, S., "Die Landreform in Äthiopien." *Afrika Spectrum*, No. 1, 1977, pp. 17-36.
Perham, M., *The Government of Ethiopia*, London, 1948, 2nd edition, 1969.
Potyka, Chr., *Haile Selassie*, Bad Honnef, 1974.
Reminick, R. A., "The Evil Eye Belief Among the Amhara of Ethiopia." *Ethnology*, Vol. 13 (1974), No. 3, pp. 279-291.
——, "The Structure and Functions of Religious Belief among the Amhara of Ethiopia." *Proceedings of the First United States Conference on Ethiopian Studies, 1973*, ed. H. G. Marcus, Michigan, 1975, pp. 25-42.
Rodinson, M., *Magie, médecine, possession en Éthiopie*, Paris, 1967.
Rubenson, S., *The Survival of Ethiopian Independence*, London, 1976.
Sahle Sellassie, *Shinega's Village: Scenes of Ethiopian Life*, Berkeley, 1964.
——, *The Afersata*, London, 1969.
——, *Warrior King*, London, 1974.

Säyfu Mättafäriya Frew, "Yäbariya səm bä'amaraw bahəl." JES, Vol. X, No. 2 (July 1972), pp. 127-200.
Sergew Hable Sellassie, *Ancient and Medieval Ethiopian History to 1270*, Addis Ababa, 1972.
Solomon Deressa, "Opaque shadows." *More Modern African Stories*, ed. C. R. Larson, London, 1975.
Strelcyn, S., *Prières magiques éthiopiennes pour délier les charmes*, Warsaw, 1955.
——, *Médecine et plantes d'Éthiopie*, Warsaw, 1968.
Taddäsä Mulat, "*Bäsärg zäfänoč wəsṭ yämmittayyu yamarəñña gəṭəmoč*", JES, Vol. VIII, No. 2, (July 1970), pp. 155-170.
Taddesse Tamrat, *Church and State in Ethiopia 1270-1527*, Oxford, 1972.
Täklä Ṣadək Mäkuriya, *Yä'ityopəya tarik kä'aṣe Tewodros əskä ḳädamawi Haylä Səllase*, Addis Ababa, 1945 E.C.
Täsämma Habtä Mika'el, *Käsatä bərhan täsämma. Yä'amarəñña mäzgäbä ḳalat*, Addis Ababa, 1951 E.C.
Trawick, B. B., *The Bible as Literature: The Old Testament and the Apocrypha*, 2nd Edition, New York, 1970.
Trimingham, J. S., *Islam in Ethiopia*, London, 1952.
Tsahai Berhane Selassie, "An Ethiopian Medical Textbook." JES, Vol. IX, No. 1 (January 1971), pp. 95-179.
Tsegaye Gabre-Medhin, "Poems." *Ethiopia Observer*, Vol. IX (1965), No. 1, pp. 50-60.
——, "Tewodros." *Ethiopia Observer*, Vol. IX (1965), No. 3, Part Two, pp. 209-226.
——, "Azmari." *Ib.*, pp. 227-239.
——, *Oda-Oak Oracle*, London, 1965.
——, *Collision of your Altars*. (Mimeographed) Addis Ababa, 1971.
Ullendorff, E., *The Ethiopians*, London, 1960, 3rd edition, 1973.
——, *The Challenge of Amharic*, London, 1965.
——, *Ethiopia and the Bible*, London, 1968.
Walker, C., *The Abyssinian at Home*, London, 1932.
Were, T., *The Orthodox Church*, (Penguin) 1963.
Young, A., "Magic as a 'Quasi-Profession': The Organization of Magic and Magical Healing Among Amhara." *Ethnology*, Vol. 14 (1975), No. 3, pp. 245-265.
Zämänfäs Ḳəddus Abrəha, *Hatäta mänafəst wä'awdä nägäst*, Addis Ababa, 1945 E.C. (6th edition, 1963 E.C.).

INDEX OF AMHARIC TERMS

abba, priest, monk; shaman
abba (or *aya*) *dəbəlbəle*, a fairy
abba ṭäḳəl(l), Haile Sellassie I's *nom-de-guerre*
abbate, monk; priest
abetu, "please" (in petition, prayer)
abənnät, magic
abəš, drink made from fenugreek seed
abəyye, uncle ("my, or little father")
abunä zäbäsämayat, the Lord's Prayer
adbar, spirit; abode of spirit
addo käbäre/käbir, a spirit, a familiar
adrus, a Muslim prayer session
afärsata, village-gathering to find a criminal
afəz adängəz, magic
aggafari, head servant, chamberlain
akfəlät/akfəlot, total fast from Friday (previously from Thursday) to Sunday in Holy Week
akrəma, straw used to weave baskets
aḳabe səray, sorcerer, wizard
aḳəm, strength; status, class
aḳəň, one who spreads Christianity and/or government influence; colonizer
aḳḳwaḳwam, church dance
aḳrab, Scorpio
alala, coloured straw used to weave baskets
aläḳa, priest; head of a main church; master-painter
aläm bäḳḳaň alä, to renounce the world
amač rämač, middleman, go-between
amättäbä, pray & make the sign of the cross
amlak, God
ammalaj, mediator, go-between
andärəbbe, poltergeist
andəmta, mode of biblical exposition
andəyye, the One God
anḳälba, cloth to carry children in
antu, you (polite form)
anṭoräṭos/anṭorṭos, hell, the deepest pit
araray, festive chant
aräḳe/aräḳi, arrack, distilled alcohol

arämäne, pagan; uncivilized
aräru, a slave-name
arb rob, the fast on Wednesdays & Fridays
arba'tu ənsəsa, the four cherubs carrying the throne of God
arbäňňa, patriot, freedom-fighter; warrior
asäd, Leo
askema, part of saintly monk's habit
asmat, magic, magic spells
asmatäňňa, sorcerer, magician, wizard
asmatä Sälomon, a magic text
asrat, tithes
aṣäfa, ritual response
aṣe, emperor
ašara bis, someone bringing misfortune
ašän kətab, kind of kətab
atete, (Galla) fertility goddess
ato, Mr.
aṭənt, bones; class, status
aṭmit, soup-like drink made from cereals
awaḳi, sorcerer, astrologer, healer
away, a spirit, a familiar
awgar, spirit; abode of spirit
awrajja, sub-province
aya, Mr. (less formal than *ato*)
ayadrəs ayadrəs, a prayer to stay evil
aynä ṭəla, evil eye; a magic text
azimam, sorcerer
azzaž, commander; royal judge
bahr aräb, fine (imported) leather
bahr zaf, eucalyptus
bahrəy, nature (of Christ); element (in man)
balambaras, noble title (under *grazmač*)
balämädhanit, medicine man; sorcerer
baläwəḳabi, spirit-medium, sorcerer
baldäras, noble title ("keeper of the king's horses")
banda, collaborator with the Italians 1935-41
barčumma/bərčumma, tripod stool made of a single piece of wood

INDEX OF AMHARIC TERMS 255

bariya, slave; 1st, 2nd, etc. generation slave: *wəlaj, fənaj, ḳənaj, asäläṭ, amäläṭ, man bete, däräba bete, dur bete*
bawaj gäbba, to receive a royal pardon
bässo, dough of soaked, ground, roasted barley
bet, house
betä əgziʾabəher, church
betä kəhənät, clergy
betä krəstiyan, church
betä krəstiyan sami, church-goer
betä ləhem, house where the elements of the Eucharist are prepared
betä nəgus, stately (circular) house
bezawitä aläm, Redemptrix of the World (the Virgin Mary)
bəḳat, holiness, perfection
bəlgənna, vulgarity, bad manners
bəlṭät, cunning, cleverness, slyness
bərəlle, decanter-like glass (for mead)
bərkumma, wooden pillow
bərz, unfermented mead
bəsanna, tree growing in the *wäynadäga* zone, croton macrostachys
blatta, title of scholar (under *blattengeta*)
blattengeta, title given to scholar
boräntəčča, animal sacrifice
bota, place, class, status
buda, one with the evil eye
buhe, (boys') feast in August
bunna bet, public bar, coffee bar
čəlot, court of law
čagula bet, home of newly-weds
čäbčäbe/čärčäbe, a magic text
čäbṭ, gonorrhea
čəbbəṭo, kind of bread
čəda, animal sacrifice
čəka šum, local headman, village elder
čərak̲, ogre, monster, chimera
čəsäñña, tenant
daba, skin mantle (worn by monks)
dabbo, (European) bread
dabbo ḳollo, small roasted dough balls
dañña, judge, arbitrator
das, bower, tent
dawəlla, measure, *c.* 100 kg.
dawit, (Book of) Psalms
däbər, main church
däbo, mutual help association

däbtära, cantor, theologian, astrologer, sorcerer
däggämä, to recite prayers, etc.
däjjač/däjjazmač, noble title (under *ras*)
däläwi, Aquarius
däm, blood, family, class
dämära, eve of *mäsḳäl*; pole burnt on this day
dämoz, temporary marriage contract
dänḳara, harmful magic or medicine
däsasa gojjo, shanty, shack
däwäl, church bell
dəba/dəbab, umbrella used in religious processions
dəbba, sorcerer's drum
dəgam, (recitation of) prayer
dəgəmt, incantation
dəggəs, feast, banquet, party
dərgo, kind of alms, food to monks, etc.
dərḳoš, dried & pounded *ənjära*
diḳala, bastard, child of master and slave
dokke, diluted *doyyo*
doyyo, pea or bean stew without butter or spices
durəyye, streetboy
əbäla bay, opportunist
əbd gäbrä kidan, Gäbrä Kidan the Fool (nickname of Tewodros II)
əbd täkle, style of church dance
əčäge, administrator of the Church
əddər, mutual help association
əgziʾabəher/əgzer, God
əgziʾota, O Lord! (said in prayer)
əjj mänša, gift; bribe; greeting
əjj nässa, to greet
əjjä säb, sorcerer, wizard; *buda*
əkkul araš, peasant who pays half the produce as tribute
əḳubat/ḳubat, concubine, mistress
ələlta, ululation
əlfəñ, stately house, main building; room
əmbušbuš ṭälla, unfermented beer
əmmä amlak, Mother of God
əmmäbet/əmmäbete/əmmät/əmmäyte/əmmete, lady, mistress of the house, Mrs.
əmmäbetaččən, Our Lady
əmmät, ashes of incense or soil touched by the blood or bones of a saint

INDEX OF AMHARIC TERMS

ənfərfər, cut-up *ənjära* mixed with spiced stew
əngočča, small *ənjära*
ənjära, pancake-like bread
ənka səlantiyya, sharp, vulgar riposte or word-game
ənnate, "my mother" (expression used among women)
ənnəbäl asra hulätt, a prayer
ərbo, basket-table
ərbo, ¼ of produce paid as tribute
ərbo araš, peasant who pays *ərbo*
ərkus mänfäs, evil spirit
ərm awäṭṭa, to lament
ərməjja, progress
ərswo/əsswo, you (polite form)
əsat, fire (one of the 4 elements in man)
ət abäba, elder sister or female relative
əṭä mäsäwwər, wand of invisibility
əzəl, solemn chant
fälač ḳorač, despot
färaj, judge
fäṭari, Creator
fäṭṭəno däraš, St. George
fəlsäta, Mary's Assumption
fəlsäṭa, demon recording man's sins
fətat/fəthat, funeral ceremony
fətfət, cut-up *ənjära* mixed with spiced stew
fətun, magic
fidäl, character of the Ethiopian syllabary
fitawrari, noble title (under *däjjazmač*)
fuka, small paneless window
gad/mugad, firewood for the kitchen where the Eucharist is prepared
gamme, (child with) tonsure; a highland tree, ehretia cymosa
ganen/ganel, demon
ganen gottač, sorcerer, wizard
garre, pancake-like bread made from sorghum and barley
gašša, land measure, *c.* 40 hectares
gašše, elder relative or other person
gäbbar, tax- or tribute-paying peasant
gäbir, magic
gädam, monastery, convent
gähannäm, hell
gähannämä əsat, hell-fire, hell
gälagay, go-between, middleman, mediator
gämäta, stipulated tribute
gännäzä, to tie thumbs & big toes of a corpse
gäwz, Gemini
getaye, sir
getoč, lord, master
gəbbi, compound, palace grounds
gəbər, tribute; banquet
gəbža, party, banquet
gəʾəz, plain chant; Geez; 1st order of *fidäl*
gəndä bäl, local noble with obligations to provide for troops
gərəmbud, armchair made of one piece of wood
gərma mogäs, a magic text
gərmawi, Majesty
gəsəggase, quick advance, rapid progress
giso, mutual help association
gobban, lover of married person
gofäre, mane (symbol that one has killed an enemy)
gojjo, hut, small house
gonj, a style of *ḳəne*
gra geta, a supervisor of church chant and dance
grazmač, noble title (under *käñnazmač*)
gubaʾe, meeting, meeting place; exposition, sermon
gubaʾe ḳana, a poem of two lines
gudd, shame, shameful deed
gugs, a kind of polo
gulləlat, inverted pot on roof-top
gullət, small local market
gult, rights to tribute
gundo, horn used as measure of honey
guš, unfiltered beer
habtäš bähabte/kabtəš bäkabte, a kind of marriage contract
hamäl, Aries
haṭʾan, sinners
haṭiʾat, sin; sperm
həbər, pun
hədar, Ethiopian month (approx. November)
həggä ləbuna, conscience
həggä mängəst, constitution (law)
həggä orit, Torah

INDEX OF AMHARIC TERMS 257

həggä wängel, (law of the) Gospel
həmamat/mamat, Holy Week
həmamatä mäskäl, the 14 sufferings of Christ, Via Dolorosa
hut, Pisces
iyyoha, a word expressing joy (in songs)
janhoy, emperor
janṭəla, umbrella used in church processions
jädi, Capricorn
jəgəl, a variety of gonorrhea
kabtəš bäkabte, see *habtəš bähabte*
karra, a sect within the Ethiopian Church
katikala/katikala aräḳe, locally brewed arrack
käffänä, to shroud a corpse
kəfu mänfäs, evil spirit
kəkk wäṭ, pea or bean stew
kətab/kitab, protective magic text, charm, amulet
kidan, covenant
kidanä məhrät, Covenant of Mercy (Virgin Mary)
kirub, cherub
kokäb koṭari, astrologer
kolba, buffalo- or ox-horn cup
kosso, tapeworm; purgative against tapeworm; a tree, hagenia abyssinica
krar, six-stringed lyre
ḳačəl, small church bell
ḳal kidan bäḳurban, (indissoluble) church marriage with the Eucharist
ḳalləčča, sorcerer
ḳäññ geta, a supervisor of church chant and dance
ḳäññazmač, noble title (under *fitawrari*)
ḳäräṭ, a tree, osyris abyssinica
ḳäṭema/ḳeṭäma, papyrus reed
ḳäwwəs, Segittarius
ḳedär, a book used at cleansing-ceremony of a profligate
ḳes, priest
ḳəbat, a division within the Ethiopian Church
ḳəddase, Mass, church service
ḳəddəst, mid-section of a church
ḳəddus, saint, holy being
ḳəddusat läḳəddusan, "holy things for saints" (said of the Eucharist)

ḳənče, boiled cereals and butter
ḳəne, traditional poetry
ḳəne mahlet, outer section of a church
ḳərrari, a drink (*ṭälla*-dregs and water)
ḳəṭər, temporary marriage contract
ḳəyyəṭ, coarse pancake-like bread
ḳiṭṭa, unfermented bread
ḳob, cap worn by monks and nuns
ḳolle, evil spirit, demon
ḳollo, roasted cereals
ḳoriṭ, a demon
ḳunna, a measure, *c.* 5 kg.
ḳurañña, demon possessing man, familiar
ḳurban, Eucharist, Holy Communion
ḳwanṭa, dried meat
läwṭ, change, social change
läyəkun, magic
leba, thief
lemat, basket-table
ləbusä səga, demon possessing a man
ləfafä ṣədḳ, protective magic text
ləjagäräd, virgin, girl
ləkura bähullu - əmmete sallu, a slave-name (call & response)
ləmat, growth, progress, development
ligaba, a palace official
liḳ, scholar; in Gondar: royal judge
liḳä ṭäbäbt, a supervisor of church chant & dance
mahbär, association, mutual help association
majrat mäči, robber
mamma, elevated platform in a field (to keep watch from)
marän, "Have mercy on me!" (a prayer)
mašəlla, millet
matäb, neck-cord worn by Christians
mädäb, earthen bench (along wall)
mädhanä aläm, Saviour of the World (common name of church)
mädhanit, medicine, magic, countermagic
mädhanitäñña, medicine man, healer, sorcerer
mäftəhe/mäftəhi, release (from magic), antidote
mäftəhe səray, countermagic
mäjlis, (Muslim) council of elders
mäḳ, the pit, hell

INDEX OF AMHARIC TERMS

mäḵamäḵ, the deep pit, hell
mäḵdäs, central part of a church
mäḵwamiya, prayer-stick
mäläñña, sorcerer
mälkäñña, representative of governor or landowner; landowner
mäls/məllaš, party at bride's home some time after a wedding
mämhər/mämər/mämre, teacher, monk, priest
mändär, village, settlement, hamlet
mängəstä sämayat, (the kingdom of) heaven; Paradise
mänṭola'ʾt, cape worn at church wedding
märäwa, church bell
märdo, death-announcement
märdufa, trousers and shirt
märet, earth (one of the 4 elements in man)
märi geta, main supervisor of church chant and dance
mäskäräm, Ethiopian month (approx. September)
mäsḵäl, Feast of the Cross (in September)
mäsob, basket-table
mäsobä wärḵ, coloured basket-table
mässallämiya, church, place of obeisance
mäswaʾətənnät, self-sacrifice
mäṣhaf gälač̣/mäṭaf gälač̣, astrologer
mäṣhafu/mäṭafu, the Book, the Bible
mäšäta bet, public bar
mätätäñña, sorcerer
mäṭäṭṭ bet, public bar
mäṭən, food given to a travelling king or noble
mäwasʾit, the Antiphons
mäwäddəs, a poem of eight lines
məkəttəl wäräda, sub-district
mənnet, monastery, convent
məntä əfrät, "for shame's sake" (begging-formula)
məntä (bäʾəntä) Maryam, "for Mary's sake" (begging-formula)
mərfaḵ, gathering to feed churchgoers from afar
məs, food/sacrifice to evil spirit
məsäso, pole, centre-pole of a hut
məslä fəkur wälda, Madonna and Child
məsläne, governor; administrator; tribute-collector
məṣat, (second) coming of Christ
məṣwat, alms
məthatäñña, magician, sorcerer
mizan, Libra
muḵ, soup-like drink made from cereals
mulmul, bread eaten at *buhe*
mwal, magic
mwart, harmful magic
mwartäñña, wizard, sorcerer
näʾakwətäkä, a magic prayer
näfas, air (one of the 4 elements in man)
nägadras, noble title ("head of the merchants")
nähase, Ethiopian month (approx. August)
näṭäla, thin shawl or cloth to drape the body
näṭäla gult, non-hereditary rights to tribute
näwr, rude, vulgar, shameful; bad form
nəgs, coronation; saint's day
nəgus, king
nəgusä nägäst, emperor, king of kings
orit, Torah
ras, highest noble title after *nəgus*
ras bitwädäd, favourite *ras*
rəʾsä däbər, a supervisor of church chant and dance
rəshat, dirt; sperm
rəst, hereditary land or cultivation rights
rəstägult, hereditary rights to tribute
rimmiṭo, roasted dough sacrificed to a spirit
säʾatat/satat, the Horologium
säbʾatu aṣwamat, the seven fasts (in the Ethiopian Church)
sädiḵ, basket-table
sägännät, stately house; balcony
sälata, Muslim prayer
sämanya, kind of marriage contract
sämay, heaven; the first to the seventh heavens are called: *Erär, Rama, Iyor, Iyärusalem sämayawit, Sämay wədud, Mänbärä mängəst, Ṣərha aryam*.
sämənna wärḵ, a poetic device; double entendre
sämonäñña, priest or deacon serving a church a week at a time

INDEX OF AMHARIC TERMS

sänbäte, gathering in the church-compound after Mass
sänbula, Virgo
säne, Ethiopian month (approx. June)
säṭṭäñ, a slave-name
säwwər, Taurus
säyṭan/seṭan, demon, evil spirit
set, woman (non-virgin)
setäñña adari, prostitute
səbkät, sermon
səga wädämu, Eucharist ("His flesh & blood")
səgdät, prostration (act of penance)
səhtät, mistake, error, sin
səlät, vow (to God or a saint)
səlaṭṭane, civilization, Western culture
səljo, stew of beans, mustard seed & garlic
səllase, Trinity; poem of six lines
səmä amlak, a magic text
səmməntäññaw si(h), last age of the world
səndädo, a grass, pennisetum sp.
siʾol, Sheol, hell
sirak, wise man; sorcerer
siso, ⅛ of produce paid as tribute
siso araš, peasant who pays *siso*
sost guləčča(woč), hearth, home
subaʾe gäbba, to be in (prayerful) seclusion (for purification)
ṣägga, a division within the Ethiopian Church
ṣäggoč, adherents of *ṣägga*
ṣälot, prayer
ṣälotäñña, prayerful, upright, devout
ṣədḳ, righteousness, completeness
ṣərha aryam, the 7th (highest) heaven
ṣom/ṭom, fast
ṣomä/ṭomä, to fast
šämma, shawl or cloth (to drape the body)
šängo, council of elders
šärmuṭa, promiscuous person; prostitute
šärṭan, Cancer
šəfta, rebel, outlaw
šəmagəlle, elder
šəro wäṭ, mash of peas and beans
tabot, Tablets of the Law, or tablets representing these; church; saint; altar
tahsas, Ethiopian month (approx. December)
täklil, church wedding
tälba, drink made from flax seed
tänkol, subterfuge, devious ways, malice
täsallämä, to pay obeisance
täsʾatu ḳəddusan, the Nine Saints
täṭäyyäḳ ləṭäyyəḳəh, litigation, prosecution; cross-examination
täwahdo, Monophysitism; Monophysite
täzkar/täskar, memory feast for the dead
təgri/təgrit, a spirit, a familiar
təhtənna, humility, modesty, politeness
təmərtä boʾat/təmhərtä həbuʾat, a magic text
ṭarä mot, death agony; angel of death
ṭawənt, lover of a married person
ṭäbäl, mineral water; holy water; beer drunk in religious gatherings; wine of the Eucharist
ṭäbäl ṭädiḳ, drink & food at religious gatherings; wine & bread of the Eucharist
ṭäggäbä, to be sated; to be haughty, to despise people
ṭäj, mead, honey wine
ṭäj bet, public bar, mead house
ṭäḳəl(l), Haile Sellassie I's *nom-de-guerre* (after his favourite horse)
ṭäḳlay gəzat, province
ṭälla, Ethiopian beer
ṭälla bet, public bar, beer house
ṭälsäm, talisman
ṭänḳway, sorcerer, magician
ṭäṭär ṭay, diviner using pebbles
ṭäyyəb, artisan (derogatory)
ṭef, a millet-like cereal, poa abyssinica
ṭəbəñña, round bread
ṭəd, African cedar, juniperus procera
ṭəgabäñña, well-fed; oppressor of the poor
ṭəla wägi, sorcerer who harms or kills through piercing a person's shadow with an iron-pointed stick
ṭənḳola, sorcery, magic
ṭərr, Ethiopian month (approx. January)

ṭos, harmful medicine or magic
ṭosäňňa, wizard, sorcerer
ṭraz näṭṭäḵ, superficially westernized
wanča, horn cup
wazema, eve (of a saint's day)
wädaja, pagan or Muslim séance
wägeša, healer of broken bones & minor injuries
wäladitä amlak, Mother of God (the Virgin Mary)
wäləy, soothsayer
wälläd aggəd, (a form of) usury
wänbär, chair; in Shoa: royal judge
wändəmme, "my brother", friendly & respectful address to a man
wänfäl, mutual help association
wäräda, district
wäsän, limit, status, class
wäṭ, stew
wäynadäga, zone 5000-7000 feet high (below *däga*, above *ḵolla*)
wäyra, olive tree, olea chrysophyla
wäyzäro, Mrs., Lady
Wəddase Maryam, a prayer-book
wəha (or *may*), water (one of the 4 elements in man)
wəḵabi, (good or bad) spirit, (guardian) angel
wərərrəd, bet, wager; fee, bribe (paid to a judge)
wəsṭä wäyra, a poetic device
wəšəmma, (paid) mistress
wzo, abbreviation of *wäyzäro*
yakfay, Easter gift
yazäbot ḵän, working-day (previously: saint's day)
(*yä'*)*aṭbiya daňňa*, neighbourhood judge
yäbäḵḵut (*yätäsäwwärut*), monks, hermits
yäbet wəld, child of master & slave
yäčən gäräd, maid and mistress
yäkkatit, Ethiopian month (approx. February)

yäkrəstənna abbat, (male) sponsor at baptism of boy
yäkrəstənna ənnat, (female) sponsor at baptism of girl
yäləmad čəlot, traditional court (using customary law)
yamadäriya märet, land given *in lieu* of a salary
yämä'at ḵän, the Day of Wrath or Judgement
yämängəst hudad, government land
yänäfs abbat, father confessor
yänägär abbat, peace-maker, arbitrator
yänəssəha abbat, father confessor
yäsäw ayn, the evil eye
yäsəlät ləjj, child born after prayer with vow; child vowed to God
yäwaza säw, someone treated without respect
yäwälad mäkanoč, parents with children who are of no use to them, who have deserted them
yäwəsṭ arbäňňa, undercover patriot
yäzämäd daňňa, family judge or peace-maker
yəluňta/yəluňňəta, fear of gossip; decency
zar, evil spirit, demon
zar färäs, spirit-medium, sorcerer
zä'amlakiyya, a poem of three lines
zäfän, secular song and music
zämänä mäsafənt, Era of the Judges (or Princes)
zängadda, sorghum
zär, seed, family, class; genealogy (father, grandfather, etc.; *abbat, ayat, ḵədmayat* (f. *əmmita*), *ḵəmat/ḵəmayat, šämmat, məzlat, əndəlat*)
zär addam, free burial service for the destitute
zəkər, feast for a saint
zəllay, jump, unorganized change, disruption

INDEX OF TRANSLATED PASSAGES

Adäfrəs, 5:9-16, 62; 6:31-7:6, 67; 7:12-24, 67f.; 8:2-23, 37; 8:25-29, 68; 9:9-14, 38; 10:22-11:16, 38; 12:1-23, 39; 28:1-11, 65f.; 29:4-8, 73; 52:20f., 154; 54:11f., 145; 64:26-30, 84; 67:2-68:5, 108; 68:23-69:8, 109; 72ult.-73:9, 23; 73:15-22, 83; 74:1-3, 83; 76:12-16, 129f.; 77:18-25, 114f.; 80:10-13, 100; 80:14-16, 83f.; 84:21-24, 83; 89:20-27, 160; 97:18-98:3, 110f.; 99:10-12, 83; 100:19-23, 80; 106:9-11, 186; 110:27-111:16, 109f.; 117:21-25, 100; 150:22-26, 175; 151:1-152ult. (paraphrase), 192f.; 156:10-17, 82; 157:31-158:6, 70; 159:12-17, 186; 168:8-12, 49; 168:13-169:5, 58; 169:20-170:19, 131f.; 172:12-14, 174f.; 173:26-175:16, 75-7; 188:25-189: 2, 62; 217:21-218:3, 62f.; 220:17-23, 63; 221:7-12, 63; 222:17-19, 63; 222:20-31, 63f.; 250:13-251:4, 55; 251:8-17, 161; 255:22-256:8, 55; 265:18-23, 104f.; 266:1-7, 105; 284:11.12f.19-24, 196f.

Addis aläm, 50:25-30, 29

Araya, 16:5-11, 137; 116:6-11, 197; 139:28-140:30,201;147:26-148:1, 183; 152:26-29, 183; 156:3-157:5, 142; 162:12-17, 161; 169: 12f., 59; 174:14-18, 69; 176:12-28, 31; 181: 28-32, 208; 185:30-32, 69; 189:4-14, 212; 227:29-31, 114; 231:16-22, 159; 306:6-8, 69; 346:20-27, 183

Arrəmuññ, 33:5-9.12-18, 179; 36:13-20, 179; 39:12-14, 179

Bərr ambar säbbärälləwo, 6:1-7:25, 147f.; 15:25-16:13, 116; 22:10-15, 80; 23:8f., 70; 23:20-24:18, 148f.; 79:7-16, 149; 79:20-25, 149; 80:9-23, 150; 81:1-3, 150; 103:22-24, 145

Fəkr əskä mäkabər, 12:16-23, 156; 13:26f., 79; 14:13-15:11, 80f.; 24:24-25:14, 122; 31:11f., 136; 32:12-18, 61; 45:18-26, 144; 55:7-9, 97; 71:8-11, 72; 86:29-87:1, 145; 156:21-32, 94; 212:16-22, 35; 212:22-29, 68; 215:10-21, 81; 220:20-25, 81f.; 221:6-31, 185; 235:22-27, 234f.; 263:31-33, 79; 273ult.-274:10, 82; 288:4-10, 135; 288:19-21, 123; 311:2-10, 27; 334:2-335:14, 173f.; 377:25-28, 59; 420:2-32, 118; 422:2-423:9, 112; 428:13-25, 113; 433:11-434:3, 209f.; 462:23-463:16, 189f.

Kaleb, 69:1-4, 85

Kä'admas bašagär, 46:5-17, 157f.; 54:16-21, 89f.; 60ult.-61:2, 156; 112:23-113:3, 144; 174:9f., 144

Ṣähay Mäsfən, 102:17-20, 92

Tarikənna məssale, Book III, 1:4-8, 94

Ṭälfo bäkise, 15:18, 137; 52:23-25, 85; 57:20-22, 120; 67:18f., 120

Yalačča gabəčča, 55:6-8, 95; 127:4-11, 114; 138:4f., 177

Yä'ənba däbdabbewoč, 52:6-20, 134; 78:11-17, 133; 98:21-27, 157; 126:12-18, 156

Yäfəkər čora, 50:2-4, 99; 172:14-173:1, 54

Yägətəm guba'e, p. 34, 180; 38:13-16, 177

Yähəllina däwäl, 86:23-87:2, 207; 91:1-6, 56; 104:16-21, 216; 109: 3f., 231; 109:9-11, 231; 179:1-6, 28; 208:13-22, 241

Yäḳəne azmära, 7:1-14, 203; 102:11-14, 216

Yäšoh aklil, 18:17-21, 175; 92:4f., 69

Yätənbit ḳäṭäro, 104:10f., 60; 104:22, 60

GENERAL INDEX

Abba Gärima, 64
Abbe Gubäñña, 2, 9, 10, 15, 32, 157, 165, 166, 167, 188, 198, 199, 212, 222, 223, 226, 229, 232, 234, 236, 239, 241
Abbo, 63n., 148
abduction, 18, 120, 177
absolution, 97, 98, 145
Abunä Arägawi, 64
Abunä Gäbrä Həywät, 63n.
Abunä Gäbrä Mänfäs Ḳəddus, 63
Abunä Peṭros, 12, 94, 167, 237
Abuyä Ṣadiḵu, 63n.
Adal 77, 83
Adäfrəs, 6, 14, 24, 26, 28, 33, 34, 36, 43, 45, 46, 48, 52, 54, 60, 65, 66, 75, 79, 80, 82, 86, 95, 104, 108, 110, 114, 119, 127, 135, 138, 159, 167, 170, 174, 176, 178, 186, 191, 195, 198, 199, 200, 202, 208, 224, 226, 232, 234, 236, 239, 240
Addis Ababa, 4, 5, 9, 10, 11, 14, 16, 17, 18, 28, 48, 52, 56, 69, 95, 125, 126, 148, 154, 172, 175, 178, 181, 186, 188, 190, 198, 207, 208, 209f., 210, 211, 212, 213, 220, 222, 223, 224, 238, 239
Addis aläm, 11, 78, 97, 169, 175, 180, 184, 202, 203, 206, 212, 218, 234, 235, 240
Addis zämän, 9, 16
Adwa, 69, 166, 237
Afäwärḳ Gäbrä Iyäsus, 8, 10, 165n.
Afäwärḳ Yoḥannəs, 195
age, 46, 50, 87, 92, 98, 129, 136, 207, 220
agriculture, 31, 44f., 138, 176, 181, 183, 188, 204, 206, 215f.
Aksum, 73, 165, 167
Aksum Ṣəyon, 86
Aläm värätäñña, 12, 199
Aləwwällädəm, 15, 32, 188, 229, 232, 236, 241
Almotkum bəyye alwašəm, 2, 13, 125, 133, 166, 179, 225, 237
alms, 61, 92, 99, 123, 150
Amanuʾel därso mäls, 17, 138, 155, 158, 177, 198, 213, 223

Amhara, 4, 83, 114
And lännatu, 14n., 16, 166n.
angels, 61, 62, 65, 70, 73, 75n., 76, 131
Ankəro, 93
apostles, 61, 73, 75n.
Araya, 2, 11, 12, 29, 31, 33, 59, 84, 114, 138, 142, 159, 161, 166f., 178, 181, 184, 195, 204, 226, 232f., 234, 237, 238, 239, 240
Arganon, 93
Arrəmuñň, 12
artisans, 27f., 128, 173f.
Arwe, 64
Asinara, 167
Asmara, 11
Asmatä Sälomon, 131
Assabənna säw, 13
astrology, 84f., 92, 102-4, 115, 116, 117, 119, 128, 130, 177, 204
Austria, 192f.
banda, 229
banquets, 31, 90, 134, 139, 141f., 189, 212
baptism, 68f., 87
barter, 38, 213
Bäʾalu Gərma, 1, 2, 9, 10, 18, 57, 157, 188, 198, 216, 224, 230, 231, 236, 238, 240
Bälg, 15, 198, 219
Bäsälamä Ḳəddus Gäbrʾel, 80, 93, 94
begging, 59, 61, 86, 92, 127, 190, 208, 214
Bərhanu Zärihun, 2, 4, 9, 10, 16, 57, 134, 138, 145, 146, 149, 153, 158, 166, 167, 172, 177, 189, 198, 208, 213, 222, 228, 236, 238
Bərr ambar säbbärälləwo, 17, 43, 115, 120, 149
Bible, 49, 79, 80f., 82, 83, 89, 91, 99, 115, 121, 149, 179, 180, 191, 205, 242
"big man", 214
birth, 128, 129, 154
Blattengeta Həruy Wäldä Səllase, 1, 2, 8, 10, 11, 41, 137, 143, 145, 149, 152, 166, 169, 180, 184, 201, 203, 235, 240

GENERAL INDEX

blessing, 50, 80, 94, 104, 149, 150, 181, 210
bravery, 42, 60, 127, 129, 161, 166f., 177, 182, 201, 237, 241
bribes, 24, 51, 53f., 125, 190, 227, 229
Brutawit/Bərutayət, 64
buhe, 90, 140
bureaucracy, 28, 30, 32, 36, 170, 178, 181, 182, 190, 191, 195, 198, 201, 204, 226, 228
burials, 78, 84, 91, 97f., 107, 115, 135, 136, 180
calendar, 61, 64, 85, 90, 148f.
cattle, 42, 44f., 50, 54, 209, 213, 215
centralization, 32, 166, 182, 184, 234f.
Cerulli, E., 7
charms, 106, 107, 115, 116, 117, 119, 130, 131
children, 11, 24, 26, 27, 36, 45, 61f., 69, 83, 87, 92, 95, 108, 109f., 119, 135-7, 176, 181, 182, 192, 206, 207, 208, 218, 220, 235
Christ, 60f., 65, 71, 75n., 88
Christianity, 4, 12, 39, 58-101, 112, 113-21, 121f., 126, 130-2, 141, 143, 159f., 161, 165, 168, 221, 243f.
church, 5, 9, 11, 14, 16, 25, 28, 30, 32, 36, 47, 49, 54, 58, 59, 61, 62, 65, 66, 72, 72-4, 77, 78, 79, 82f., 84, 86f., 90, 91, 93, 94, 95, 96, 98, 99f., 113, 116, 119, 132, 134, 149f., 160, 180f., 203, 221, 222, 227, 233, 236, 239f., 243f., 245
church compound, 54, 77, 92, 93
church schools, 10, 14, 91, 99-101, 113, 117, 194, 201, 210, 236, 239, 244
class, 23ff., 51, 144f., 172, 173f., 189, 192f., 201, 203, 221, 244
clergy, 12, 23, 25, 28, 36, 41, 72, 74, 76f., 77-84, 88, 90, 95, 97, 99f., 111, 112, 113, 115, 116, 131, 146-8, 149f., 160, 176, 180f., 189f., 202, 210, 212, 213, 240, 243, 244
Comba, P., 7
communal life, 133-5
confessor, see father confessor
conservatism, 132, 172-80, 195, 196f., 220
corruption, 53, 190, 228f., 230, 238, 240, 243, 244, 245
courts, 30, 51-7, 185, 189, 227, 229
covenant, 61n.

crimes, 17, 51-7, 178, 199, 202, 210f., 219, 225-30
Čäbčäbe/Čärčäbe, 131
Čäräka sətwäṭa, 17, 177, 222, 238
dance, 74, 78, 98, 100, 129, 134, 153, 221, 222
Daññaččäw Wärku, 2, 9, 10, 14, 108, 127, 170, 186, 200, 224, 230, 236, 239
David, 13
Dawit III, 13
Däbrä Bərhan, 230
Däbrä Bizän, 83, 86
Däbrä Damo, 64
Däbrä Libanos, 86, 95, 116n.
Däbrä Sina, 28, 52, 76, 170, 191
Däbrä Wärk, 60
däbtära, 28, 69, 74, 84f., 98, 113, 114, 115, 116, 117, 119, 120, 130, 131, 145, 152, 181, 221
Däkkä Ǝsṭifa, 117
dämära, 89
deacons, 78, 88, 113, 149
death, 50, 71, 84, 92f., 94, 96-9, 109f., 128
decay, 70f., 217-30, 238f.
deceit, 9, 124, 125, 178, 214, 221, 225-30
demons, see spiritsevil
Dessie, 217
detective stories, 17, 228
development, 9, 10, 15, 30f., 32, 45, 56, 165, 169, 178, 179, 182, 183, 184, 186, 199, 203, 215f., 217, 225, 228, 234, 235, 239, 240f., 243
devil, 62, 63f., 70, 76, 81, 94, 111, 120, 130
Dəll kämot bähwala, 17
Dərsanä Mika'el, 93
Dhu Nuwas, 12, 165
Dima, 72, 90, 101
Dire Dawa, 208, 209, 238
dirges, 98n.
divination, 102-4, 115, 117, 177
divorce, 51, 52, 120, 124, 133, 137, 153f., 156, 177, 208, 214, 224
Djibouti, 32, 178, 195, 197
Dogali, 116, 237
dowry, 146, 152f.
dragon, 64, 168
dreams, 128, 138
drink, 32, 88f., 89f., 132, 133, 138-43, 175, 192, 199, 209, 212, 221, 222f.

drunkenness, 15, 17, 99n., 124, 125, 131f., 155, 180, 208, 209, 213, 222, 244
East, The, 169, 171
economics, 3, 169, 171, 172, 180, 181, 182f., 188, 206f., 210, 211-7, 225, 234, 236, 240f.
education, 11, 17, 18, 28, 30, 32, 42, 44, 56, 83, 86, 92, 99-101, 117, 137f., 145, 154, 170, 171, 174, 176, 178, 181, 182, 183, 186f., 193, 196, 197, 200, 201-6, 207, 210, 222, 223, 224, 225, 232, 233, 234, 235-7, 239, 241, 244
Egypt, 30, 63, 73, 82f.
elders, 46, 52, 81, 146, 149, 220
elopement, 14, 185
emperor, 25, 28-33, 38, 40, 41, 68, 160, 172, 183f., 187, 191, 244
end of the world, 70f., 72, 75n., 92, 126, 176, 218
England, 17, 170
envy, 125, 157, 206, 226, 230
epilepsy, 130
Era of the Judges (or Princes), 16, 165f.
escapism, 190-200
ethics, 39, 63, 90, 91, 92, 121-7, 165f., 188, 222-5, 238-40, 243f., 245
Eucharist, 73, 77, 81, 83, 87f., 126, 149, 150
eviction, 34, 176
evil eye, 28, 107, 117, 128, 205
evil spirits, 59, 65f., 84, 96, 102, 105-12, 113, 115, 119, 124, 126, 130, 154, 221
excommunication, 79, 150
exorcism, 59, 66, 112, 130
exploitation, 36-40, 170, 244
Əddəl näw? bädäl?, 16, 26, 33, 56, 212, 223, 226, 229
Əretənna mar, 16, 167
Əsat wäy abäba, 15, 210f.
family, 23, 46, 47, 50, 104, 123, 133, 135-8, 152, 160, 172f., 174, 194f., 214, 217f., 220
Fascism, 167f., 226, 229
fasting, 59, 67, 69, 72, 85, 86, 88f., 122, 126, 128, 139, 143, 221
fatalism, 68f., 87, 102, 104, 128, 186, 242
father confessor, 65f., 68, 78, 79, 79n., 81, 82, 124, 146, 150, 213

feasts, 31, 35, 64, 72, 82, 87, 88, 89f., 98f., 107, 132, 134, 139, 140f., 143, 143f., 148, 152f., 203, 212, 218
Fəkkare Iyäsus, 70, 70n.
Fəḳr əskä mäḳabər, 2, 6, 14, 24, 25, 26, 27, 28, 31, 33, 34, 35, 39, 41, 43, 46, 53, 60, 79, 81, 85, 86, 94, 101, 112, 113, 116, 117, 120, 122, 126, 173, 176, 184, 189, 194, 195, 200, 209, 213, 227, 228, 236, 239
folk tales, 14, 127, 227f.
food, 31, 32, 34, 39, 44, 45, 51, 67f., 88f., 89f., 98, 99, 101, 104, 109, 111, 122, 132, 134, 137, 138-43, 152f., 175, 179, 212
France, 11, 12, 32, 169f., 176, 180, 181, 182, 191, 193, 194, 201, 203, 204, 219, 231, 236
fruit, 45, 141
funerals, see burials
Galla, 4, 83, 104, 106, 114
Gandhi, 169
Geez, 10, 87, 99, 149, 180
Gérard, A., 7
Gərmaččäw Täklä Hawaryat, 2, 8, 10, 11, 12, 29, 31, 40, 160, 166, 169, 181, 183, 184, 236, 237, 239
Gərmame Nəway, 180
Gərma Mogäs, 131
Gərma Taddäsä, 2
Gəšän, 86
gifts, 35, 51, 53, 82, 95, 238
Gobland aṭbärbariw ṭoṭa, 16, 226n.
God, 5, 23, 25, 30, 32, 33, 37-40, 47, 49, 50, 53, 58-60, 63f., 67-9, 70, 72, 73, 79, 82, 85, 93f., 97, 110f., 113, 115, 116, 118f., 120, 121, 130, 141, 149, 159, 165, 172, 190, 193f., 217, 221, 232, 234, 241
Gojjam, 4, 28, 46, 101, 113, 117, 173, 209, 213
Gondar, 4, 172
government, 18, 23, 25, 28, 38f., 100, 160, 166, 170, 172, 178f., 181, 182, 184, 187, 188f., 191, 195, 198f., 230, 234, 235, 244
government land, 25, 36
greetings, 31, 33, 48, 50, 51, 58, 129, 210
grief, see mourning
Haddis Alämayyähu, 2, 9, 10, 14, 184, 190, 200, 227, 234, 236, 239

GENERAL INDEX

Haile Sellassie I, 28-33, 40, 80, 83, 172, 183f., 187, 191, 235
hanging, 54, 202
Harar, 95
Hararge, 4, 13, 69, 181, 187, 191, 204
health, 56, 61, 69f., 91f., 95f., 102, 104, 106, 107, 109, 110f., 119, 130-2, 142f., 169, 181, 202, 206, 221, 235, 241
heaven, 60, 71, 82, 83, 85, 92, 160
hell, 63f., 71f., 84, 161
Həruy Wäldä Səllase, see Blattengeta Həruy W/S
holidays, 82, 134, 139, 140, 144, 221, 241
holiness, 62f., 70, 74, 95f., 126
holy water, 66, 91, 95, 111, 115, 130, 136
honour, 37, 38, 42, 124, 214f., 240
horse-names, 29
hospitality, 50, 51, 129, 133, 138, 193, 238
houses, 43f., 49, 50, 151, 152, 186, 209, 215
Hulätt yäʾənba däbdabbewoč, 17n.
ideals, 127-30, 137, 161, 184, 187, 196, 197, 231-42, 244
Illubabor, 4, 52, 118, 188, 232
India, 17
insults, 28, 41, 42, 50n., 51, 124, 127f., 173, 174, 189, 194, 204, 210
intellectuals, 5, 18, 167, 186-9, 197-9, 223, 232, 238, 241, 243, 244, 245
Iskinder (Emperor), 117
Italian occupation, 2, 12, 13, 30, 32, 84, 125, 133, 134, 138, 166f., 167f., 172, 183, 191, 209, 225, 226, 229, 234, 237
Japan, 169, 182
Joro ṭäbi, 13, 57
Judaism, 168
judges, 30, 52-7, 63, 195, 196, 229
justice, 17, 33, 53, 54, 68, 122, 161, 173f., 189f., 226f., 228, 229, 234, 235
Kaleb, 85, 165
Kaleb, 11, 165
Kane, T.L., 7
Käʾadmas bašagär, 18, 57, 170, 198, 219, 223, 224, 236, 238
Käbbädä Mikaʾel, 2, 8, 10, 11, 30, 60, 165, 166, 167, 168, 184, 203, 216, 218, 236, 237, 239, 240

Kältammawa əhəte, 15, 137, 157, 199, 224
king, 13, 25, 29, 30, 37, 40, 47, 52f., 64, 68, 80, 83, 134, 151, 161, 165, 168, 172, 174f., 184, 189, 192f., 238
kissing, 48, 49, 50, 74, 86f., 94, 112, 120, 150
Krəstos Sämra, 63f.
Kulubi, 95, 117
Ḳedär (Book of), 91, 91n.
ḳəne (poetry), 10, 16, 99, 101, 116f., 167
Lalibela, 86
landlords, 5, 6, 14, 23, 24-6, 33-40, 42, 45, 48, 52, 65, 67f., 81f., 82, 174-6, 184-6, 189, 220
landownership, 5, 25, 33-40, 51, 194, 196, 213, 214, 230, 232, 241
land reform, 33f., 40, 232, 241
lawsuits, 16, 51-7, 189, 221, 229
leadership, 13, 16, 30, 32, 166, 178f., 182, 184, 189, 193, 196, 233f., 235, 241, 244, 245
Lelaw mängäd, 14, 189, 198, 212, 219
Ləbb wälläd tarik, 8
Ləbnä Dəngəl, 185
litigation, 51-7, 95, 226f.
locale, 4
Lord's Prayer, 80, 93, 94, 148
love, 14, 15, 18, 47f., 92, 102, 111, 112, 117, 119, 135, 137, 139, 145, 153, 156, 161, 172, 177, 179, 199, 203, 219, 223, 224, 230
luck, 68f., 128, 216, 234
madness, 17, 110, 130, 155, 174, 185, 194f., 222, 224
magic, 28, 66, 84, 86, 102, 105-12, 113, 115, 116, 117, 118, 119, 120, 121, 130, 210
man (view of), 65-7, 70, 96, 126, 179, 186, 192, 230
Maoism, 232
marriage, 11, 13, 14, 15, 17, 18, 24, 41, 51, 52, 72, 79, 80f., 85, 103, 115, 116, 120, 124, 126, 129, 135, 137f., 143-54, 155, 156, 173, 174, 177, 180, 181, 185, 187, 192, 199, 208, 217, 218f., 220, 223f., 235
martyrs, 61, 64, 73, 75n.
Marxism, 180, 232
Mary, see Virgin Mary
Mass, 74, 78, 84, 86, 87, 91, 92, 134, 150

Mayčäw/May Čäw, 13, 31, 32, 166, 237
Mäkonnən Əndalkaččäw, 2, 8, 10, 12, 31, 40, 92, 126, 127, 133, 165, 166, 167, 170, 172, 179, 201, 216, 222, 224, 227, 236, 237, 238, 239
Mäḵdäla, 237
Mälkä Guba'e, 93
Mälkä Maryam, 99
Mälkä Rufa'el, 93
Mängəstu Gädamu, 2
Mängəstu Lämma, 2, 6, 9, 17, 158, 167, 170, 177, 179, 187, 204, 223, 232, 236, 238
Mäskäräm, 14, 189, 198, 219, 226
Mäskot, 16, 167
Mäsḵäl, 89, 107
Mäṣhafä sä'atat, 93
Mätolomi/Motälämi, 62
Mäwas'it, 98
medicine, 11, 84, 106f., 111, 116, 118, 130, 131, 132, 142, 172, 181, 206, 217, 221
memory feasts for the dead, 98f., 139, 180, 212, 213, 221
Menelik II, 13, 30, 169
merchants, 28, 32, 71, 82, 170, 191, 209, 210f., 213
Məlkam säyfä näbälbal, 15, 32, 188, 226n., 230, 232, 236, 241
Middle East, 168
migrant workers, 215
miracles, 62f., 64, 75n., 160
monasticism, 12, 13, 39, 64, 70, 79, 85f., 92, 101, 113, 114, 119, 126, 155, 187, 195, 199f., 210, 239
money, 12, 13, 17, 33, 54, 71, 92, 110, 120, 124f., 138, 151, 157, 177f., 179, 180f., 182, 188, 192, 202-7, 220, 221, 222, 223, 225-30, 244
morals, 3, 9, 14, 16, 66, 70f., 93, 121-7, 165f., 167, 169, 172, 176, 177f., 179, 183, 202, 217-25, 236, 238-40, 243, 245
Moreno, M. M., 7
mourning, 50, 72, 96-9, 180
music, 65f., 74, 78, 87, 89, 97f., 100, 107, 124, 129, 134, 149, 153, 171, 180, 234
Muslims, 4, 83, 114, 119, 120, 159, 165, 168, 221
mutual help associations, 129, 135, 143, 216f., 234

names, 27, 29, 66, 85, 87, 102, 103, 105, 105n., 115, 136
neck-cord, 83f., 87, 91n., 115, 116, 119, 121
négritude, 167f.
neighbours, 133-5
nepotism, 189f., 214
Nine Saints, The, 64
nobility, 6, 9, 12, 13, 14, 15, 24f., 30, 37, 40-5, 46, 47, 73, 79, 80, 82, 92, 134, 148, 151, 172-4, 176, 181f., 182, 185f., 189, 192f., 201, 204, 212, 215, 221, 226f., 240, 243, 245
nom-de-guerre, 29
oaths, 29, 30, 58f., 60, 61, 79f., 95, 109, 150f.
Oromo, 4
paganism, 12, 62, 66, 73, 84, 92, 101-12, 113-21, 159, 176, 192
painting, 61, 73, 74-7, 119, 129, 170
parliament, 33, 241
patriotism, 12, 16, 33, 160, 165-8, 191, 228, 234, 237f., 240, 245
patriots, 13, 32, 41, 84, 120, 167, 177, 191, 229, 237, 238, 241
peasants, 16, 25f., 33-40, 41, 45, 52, 53, 54, 81f., 118, 139, 172, 176, 184-6, 213, 220, 226f., 229, 244
petitions, 30, 47, 54
pilgrimage, 86, 95, 136
police, 56, 178, 189, 230
politeness, 42, 45-51, 58, 123, 138, 173, 210
Portuguese missionaries, 8
possession of spirits, 66, 104-6, 110f., 112, 118
poverty, 40, 42, 46, 50, 67, 92, 98, 99, 124, 139f., 151, 174, 176, 208, 212, 213, 215, 216, 234
prayers, 44, 47, 62, 63, 69, 72, 74, 77, 78, 80, 85, 86f., 89, 91, 92, 93-5, 97f., 111, 114, 118f., 122, 126, 131, 148, 150, 213, 232
preachers, 86, 87, 98n., 181
priests, see clergy
progress, 166, 169, 176, 178, 179, 181, 182f., 184, 186, 188, 191, 195, 201-17, 232, 233, 234, 235, 240f., 245
prophets, 61, 73, 114, 165
prostitution, 15, 17, 119, 124f., 134, 154, 155, 156-8, 177, 187, 199, 200, 208, 214, 217, 223, 224f., 241

proverbs, 24, 37, 38, 39, 53, 71, 127, 174, 174f., 194
Psalms, 33, 86, 91, 93, 98, 99, 159, 186, 191, 232f.
Pawlos Ñoñño, 2, 9n.
radicalism, 32, 180-90, 231-5
readership, 4f.
rebels, 184f., 234f.
reforms, 11, 12, 40, 165, 169, 170, 171, 178, 180f., 184, 192, 196, 204, 221, 231, 234, 236, 244
revolution, 170, 181f., 184, 192, 201, 202, 231, 232, 233
Ricci, L., 7
righteousness, 71, 85, 89, 92, 96, 121
royal chronicles, 8
royal praise poetry, 8
Russia, 180, 232
sacrifice, 92, 104, 106f., 109f., 110f., 114, 115, 119, 123, 126, 130, 131, 199, 205, 218
St. Ephraim, 75n.
St. Gabriel, 61, 64, 80, 94, 95, 117
St. George, 61, 64, 65, 75n., 94, 122, 147
St. John, 61
St. Michael, 58, 61, 62, 65, 73, 75-7, 131f.
St. Rufa'el, 75n.
saints, 47, 49, 58, 61-5, 72, 73, 90, 91, 93, 95, 96, 114, 119, 122, 135
St. Yared, 100
Salsawi Dawit, 13, 165
Säw allä bəyye, 14, 224, 230
serpent, 64, 128, 168
servants, 18, 23, 24, 26f., 41, 43, 44, 51, 108, 111, 137, 140, 151, 174, 199f., 204, 219, 220
sex, 13, 15, 17, 24, 26, 27, 42, 56, 63, 66, 87, 88, 110, 122, 124f., 126, 130, 133, 143-54, 155, 157, 177, 187, 198, 213, 219f., 222-4, 225, 236, 244
Səmä amlak, 131
shepherds, 26, 36, 84, 108, 137, 140, 192
Shoa, 4, 46, 52, 62, 119, 172, 186
shrines, 95
sin, 69f., 71, 92, 121, 123f., 125, 126, 135, 176, 179
slavery, 26, 27, 55, 130, 173f., 210
social change, 3, 9, 29, 32, 70, 72, 80, 163ff., 243, 244

socialism, 179f., 232
soldiers, 25, 28, 30, 36, 41, 199, 241
Solomon Deressa, 6, 128n.
sorcerers, 84, 85, 102, 105, 107, 109, 111, 114, 117, 119, 120, 121, 140, 145, 176, 181, 202
sorcery, 108f., 113, 116
South Africa, 17
spirits, 65, 89f., 104-12, 114, 119, 130 (see also: evil spirits)
status symbols, 40-5, 49f., 51, 153
Stephanites, 117
students, 4, 18, 23, 32, 99-101, 108, 113, 174, 186f., 188f., 202-6, 211, 220, 232, 233f., 245
style, 5, 8, 9, 10f.
syncretism, 112, 113-21
Şäggaye Gäbrä Mädhən, 2, 9, 10, 15, 166, 198, 208, 210, 236, 237
Şähay Mäsfən, 13, 92, 126, 170, 179, 219, 236
Şomä Dəggwa, 99
tabot, 47, 73f., 95, 147
Taddäsä Libän, 2, 9, 14, 189, 198, 205, 212, 213, 214, 218, 219, 223, 225, 236, 239
talisman, 107, 115, 119
tapeworm, 142f.
Tarikənna məssale, Book III, 11, 184, 236
Täklä Alfa, 90
Täklä Haymanot, 62f., 65, 90
Tärät tärät yämäsärät, 14, 227f.
Täwänäy, 116f.
tenants, 5, 6, 24, 26, 33-40, 42, 45, 46, 48, 67f., 109, 176, 220, 244
Ten Commandments, 121, 121n.
Tewodros, 12, 166n.
Tewodros II, 3, 4, 8, 12, 13, 16, 17, 32, 166, 184, 195, 234, 235, 237f., 244
Təmhərtä həbu'at, 131
titles, 30, 40f., 42, 47, 78, 182, 201, 234
Torah, 60, 91, 116, 121
trade, 31, 171, 183, 210f., 215f.
tribute, 25, 26, 33-40, 42, 45, 81, 139, 172, 220, 226f.
Ṭaytu Bəṭul, 13, 166
Ṭälfo bäkise, 18, 84, 120, 158, 177, 223, 238, 242
Ṭobbiya, 8, 165n.
unemployment, 213f., 241

United States, 168, 170, 219
urbanization, 9, 15, 47, 52, 138, 143, 154, 156, 174, 177, 189, 201, 206-11, 213, 217, 224, 239
usury, 38, 170, 215, 230
vices, 67, 123f., 125, 126, 244
virginity, 110, 124, 145, 153, 154, 156, 220, 226
Virgin Mary, 47, 50, 61f., 64f., 73, 75n., 79, 90, 91, 92, 93, 148
virtues, 67, 123, 126, 135
vows, 61, 85, 92, 95, 110, 119, 126, 136
Wädaje ləbbe, 8
Wäldä Giorgis Wäldä Yohannəs, 7n.
wealth, 13, 28, 40-5, 68, 92, 102, 125, 126, 145, 156, 158, 161, 183, 188, 197, 201, 207, 210, 212-7, 227-30, 238, 240f., 245
weddings, 74, 134, 139, 144, 149f., 152f., 180f., 212
West, The, 4, 9, 10, 57, 69, 77, 82, 130, 167, 168-71, 172, 175, 187, 188, 196, 197, 201, 203f., 205, 206, 207, 208, 209, 212, 218, 221, 223, 231, 235, 238, 239, 242, 243, 245
Wəddase amlak, 93
Wəddase Maryam, 75n., 91, 93, 99
women, 11, 24, 27, 33, 36f., 43, 44, 48, 49, 51, 62, 80f., 89, 96, 97, 98, 99, 104, 124, 125, 129, 133, 135f., 138, 141, 151, 154, 154-8, 177, 181, 189, 198, 199f., 213, 214, 222f.
work, 28, 30, 35, 45, 90, 123, 126, 137, 154, 182, 183, 186, 191, 207, 210f., 213f., 216, 220, 222, 232, 233, 240f.

worship, 72ff., 118
Wright, S., 7
Yalačča gabəčča, 17, 24, 33, 52, 56, 66, 95, 103, 114, 115, 119, 120, 135, 158, 170, 175, 177, 187, 204, 212, 219, 221, 236
Yä'amäṣ nuzaze, 15, 222
Yäbädäl fəṣṣame, 17, 57, 158, 178, 228f.
Yädäkamoč wäṭmäd, 16, 165
Yädäm dəmṣ, 12, 237
Yädəhoč kätäma, 12, 92, 126, 170, 179, 222, 238
Yä'ənba däbdabbewoč, 17, 125, 133, 138, 155, 158, 177, 189, 224, 226, 236
Yäfəkər čora, 13, 54, 126, 170, 224, 236
Yägəṭəm guba'e, 17, 170
Yähamet susäññoč, 16, 226n.
Yähəllina däwäl, 1, 18, 28, 34, 40, 56, 57, 176, 178, 188, 203, 204, 206, 216, 217, 224, 230, 232, 233, 234, 236, 240
Yäkärmo säw, 15, 198, 208
Yäḵayäl dəngay, 12, 179
Yäḵəne azmära, 11
Yäləbb hassab, 1, 11, 137, 169, 181, 201, 206, 219, 235
Yäräggäfu abäboč, 16, 198, 222
Yašoh aklil, 15, 175, 198, 219
Yätewodros ənba, 17, 166n.
Yätənbit ḵäṭäro, 12, 165, 184
Yohannes IV, 166
Zär'a Ya'kob, 185
Zəkwala, 63, 86
Zodiac, 103, 103n.